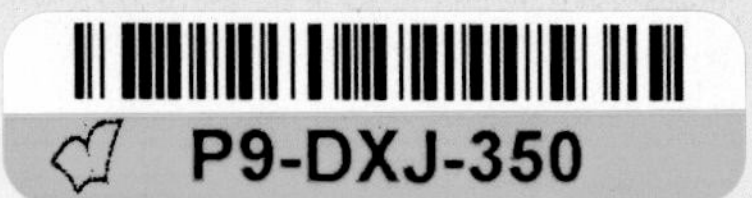
P9-DXJ-350

CONFORMITY AND CONFLICT

Readings in Cultural Anthropology

NINTH EDITION

James Spradley

David W. McCurdy
Macalester College

LONGMAN

An imprint of Addison Wesley Longman, Inc.

New York • Reading, Massachusetts • Menlo Park, California • Harlow, England
Don Mills, Ontario • Sydney • Mexico City • Madrid • Amsterdam

Acquisitions Editor: Margaret Loftus
Supplements Editor: Tom Kulesa
Project Coordination and Text Design: York Production Services
Cover Designer: Kay Petronio
Cover Photos: Photodisk, Inc.
Art Coordination: York Production Services
Photo Researcher: Karen Koblik
Electronic Production Manager: Valerie Zaborski
Manufacturing Manager: Helene G. Landers
Electronic Page Makeup: York Production Services
Printer and Binder: R. R. Donnelley & Sons Company
Cover Printer: Phoenix Color Corp.

For permission to use copyrighted material, grateful acknowledgment is made to the copyright holders on page 408, which are hereby made part of this copyright page.

Library of Congress Cataloging-in-Publication Data

Conformity and conflict: readings in cultural anthropology/James P. Spradley, David W. McCurdy, [editors]. —9th ed.
p. cm.
Includes index.
ISBN 0-673-52510-4
1. Ethnology. I. Spradley, James P. II. McCurdy, David W.
GN325.C69 1996
305.8—dc20 96-27415
CIP

Copyright © 1997 by Barbara A. Spradley and David W. McCurdy

All rights reserved. No part of this publication may be reproduced, stored in a retrieval system, or transmitted, in any form or by any means, electronic, mechanical, photocopying, recording, or otherwise, without the prior written permission of the publisher. Printed in the United States.

ISBN 0-673-52510-4

1234567890—DOC—99989796

Contents

World Map and Geographical Placement of Readings x

Preface xiii

Part 1
Culture and the Contemporary World 3

Part 2
Culture and Ethnography 13

1 **Ethnography and Culture** 18
James P. Spradley

To discover culture, the ethnographer must relate to the informant as a teacher.

2 **Eating Christmas in the Kalahari** 26
Richard Borshay Lee

The "generous" gift of a Christmas ox involves the anthropologist in a classic case of cross-cultural misunderstanding.

3 **Shakespeare in the Bush** 34
Laura Bohannan

Cross-cultural communication breaks down when the anthropologist attempts to translate the meaning of Hamlet to the Tiv.

4 **Lessons from the Field** 44
George Gmelch

Fieldwork in Barbados gives students a greater understanding of their own culture and personal life.

Part 3
Language and Communication 57

5 **The Sounds of Silence** 61
Edward T. Hall and Mildred Reed Hall

The frown, the smile, the dilated pupil, the distance at which people converse, and other forms of nonverbal behavior all serve to convey meaning in social encounters.

6 **Conversation Style: Talking on the Job** 71
Deborah Tannen

On the job, men and women use distinctive conversation styles to ask for help leading them to evaluate performance and character differently.

7 **The Sapir-Whorf Hypothesis: Worlds Shaped by Words** 80
David S. Thomson

To what extent does Whorf's hypothesis that language creates reality apply in daily life?

8 **Teleconditioning and the Postmodern Classroom** 93
Conrad Phillip Kottak

Long hours watching television has modified the cultural behavior of viewers, partly explaining the casual way university students act during class.

Part 4
Ecology and Subsistence 101

9 **The Hunters: Scarce Resources in the Kalahari** 105
Richard Borshay Lee

!Kung and other foragers traditionally worked less and ate better than many other people with more "advanced" food producing techniques. Today, however, their survival depends more on drilling wells and keeping cattle than collecting wild foods.

10 Cultivating the Tropical Forest 120
Richard K. Reed

South American governments could learn much about tropical forest "development" from the Amazonian Indians who live there.

11 India's Sacred Cow 130
Marvin Harris

India's religious restrictions on cattle slaughter evolved to ensure an adequate supply of this valuable animal in an intensive agricultural society.

12 Adaptive Failure: Easter's End 141
Jared Diamond

Polynesian settlers on Easter Island prospered and multiplied until they eventually destroyed their island habitat, and with it their civilization.

Part 5

Economic Systems 153

13 Reciprocity and the Power of Giving 157
Lee Cronk

Gifts not only function to tie people together, they may also be used to "flatten" an opponent and control the behavior of others.

14 The Shadow Economy: Cleaners in Bombay 164
Sara S. Mitter

Low-caste women who clean the apartments of more affluent Indians are caught in a shadow economy without hope of advancement.

15 Workaday World—Crack Economy 171
Philippe Bourgois

Work selling crack is neither lucrative nor glamorous, but for many African-American men it is the only employment available.

16 Subsistence and Market: When the Turtle Collapses 180
Bernard Nietschmann

The world demand for green sea turtles thrusts Miskito Indians into a conflict between cash and subsistence.

Part 6
Kinship and Family 191

17 Mother's Love: Death Without Weeping 195
Nancy Scheper-Hughes

Close mother-child bonds suffer in the presence of high infant mortality in a Brazilian shanty town.

18 Family and Kinship in Village India 205
David W. McCurdy

Kinship still organizes the lives of Bhil villagers despite economic opportunities that draw people away from their community and dependence on relatives.

19 Polyandry: When Brothers Take a Wife 214
Melvyn C. Goldstein

By jointly marrying one woman, Tibetan brothers preserve family resources and the "good life."

20 Uterine Families and the Women's Community 222
Margery Wolf

To succeed in a traditional patrilineal family, a Chinese woman must form her own informal uterine family inside her husband's household.

Part 7
Roles and Inequality 231

21 Symbolizing Roles: Behind the Veil 235
Elizabeth W. Fernea and Robert A. Fernea

The women's veil stands for everything from personal protection to female honor in Mediterranean societies.

22 Society and Sex Roles 243
Ernestine Friedl

Given access to public resources, women can attain equal or dominant status in any society.

23 Culture, Rank, and IQ: The Bell Curve Phenomenon 252
Mark Nathan Cohen

No matter what the book *The Bell Curve* says, IQ is not a "real" thing that can be measured cross-culturally and used to stigmatize groups.

24 The Vice Lord Phoenix 259
Lincoln Keiser

Despite official efforts to eradicate them, gangs reappear because they adapt their members to life on the street and in the penitentiary.

Part 8
Law and Politics 267

25 Why Women Take Men to Magistrate's Court 270
Mindie Lazarus-Black

Antiguan women use a law designed to ensure child support as a way to demand justice and respect in their kinship relations.

26 Cross-cultural Law: The Case of the Gypsy Offender 282
Anne Sutherland

Legal cultures clash when a young Gypsy is convicted of using someone else's social security number to apply for a car loan.

27 Navigating Nigerian Bureaucracies 290
Elizabeth A. Eames

In Nigeria, it's who you know, not what you know, that defines bureaucratic process.

28 Government, Oil, and Political Transformation: The Iñupiat Eskimo Case 299
Norman A. Chance

Over the past 30 years the Iñupiat have had to adjust to the discovery of oil on their lands.

Part 9
Religion, Magic, and Worldview 307

29 God's Saviours in the Sierra Madre 310
William L. Merrill

The Rarámuri of Mexico have transformed the Christian God, Devil, and Easter to fit their own religious values on balance and harmony.

30 Baseball Magic 320
George Gmelch

American baseball players employ magical practices as they try to deal with the uncertainty of the game.

31 Revitalization Drives American Militias 330
William O. Beeman

Stressed by rapid change, both American militia members and Middle Eastern fundamentalist Muslims create revitalization movements to restore an idealized past.

32 Cargo Beliefs and Religious Experience 337
Stephen C. Leavitt

New Guinea cargo movements serve not only as a strategy to acquire cargo (Western goods) but also as a way to contact the ancestors.

Part 10
Culture Change and Applied Anthropology 349

33 Cocaine and the Economic Deterioration of Bolivia 354
Jack McIver Weatherford

The world market for cocaine robs Bolivian villages of their men and causes problems for health, nutrition, transportation, and family.

34 The Kayapo Resistance 365

Terence Turner

Using everything from airplanes to the world environmental movement, the Kayapo Indians of Brazil have managed to prevent the building of a dam that would have flooded their Amazonian habitat.

35 Using Anthropology 383

David W. McCurdy

Professional anthropologists do everything from ethnographies of automobile production lines to famine relief, but even the neophyte may be able to use the idea of culture to understand the workplace.

36 The Medical Anthropologist as Consultant 395

Eric J. Bailey

A medical anthropologist tells how he learned to design health fairs for African Americans and eventually started his own consulting business.

Glossary 401

Photo Credits 408

Index 409

World Map and Geographical Placement of Readings

The numbers on this map correspond to the reading numbers and indicate the places on which the articles focus. Screened maps also accompany readings themselves, and white areas on these maps highlight the subject locations. Readings labeled as world on this global map do not include white areas.

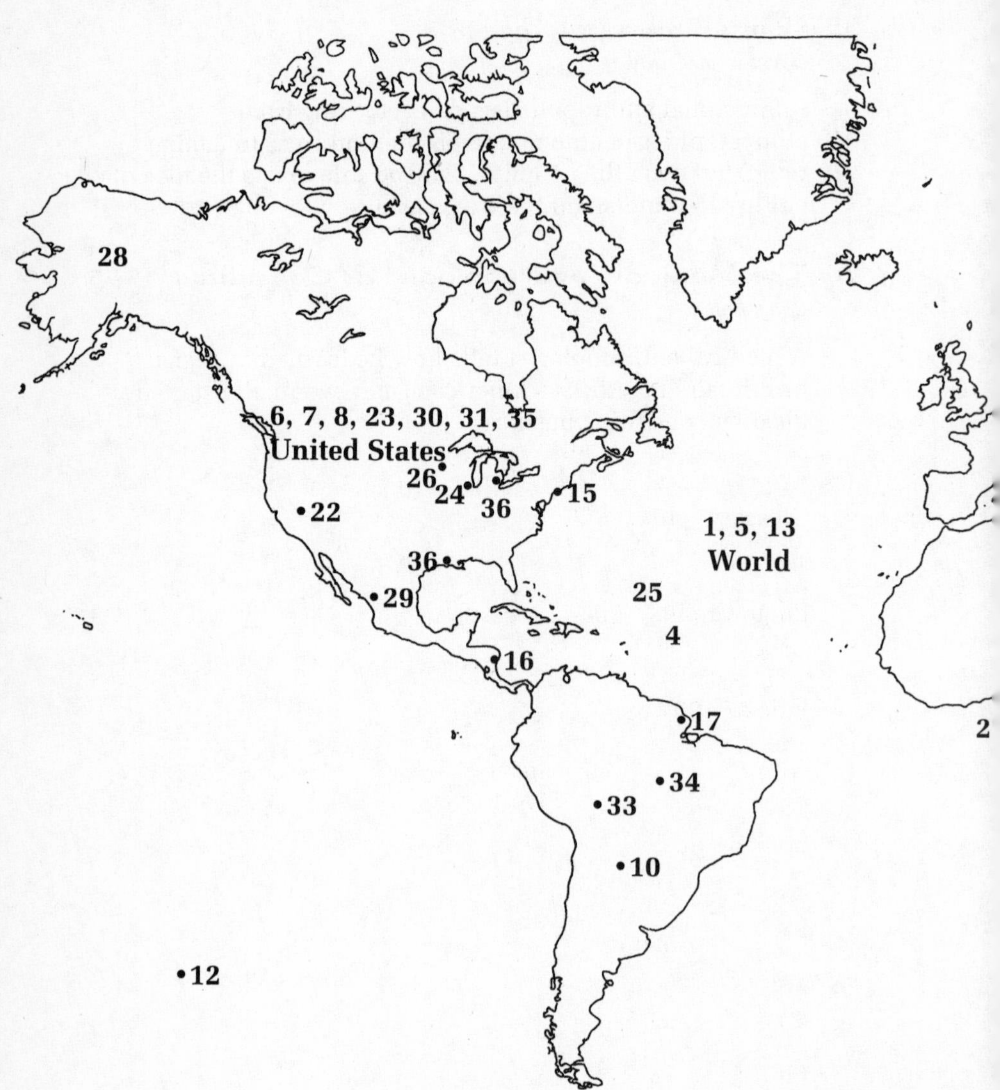

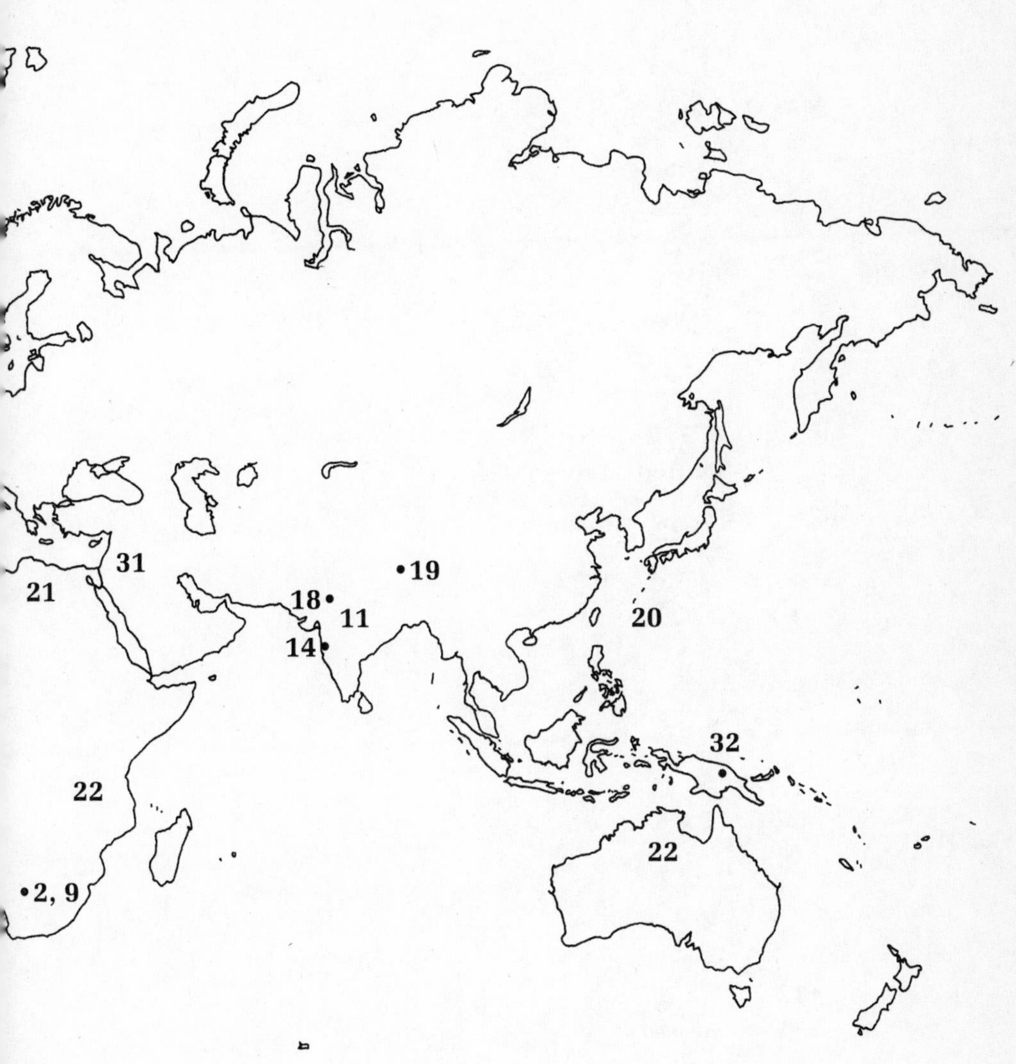

31
21
19
18
11
14
20
32
22
22
2, 9

Preface

Cultural anthropology has a twofold mission—to understand other cultures and to communicate that understanding. When preparing the first edition of this book twenty-seven years ago, we sought to make communication easier and more enjoyable for teachers and students alike. We focused on the twin themes stated in the title—conformity, or order, and conflict, or change—while organizing selections into parts based on traditional topics. We balanced the coverage of cultures between non-Western and Western (including American), so students could make their own cultural comparisons and see the relationship between anthropology and their lives. We chose articles that reflected interesting topics in anthropology, but we also looked for selections that illustrated important concepts and theories because we believed that anthropology provides a unique and powerful way to look at experience. We searched extensively for scholarly articles written with insight and clarity. Students and instructors in hundreds of colleges and universities responded enthusiastically to our efforts, and a pattern was set that carried through eight subsequent editions.

This ninth edition retains the features of earlier edition—the focus on stability and change, the coverage of a broad range of societies, the combination of professionalism and readability in selections, the view that anthropology provides a perspective on experience, and carefully integrated organization. As in previous editions, I have revamped topics and added or subtracted selections in response to the suggestions of instructors and students across the country. Anthropology and the world it seeks to understand have changed since the first edition of *Conformity and Conflict*. Most new articles have been written in the last four years. Several articles were created especially for this volume, and three are substantially revised versions of previous selections. There are major revisions to the parts on language and communication, ecology and subsistence, economic systems, roles and inequality, law and politics, religion and worldview, and culture change and applied anthropology. In all, out of thirty-six articles, fourteen are new, three have been extensively revised, and one has been brought back from earlier editions. Every part has a least one new or revised selection.

I have also continued the expanded special features that have appeared in past editions. Part introductions include discussion of many basic anthropological definitions for instructors who do not wish to use a standard textbook but find it useful to provide students with a terminological foundation. Article introductions seek to tie selections to anthropological concepts and explanations in a coherent and systematic way.

Several student aids have been retained in the ninth edition. Lists of key terms accompany each part introduction. Each article is followed by several review questions. Maps locating societies discussed in articles accompany each selection. There is also a glossary and subject index at the end of the book.

A complimentary instructor's manual and test bank is available from the publisher. The manual contains a summary of each article, as well as a large selection of true or false and multiple-choice questions for articles and part introductions.

It has always been my aim to provide a book that meets the needs of students and instructors. To help with this goal, I encourage you to send your comments and ideas for improving *Conformity and Conflict* to me at mccurdy@macalester.edu.

Many people have made suggestions that guided this revision of *Conformity and Conflict.* I am especially grateful to George Gmelch, Steven Leavitt, Kathleen Barlow, University of Minnesota; Kevin K. Birth, Queens College-The University of New York; Marie J. Boutts, University of Nevada; Donald N,. Brown, Oklahoma State University; Charles Ellenbaum, College of DuPage; Risa Ellovich, North Carolina State University; Michael D. Olien, University of Georgia; and Ann Popplestone, Cuyahoga Community College, for their advice. I would also like to thank Alan McClare and Margaret Loftus of Addison Wesley Longman for their editorial support and Kathryn Hyduke for her advice and help in production. Finally, I am grateful to my students at Macalester College for their advice and inspiration and those at Union College for their advice.

D.W.M.

CONFORMITY

AND

CONFLICT

1

CULTURE AND THE CONTEMPORARY WORLD

Viewed as a whole discipline, anthropology is a wide-ranging social and biological science concerned with most aspects of human existence. It includes *physical* (biological) *anthropology,* the study of human biology and paleontology; *archaeology,* the reconstruction of past cultures through the investigation of things people have left behind; and *anthropological linguistics,* the study of language structure, meaning, and history. It also includes the subfield, *cultural anthropology.*

Cultural anthropology emerged as an academic discipline by the middle 1800s, although the first American anthropology department did not appear until the turn of the century. The discipline was formed by a few inquisitive Europeans and Americans who became interested in the varied customs of nonwestern peoples. These early anthropologists coined the term *culture* to stand for the system of learned beliefs and customs that characterized the total way of life for a particular society. Differences among societies could be explained as the outcome of different learned cultures. Although the definition of culture has been modified over the years, as we will see below, the concept remains central to the discipline.

Few of the first anthropologists studied culture in the field. Instead, they relied on the reports of colonial officials, travelers, and missionaries. By the late 1800s, however, anthropologists began to stress the importance of firsthand observation and inquiry. This resulted in a strong fieldwork tradition, called *ethnography* (the discovery and description of a culture) that persists to this day, which sets anthropology off from other social sciences.

For much of its history, cultural anthropology largely involved the study of nonwestern societies. American anthropologists, for example, worked hard to record the traditional cultures of Native American groups during the early part of the century. British ethnographers studied the diverse cultures of African kingdoms and tribes, as well a large number of societies found in other parts of what was then the British empire. Indigenous peoples from every part of the world were the subject of anthropological inquiry.

During more recent decades, however, anthropologists have become interested in a wider variety of societies and social groups. As indigenous groups have become part of larger nation states, anthropologists have increasingly studied subcultures within more complex societies. Certainly World War II and the Cold War stimulated this trend. The United States government employed anthropologists to describe societies in whose territories it fought and where it would later administrate. The Cold War, marked by competition with Russians for influence in developing nations, stimulated an unprecedented growth in the number of U.S. academic anthropology programs. It also forced anthropologists to identify new groups to study. Anthropologists concerned with India, for example, began to study peasant villages or city wards.

Today, the problem of what to study in anthropology is even more complex. Most groups around the world are part of much larger social systems. African tribes or Indian villagers who once led relatively separate, isolated lives now find themselves participating in national politics and world markets.

But how can a discipline originally dedicated to the study of small, contained societies contribute to an understanding of today's world? Other social scientists have carried on research in complex societies for decades and have evolved special methodologies to do so. Is there anything special that anthropology can contribute to an understanding of human behavior in the contemporary world?

In many ways the answer to this question is no. The various social sciences often share the same interests. Yet, as a result of their intensive cross-cultural experience, anthropologists have developed a unique perspective on the nature and the significance of *culture.* This view has emerged from over a century of fieldwork among populations whose behavior was dramatically different from the anthropologists' own. Why, for example, did Iroquois women participate with apparent relish in the gruesome torture of prisoners? How could Bhil tribesmen put chili powder in the eyes of witches, blindfold them, and swing them over a smoky fire by their feet? What possessed Kwakiutl chiefs to destroy their wealth publicly at potlatch ceremonies? Why did Rajput widows cast themselves upon their husbands' funeral pyres? Why did Nagas engage in raids to acquire human heads? In every case, anthropologists were impressed by the fact that this "bizarre" behavior was intentional and meaningful to the participants. Bhils wanted to swing witches; to them it was appropriate. Kwakiutl chiefs made careful investments to increase the wealth they destroyed. These acts were planned; people had a notion of what they were going to do before they did it, and others shared their expectations.

Culture

The acquired knowledge that people use to interpret their world and generate social behavior is called *culture.* Culture is not behavior itself, but the knowledge used to construct and understand behavior. It is learned as children grow up in society and discover how their parents, and others around them, interpret the world. In our society we learn to distinguish objects such as cars, windows, houses, children, and food; to recognize attributes like sharp, hot, beautiful, and humid; to classify and perform different kinds of acts; to evaluate what is good and bad and to judge when an unusual action is appropriate or inappropriate. How often have you heard parents explain something about life to a child? Why do you think children are forever asking why? During socialization children learn a culture, and because they learn it from others, they share it with others, a fact that makes human social existence possible.

Culture is thus the system of knowledge by which people design their own actions and interpret the behavior of others. It tells an American that eating with one's mouth closed is proper, while an Indian knows that to be polite one must chew with one's mouth open. There is nothing preordained about culture categories; they are arbitrary. The same act can have different meanings in various cultures. For example, when adolescent Hindu boys walk holding hands, it signifies friendship, while to Americans the same act may suggest homosexuality. This arbitrariness is particularly important to remember if we are to understand our own complex society. We tend to think that the norms we follow represent the "natural" way human beings do things. Those who behave otherwise are judged as being morally wrong. This viewpoint is *ethnocentric,* which means that people think their own culture represents the best, or at least the most appropriate, way for human beings to live.

Although in our complex society we share many cultural norms with everyone, each of us belongs to a number of groups possessing exclusive cultural knowledge. We share some categories and plans with family members alone. And our occupational group, ethnic group, voluntary society, and age group each have their distinctive culture. Instead of assuming that peoples' behavior is reasonable to them, or her, that it is motivated by a different set of cultural norms, we frequently assume that they have intentionally violated accepted conventions. In their attempt to build bridges of understanding across cultural barriers, anthropologists identified the universality of ethnocentrism many years ago. The study of subcultures in our own society is another attempt to further mutual understanding, as some of the selections in this volume indicate.

How do anthropologists discover and map another culture? Are their methods applicable in the United States? Typically, anthropologists live among the people of the society that interests them. They learn the culture by observing, asking questions, and participating in daily activities—a process resembling childhood socialization or enculturation. Obviously, the anthropologist cannot become a child and must try to learn the norms in a strange group despite his or her foreign appearance and advanced age. Those who study in the United States have followed a similar procedure.

More than anything else, the study of culture separates anthropologists from other social scientists. Other scholars do not ignore culture; they assume their subjects have it, but their main interest is to account for human behavior by plotting correlations among variables. Some social scientists have explained the rise in the American divorce rate as a function of industrialization; this hypothesis can be tested by seeing if higher divorce rates are associated with industrialization and mobility. Anthropologists share a concern with this kind of explanation; for example, many have employed the Human Relations Area Files, a collection of ethnographies describing several hundred societies, as data for testing more general hypotheses. Almost every anthropologist starts with an ethnography, the description of a particular culture, and such studies are required to understand the complexity within American society.

As anthropologists have encountered, studied, and compared the world's societies, they have learned more about the concept of culture itself. As we have seen, culture is the knowledge people use to generate behavior, not behavior itself; it is arbitrary, learned, and shared. In addition, culture is adaptive. Human beings cope with their natural and social environment by means of their traditional knowledge. Culture allows for rapid adaptation because it is flexible and permits the invention of new strategies—although change often appears to be painfully slow to those who are in a hurry for it. By the same token, the adaptive nature of culture accounts for the enormous variety of the world's distinct societies.

Culture is a system of interrelated parts. If Americans were to give up automobiles, then other modes of travel, places for courtship, marks of status, and sources of income would have to be found. Culture meets personal needs; through it, people seek security and a sense of control over experience. Indeed, every tradition includes ways to cure the sick, to prepare for the unexpected, and to support the individual. In a complex society with many ways of life in contact with each other, change is persistent. It may be illusion to think that people can control the course of change or can modify the resulting culture conflict. But if we can understand human cultures—including our own—the illusion may become reality.

It is easy for people to feel that their own way of life is natural and God-given. One's culture is not like a suit of clothing that can be discarded easily or exchanged for each new lifestyle that comes along. It is rather like a security blanket, and though to some it may appear worn and tattered, outmoded and ridiculous, it has great meaning to its owner. Although there are many reasons for this fact, one of the most important is the value-laden nature of what we learn as members of society. Whether it is acquired in a tribal band, a peasant village, or an urban neighborhood, each culture is like a giant iceberg. Beneath the surface of rules, norms, and behavior patterns there is a system of values. Some of these premises are easily stated by members of a society, while others are outside their awareness. Because many difficulties in the modern world involve values, we must examine this concept in some detail.

A value is an arbitrary conception of what is *desirable* in human experience. During socialization all children are exposed to a constant barrage of evaluations—the arbitrary "rating system" of their culture. Nearly everything they learn is labeled in terms of its desirability. The value attached to each bit of information may result from the pain of a hot stove, the look of disapproval from a parent, the smile of appreciation from a teacher, or some specific verbal instruction. When parents tell a child, "You should go to college and get a good education," they are expressing a value. Those who do not conform to society's rating system are identified with derogatory labels or are punished in a more severe way. When a Tlingit Indian says to his nephew, "You should marry your father's sister," he is expressing one of the core values of his culture. When a young couple save income for future emergencies, they are conforming to the American value that the future is more important than the present. When a tramp urinates in an alley, he is violating the value attached to privacy. All these concepts of what is desirable combine cognitive and affective meanings. Individuals internalize their ideas about right and wrong, good and bad, and invest them with strong feelings.

Why do values constitute an inevitable part of all human experience? It is well known that human potential is at odds with the requirements of social life. Behavior within the realm of possibility is often outside the realm of necessity. There are numerous ways to resolve the conflict between what people *can do* by themselves and what they *must do* as members of society. It is a popular notion that prisons and other correctional institutions are the primary means by which our society enforces conformity, but this is not the case. Socialization may be ineffective for a few who require such drastic action, but for the vast majority in any society, conformity results from the internalization of values. As we learn through imitation, identification, and instruction, values are internalized. They provide security and contribute to a sense of personal and social identity. For this reason, individuals in every society cling tenaciously to the values they have acquired and feel threatened when confronted with others who live according to different conceptions of what is desirable.

Cultural Relativism

A misconception about values has been spawned by science and, in particular, by the anthropological doctrine of cultural relativism. Some have maintained that it is possible to separate values from facts and, since science is limited to facts, that it is possible to do "value-free" research. By an exercise in mental gymnastics, the very scholars who admit the influence of values in the behavior of others sometimes deny it in themselves. Preferences operate whenever an individual must *select* one action from a multitude of possible courses. Anyone who decides to observe one thing and not another is making that decision on the basis of an implicit or explicit conception of desirability. Science is an activity that makes many value judgments—including which approaches to information gathering are the best. When biologists decide to examine the structure of the DNA molecule using an empirical approach, rather than a mystical, intuitive, or religious one, they are doing so with reference to their sense of what is desirable. Even the decision to study DNA rather than some other substance involves an exercise of values. When doing research on human behavior, the influence of one's values is undeniable. The "objective observer" who is detached from the subject matter, who refrains from allowing values to influence observations, is a myth. This fact does not suggest a retreat from the *quest for objectivity.* It does not mean that social scientists are free to disparage the customs encountered in other societies or to impose their morals on those being studied. Skilled anthropologists are aware of their own values and then approach other cultures with tolerance and respect. They *identify* rather than *deny* the influence of their own viewpoints. They strive to achieve the ideal of value-free research but realize that it would be naive to assume that such a goal is possible.

Cultural relativism rests on the premise that it is possible to remain aloof and free from making value judgments. Put simply, this doctrine is based on four interrelated propositions.

1. Each person's value system is a result of his or her experience; that is, it is learned.
2. The values that individuals learn differ from one society to another because of different learning experiences.
3. Values, therefore, are relative to the society in which they occur.
4. There are no universal values, but we should respect the values of each of the world's cultures.

Cultural relativism has enabled the uninformed to understand what appears to be strange and immoral behavior. Although we may not believe it is good to kill infants, for example, we have found it intelligible in the context of a native Australian band. Although Americans generally believe in the desirability of monogamous marriage (or at least serial monogamy), we have found the practice of polygamy in other societies to be comprehensible when related to their *cultures.* This view presents numerous difficulties. Does one respect a society that believes it best to murder six million of its members who happen to be Jewish? How do anthropologists respect the values of a head-hunting tribe when their own heads are at stake?

Moreover, all the statements in this doctrine of relativism are either based on implicit values (that is, empiricism), or they are outright statements of desirability. The belief that it is good to *respect* the ideals of each of the world's cultures is itself a "relative" value. An extreme relativism is based on the philosophy that it is best to "let everyone do his or her own thing." Given unlimited resources and space this might have been possible, but in the modern world this philosophy represents a retreat from the realities facing us. It absolves the believer from the responsibility of finding some way to resolve conflicts among the world's different value systems. What is needed today is not a "live and let live" policy but a commitment to a higher, more inclusive value system, and this requires changes that are extremely difficult to achieve.

Conformity and Conflict

Every social system is a moral order; shared values act as the mortar binding together the structure of each human community. Rewards and punishments are based on commonly held values; those persons achieving high status do so in terms of cultural rating systems. These values are expressed in symbolic ways—through food, clothing, wealth, language, behavior—all of which carry implicit messages about good and bad. The pervasiveness of values gives each person a sense of belonging, a sense of being a member of a community, the feeling of joining other human beings who share a commitment to the good life. But the moral nature of every culture has two sides: it facilitates adaptation and survival on the one hand, but it often generates conflict and destruction on the other. Let us examine each of these possibilities.

For almost a million years, people have successfully adapted to a variety of terrestrial environments. From the frozen tundra to the steaming jungle, people have built their homes, reared their children, performed their rituals, and buried their dead. In recent years we have escaped the thin layer of atmosphere surrounding the earth to live, if only for a few days, in outer space and beneath the ocean. All these achievements have been possible because of a unique endowment, our capacity for culture. Wherever people wandered, they developed patterns for organizing behavior, using natural resources, relating to others, and creating a meaningful life. A genetic inheritance did not channel behavior into specialized responses but instead provided a reservoir of plasticity that was shaped by values into one of the many ways to be human. Children in every society do not learn the entire range of potential human behavior—they are taught to *conform* to a very limited number of behavior patterns that are appropriate to a particular society. Human survival depends on cultural conformity, which requires that every individual become a specialist, be committed to a few values, and acquire knowledge and skills of a single society.

This very specialization has led to diversity, resulting in a myriad of contrasting cultures. This volume contains only a small sample of the different symbolic worlds created by people in their attempt to cope with the common problems of human existence. We will see how the generosity of the American Christmas spirit stands in contrast to the daily sharing among the !Kung. Chicago suburbanites and natives of the Brazilian jungle both adorn their bodies with paint, clothing, and rings, but neither can comprehend how the other defines these symbols. All elements of human experience—kinship, marriage, age, race, sexuality, food, warfare—are socially defined and valued. The difficulty of moving from one cultural world to another is immense.

Cultural diversity has fascinated people for centuries. The study of strange and exotic peoples has attracted the curious for many generations. In the isolation of a remote jungle village or South Sea island, anthropologists found a natural laboratory for carrying out research. Their research reports often seemed more like novels than scientific studies and were read by both professionals and laypeople; seldom did any reader feel threatened by the strange behavior of far-off "savages."

But isolation rapidly disappeared, sometimes by virtue of the anthropologists' intrusion! Exploration gave way to colonization, trade, and the massive troop movements of modern warfare. Today it is impossible to find groups of people who are isolated from the remainder of the world. Instead we have a conglomeration of cultures within a single nation, and often within a single city. Anthropologists need only walk down the street from the university to encounter those who have learned a culture unlike their own. Individuals with different language styles, sexual practices, religious rituals, and a host of other strange behavior patterns sit in their classrooms or play with their children on the urban playgrounds. Anthropology today is a science concerned with understanding how people can survive in a world where village, hamlet, city, and nation are all *multicultural.* In isolation, each value system is interesting. Crowded into close and intimate contact, these distinct culture patterns often lead to conflict, oppression, and warfare. Barbara Ward has eloquently summed up our situation:

> In the last few decades, mankind has been overcome by the most change in its entire history. Modern science and technology have created so close a network of communication, transport, economic interdependence—and potential nuclear destruction—that planet Earth, on its journey through infinity, has acquired the intimacy, the fellowship and the vulnerability of a spaceship.[1]

In a sense, our greatest resource for adapting to different environments—the capacity to create different cultures—has become the source of greatest danger. Diversity is required for survival in the ecological niches of earth, but it can be destructive when all people suddenly find themselves in the same niche. Numerous species have become extinct because of their inability to adapt to a changing *natural* environment. Culture was the survival kit that enabled us to meet fluctuating natural conditions with flexibility, but now we are faced with a radically altered *human* environment. Successful adaptation will require changes that fly in the face of thousands of years of cultural specialization. Our ingenuity has been used to develop unique cultures, but thus far we have failed to develop satisfactory patterns and rules for articulating these differences. Can we survive in a world where our neighbors and even our children have different cultures? Can we adapt to the close, intimate fellowship of a spaceship when each group of passengers lives by different values?

Toward a Multicultural Society

What is required? In the first place, instead of suppressing cultural diversity by stressing assimilation into the mainstream of American life, we must recognize the extent to which our culture is pluralistic. We must accept the fact that groups within our society are committed to disparate and sometimes conflicting values. The second requirement for a truly multicultural society is that we continuously examine the *consequences* of each value system. What is the long-range effect of our commitment to a "gospel of growth"? What are the results of a belief in male superiority? How do our values of privacy affect those without homes? What is the consequence for minority

---

[1] Barbara Ward, *Spaceship Earth* (New York: Columbia University Press, 1966), vii.

groups when all students are taught to use "standard English"? As we study American culture we must discover the effect of our dominant values on every sector of life. The ideals that have made this country what it is have also been destructive to some citizens. In our efforts to assimilate ethnic groups, we have destroyed their pride and self-identity. In our attempt to offer the advantages of education to American Indians, we have induced them to become failures because our schools are not able to educate for diversity. In order to demonstrate the tolerance built into American values, we have created the "culturally deprived," but the sophistication of labels does not conceal our prejudice. The absence of men in the families of the urban poor is a logical consequence of welfare institutions created from a single value system. The consumer suffers from dangerous products because in our culture productive enterprise is more important than consumer protection. We have only begun to understand some of the consequences of our values, and during the next few decades our survival will demand that the study of values be given top priority.

Finally, the most difficult task for the contemporary world is to induce people to relinquish those values with destructive consequences. This will not be simple, and it probably will not occur without a better understanding of the nature and the function of the world's many value systems. People's capacity to learn has not yet reached its full potential. In every society, children learn to shift from *egocentric* behavior to *ethnocentric* behavior. In deference to desirable community standards, individuals give up those things they desire, and life in a particular society becomes secure and meaningful, with conventional values acting as warp and woof of social interaction.

Can we now learn to shift from *ethnocentric* to *homocentric* behavior? Can we relinquish values desirable from the standpoint of a single community but destructive to the wider world? This change will require a system of ideals greater than the conventions of any localized culture. The change will necessitate a morality that can articulate conflicting value systems and create a climate of tolerance, respect, and cooperation. Only then can we begin to create a culture that will be truly adaptive in today's world.

2

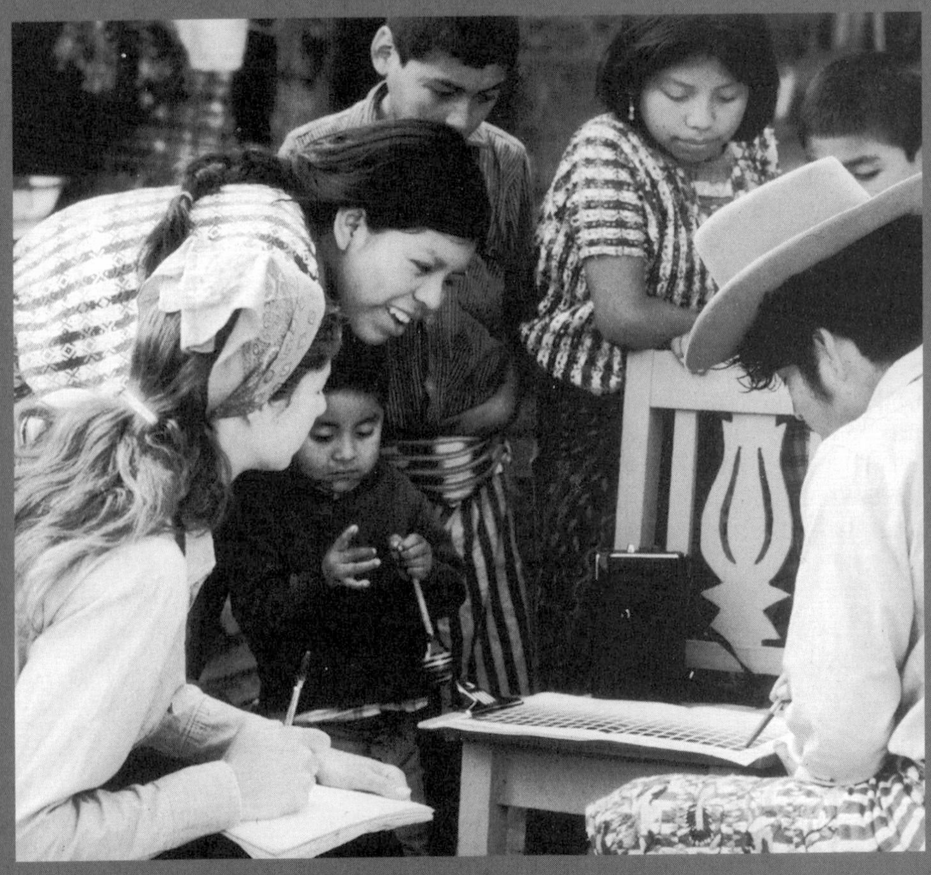

CULTURE AND ETHNOGRAPHY

Culture, as its name suggests, lies at the heart of cultural anthropology. And the concept of *culture,* along with ethnography, sets anthropology apart from other social and behavioral sciences. Let us look more closely at these concepts.

To understand what anthropologists mean by culture, imagine yourself in a foreign setting, such as a market town in India, forgetting what you might already know about that country. You step off a bus onto a dusty street where you are immediately confronted by strange sights, sounds, and smells. Men dress in Western clothes, but of a different style. Women drape themselves in long shawls that entirely cover their bodies. They peer at you through a small gap in this garment as they walk by. Buildings are one- or two-story affairs, open at the front so you can see inside. Near you some people sit on wicker chairs eating strange foods. Most unusual is how people talk. They utter vocalizations unlike any you have ever heard, and you wonder how they can possibly understand each other. But obviously they do, since their behavior seems organized and purposeful.

Scenes such as this confronted early explorers, missionaries, and anthropologists, and from their observations an obvious point emerged. People living in various parts of the world looked and behaved in dramatically different ways. And these differences correlated with groups. The people of India had customs different from those of the Papuans; the British did not act and dress like the Iroquois.

Two possible explanations for group differences came to mind. Some argued that group behavior was inherited. Dahomeans of the African Gold Coast, for example, were characterized as particularly "clever and adaptive" by one British colonial official, while, according to the same authority, another African group was "happy-go-lucky and improvident." Usually implied in such statements was the idea that group members were born that way. Such thinking persists to the present and in its least discriminating guise takes the form of racism.

But a second explanation also emerged. Perhaps, rather than a product of inheritance, the behavior characteristic of a group was learned. The way people dressed, what they ate, how they talked—all these could more easily be explained as acquisitions. Thus a baby born on the African Gold Coast would, if immediately transported to China and raised like other children there, grow up to dress, eat, and talk like a Chinese. Cultural anthropologists focus on the explanation of learned behavior.

The idea of learning, and a need to label the lifestyles associated with particular groups, led to the definition of culture. In 1871, British anthropologist Sir Edward Burnet Tylor argued that "Culture . . . is that complex whole which includes knowledge, belief, art, law, morals, custom, and any other capabilities and habits acquired by man as a member of society."[1] The definition we present here places more emphasis on the importance of knowledge than does Tylor's. We will say that *culture is the acquired knowledge that people use to generate behavior and interpret experience.*

Important to this definition is the idea that culture is a kind of knowledge, not behavior. It is in people's heads. It reflects the mental categories they learn from others as they grow up. It helps them *generate* behavior and *interpret* what they experience. At the moment of birth, we lack a culture. We don't yet have a system of beliefs, knowledge, and patterns of customary behavior. But from that moment until we die, each of us participates in a kind of universal schooling that teaches us our native culture. Laughing and smiling are genetic responses, but as infants we soon learn when to smile, when to laugh, and even how to laugh. We also inherit the potential to cry, but we must learn our cultural rules for when crying is appropriate.

As we learn our culture, we acquire a way to interpret experience. For example, we Americans learn that dogs are like little people in furry suits. Dogs live in our houses, eat our food, share our beds. They hold a place in our hearts; their loss causes us to grieve. Villagers in India, on the other hand, view dogs as pests, that admittedly are useful for hunting in those few parts of the country where one still can hunt, and as watchdogs. Quiet days in Indian villages are often punctuated by the yelp of a dog that has been threatened or actually hurt by its master or a bystander.

Clearly, it is not the dogs that are different in these two societies. Rather, it is the meaning that dogs have for people that varies. And such meaning is cultural; it is learned as part of growing up in each group.

Ethnography is the process of discovering and describing a particular culture. It involves anthropologists in an intimate and personal activity as they attempt to learn how the members of a particular group see their worlds.

But which groups qualify as culture-bearing units? How does the anthropologist identify the existence of a culture to study? This was not a difficult question when anthropology was a new science. As Tylor's definition notes, culture was the whole way of life of a people. To find it, one sought out dis-

---

[1] Edward Burnet Tylor, *Primitive Culture* (New York: Harper Torchbooks, Harper & Row, 1958; originally published by John Murray, London, 1871), 1.

tinctive ethnic units, such as Bhil tribals in India or Apaches in the American Southwest. Anything one learned from such people would be part of their culture.

But discrete cultures of this sort are becoming more difficult to find. The world is increasingly divided into large national societies, each subdivided into a myriad of subgroups. Anthropologists are finding it increasingly attractive to study such subgroups, because they form the arena for most of life in complex society. And this is where the concept of the microculture enters the scene.

Microcultures are systems of cultural knowledge characteristic of subgroups within larger societies. Members of a microculture will usually share much of what they know with everyone in the greater society but will possess a special cultural knowledge that is unique to the subgroup. For example, a college fraternity has a microculture within the context of a university and a nation. Its members have special daily routines, jokes, and meanings for events. It is this shared knowledge that makes up their microculture and that can serve as the basis for ethnographic study. More and more, anthropologists are turning to the study of microcultures, using the same ethnographic techniques they employ when they investigate the broader culture of an ethnic or national group.

More than anything else, it is ethnography that is anthropology's unique contribution to social science. Most scientists, including many who view people in social context, approach their research as *detached observers*. As social scientists, they observe the human subjects of their study, categorize what they see, and generate theory to account for their findings. They work from the outside, creating a system of knowledge to account for other people's behavior. Although this is a legitimate and often useful way to conduct research, it is not the main task of ethnography.

Ethnographers seek out the insider's viewpoint. Because culture is the knowledge people use to generate behavior and interpret experience, the ethnographer seeks to understand group members' behavior from the inside, or cultural, perspective. Instead of looking for a *subject* to observe, ethnographers look for an *informant* to teach them the culture. Just as a child learns its native culture from parents and other people in its social environment, the ethnographer learns another culture by inferring folk categories from the observation of behavior and by asking informants what things mean.

Anthropologists employ many strategies during field research to understand another culture better. But all strategies and all research ultimately rest on the cooperation of *informants*. An informant is neither a subject in a scientific experiment nor a *respondent* who answers the investigator's questions. An informant is a teacher who has a special kind of pupil: a professional anthropologist. In this unique relationship a transformation occurs in the anthropologist's understanding of an alien culture. It is the informant who transforms the anthropologist from a tourist into an ethnographer. The informant may be a child who explains how to play hopscotch, a cocktail waitress who teaches the anthropologist to serve drinks and to encourage customers to leave tips, an elderly man who teaches the anthropologist to build an igloo, or a grandmother who explains the intricacies of Zapotec kinship. Almost any individual who has acquired a repertoire of cultural behavior can become an informant.

Ethnography is not as easy to do as we might think. For one thing, Americans are not taught to be good listeners. We prefer to observe and draw our own conclusions. We like a sense of control in social contexts; passive listening is a sign of weakness in our culture. But listening and learning from others is at the heart of ethnography, and we must put aside our discomfort with the student role.

It is also not easy for informants to teach us about their cultures. Culture is often *tacit*; it is so regular and routine that it lies below a conscious level. A major ethnographic task is to help informants remember their culture, to make their knowledge part of their *explicit culture.*

But, in some cases, it is necessary to infer cultural knowledge by observing an informant's behavior because the cultural rules governing it cannot be expressed in language. Speaking distances, which vary from one culture to the next, and language sound categories, called *phonemes,* are good examples of this kind of tacit culture.

Naive realism may also impede ethnography. *Naive realism* is the belief that people everywhere see the world in the same way. It may, for example, lead the unwary ethnographer to assume that beauty is the same for all people everywhere or, to use our previous example, that dogs should mean the same thing in India as they do in the United States. If an ethnographer fails to control his or her own naive realism, inside cultural meanings will surely be overlooked.

Culture shock and ethnocentrism may also stand in the way of ethnographers. *Culture shock* is a state of anxiety that results from cross-cultural misunderstanding. Immersed alone in another society, the ethnographer understands few of the culturally defined rules for behavior and interpretation used by his or her hosts. The result is anxiety about proper action and an inability to interact appropriately in the new context.

Ethnocentrism can be just as much of a liability. *Ethnocentrism* is the belief and feeling that one's own culture is best. It reflects our tendency to judge other people's beliefs and behavior using values of our own native culture. Thus if we come from a society that abhors painful treatment of animals, we are likely to react with anger when an Indian villager hits a dog with a rock. Our feeling is ethnocentric.

It is impossible to rid ourselves entirely of the cultural values that make us ethnocentric when we do ethnography. But it is important to control our ethnocentric feeling in the field if we are to learn from informants. Informants resent negative judgment.

Finally, the role assigned to ethnographers by informants affects the quality of what can be learned. Ethnography is a personal enterprise, as all the articles in this section illustrate. Unlike survey research using questionnaires or short interviews, ethnography requires prolonged social contact. Informants will assign the ethnographer some kind of role and what that turns out to be will affect research.

The selections in Part 2 illustrate several points about culture and ethnography discussed in the preceding section. The first piece, by the late James Spradley, takes a close look at the concept of culture and its role in ethnographic research. The second, by Richard Lee, illustrates how a simple act of giving can have a dramatically different cultural meaning in two societies, leading to cross-cultural misunderstanding. Laura Bohannan's article deals with the concept of naive realism and its role in cross-cultural misunderstanding. When she tells the classic story of *Hamlet* to African Tiv elders, the plot takes on an entirely different meaning as they use their own cultural knowledge in its interpretation. Finally, the fourth article, by George Gmelch, explores how fieldwork in another culture can increase understanding of one's own.

Key Terms

culture
ethnocentrism
ethnography
microculture
detached observer
subject
informant
respondent
tacit culture
explicit culture
naive realism
culture shock

Readings in This Section

Ethnography and Culture *James P. Spradley,* page 18

Eating Christmas in the Kalahari *Richard Borshay Lee,* page 26

Shakespeare in the Bush *Laura Bohannan,* page 34

Lessons from the Field *George Gmelch,* page 44

1

Ethnography and Culture

James P. Spradley

Most Americans associate science with detached observation; we learn to observe whatever we wish to understand, introduce our own classification of what is going on, and explain what we see in our own terms. In this selection, James Spradley argues that cultural anthropologists work differently. Ethnography is the work of discovering and describing a particular culture; culture is the learned, shared knowledge that people use to generate behavior and interpret experience. To get at culture, ethnographers must learn the meanings of action and experience from the insider's or informant's point of view. Many of the examples used by Spradley also show the relevance of anthropology to the study of culture in this country.

Ethnographic fieldwork is the hallmark of cultural anthropology. Whether in a jungle village in Peru or on the streets of New York, the anthropologist goes to where people live and "does fieldwork." This means participating in activities, asking questions, eating strange foods, learning a

"Ethnography and Culture" from *Participant Observation* by James Spradley. Copyright © by Holt, Rinehart, and Winston, Inc., 1980. Reprinted by permission of the publishers.

new language, watching ceremonies, taking fieldnotes, washing clothes, writing letters home, tracing out genealogies, observing play, interviewing informants, and hundreds of other things. This vast range of activities often obscures the nature of the most fundamental task of all fieldwork: doing ethnography.

Ethnography is the work of describing a culture. The central aim of ethnography is to understand another way of life from the native point of view. The goal of ethnography, as Malinowski put it, is "to grasp the native's point of view, his relation to life, to realize *his* vision of *his* world."[1] Fieldwork, then, involves the disciplined study of what the world is like to people who have learned to see, hear, speak, think, and act in ways that are different. Rather than *studying people,* ethnography means *learning from people.* Consider the following illustration.

George Hicks set out, in 1965, to learn about another way of life, that of the mountain people in an Appalachian valley.[2] His goal was to discover their culture, to learn to see the world from their perspective. With his family he moved into Little Laurel Valley, his daughter attended the local school, and his wife became one of the local Girl Scout leaders. Hicks soon discovered that stores and storekeepers were at the center of the valley's communication system, providing the most important social arena for the entire valley. He learned this by watching what other people did, by following their example, and slowly becoming part of the groups that congregated daily in the stores. He writes:

> At least once each day I would visit several stores in the valley, and sit in on the groups of gossiping men or, if the storekeeper happened to be alone, perhaps attempt to clear up puzzling points about kinship obligations. I found these hours, particularly those spent in the presence of the two or three excellent storytellers in the Little Laurel, thoroughly enjoyable. . . . At other times, I helped a number of local men gather corn or hay, build sheds, cut trees, pull and pack galax, and search for rich stands of huckleberries. When I needed aid in, for example, repairing frozen water pipes, it was readily and cheerfully provided.[3]

In order to discover the hidden principles of another way of life, the researcher must become a *student.* Storekeepers and storytellers and local farmers become *teachers.* Instead of studying the "climate," the "flora," and the "fauna" that made up the environment of this Appalachian valley, Hicks tried to discover how these mountain people defined and evaluated trees and galax and huckleberries. He did not attempt to describe social life in terms of what most Americans know about "marriage," "family," and "friendship"; instead he sought to discover how these mountain people identified relatives and friends. He tried to learn the obligations they felt toward kinsmen and

---

[1] Bronislaw Malinowski, *Argonauts of the Western Pacific* (London: Routledge, 1922), 22.
[2] George Hicks, *Appalachian Valley* (New York: Holt, Rinehart, and Winston, 1976).
[3] Hicks, 3.

discover how they felt about friends. Discovering the *insider's view* is a different species of knowledge from one that rests mainly on the outsider's view, even when the outsider is a trained social scientist.

Consider another example, this time from the perspective of a non-Western ethnographer. Imagine an Eskimo woman setting out to learn the culture of Macalester College. What would she, so well schooled in the rich heritage of Eskimo culture, have to do in order to understand the culture of Macalester College students, faculty, and staff? How would she discover the patterns that made up their lives? How would she avoid imposing Eskimo ideas, categories, and values on everything she saw?

First, and perhaps most difficult, she would have to set aside her belief in *naive realism,* the almost universal belief that all people define the *real* world of objects, events, and living creatures in pretty much the same way. Human languages may differ from one society to the next, but behind the strange words and sentences, all people are talking about the same things. The naive realist assumes that love, snow, marriage, worship, animals, death, food, and hundreds of other things have essentially the same meaning to all human beings. Although few of us would admit to such ethnocentrism, the assumption may unconsciously influence our research. Ethnography starts with a conscious attitude of almost complete ignorance: "I don't know how the people at Macalester College understand their world. That remains to be discovered."

This Eskimo woman would have to begin by learning the language spoken by students, faculty, and staff. She could stroll the campus paths, sit in classes, and attend special events, but only if she consciously tried to see things from the native point of view would she grasp their perspective. She would need to observe and listen to first-year students during their weeklong orientation program. She would have to stand in line during registration, listen to students discuss the classes they hoped to get, and visit departments to watch faculty advising students on course selection. She would want to observe secretaries typing, janitors sweeping, and maintenance personnel plowing snow from walks. She would watch the more than 1600 students crowd into the post office area to open their tiny mailboxes, and she would listen to their comments about junk mail and letters from home or no mail at all. She would attend faculty meetings to watch what went on, recording what professors and administrators said and how they behaved. She would sample various courses, attend "keggers" on weekends, read the *Mac Weekly,* and listen by the hour to students discussing things like their "relationships," the "football team," and "work study." She would want to learn the *meanings* of all these things. She would have to listen to the members of this college community, watch what they did, and participate in their activities to learn such meanings.

The essential core of ethnography is this concern with the meaning of actions and events to the people we seek to understand. Some of these meanings are directly expressed in language; many are taken for granted and communicated only indirectly through word and action. But in every society people make constant use of these complex meaning systems to organize their behavior, to understand themselves and others, and to make sense out of the world in which they live. These systems of meaning constitute their culture; ethnography always implies a theory of culture.

Culture

When ethnographers study other cultures, they must deal with three fundamental aspects of human experience: what people do, what people know, and the things people make and use. When each of these is learned and shared by members of some group, we speak of them as *cultural behavior, cultural knowledge,* and *cultural artifacts.* Whenever you do ethnographic fieldwork, you will want to distinguish among these three, although in most situations they are usually mixed together. Let's try to unravel them.

Recently I took a commuter train from a western suburb to downtown Chicago. It was late in the day, and when I boarded the train, only a handful of people were scattered about the car. Each was engaged in a common form of *cultural behavior: reading.* Across the aisle a man held the *Chicago Tribune* out in front of him, looking intently at the small print and every now and then turning the pages noisily. In front of him a young woman held a paperback book about twelve inches from her face. I could see her head shift slightly as her eyes moved from the bottom of one page to the top of the next. Near the front of the car a student was reading a large textbook and using a pen to underline words and sentences. Directly in front of me I noticed a man looking at the ticket he had purchased and reading it. It took me an instant to survey this scene, and then I settled back, looked out the window, and read a billboard advertisement for a plumbing service proclaiming it would open any plugged drains. All of us were engaged in the same kind of cultural behavior: reading.

This common activity depended on a great many *cultural artifacts,* the things people shape or make from natural resources. I could see artifacts like books and tickets and newspapers and billboards, all of which contained tiny black marks arranged into intricate patterns called "letters." And these tiny artifacts were arranged into larger patterns of words, sentences, and paragraphs. Those of us on that commuter train could read, in part, because of still other artifacts: the bark of trees made into paper; steel made into printing presses; dyes of various colors made into ink; glue used to hold book pages together; large wooden frames to hold billboards. If an ethnographer wanted to understand the full cultural meaning in our society, it would involve a careful study of these and many other cultural artifacts.

Although we can easily see behavior and artifacts, they represent only the thin surface of a deep lake. Beneath the surface, hidden from view, lies a vast reservoir of *cultural knowledge.* Think for a moment what the people on that train needed to know in order to read. First, they had to know the grammatical rules for at least one language. Then they had to learn what the little marks on paper represented. They also had to know the meaning of space and lines and pages. They had learned cultural rules like "move your eyes from left to right, from the top of the page to the bottom." They had to know that a sentence at the bottom of a page continues on the top of the next page. The man reading a newspaper had to know a great deal about columns and the spaces between columns and what headlines mean. All of us needed to know what kinds of messages were intended by whoever wrote what we read. If a person cannot distinguish the importance of a message on a billboard from one that comes in a letter from a spouse or child, problems would develop. I knew how to recognize when other people were reading. We all knew it was impolite to read aloud on a train. We all knew how to feel when reading things like jokes or calamitous news in the paper. Our culture has a large body of shared knowledge that people learn and use to engage in this behavior called *reading* and make proper use of the artifacts connected with it.

Although cultural knowledge is hidden from view, it is of fundamental importance because we all use it constantly to generate behavior and interpret our experience. Cultural knowledge is so important that I will frequently use the broader term *culture* when speaking about it. Indeed, I will define culture as *the acquired knowledge people use to interpret experience and generate behavior.* Let's consider another example to see how people use their culture to interpret experience and do things.

One afternoon in 1973 I came across the following news item in the *Minneapolis Tribune:*

> Crowd Mistakes Rescue Attempt, Attacks Police
>
> *Nov. 23, 1973. Hartford, Connecticut.* Three policemen giving a heart massage and oxygen to a heart attack victim Friday were attacked by a crowd of 75 to 100 persons who apparently did not realize what the policemen were doing.
>
> Other policemen fended off the crowd of mostly Spanish-speaking residents until an ambulance arrived. Police said they tried to explain to the crowd what they were doing, but the crowd apparently thought they were beating the woman.
>
> Despite the policemen's efforts the victim, Evangelica Echevacria, 59, died.

Here we see people using their culture. Members of two different groups observed the same event, but their *interpretations* were drastically different. The crowd used their cultural knowledge (a) to interpret the behavior of the policemen as cruel and (b) to act on the woman's behalf to put a stop to what they perceived as brutality. They had acquired the cultural principles for acting and interpreting things in this way through a particular shared experience.

The policemen, on the other hand, used their cultural knowledge (a) to interpret the woman's condition as heart failure and their own behavior as a life-saving effort and (b) to give her cardiac massage and oxygen. They used artifacts like an oxygen mask and an ambulance. Furthermore, they interpreted the actions of the crowd in an entirely different manner from how the crowd saw their own behavior. The two groups of people each had elaborate cultural rules for interpreting their experience and for acting in emergency

Figure 1

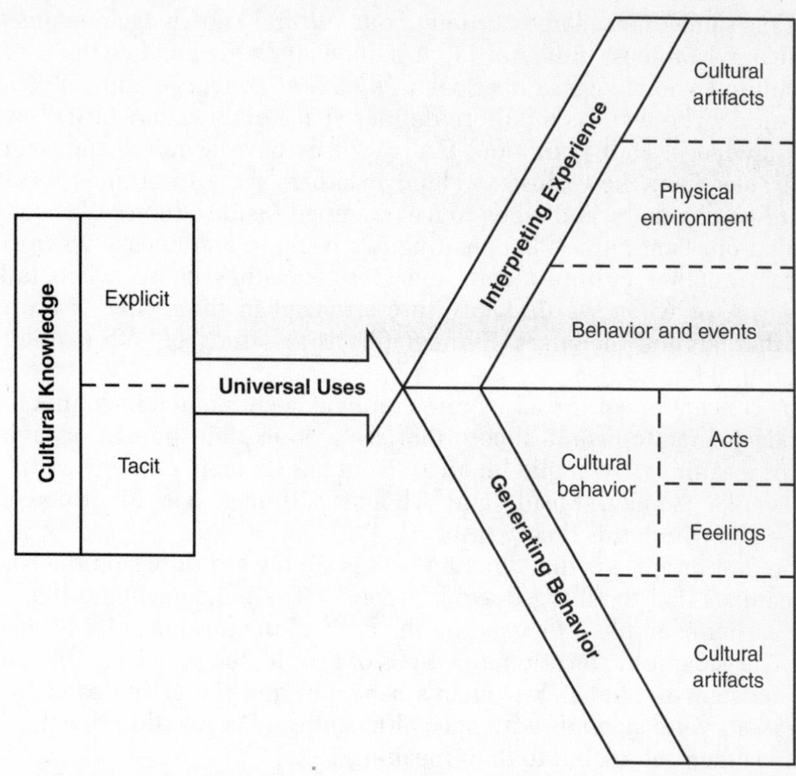

situations, and the conflict arose, at least in part, because these cultural rules were so different.

We can now diagram this definition of culture and see more clearly the relationships among knowledge, behavior, and artifacts (Figure 1). By identifying cultural knowledge as fundamental, we have merely shifted the emphasis from behavior and artifacts to their *meaning*. The ethnographer observes behavior but goes beyond it to inquire about the meaning of that behavior. The ethnographer sees artifacts and natural objects but goes beyond them to discover what meanings people assign to these objects. The ethnographer observes and records emotional states but goes beyond them to discover the meaning of fear, anxiety, anger, and other feelings.

As represented in Figure 1, cultural knowledge exists at two levels of consciousness. *Explicit culture* makes up part of what we know, a level of knowledge people can communicate about with relative ease. When George Hicks asked storekeepers and others in Little Laurel Valley about their relatives, he discovered that any adult over fifty could tell him the genealogical connections among large numbers of people. They knew how to trace kin relationships and the cultural rules for appropriate behavior among kins. All of us have acquired large areas of cultural knowledge such as this which we can talk about and make explicit.

At the same time, a large portion of our cultural knowledge remains *tacit,* outside our awareness. Edward Hall has done much to elucidate the nature of tacit cultural knowledge in his books *The Silent Language* and *The Hidden Dimension.*[4] The way each culture defines space often occurs at the level of tacit knowledge. Hall points out that all of us have acquired thousands of spatial cues about how close to stand to others, how to arrange furniture, when to touch others, and when to feel cramped inside a room. Without realizing that our tacit culture is operating, we begin to feel uneasy when someone from another culture stands too close, breathes on us when talking, touches us, or when we find furniture arranged in the center of the room rather than around the edges. Ethnography is the study of both explicit and tacit cultural knowledge. . . .

The concept of culture as acquired knowledge has much in common with symbolic interactionism, a theory that seeks to explain human behavior in terms of meanings. Symbolic interactionism has its roots in the work of sociologists like Cooley, Mead, and Thomas. Blumer has identified three premises on which this theory rests.

The first premise is that "human beings act toward things on the basis of the meanings that the things have for them."[5] The policemen and the crowd in our earlier example interacted on the basis of the meanings things had for them. The geographic location, the types of people, the police car, the policemen's movements, the sick woman's behavior, and the activities of the onlookers—all were *symbols* with special meanings. People did not act toward the things themselves, but to their meanings.

The second premise underlying symbolic interactionism is that the "meaning of such things is derived from, or arises out of, the social interaction that one has with one's fellows."[6] Culture, as a shared system of meanings, is learned, revised, maintained, and defined in the context of people interacting. The crowd came to share their definitions of police behavior through interacting with one another and through past associations with the police. The police officers acquired the cultural meanings they used through interacting with other officers and members of the community. The culture of each group was inextricably bound up with the social life of their particular communities.

The third premise of symbolic interactionism is that "meanings are handled in, and modified through, an interpretive process used by the person dealing with the things he encounters."[7] Neither the crowd nor the policemen were automatons, driven by their culture to act in the way they did. Rather,

---

[4] Edward T. Hall, *The Silent Language* (Garden City, NY: Doubleday, 1959); *The Hidden Dimension* (Garden City, NY: Doubleday, 1966).

[5] Herbert Blumer, *Symbolic Interactionism* (Englewood Cliffs, NJ: Prentice-Hall, 1969), 2.

[6] Blumer, 2.

[7] Blumer, 2.

they used their cultural knowledge to interpret and evaluate the situation. At any moment, a member of the crowd might have interpreted the behavior of the policemen in a slightly different way, leading to a different reaction.

We may see this interpretive aspect more clearly if we think of culture as a cognitive map. In the recurrent activities that make up everyday life, we refer to this map. It serves as a guide for acting and for interpreting our experience; it does not compel us to follow a particular course. Like this brief drama between the policemen, a dying woman, and the crowd, much of life is a series of unanticipated social occasions. Although our culture may not include a detailed map for such occasions, it does provide principles for interpreting and responding to them. Rather than a rigid map that people must follow, culture is best thought of as

> a set of principles for creating dramas, for writing script, and of course, for recruiting players and audiences. . . . Culture is not simply a cognitive map that people acquire, in whole or in part, more or less accurately, and then learn to read. People are not just map-readers; they are map-makers. People are cast out into imperfectly charted, continually revised sketch maps. Culture does not provide a cognitive map, but rather a set of principles for map making and navigation. Different cultures are like different schools of navigation to cope with different terrains and seas.[8]

If we take *meaning* seriously, as symbolic interactionists argue we must, it becomes necessary to study meaning carefully. We need a theory of meaning and a specific methodology designed for the investigation of it . . . .

Review Questions

1. What is the definition of *culture?* How is this definition related to the way anthropologists do ethnographic fieldwork?
2. What is the relationship among cultural behavior, cultural artifacts, and cultural knowledge?
3. What is the difference between tacit and explicit culture? How can anthropologists discover these two kinds of culture?
4. What are some examples of naive realism in the way Americans think about people in other societies?

---

[8] Charles O. Frake, "Plying Frames Can Be Dangerous: Some Reflections on Methodology in Cognitive Anthropology," *Quarterly Newsletter of the Institute for Comparative Human Development* 3 (1977): 6–7.

2

Eating Christmas in the Kalahari

Richard Borshay Lee

What happens when an anthropologist living among the !Kung of Africa decides to be generous and to share a large animal with everyone at Christmastime? This compelling account of the misunderstanding and confusion that resulted takes the reader deeper into the nature of culture. Richard Lee carefully traces how the natives perceived his generosity and taught the anthropologist something about his own culture.

The !Kung Bushmen's knowledge of Christmas is thirdhand. The London Missionary Society brought the holiday to the southern Tswana tribes in the early nineteenth century. Later, native catechists spread the idea far and wide among the Bantu-speaking pastoralists, even in the remotest corners of the Kalahari Desert. The Bushmen's idea of the Christmas story,

Originally published as "A Naturalist at Large: Eating Christmas in the Kalahari." With permission from *Natural History,* December 1969. Copyright © by the American Museum of Natural History, 1969.

stripped to its essentials, is "praise the birth of white man's god-chief"; what keeps their interest in the holiday high is the Tswana-Herero custom of slaughtering an ox for his Bushmen neighbors as an annual goodwill gesture. Since the 1930s, part of the Bushmen's annual round of activities has included a December congregation at the cattle posts for trading, marriage brokering, and several days of trance dance feasting at which the local Tswana headman is host.

As a social anthropologist working with !Kung Bushmen, I found that the Christmas ox custom suited my purposes. I had come to the Kalahari to study the hunting and gathering subsistence economy of the !Kung, and to accomplish this it was essential not to provide them with food, share my own food, or interfere in any way with their food-gathering activities. While liberal handouts of tobacco and medical supplies were appreciated, they were scarcely adequate to erase the glaring disparity in wealth between the anthropologist, who maintained a two-month inventory of canned goods, and the Bushmen, who rarely had a day's supply of food on hand. My approach, while paying off in terms of data, left me open to frequent accusations of stinginess and hardheartedness. By their lights, I was a miser.

The Christmas ox was to be my way of saying thank you for the cooperation of the past year; and since it was to be our last Christmas in the field, I was determined to slaughter the largest, meatiest ox that money could buy, insuring that the feast and trance dance would be a success.

Through December I kept my eyes open at the wells as the cattle were brought down for watering. Several animals were offered, but none had quite the grossness that I had in mind. Then, ten days before the holiday, a Herero friend led an ox of astonishing size and mass up to our camp. It was solid black, stood five feet high at the shoulder, had a five-foot span of horns, and must have weighed 1,200 pounds on the hoof. Food consumption calculations are my specialty, and I quickly figured that bones and viscera aside, there was enough meat—at least four pounds—for every man, woman, and child of the 150 Bushmen in the vicinity of /ai/ai who were expected at the feast.

Having found the right animal at last, I paid the Herero £20 ($56) and asked him to keep the beast with his herd until Christmas day. The next morning word spread among the people that the big solid black one was the ox chosen by /ontah (my Bushman name; it means, roughly, "whitey") for the Christmas feast. That afternoon I received the first delegation. Ben!a, an outspoken sixty-year-old mother of five, came to the point slowly.

"Where were you planning to eat Christmas?"

"Right here at /ai/ai," I replied.

"Alone or with others?"

"I expect to invite all the people to eat Christmas with me."

"Eat what?"

"I have purchased Yehave's black ox, and I am going to slaughter and cook it."

"That's what we were told at the well but refused to believe it until we heard it from yourself."

"Well, it's the black one," I replied expansively, although wondering what she was driving at.

"Oh, no!" Ben!a groaned, turning to her group. "They were right." Turning back to me she asked, "Do you expect us to eat that bag of bones?"

"Bag of bones! It's the biggest ox at /ai/ai."

"Big, yes, but old. And thin. Everybody knows there's no meat on that old ox. What did you expect us to eat off it, the horns?"

Everybody chuckled at Ben!a's one-liner as they walked away, but all I could manage was a weak grin.

That evening it was the turn of the young men. They came to sit at our evening fire. /gaugo, about my age, spoke to me man-to-man.

"/ontah, you have always been square with us," he lied. "What has happened to change your heart? That sack of guts and bones of Yehave's will hardly feed one camp, let alone all the Bushmen around /ai/ai." And he proceeded to enumerate the seven camps in the /ai/ai vicinity, family by family. "Perhaps you have forgotten that we are not few, but many. Or are you too blind to tell the difference between a proper cow and an old wreck? That ox is thin to the point of death."

"Look, you guys," I retorted, "that is a beautiful animal, and I'm sure you will eat it with pleasure at Christmas."

"Of course we will eat it; it's food. But it won't fill us up to the point where we will have enough strength to dance. We will eat and go home to bed with stomachs rumbling."

That night as we turned in, I asked my wife, Nancy, "What did you think of the black ox?"

"It looked enormous to me. Why?"

"Well, about eight different people have told me I got gypped; that the ox is nothing but bones."

"What's the angle?" Nancy asked. "Did they have a better one to sell?"

"No, they just said that it was going to be a grim Christmas because there won't be enough meat to go around. Maybe I'll get an independent judge to look at the beast in the morning."

Bright and early, Halingisi, a Tswana cattle owner, appeared at our camp. But before I could ask him to give me his opinion on Yehave's black ox, he gave me the eye signal that indicated a confidential chat. We left the camp and sat down.

"/ontah, I'm surprised at you; you've lived here for three years and still haven't learned anything about cattle."

"But what else can a person do but choose the biggest, strongest animal one can find?" I retorted.

"Look, just because an animal is big doesn't mean that it has plenty of meat on it. The black one was a beauty when it was younger, but now it is thin to the point of death."

"Well, I've already bought it. What can I do at this stage?"

"Bought it already? I thought you were just considering it. Well, you'll have to kill it and serve it, I suppose. But don't expect much of a dance to follow."

My spirits dropped rapidly. I could believe that Ben!a and /gaugo just might be putting me on about the black ox, but Halingisi seemed to be an impartial critic. I went around that day feeling as though I had bought a lemon of a used car.

In the afternoon it was Tomazo's turn. Tomazo is a fine hunter, a top trance performer . . . and one of my most reliable informants. He approached the subject of the Christmas cow as part of my continuing Bushman education.

"My friend, the way it is with us Bushmen," he began, "is that we love meat. And even more than that, we love fat. When we hunt we always search for the fat ones, the ones dripping with layers of white fat: fat that turns into a clear, thick oil in the cooking pot, fat that slides down your gullet, fills your stomach and gives you a roaring diarrhea," he rhapsodized.

"So, feeling as we do," he continued, "it gives us pain to be served such a scrawny thing as Yehave's black ox. It is big, yes, and no doubt its giant bones are good for soup, but fat is what we really crave, and so we will eat Christmas this year with a heavy heart."

The prospect of a gloomy Christmas now had me worried, so I asked Tomazo what I could do about it.

"Look for a fat one, a young one . . . smaller, but fat. Fat enough to make us *//gom* (evacuate the bowels), then we will be happy."

My suspicions were aroused when Tomazo said that he happened to know a young, fat, barren cow that the owner was willing to part with. Was Tomazo working on commission, I wondered? But I dispelled this unworthy thought when we approached the Herero owner of the cow in question and found that he had decided not to sell.

The scrawny wreck of a Christmas ox now became the talk of the /ai/ai water hole and was the first news told to the outlying groups as they began to come in from the bush for the feast. What finally convinced me that real trouble might be brewing was the visit from u!au, an old conservative with a reputation for fierceness. His nickname meant spear and referred to an incident thirty years ago in which he had speared a man to death. He had an intense manner; fixing me with his eyes, he said in clipped tones:

"I have only just heard about the black ox today, or else I would have come here earlier. /ontah, do you honestly think you can serve meat like that to people and avoid a fight?" He paused, letting the implications sink in. "I don't mean fight you, /ontah; you are a white man. I mean a fight between Bushmen. There are many fierce ones here, and with such a small quantity of meat to distribute, how can you give everybody a fair share? Someone is sure to accuse another of taking too much or hogging all the choice pieces. Then you will see what happens when some go hungry while others eat."

The possibility of at least a serious argument struck me as all too real. I had witnessed the tension that surrounds the distribution of meat from a kudu or gemsbok kill, and had documented many arguments that sprang up from a real or imagined slight in meat distribution. The owners of a kill may spend up to two hours arranging and rearranging the piles of meat under the gaze of a circle of recipients before handing them out. And I knew that the Christmas feast at /ai/ai would be bringing together groups that had feuded in the past.

Convinced now of the gravity of the situation, I went in earnest to search for a second cow; but all my inquiries failed to turn one up.

The Christmas feast was evidently going to be a disaster, and the incessant complaints about the meagerness of the ox had already taken the fun out of it for me. Moreover, I was getting bored with the wisecracks, and after losing my temper a few times, I resolved to serve the beast anyway. If the meat fell short, the hell with it. In the Bushmen idiom, I announced to all who would listen:

"I am a poor man and blind. If I have chosen one that is too old and too thin, we will eat it anyway and see if there is enough meat there to quiet the rumbling of our stomachs."

On hearing this speech, Ben!a offered me a rare word of comfort. "It's thin," she said philosophically, "but the bones will make a good soup."

At dawn Christmas morning, instinct told me to turn over the butchering and cooking to a friend and take off with Nancy to spend Christmas alone in the bush. But curiosity kept me from retreating. I wanted to see what such a scrawny ox looked like on butchering, and if there *was* going to be a fight, I wanted to catch every word of it. Anthropologists are incurable that way.

The great beast was driven up to our dancing ground, and a shot in the forehead dropped it in its tracks. Then, freshly cut branches were heaped around the fallen carcass to receive the meat. Ten men volunteered to help with the cutting, I asked /gaugo to make the breast bone cut. This cut, which begins the butchering process for most large game, offers easy access for removal of the viscera. But it also allows the hunter to spot-check the amount of fat on an animal. A fat game animal carries a white layer up to an inch thick on the chest, while in a thin one, the knife will quickly cut to bone. All eyes fixed on his hand as /gaugo, dwarfed by the great carcass, knelt to the breast. The first cut opened a pool of solid white in the black skin. The second and third cut widened and deepened the creamy white. Still no bone. It was pure fat; it must have been two inches thick.

"Hey /gau," I burst out, "that ox is loaded with fat. What's this about the ox being too thin to bother eating? Are you out of your mind?"

"Fat?" /gau shot back. "You call that fat? This wreck is thin, sick, dead!" And he broke out laughing. So did everyone else. They rolled on the ground, paralyzed with laughter. Everybody laughed except me; I was thinking.

I ran back to the tent and burst in just as Nancy was getting up. "Hey, the black ox. It's fat as hell! They were kidding about it being too thin to eat. It was a joke or something. A put-on. Everyone is really delighted with it."

"Some joke," my wife replied. "It was so funny that you were ready to pack up and leave /ai/ai."

If it had indeed been a joke, it had been an extraordinarily convincing one, and tinged, I thought, with more than a touch of malice, as many jokes are. Nevertheless, that it was a joke lifted my spirits considerably, and I returned to the butchering site where the shape of the ox was rapidly disappearing under the axes and knives of the butchers. The atmosphere had become festive. Grinning broadly, their arms covered with blood well past the elbow, men packed chunks of meat into the big cast-iron cooking pots, fifty pounds to the load, and muttered and chuckled all the while about the thinness and worthlessness of the animal and /ontah's poor judgment.

We danced and ate that ox two days and two nights; we cooked and distributed fourteen potfuls of meat and no one went home hungry and no fights broke out.

But the "joke" stayed in my mind. I had a growing feeling that something important had happened in my relationship with the Bushmen and that the clue lay in the meaning of the joke. Several days later, when most of the people had dispersed back to the bush camps, I raised the question with Hakekgose, a Tswana man who had grown up among the !Kung, married a !Kung girl, and who probably knew their culture better than any other non-Bushman.

"With us whites," I began, "Christmas is supposed to be the day of friendship and brotherly love. What I can't figure out is why the Bushmen went to such lengths to criticize and belittle the ox I had bought for the feast. The animal was perfectly good and their jokes and wisecracks practically ruined the holiday for me."

"So it really did bother you," said Hakekgose. "Well, that's the way they always talk. When I take my rifle and go hunting with them, if I miss, they laugh at me for the rest of the day. But even if I hit and bring one down, it's no better. To them, the kill is always too small or too old or too thin; and as we sit down on the kill site to cook and eat the liver, they keep grumbling, even with their mouths full of meat. They say things like, 'Oh, this is awful! What a worthless animal! Whatever made me think that this Tswana rascal could hunt!' "

"Is this the way outsiders are treated?" I asked.

"No, it is their custom; they talk that way to each other, too. Go and ask them."

/gaugo had been one of the most enthusiastic in making me feel bad about the merit of the Christmas ox. I sought him out first.

"Why did you tell me the black ox was worthless, when you could see that it was loaded with fat and meat?"

"It is our way," he said, smiling. "We always like to fool people about that. Say there is a Bushman who has been hunting. He must not come home and announce like a braggart, 'I have killed a big one in the bush!' He must first sit down in silence until I or someone else comes up to his fire and asks, 'What did you see today?' He replies quietly, 'Ah, I'm no good for hunting. I saw nothing at all [pause] just a little tiny one.' Then I smile to myself," /gaugo continued, "because I know he has killed something big.

"In the morning we make up a party of four or five people to cut up and carry the meat back to the camp. When we arrive at the kill we examine it and cry out, 'You mean to say you have dragged us all the way out here in order to make us cart home your pile of bones? Oh, if I had known it was this thin I wouldn't have come.' Another one pipes up, 'People, to think I gave up a nice day in the shade for this. At home we may be hungry, but at least we have nice cool water to drink.' If the horns are big, someone says, 'Did you think that somehow you were going to boil down the horns for soup?'

"To all this you must respond in kind. 'I agree,' you say, 'this one is not worth the effort; let's just cook the liver for strength and leave the rest for the hyenas. It is not too late to hunt today and even a duiker or a steenbok would be better than this mess.'

"Then you set to work nevertheless; butcher the animal, carry the meat back to the camp and everyone eats," /gaugo concluded.

Things were beginning to make sense. Next, I went to Tomazo. He corroborated /gaugo's story of the obligatory insults over a kill and added a few details of his own.

"But," I asked, "why insult a man after he has gone to all that trouble to track and kill an animal and when he is going to share the meat with you so that your children will have something to eat?"

"Arrogance," was his cryptic answer.

"Arrogance?"

"Yes, when a young man kills much meat he comes to think of himself as a chief or a big man, and he thinks of the rest of us as his servants or inferiors. We can't accept this. We refuse one who boasts, for someday his pride will make him kill somebody. So we always speak of his meat as worthless. This way we cool his heart and make him gentle."

"But why didn't you tell me this before?" I asked Tomazo with some heat.

"Because you never asked me," said Tomazo, echoing the refrain that has come to haunt every field ethnographer.

The pieces now fell into place. I had known for a long time that in situations of social conflict with Bushmen I held all the cards. I was the only source of tobacco in a thousand square miles, and I was not incapable of cutting an individual off for noncooperation. Though my boycott never lasted longer than a few days, it was an indication of my strength. People resented my presence at the water hole, yet simultaneously dreaded my leaving. In short I was a perfect target for the charge of arrogance and for the Bushman tactic of enforcing humility.

I had been taught an object lesson by the Bushmen; it had come from an unexpected corner and had hurt me in a vulnerable area. For the big black ox was to be the one totally generous, unstinting act of my year at /ai/ai and I was quite unprepared for the reaction I received.

As I read it, their message was this: There are no totally generous acts. All "acts" have an element of calculation. One black ox slaughtered at Christmas does not wipe out a year of careful manipulation of gifts given to serve your own ends. After all, to kill an animal and share the meat with people is really no more than the Bushmen do for each other every day and with far less fanfare.

In the end, I had to admire how the Bushmen had played out the farce—collectively straight-faced to the end. Curiously, the episode reminded me of the *Good Soldier Schweik* and his marvelous encounters with authority. Like Schweik, the Bushmen had retained a thoroughgoing skepticism of good intentions. Was it this independence of spirit, I wondered, that had kept them culturally viable in the face of generations of contact with more powerful societies, both black and white? The thought that the Bushmen were alive and well in the Kalahari was strangely comforting. Perhaps, armed with that independence and with their superb knowledge of their environment, they might yet survive the future.

Review Questions

1. What was the basis of the misunderstanding experienced by Lee when he gave an ox for the Christmas feast held by the !Kung?
2. Construct a model of cross-cultural misunderstanding, using the information presented by Lee in this article.
3. Why do you think the !Kung ridicule and denigrate people who have been successful hunters or who have provided them with a Christmas ox? Why do Americans expect people to be grateful to receive gifts?

3

Shakespeare in the Bush

Laura Bohannan

All of us use the cultural knowledge we acquire as members of our own society to organize our perception and behavior. Most of us are also naive realists: we tend to believe our culture mirrors a reality shared by everyone. But cultures are different, and other people rarely behave or interpret experience according to our cultural plan. In this article, Laura Bohannan describes her attempt to tell the classic story of Hamlet *to Tiv elders in West Africa. At each turn in the story, the Tiv interpret the events and motives in* Hamlet *using their own cultural knowledge. The result is a very different version of the classic play.*

Just before I left Oxford for the Tiv in West Africa, conversation turned to the season at Stratford. "You Americans," said a friend, "often have difficulty with Shakespeare. He was, after all, a very English poet, and one can easily misinterpret the universal by misunderstanding the particular."

I protested that human nature is pretty much the same the whole world over; at least the general plot and motivation of the greater tragedies would

---

Reprinted with permission by the author from *Natural History,* August/September 1966. Copyright © by Laura Bohannan, 1966.

always be clear—everywhere—although some details of custom might have to be explained and difficulties of translation might produce other slight changes. To end an argument we could not conclude, my friend gave me a copy of *Hamlet* to study in the African bush: it would, he hoped, lift my mind above its primitive surroundings, and possibly I might, by prolonged meditation, achieve the grace of correct interpretation.

It was my second field trip to that African tribe, and I thought myself ready to live in one of its remote sections—an area difficult to cross even on foot. I eventually settled on the hillock of a very knowledgeable old man, the head of a homestead of some hundred and forty people, all of whom were either his close relatives or their wives and children. Like the other elders of the vicinity, the old man spent most of his time performing ceremonies seldom seen these days in the more accessible parts of the tribe. I was delighted. Soon there would be three months of enforced isolation and leisure, between the harvest that takes place just before the rising of the swamps and the clearing of new farms when the water goes down. Then, I thought, they would have even more time to perform ceremonies and explain them to me.

I was quite mistaken. Most of the ceremonies demanded the presence of elders from several homesteads. As the swamps rose, the old men found it too difficult to walk from one homestead to the next, and the ceremonies gradually ceased. As the swamps rose even higher, all activities but one came to an end. The women brewed beer from maize and millet. Men, women, and children sat on their hillocks and drank it.

People began to drink at dawn. By midmorning the whole homestead was singing, dancing, and drumming. When it rained, people had to sit inside their huts: there they drank and sang or they drank and told stories. In any case, by noon or before, I either had to join the party or retire to my own hut and my books. "One does not discuss serious matters when there is beer. Come, drink with us." Since I lacked their capacity for the thick native beer, I spent more and more time with *Hamlet*. Before the end of the second month, grace descended on me. I was quite sure that *Hamlet* had only one possible interpretation, and that one universally obvious.

Early every morning, in the hope of having some serious talk before the beer party, I used to call on the old man at his reception hut—a circle of posts supporting a thatched roof above a low mud wall to keep out wind and rain. One day I crawled through the low doorway and found most of the men of the homestead sitting huddled in their ragged cloths on stools, low plank beds, and reclining chairs, warming themselves against the chill of the rain around a smoky fire. In the center were three pots of beer. The party had started.

The old man greeted me cordially. "Sit down and drink." I accepted a large calabash full of beer, poured some into a small drinking gourd, and tossed it down. Then I poured some more into the same gourd for the man second in seniority to my host before I handed my calabash over to a young man for further distribution. Important people shouldn't ladle beer themselves.

"It is better like this," the old man said, looking at me approvingly and plucking at the thatch that had caught in my hair. "You should sit and drink with us more often. Your servants tell me that when you are not with us, you sit inside your hut looking at a paper."

The old man was acquainted with four kinds of "papers": tax receipts, bride price receipts, court fee receipts, and letters. The messenger who brought him letters from the chief used them mainly as a badge of office, for he always knew what was in them and told the old man. Personal letters for the few who had relatives in the government or mission stations were kept until someone went to a large market where there was a letter writer and reader. Since my arrival, letters were brought to me to be read. A few men also brought me bride price receipts, privately, with requests to change the figures to a higher sum. I found moral arguments were of no avail, since in-laws are fair game, and the technical hazards of forgery difficult to explain to an illiterate people. I did not wish them to think me silly enough to look at any such papers for days on end, and I hastily explained that my "paper" was one of the "things of long ago" of my country.

"Ah," said the old men. "Tell us."

I protested that I was not a storyteller. Storytelling is a skilled art among them; their standards are high, and the audiences critical—and vocal in their criticism. I protested in vain. This morning they wanted to hear a story while they drank. They threatened to tell me no more stories until I told them one of mine. Finally, the old man promised that no one would criticize my style "for we know you are struggling with our language." "But," put in one of the elders, "you must explain what we do not understand, as we do when we tell you our stories." Realizing that here was my chance to prove *Hamlet* universally intelligible, I agreed.

The old man handed me some more beer to help me on with my storytelling. Men filled their long wooden pipes and knocked coals from the fire to place in the pipe bowls; then, puffing contentedly, they sat back to listen. I began in the proper style, "Not yesterday, not yesterday, but long ago, a thing occurred. One night three men were keeping watch outside the homestead of the great chief, when suddenly they saw the former chief approach them."

"Why was he no longer their chief?"

"He was dead," I explained. "That is why they were troubled and afraid when they saw him."

"Impossible," began one of the elders, handing his pipe on to his neighbor, who interrupted, "Of course it wasn't the dead chief. It was an omen sent by a witch. Go on."

Slightly shaken, I continued. "One of these three was a man who knew things"—the closest translation for scholar, but unfortunately it also meant witch. The second elder looked triumphantly at the first. "So he spoke to the dead chief, saying, 'Tell us what we must do so you may rest in your grave,' but the dead chief did not answer. He vanished, and they could see him no more. Then the man who knew things—his name was Horatio—said this event was the affair of the dead chief's son, Hamlet."

There was a general shaking of heads around the circle. "Had the dead chief no living brothers? Or was this son the chief?"

"No," I replied. "That is, he had one living brother who became the chief when the elder brother died."

The old men muttered: such omens were matters for chiefs and elders, not for youngsters; no good could come of being behind a chief's back; clearly Horatio was not a man who knew things.

"Yes, he was," I insisted, shooing a chicken away from my beer. "In our country the son is next to the father. The dead chief's younger brother had become the great chief. He had also married his elder brother's widow only about a month after the funeral."

"He did well," the old man beamed and announced to the others, "I told you that if we knew more about Europeans, we would find they really were very like us. In our country also," he added to me, "the younger brother marries the elder brother's widow and becomes the father of his children. Now, if your uncle, who married your widowed mother, is your father's full brother, then he will be a real father to you. Did Hamlet's father and uncle have one mother?"

His question barely penetrated my mind; I was too upset and thrown too far off balance by having one of the most important elements of *Hamlet* knocked straight out of the picture. Rather uncertainly I said that I thought they had the same mother, but I wasn't sure—the story didn't say. The old man told me severely that these genealogical details made all the difference and that when I got home I must ask the elders about it. He shouted out the door to one of his younger wives to bring his goatskin bag.

Determined to save what I could of the mother motif, I took a deep breath and began again. "The son Hamlet was very sad because his mother had married again so quickly. There was no need for her to do so, and it is our custom for a widow not to go to her next husband until she has mourned for two years."

"Two years is too long," objected the wife, who had appeared with the old man's battered goatskin bag. "Who will hoe your farms for you while you have no husband?"

"Hamlet," I retorted without thinking, "was old enough to hoe his mother's farms himself. There was no need for her to remarry." No one looked convinced. I gave up. "His mother and the great chief told Hamlet not to be sad, for the great chief himself would be a father to Hamlet. Furthermore, Hamlet would be the next chief: therefore he must stay to learn the things of a chief. Hamlet agreed to remain, and all the rest went off to drink beer."

While I paused, perplexed at how to render Hamlet's disgusted soliloquy to an audience convinced that Claudius and Gertrude had behaved in the best possible manner, one of the younger men asked me who had married the other wives of the dead chief.

"He had no other wives," I told him.

"But a chief must have many wives! How else can he brew beer and prepare food for all his guests?"

I said firmly that in our country even chiefs had only one wife, that they had servants to do their work, and that they paid them from tax money.

It was better, they returned, for a chief to have many wives and sons who would help him hoe his farms and feed his people; then everyone loved the chief who gave much and took nothing—taxes were a bad thing.

I agreed with the last comment, but for the rest fell back on their favorite way of fobbing off my questions: "That is the way it is done, so that is how we do it."

I decided to skip the soliloquy. Even if Claudius was here thought quite right to marry his brother's widow, there remained the poison motif, and I knew they would disapprove of fratricide. More hopefully I resumed, "That night Hamlet kept watch with the three who had seen his dead father. The dead chief again appeared, and although the others were afraid, Hamlet followed his dead father off to one side. When they were alone, Hamlet's dead father spoke."

"Omens can't talk!" The old man was emphatic.

"Hamlet's dead father wasn't an omen. Seeing him might have been an omen, but he was not." My audience looked as confused as I sounded. "It *was* Hamlet's dead father. It was a thing we call a 'ghost.'" I had to use the English word, for unlike many of the neighboring tribes, these people didn't believe in the survival after death of any individuating part of the personality.

"What is a 'ghost'? An omen?"

"No, a 'ghost' is someone who is dead but who walks around and can talk, and people can hear him and see him but not touch him."

They objected. "One can touch zombis."

"No, no! It was not a dead body the witches had animated to sacrifice and eat. No one else made Hamlet's dead father walk. He did it himself."

"Dead men can't walk," protested my audience as one man.

I was quite willing to compromise. "A 'ghost' is a dead man's shadow."

But again they objected. "Dead men cast no shadows."

"They do in my country," I snapped.

The old man quelled the babble of disbelief that rose immediately and told me with that insincere, but courteous, agreement one extends to the fancies of the young, ignorant, and superstitious, "No doubt in your country the dead can also walk without being zombis." From the depths of his bag he produced a withered fragment of kola nut, bit off one end to show it wasn't poisoned, and handed me the rest as a peace offering.

"Anyhow," I resumed, "Hamlet's dead father said that his own brother, the one who became chief, had poisoned him. He wanted Hamlet to avenge him. Hamlet believed this in his heart, for he did not like his father's brother." I took another swallow of beer. "In the country of the great chief, living in the same homestead, for it was a very large one, was an important elder who was often with the chief to advise and help him. His name was Polonius. Hamlet was courting his daughter, but her father and her brother ... [I cast hastily about for some tribal analogy] warned her not to let Hamlet visit her when she was alone on her farm, for he would be a great chief and so could not marry her."

"Why not?" asked the wife, who had settled down on the edge of the old man's chair. He frowned at her for asking stupid questions and growled, "They lived in the same homestead."

"That was not the reason," I informed them. "Polonius was a stranger who lived in the homestead because he helped the chief, not because he was a relative."

"Then why couldn't Hamlet marry her?"

"He could have," I explained, "but Polonius didn't think he would. After all, Hamlet was a man of great importance who ought to marry a chief's daughter, for in his country a man could have only one wife. Polonius was afraid that if Hamlet made love to his daughter, then no one else would give a high price for her."

"That might be true," remarked one of the shrewder elders, "but a chief's son would give his mistress's father enough presents and patronage to more than make up the difference. Polonius sounds like a fool to me."

"Many people think he was," I agreed. "Meanwhile Polonius sent his son Laertes off to Paris to learn the things of that country, for it was the homestead of a very great chief indeed. Because he was afraid that Laertes might waste a lot of money on beer and women and gambling, or get into trouble by fighting, he sent one of his servants to Paris secretly, to spy out what Laertes was doing. One day Hamlet came upon Polonius's daughter Ophelia. He behaved so oddly he frightened her. Indeed"—I was fumbling for words to express the dubious quality of Hamlet's madness—"the chief and many others had also noticed that when Hamlet talked one could understand the words but not what they meant. Many people thought that he had become mad." My audience suddenly became much more attentive. "The great chief wanted to know what was wrong with Hamlet, so he sent for two of Hamlet's age mates [school friends would have taken long explanation] to talk to Hamlet and find out what troubled his heart. Hamlet, seeing that they had been bribed by the chief to betray him, told them nothing. Polonius, however, insisted that Hamlet was mad because he had been forbidden to see Ophelia, whom he loved."

"Why," inquired a bewildered voice, "should anyone bewitch Hamlet on that account?"

"Bewitch him?"

"Yes, only witchcraft can make anyone mad, unless, of course, one sees the beings that lurk in the forest."

I stopped being a storyteller, took out my notebook and demanded to be told more about these two causes of madness. Even while they spoke and I jotted notes, I tried to calculate the effect of this new factor on the plot. Hamlet had not been exposed to the beings that lurk in the forest. Only his relatives in the male line could bewitch him. Barring relatives not mentioned by Shakespeare, it had to be Claudius who was attempting to harm him. And, of course, it was.

For the moment I staved off questions by saying that the great chief also refused to believe that Hamlet was mad for the love of Ophelia and nothing else. "He was sure that something much more important was troubling Hamlet's heart."

"Now Hamlet's age mates," I continued, "had brought with them a famous storyteller. Hamlet decided to have this man tell the chief and all his homestead a story about the man who had poisoned his brother because he desired his brother's wife and wished to be chief himself. Hamlet was sure the great chief could not hear the story without making a sign if he was indeed guilty, and then he would discover whether his dead father had told him the truth."

The old man interrupted, with deep cunning. "Why should a father lie to his son?" he asked.

I hedged: "Hamlet wasn't sure that it really was his dead father." It was impossible to say anything, in that language, about devil-inspired visions.

"You mean," he said, "it actually was an omen, and he knew witches sometimes send false ones. Hamlet was a fool not to go to one skilled in reading omens and divining the truth in the first place. A man-who-sees-the-truth could have told him how his father died, if he really had been poisoned, and if there was witchcraft in it; then Hamlet could have called the elders to settle the matter."

The shrewd elder ventured to disagree. "Because his father's brother was a great chief, one-who-sees-the-truth might therefore have been afraid to tell it. I think it was for that reason that a friend of Hamlet's father—a witch and an elder—sent an omen so his friend's son would know. Was the omen true?"

"Yes," I said, abandoning ghosts and the devil; a witch-sent omen it would have to be. "It was true, for when the storyteller was telling his tale before all the homestead, the great chief rose in fear. Afraid that Hamlet knew his secret, he planned to have him killed."

The stage set of the next bit presented some difficulties of translation. I began cautiously. "The great chief told Hamlet's mother to find out from her son what he knew. But because a woman's children are always first in her heart, he had the important elder Polonius hide behind a cloth that hung against the wall of Hamlet's mother's sleeping hut. Hamlet started to scold his mother for what she had done."

There was a shocked murmur from everyone. A man should never scold his mother.

"She called out in fear, and Polonius moved behind the cloth. Shouting 'A rat!' Hamlet took his machete and slashed through the cloth." I paused for a dramatic effect. "He had killed Polonius!"

The old men looked at each other in supreme disgust. "That Polonius truly was a fool and a man who knew nothing! What child would not know enough to shout, 'It's me!' " With a pang, I remembered that these people are ardent hunters, always armed with bow, arrow, and machete; at the first rustle in the grass an arrow is aimed and ready, and the hunter shouts "Game!" If no human voice answers immediately, the arrow speeds on its way. Like a good hunter Hamlet had shouted, "A rat!"

I rushed in to save Polonius's reputation. "Polonius did speak. Hamlet heard him. But he thought it was the chief and wished to kill him to avenge his father. He had meant to kill him earlier that evening . . . ." I broke down, unable to describe to these pagans, who had no belief in individual afterlife, the difference between dying at one's prayers and dying "unhousell'd, disappointed, unaneled."

This time I had shocked my audience seriously. "For a man to raise his hands against his father's brother and the one who has become his father—that is a terrible thing. The elders ought to let such a man be bewitched."

I nibbled at my kola nut in some perplexity, then pointed out that after all the man had killed Hamlet's father.

"No," pronounced the old man, speaking less to me than to the young men sitting behind the elders. "If your father's brother has killed your father, you must appeal to your father's age mates; *they* may avenge him. No man may use violence against his senior relatives." Another thought struck him. "But if his father's brother had indeed been wicked enough to bewitch Hamlet and make him mad, that would be a good story indeed, for it would be his fault that Hamlet, being mad, no longer had any sense and thus was ready to kill his father's brother."

There was a murmur of applause. *Hamlet* was again a good story to them, but it no longer seemed quite the same story to me. As I thought over the coming complications of plot and motive, I lost courage and decided to skim over dangerous ground quickly.

"The great chief," I went on, "was not sorry that Hamlet had killed Polonius. It gave him a reason to send Hamlet away, with his two treacherous age mates, with letters to a chief of a far country, saying that Hamlet should be killed. But Hamlet changed the writing on their papers, so that the chief killed his age mates instead." I encountered a reproachful glare from one of the men whom I had told undetectable forgery was not merely immoral but beyond human skill. I looked the other way.

"Before Hamlet could return, Laertes came back for his father's funeral. The great chief told him Hamlet had killed Polonius. Laertes swore to kill Hamlet because of this, and because his sister Ophelia, hearing her father had been killed by the man she loved, went mad and drowned in the river."

"Have you already forgotten what we told you?" The old man was reproachful. "One cannot take vengeance on a madman; Hamlet killed Polonius in his madness. As for the girl, she not only went mad, she was drowned. Only witches can make people drown. Water itself can't hurt anything. It is merely something one drinks and bathes in."

I began to get cross. "If you don't like the story, I'll stop."

The old man made soothing noises and himself poured me some more beer. "You tell the story well, and we are listening. But it is clear that the elders of your country have never told you what the story really means. No, don't interrupt! We believe you when you say your marriage customs are different, or your clothes and weapons. But people are the same everywhere; therefore, there are always witches and it is we, the elders, who know how witches work. We told you it was the great chief who wished to kill Hamlet, and now your own words have proved us right. Who were Ophelia's male relatives?"

"There were only her father and her brother." Hamlet was clearly out of my hands.

"There must have been many more; this also you must ask of your elders when you get back to your country. From what you tell us, since Polonius was dead, it must have been Laertes who killed Ophelia, although I do not see the reason for it."

We had emptied one pot of beer, and the old men argued the point with slightly tipsy interest. Finally one of them demanded of me, "What did the servant of Polonius say on his return?"

With difficulty I recollected Reynaldo and his mission. "I don't think he did return before Polonius was killed."

"Listen," said the elder, "and I will tell you how it was and how your story will go, then you may tell me if I am right. Polonius knew his son would get into trouble, and so he did. He had many fines to pay for fighting, and debts from gambling. But he had only two ways of getting money quickly. One was to marry off his sister at once, but it is difficult to find a man who will marry a woman desired by the son of a chief. For if the chief's heir commits adultery with your wife, what can you do? Only a fool calls a case against a man who will someday be his judge. Therefore Laertes had to take the second way: he killed his sister by witchcraft, drowning her so he could secretly sell her body to the witches."

I raised an objection. "They found her body and buried it. Indeed Laertes jumped into the grave to see his sister once more—so, you see, the body was truly there. Hamlet, who had just come back, jumped in after him."

"What did I tell you?" The elder appealed to the others. "Laertes was up to no good with his sister's body. Hamlet prevented him, because the chief's heir, like a chief, does not wish any other man to grow rich and powerful. Laertes would be angry, because he would have killed his sister without benefit to himself. In our country he would try to kill Hamlet for that reason. Is this not what happened?"

"More or less," I admitted. "When the great chief found Hamlet was still alive, he encouraged Laertes to try to kill Hamlet and arranged a fight with machetes between them. In the fight both the young men were wounded to death. Hamlet's mother drank the poisoned beer that the chief meant for Hamlet in case he won the fight. When he saw his mother die of poison, Hamlet, dying, managed to kill his father's brother with his machete."

"You see, I was right!" exclaimed the elder.

"That was a very good story," added the old man, "and you told it with very few mistakes. There was just one more error, at the very end. The poison Hamlet's mother drank was obviously meant for the survivor of the fight, whichever it was. If Laertes had won, the great chief would have poisoned him, for no one would know that he arranged Hamlet's death. Then, too, he need not fear Laertes's witchcraft; it takes a strong heart to kill one's only sister by witchcraft.

"Sometime," concluded the old man, gathering his ragged toga about him, "you must tell us some more stories of your country. We, who are elders, will instruct you in their true meaning, so that when you return to your own land your elders will see that you have not been sitting in the bush, but among those who know things and who have taught you wisdom."

Review Questions

1. In what ways does Bohannan's attempt to tell the story of *Hamlet* to the Tiv illustrate the concept of naive realism?
2. Using Bohannan's experience of telling the story of *Hamlet* to the Tiv and the response of the Tiv elders to her words, illustrate cross-cultural misunderstanding.
3. What are the most important parts of *Hamlet* that the Tiv found it necessary to reinterpret?

4

Lessons from the Field

George Gmelch

Ethnographic fieldwork is a valued tradition in anthropology. Most anthropologists believe that the experience of living and working in another culture is essential to successful research. They also realize, however, that there is more to the experience than discovering and describing the culture of others. Like a rite of passage, fieldwork is an intense personal experience, one that yields deeper insight into one's own culture and personal life. It is this reflexive power of fieldwork that George Gmelch discusses below. He bases his analysis on the experiences of undergraduate students he has sent to do fieldwork in Barbados since 1978. He argues that, after a stressful beginning, students gain valuable new insight into their own views on materialism, gender, race, social class, the United States, and the value of education as well as Barbadian culture.

Sara, Eric, and Kristen heave their backpacks and suitcases—all the gear they'll need for the next ten weeks—into the back of the Institute's battered Toyota pick-up. Sara, a tense grin on her face, gets up front with me, the others climb in the back and make themselves comfortable on the soft luggage.

This article is a revision of one published by the author in the previous edition of this book. Copyright © by George Gmelch, 1997. Reprinted by permission of the author.

Leaving Bellairs Research Institute on the west coast of the island of Barbados, we drive north past the posh resort hotels. The scene changes abruptly as we move from tourism to agriculture, from the hustle and noise of the coast to the green and quiet of rolling sugar cane fields. There are no more white faces.

Graceful cabbage palms flank a large plantation house, one of the island's "great houses." On the edge of its cane fields is a tenantry, a cluster of small board houses whose inhabitants are the descendants of the slaves who once worked on the plantation.

Entering the village of Mile and a Quarter, so named because that is the distance from the village to nearby Speightstown, I point out the small orange and blue board house that one of my first students lived in. Sara and the others know of Ellen, as she became a documentary film maker and has made several films about the island that they have seen.

Two monkeys emerge from a cane field and scamper across the road. I mention that monkeys came to Barbados on early slave ships, 300 years ago. But Sara, absorbed in her own thoughts, doesn't seem to hear me. I've taken enough students to the "field" to have an idea of what's on her mind. She is wondering what her village will be like—the one we just passed through looked unusually poor. And will she like the family she is going to live with? Will they like her? Many people are walking along the road; clusters of men sit outside a rum shop shouting loudly while slamming dominoes on a wobbly plywood table. She is wondering how she will ever make friends with these people and gain their acceptance, which as a student anthropologist she must do.

Earlier in the day, Eric told me that many of the ten students on the field program thought they had made a mistake coming to Barbados. If they had chosen to go on the term abroad to Greece, or England, or even Japan, they mused, they would be together on campus, among friends, and safe. They wouldn't have to live in a village, they wouldn't have to go out and make friends with all these strange people; and to do it all alone now seemed more of a challenge than many wanted.

We drive toward the northeastern corner of the island to the village of Pie Corner, where I had arranged for Sara to live with a family. This is the unsheltered side of the island. From several miles off we could see huge swells rolling in off the Atlantic and beat against the cliffs. The village only has a few hundred people but six small wooden churches, one of which is Bennett's Temple has windows painted on the wall instead of real glass. Marcus Hinds and his family all come out to the truck to welcome Sara. Mrs Hinds gives her a big hug, as though she were a returning relative, and daughter Yvette takes Sara into the backyard to show her the pigs and chickens. I explain to the Hinds, for a second time, the nature of the program, that Sara, like the other students, would be spending most of her time in the village talking to people and as much as possible participating in the life of the community, which meant everything from attending church to cutting sugar cane. He is puzzled as my description doesn't fit his conception of what a university education is all about. The lives of Caribbean villagers is not something he thinks worthy of a university student's attention.

Back in the truck Eric and Kristen commented on the curiosity of the children, and the stares from the houses we'd passed. But they also appeared relieved at seeing the warm welcome and friendliness of the family.

Things were different at Eric's village. Chalky Mount sits high on a narrow ridge, on land unsuitable for cultivation. The land drops away so abruptly that most residents have little flat ground, so many activities take place on the road. Most houses are simple wooden affairs with corrugated metal roofs. Eric's host "mother" shows him around. I see the disappointment in Eric's face when we are shown his bedroom. It is more cramped than he had ever imagined, barely larger than the bed. His new "mother," mostly out of her nervousness and uncertain over what to do with a foreigner, much less a white man, seems aloof and uncaring. Later, Eric wrote about his arrival in his field notes:

> It was just awful. I expected my home stay mother to welcome me with open arms and be so excited. But she had nothing to say. The only solution was to go to my room and unpack.

Back in the truck, Kristen, who had seemed more relaxed after the first drop off, after meeting Sara's family, began to bite her nails.

For fifteen years I have been taking students to the field, and like most anthropologists I know a good deal about what they learn about the foreign culture in which they live. But it wasn't until serving on a committee that evaluated my college's foreign study programs, that I ever thought much about what it is that they learn about their own culture by living in another. The notion that you have to live in another culture before you can understand your own has gained wide acceptance. But what is it that we learn?

I questioned other anthropologists who also took students to the field, and they too were unclear about its lessons. A search through the literature didn't help. All the research on the educational outcomes of foreign study has been done among students who study at universities in foreign countries.

As a result, I decided to examine the experiences of my own students in Barbados. Using a variety of techniques, including questionnaires, tape recorded interviews, and analysis of their daily field notes and journals, I looked at their adjustment to the new culture, their adjustment to being student anthropologists, and what they learned about themselves and their own culture while living in Barbados. It is primarily the latter that I wish to address here.

Typically, my students go to Barbados expecting to learn a great deal about how people in this Caribbean society live and think. What they don't expect is that they will also learn much about themselves and their own society. Nor do they imagine that they will discover attitudes and perspectives that they will take back home and incorporate into their own lives.

Rural Life

Living in a Barbadian village brings many lessons in the difference between rural and urban. Over 80 percent of my students come from suburbs or cities and have never lived in the countryside before. For them a significant part of their experience in Barbados is living among people who are close to the land. The host families, like most villagers, grow crops and raise animals. Each morning, before dawn, the students are awakened by the sounds of animals in the yard. They quickly begin to learn about the behavior of chickens, pigs, sheep, and cows. They witness animals giving birth and being slaughtered. They see the satisfaction families get from consuming food they have produced themselves. One student described the effect an everyday occurrence had on her:

> I was in Mrs S's kitchen and she was making sugar cakes. The recipe calls for a lime, and when she didn't have any in the kitchen she just walked into the yard and pulled a few off the nearest tree. It was nothing to her but I was amazed, and I thought how in that situation I would have had to drive to the supermarket.

In the villages, most students live close to nature for a prolonged period of time. They may share their bedrooms with a green lizard or two, mice, cockroaches, and sometimes a whistling frog. They become aware of the different sounds of the countryside and are struck by the darkness of the sky and the brightness of the stars with no city lights to diminish their intensity. A student from Long Island described it as "like living in a planetarium."

The social world of the village is unlike anything most students know. In doing a household survey, for example, students discover that not only does everybody seem to know everybody else, and that many families are related to one another, but they know one another in more than one context—that people are tied to one another in multiple ways. Relationships are not single stranded as they often are in the urban America the students come from.

Students have never known a place of such intimacy, where relationships are so embedded with different meanings and a shared history. Some students reflect upon and compare the warmth, friendliness, and frequent sharing of food and other resources with the impersonality, individualism, and detachment of suburban life at home. But they also learn the drawbacks to living in small communities: there is no anonymity. People are nosy and unduly interested in the affairs of their neighbors. As the students become integrated into the community, they soon discover that they too may be the object of local gossip. Several female students learned from village friends that there were stories afoot that they were either mistresses to their host fathers or sleeping with their host brothers. The gossip hurt, for the students had worked hard to gain acceptance, greatly valued the friendships they had made, and naturally were concerned about the damage such rumors might do to their reputations (even though the students spend only ten weeks in their villages and most will never return, they still care greatly that villagers think well of them).

One of the biggest adjustments students must make to village life is to its slow pace, and the absence of the diversions and entertainment that they are accustomed to at home. Early in their stay there seems to be little to do apart from their research. At times they are desperate to escape the village but they are not allowed to leave except on designated days (all students initially hate this restriction, but by the end of the term they recommend that it be continued). The outcome of their forced isolation from other students is that they must satisfy their needs for companionship and recreation within their communities. They must learn to be resourceful in finding ways to entertain themselves. The outcome is that they spend a good deal of time hanging out—socializing—with people in the village, a practice which strengthens friendships and results in a good deal of informal education about culture. By the midpoint in the term most students have adapted so well to village life that they no longer report being bored or desperate to get away. And many no longer leave the village on their day off.

Materialism

Many students arrive at a new awareness of wealth and materialism. One of the strongest initial perceptions the students have of their villages is that the people are poor—that most of their houses are tiny, that their diets are restricted, and that they have few of the amenities and comforts the students are accustomed to. Even little things may remind students of the difference in wealth, as anthropology major Betsy recounted after her first week in the field:

> At home [Vermont] when I go into a convenience store and buy a soda, I don't think twice about handing the clerk a $20 dollar bill. But here when you hand a man in the rum shop a $20 dollar bill [equals $10 U.S.] they often ask if you have something smaller. It makes me self conscious of how wealthy I appear, and of how little money the rum shop man makes in a day.

The initial response of the students to such incidents and to the poverty they perceive around them is often to feel embarrassed and even guilty that they, like many Americans, have so much wealth. However, such feelings are short-lived for as the students get to know the families better they no longer see poverty, even the houses no longer seem so small. They discover that most people not only manage quite well on what they have but that they are reasonably content. In fact, most students eventually come to believe that the villagers are, on the whole, actually more satisfied with their lives than are most Americans. Whether or not this is true, it's an important perception for students whose ideas about happiness have been shaped by an ethos which measures success and satisfaction by material gain. About his host family, Dan said:

> I ate off the same plate and drank from the same cup every night. We only had an old fridge, an old stove, and an old TV, and a few dishes and pots and pans. But

that was plenty. Mrs. H. never felt like she needed any more. And after awhile I never felt like I needed any more either.

Many students say that after Barbados they became less materialistic. Many said that when they returned home from Barbados they were surprised at how many possessions they owned; and that when they came back to campus after Barbados they didn't bring nearly as many things with them as they usually do. A few had gone through their drawers and closets and given away to the Goodwill or Salvation Army the things they didn't really need. Most said they would no longer take for granted the luxuries, such as hot showers, that they are accustomed to at campus and home. Amy said:

> When I came back I saw how out of control the students here are. It's just crazy. They want so much, they talk about how much money they need to make, as if these things are necessities and you'll never be happy without them. Maybe I was like that too, but now I know I don't need those things; sure I'd like a great car, but I don't need it.

When alumni of the program were asked in a survey—conducted years after their return from Barbados—how their attitudes had been changed by their experience in a Bajan (Barbadian) village, most said they were less materialistic today.

Gender

Female students quickly learn that gender relations are quite different in Barbados. Indeed, the most difficult adjustment for many women students is learning how to deal with the frequent and aggressive advances of Bajan men. At the end of her first week in the field, Jenny described a plight common to the students:

> When I walk through the village, the guys who hang out at the rum shop yell comments. I have never heard men say some of the things they tell me here. My friend Andrew tells me that most of the comments are actually compliments. Yet I still feel weird . . . I am merely an object that they would like to conquer. I hate that feeling, so I am trying to get to know these guys. I figure that if they know me as a person and a friend, they will stop with the demeaning comments. Maybe its a cultural thing they do to all women.

Indeed, many Bajan men feel it is their right—as males—to accost women in public places with hissing, appreciative remarks, and offers of sexual services. This sexual bantering is tolerated by Bajan women who generally ignore the men's comments. Most women consider it harmless, if annoying; some consider it flattering. Students like Jenny, however, are not sure what to make of it. They do not know whether it is being directed at them because local men think white girls are "loose" or whether Bajan men behave in this fashion toward all women. Anxious to be accepted and not wanting to be rude or culturally insensitive, most female students tolerate the remarks the best they can, while searching for a strategy to politely discourage them. Most find that as people get to know them by name, the verbal harassment subsides.

But they still must become accustomed to other sexual behavior. For example, when invited to their first neighborhood parties most are shocked at the sexually explicit dancing, in which movements—"grinding"—imitate intercourse. One female student wrote, after having been to several fetes (parties):

> I was watching everyone dance when I realized that even the way we dance says a lot about culture. We are so conservative at home. Inhibited. In the U.S. one's body is a personal, private thing, and when it is invaded we get angry. We might give a boyfriend some degree of control over our bodies, but no one else. Bajans aren't nearly as possessive about their bodies. Men and women can freely move from one dance partner to the next without asking, and then grind the other person—it's like having sex with your clothes on.

Students discover that, to an even greater degree than in the United States, women are regarded by men as both subordinates and sexual objects. Masculinity is largely based on men's sexual conquest of women and on their ability to give them pleasure. Being sexually active, a good sex partner, and becoming a father all enhance young men's status among male peers. As time passes, the students discover male dominance in other areas of Barbadian life as well—that women earn less than men, are more likely to be unemployed, and far fewer seek or are able to attain political office. They conclude that while their own society is sexist Barbados is far more so.

Race

In Barbados my students become members of a racial minority for the first time in their lives. Everyone in the villages in which they live is black, while nearly all of my students have been white. Before going to Barbados, most of my students have had little contact with Blacks and as a result they feel awkward and in some cases hold negative stereotypes. The students have never experienced racial prejudice themselves. During their first few weeks in the field, however, they become acutely aware of their own "race," of their being white while everyone around them is dark. Females students are often called "white girl" by people in the village until they get to know them personally. Village children ask if they can touch the students skin, some want to feel the students straight hair; they marvel at the blue veins which show through the students white skin, and sometimes ask those with freckles if they have a skin disease.

Characteristically, during the second week one student wrote:

> I have never been in a situation before where I was a minority purely due to the color of my skin, and treated differently because of it. When I approach people I am very conscious of having white skin. Before I never thought of myself as having color.

A few students become hypersensitive to race during the early weeks of their stay. When students leave their villages, they travel by bus. The buses are often crowded, with the students usually being the only white people on board. Often they are stared at (sometimes because as the buses head into the countryside the passengers assume the student has missed her stop or taken the wrong bus). The students notice that as the bus fills up, the seat next to them is often the last to be taken, and the reaction of some is to feel shame or guilt. Here is the extreme reaction of one female student who has gone by bus to a remote area during her first week in Barbados. There she encounters a woman who stares at her:

> The woman glared at me as if she was seeing the evil white woman who has been responsible for the oppression of her people. I felt like I had chained, maimed, and enslaved every black person who had ever lived. The feelings were so strange . . . somehow I felt responsible for the entire history of the relationship between blacks and whites. I carried this woman's face with me for the rest of the day. When I got on the bus to go back to my village I felt very alone and very unwanted, like the mere presence of my color was making a lot of people very uneasy.

But concerns about race, even the very awareness of race, diminishes rapidly as the students make friends and become integrated into their villages. In fact, by the end of the term most said they were "rarely" aware of being white. Several students described incidents in which they had become so unaware of skin color that they were shocked when someone made a remark or did something to remind them of their being different. Sara was startled when, after shaking the hand of someone in her village, the person remarked that she had never touched the hand of a white person before. Several students reported being surprised when they walked by a mirror and got a glimpse of their white skin. One student wrote that although she knew she wasn't black, she no longer felt white.

What is the outcome of all this? Do students now have an understanding of what it means to be a minority, and does this translate into their having more empathy at home? I think so. All the students from the previous Barbados programs whom I questioned about the impact of their experiences mentioned a heightened empathy for Blacks, and some said other minorities as well. Several said that when they first returned home, they wanted to go up to any black person they saw and have a conversation. "But I kept having to remind myself," said one student, "that most Blacks in America are not West Indians and they wouldn't understand where I am coming from."

Social Class

American students, particularly compared to their European counterparts, have little understanding of social class. Even after several weeks in Barbados, most students are fairly oblivious to class and status distinctions in their villages. The American suburbs that my students grow up in are fairly homogenous in social composition and housing—most homes fall in the same general price range. In contrast, the Barbadian villages the students now live in exhibit a broad spectrum, ranging from the large two-story masonry homes of return migrants to tiny board houses of small farmers who eke out a living from a few acres of sugar cane and a kitchen garden. The students are slow to translate such differences in the material conditions of village households into status and/or class differences. Also, Barbadians' well-developed class consciousness, fostered by three centuries of British rule, is foreign to American students steeped in a culture that stresses, at least on an ideological level, egalitarianism. Hence, the students, who have never given much thought to social class, tend to view the population of the villages as all the same.

It is largely from the comments that their host families make about other people, that students gradually become aware of status distinctions. But equally, they learn about class and status from making mistakes, from violating norms concerning relationships between different categories of people. Kristen learned that there are different standards of behavior for the more affluent families after she walked home through the village carrying a bundle on her head: "Mrs C. told me never to do that again, that only poor people carry things on their heads, and that my doing it reflected badly on her family."

As in most field situations, the first villagers to offer the student friendship are sometimes marginal members of the community and this creates special problems in that the students are usually guests in the homes of "respectable" and often high status village families. The host parents become upset when they discover their student has been seeing a disreputable man or woman (e.g., beach bum, drug user, or loose woman). Most serious were, in the early years of the field program, female students who went out with lower-class local men. The women entered into these relationships oblivious to what the local reaction might be, and equally oblivious to how little privacy there is in a village where everyone knows everyone else's business. One student said she wrongly assumed that people would look favorably upon her going with a local man because it would show she wasn't prejudiced and that she found blacks just as desirable as whites. Another female student was befriended by some Rastafarians—orthodox Rastas who wore no clothes, lived off the land, and slept in caves in the hills above her village. When villagers discovered she had been seeing the Rastas, her host mother nearly evicted her and others gave her the cold shoulder. The student wrote:

> I have discovered the power of a societal norm: nice girls don't talk to Rastas. When girls who were formerly nice talk to Rastas, they cease to be known as nice. Exceptions none.

New Perspectives on North America

In learning about Barbadian society, students inevitably make comparisons with their own culture. Especially in the early stages of fieldwork, students think about Barbadian customs in terms of how similar or different they are from customs at home. The students are often assisted in such comparisons by villagers who know a lot about America from television, tourism, and for some, travel. Students quickly discover, however, that the villagers' perspectives on America are often at odds with their own. Based on a steady diet of American soap operas, many villagers, for example, believe that all students are wealthy, own late model cars, vacation in exotic places, etc.

Early in the term, many students find themselves defending the United States from criticism and from stereotypes. For example, one student described getting very annoyed when a guest at his host family's dinner table criticized the United States and talked about the chemical adulteration of American chicken. He knew this to be true, but later he said, "I couldn't take it anymore and fought back. I felt like an idiot afterward, defending American chicken."

Over time the students become less eager to defend their own society. Indeed, many become quite critical of the United States, or at least aspects of it. Why? What makes them question their own society after a few months in Barbados? Part of the answer is found in their growing appreciation for Bajan life and their identification with local people. They come to see many things from the perspective of their village friends. Another factor is the students' exposure to North American tourists. When students go to the beach or town on their free day they encounter tourists and are sometimes disappointed or embarrassed by what they see and hear—tourists entering shops and walking the street in skimpy beach attire, and their loud and intrusive voices. From a variety of sources, students learn about the social impacts of tourism—drug trafficking, materialism, crime, environmental damage, and American cultural penetration. Viewing tourism as part of a broader Americanization of the region, many students become critical not only of tourists but of America's presence abroad generally.

Fieldwork and Education

Students learn more than about just cultural differences from their experience of living and doing anthropology alone in a Caribbean village. Most returned from Barbados with a more positive attitude toward education. This appears to stem both from their own experiences in doing research and from seeing the high value that villagers place on formal education, which is their chief means of upward mobility. They see that they are accorded respect and adult status largely because they are working toward a university degree. Also, as the weeks pass, most students become deeply involved in their own research. They are surprised at how much satisfaction they get from doing something that they previously regarded as "work." A number of the students from past terms have said they didn't see education as an end in itself, something to be enjoyed, until doing fieldwork in Barbados. One student wrote about her attitude after returning from the field:

> I feel isolated from many of my old friends on campus, and I no longer feel guilty missing social events . . . I appreciate my education more and I do much more work for my own understanding and enjoyment rather than just for the exam or

> grades. I find myself on a daily basis growing agitated with those who don't appreciate what is being offered to them here. Several of my classmates blow off class and use other peoples' notes. A lot of what I feel is from seeing how important education was to my Bajan friends in Barbados compared to the lax attitude of my Union friends here.

Students spend much of their time in the field talking to people; a good part of each day is spent in conversations which they must direct onto the topics that they are investigating. To succeed at their studies, they must learn to be inquisitive, to probe sensitively and dig deep into another person's knowledge or memory of particular events or aspects of culture, and to concentrate, to listen to what they are being told, and later to be able to recall it so that they can record it in field notes. The students become proficient at maintaining lengthy conversations with adults and at asking pertinent questions. These are interpersonal skills they bring back with them and make use of in many aspects of their own lives.

While the students spend a semester discovering and making sense of the differences between their own culture and the Barbadians around them, most arrive at the notion that beneath differences in race and culture, Barbadians and Americans are basically alike, that beneath the veneer of custom there is something fundamental about "human nature" which is shared by everyone. In the words of one student, who is now an anthropologist:

> If I had to sum up my whole trip in one experience it would be this. It was late at night, a full moon, and I sat in a pasture with a local Rastafarian. After hours of talking, about everything from love to politics, the two of us came to an interesting conclusion. Although we lived a thousand miles away from each other, and that our skin color, hair style, and many personal practices were quite different, at heart we were the same people.

While this may seem like common sense it is surprisingly not a notion that many college students share today.

As the world's economies intertwine and its societies move closer to the "global village" Marshall McLuhan envisioned, it is more imperative than ever that we seek to understand other peoples and cultures. Without understanding there can be neither respect, nor prosperity, nor lasting peace. "The tragedy about Americans," noted Mexican novelist Carlos Fuentes, "is that they understand others so little." Students who study abroad, like those described in these pages, not only enrich themselves but in countless small ways help bridge the gulf between "us" and "them." And, in getting to know another culture is to look in the proverbial mirror and get glimpse of oneself and of what it means to be an "American."

Review Questions

1. What are the main ways that fieldwork in Barbados has changed students' perceptions of their own culture and personal lives?

2. How has the behavior of U.S. tourists in Barbados changed students' perception of their own nation?
3. How has life in a Barbadian rural community affected students' views of U.S. materialism, gender, and social class?
4. How do you think fieldwork achieves the personal transformations described by Gmelch in the students he has sent to Barbados?

3

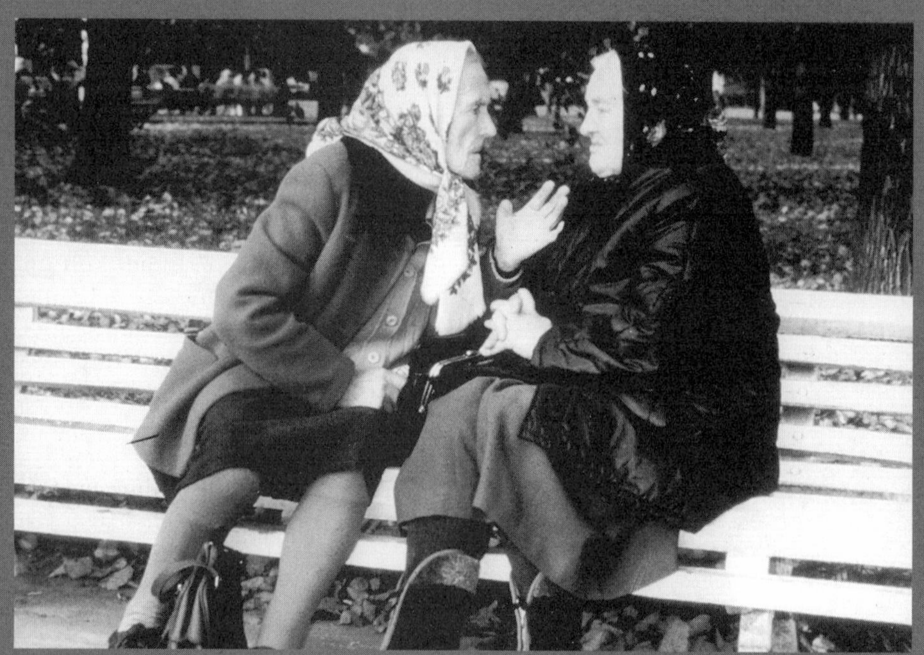

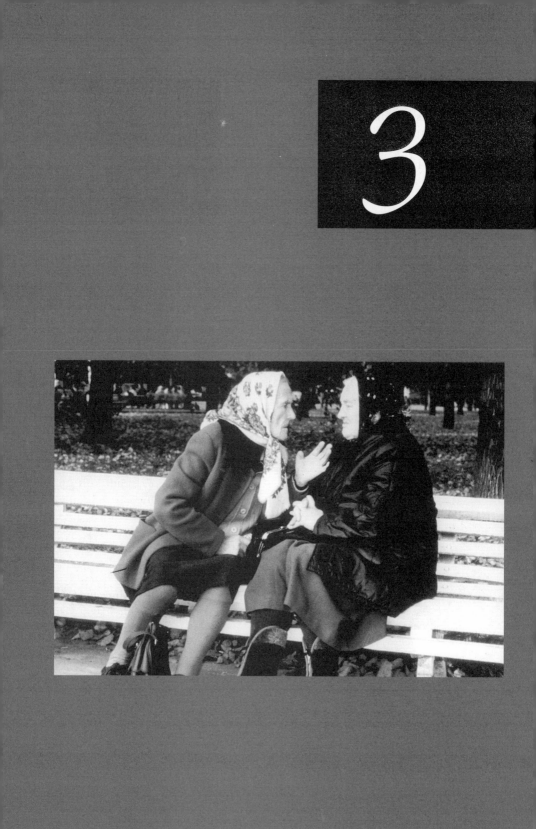

LANGUAGE AND COMMUNICATION

Culture is a system of symbols that allows us to represent and communicate our experience. We are surrounded by symbols: the flag, a new automobile, a diamond ring, billboard pictures, and, of course, spoken words.

A *symbol* is anything that we can perceive with our senses that stands for something else. Almost anything we experience can come to have symbolic meaning. Every symbol has a referent that it calls to our attention. The term *mother-in-law* refers to a certain kind of relative, the mother of a person's spouse. When we communicate with symbols, we call attention not only to the referent but also to numerous connotations of the symbol. In our culture, *mother-in-law* connotes a stereotype of a person who is difficult to get along with, who meddles in the affairs of her married daughter or son, and who is to be avoided. Human beings have the capacity to assign meaning to anything they experience in an arbitrary fashion. This fact gives rise to limitless possibilities for communication.

Symbols greatly simplify the task of communication. Once we learn that a word like *barn,* for example, stands for a certain type of building, we can communicate about a whole range of specific buildings that fit into the category. And we can communicate about barns in their absence; we can even invent flying barns and dream about barns. Symbols make it possible to communicate the immense variety of human experience, whether past or present, tangible or intangible, good or bad.

Many channels are available to human beings for symbolic communication: sound, sight, touch, and smell. Language, our most highly developed communication system, uses the channel of sound (or, for some deaf people, sight). *Language* is a system of cultural knowledge used to generate and interpret speech. It is a feature of every culture and a distinctive characteristic of the human animal. *Speech* refers to the behavior that produces vocal sounds. Our distinction between language and speech is like the one made between culture and behavior. Language is part of culture, the system of knowledge that generates behavior. Speech is the behavior generated and interpreted by language.

Every language is composed of three subsystems for dealing with vocal symbols: phonology, grammar, and semantics. Let's look briefly at each of these.

Phonology consists of the categories and rules for forming vocal symbols. It is concerned not directly with meaning but with the formation and recognition of the vocal sounds to which we assign meaning. For example, if you utter the word *bat,* you have followed a special set of rules for producing and ordering sound categories characteristic of the English language.

A basic element defined by phonological rules for every language is the phoneme. *Phonemes* are the minimal categories of speech sounds that serve to keep utterances apart. For example, speakers of English know that the words *bat, cat, mat, hat, rat,* and *fat* are different utterances because they hear the sounds /b/, /c/, /m/, /h/, /r/, and /f/ as different categories of sounds. In English, each of these is a phoneme. Our language contains a limited number of phonemes from which we construct all our vocal symbols.

Phonemes are arbitrarily constructed, however. Each phoneme actually classifies slightly different sounds as though they were the same. Different languages may divide up the same range of speech sounds into different sound categories. For example, speakers of English treat the sound /t/ as a single phoneme. Hindi speakers take the same general range and divide it into four phonemes: /t/, /t^h/, /T/, and /T^h/. (The lowercase *t*'s are made with the tongue against the front teeth, while the uppercase *T*'s are made by touching the tongue to the roof of the mouth further back than would be normal for an English speaker. The *h* indicates a puff of air, called *aspiration,* associated with the *t* sound.) Americans are likely to miss important distinctions among Hindi words because they hear these four different phonemes as a single one. Hindi speakers, on the other hand, tend to hear more than one sound category as they listen to English speakers pronounce *t*'s. The situation is reversed for /w/ and /v/. We treat these as two phonemes, whereas Hindi speakers hear them as one. For them, the English words *wine* and *vine* sound the same.

Phonology also includes rules for ordering different sounds. Even when we try to talk nonsense, we usually create words that follow English phonological rules. It would be unlikely, for example, for us ever to begin a word with the phoneme /ng/ usually written in English as "ing." It must come at the end or in the middle of words.

Grammar is the second subsystem of language. *Grammar* refers to the categories and rules for combining vocal symbols. No grammar contains rules for combining every word or element of meaning in the language. If this were the case, grammar would be so unwieldy that no one could learn all the rules in a lifetime. Every grammar deals with *categories* of symbols, such as the ones we call *nouns* and *verbs.* Once you know the rules covering a particular category, you can use it in appropriate combinations.

Morphemes are the categories in any language that carry meaning. They are minimal units of meaning that cannot be subdivided. Morphemes occur in more complex patterns than you may think. The term *bats,* for example, is actually two morphemes, /bat/ meaning a flying mammal and /s/ meaning plural. Even more confusing, two different morphemes may have the same sound shape. /Bat/ can refer to a wooden club used in baseball as well as a flying mammal.

The third subsystem of every language is semantics. *Semantics* refers to the categories and rules for relating vocal symbols to their referents. Like the rules of grammar, semantic rules are simple instructions for combining things; they instruct us to combine words with what they refer to. A symbol can be said to *refer* because it focuses our attention and makes us take account of something. For example, /bat/ refers to a family of flying mammals, as we have already noted.

Language regularly occurs in a social context, and to understand its use fully it is important to recognize its relation to sociolinguistic rules. *Sociolinguistic rules* combine meaningful utterances with social situations into appropriate messages.

Although language is the most important human vehicle for communication, almost anything we can sense may represent a *nonlinguistic symbol* that conveys meaning. The way we sit, how we use our eyes, how we dress, the car we own, the number of bathrooms in our house—all these things carry symbolic meaning. We learn what they mean as we acquire culture. Indeed, a major reason we feel so uncomfortable when we enter a group from a strange culture is our inability to decode our hosts' symbolic world.

The articles in this part illustrate several important aspects of language and communication. The first selection, by Edward and Mildred Hall, shows the significance of nonverbal symbols. The authors describe how tacit behaviors, such as eye contact and speaking distance, form powerful channels for communication in human groups. The second piece, by Deborah Tannen, looks at another aspect of language, communication styles. Focusing on the different styles of men and women in the workplace, she describes and analyzes how conversational styles themselves carry meaning and that may create misunderstanding. In the third article, David Thomson describes the hypothesis generated in the 1930s by a young linguist named Benjamin Lee Whorf. Whorf argued that, instead of merely labeling reality, the words and grammatical structure of a language can actually determine the way its speakers perceive the world. Thomson reviews and evaluates this hypothesis and asserts that, although language may not create reality, it affects our perceptions, as illustrated by the use of words in American advertising and political doublespeak. Finally, Conrad Kottak looks at the role played by *teleconditioning* in the creation of American cultural behavior. He argues that the ways people relate to their television sets inappropriately carry over into other social settings, such as university classrooms. Classrooms are *postmodern,* marked by a blurring of categories and boundaries, the product of teleconditioning.

Key Terms

symbol
language
speech
phonology
phonemes
grammar
morphemes
semantics
sociolinguistic rules
nonlinguistic symbols
teleconditioning
postmodern

Readings in This Section

The Sounds of Silence *Edward T. Hall and Mildred Reed Hall,* page 61

Conversation Style: Talking on the Job *Deborah Tannen,* page 71

The Sapir-Whorf Hypothesis: Worlds Shaped by Words *David S. Thomson,* page 80

Teleconditioning and the Postmodern Classroom *Conrad Phillip Kottak,* page 93

5

The Sounds of Silence

Edward T. Hall and Mildred Reed Hall

People communicate with more than just words. An important part of every encounter is the messages we send with our bodies and faces: the smile, the frown, the slouch of the shoulders, or the tightly crossed legs are only a few gestures that add another dimension to our verbal statements. These gestures as well as their cultural meaning change from one culture to another. They also vary over time as styles and meanings change. Often, nonverbal symbols, such as speaking distances, operate outside the awareness of actors and represent good examples of tacit culture *(see Part II). In this classic article, Edward and Mildred Hall, pioneers in the study of nonverbal communication, describe and explain the function of nonverbal symbols and their meanings for social encounters observed by them and other researchers during the 1960s.*

Bob leaves his apartment at 8:15 A.M. and stops at the corner drugstore for breakfast. Before he can speak, the counterman says, "The usual?" Bob nods yes. While he savors his Danish, a fat man pushes onto the adjoin-

---

Originally appeared in *Playboy* Magazine. Copyright © by Edward T. Hall and Mildred Reed Hall, 1971. Reprinted with permission of the authors.

ing stool and overflows into his space. Bob scowls and the man pulls himself in as much as he can. Bob has sent two messages without speaking a syllable.

Henry has an appointment to meet Arthur at 11 o'clock; he arrives at 11:30. Their conversation is friendly, but Arthur retains a lingering hostility. Henry has unconsciously communicated that he doesn't think the appointment is very important or that Arthur is a person who needs to be treated with respect.

George is talking to Charley's wife at a party. Their conversation is entirely trivial, yet Charley glares at them suspiciously. Their physical proximity and the movements of their eyes reveal that they are powerfully attracted to each other.

José Ybarra and Sir Edmund Jones are at the same party and it is important for them to establish a cordial relationship for business reasons. Each is trying to be warm and friendly, yet they will part with mutual distrust and their business transaction will probably fall through. José, in Latin fashion, moved closer and closer to Sir Edmund as they spoke, and this movement was miscommunicated as pushiness to Sir Edmund, who kept backing away from this intimacy, and this was miscommunicated to José as coldness. The silent languages of Latin and English cultures are more difficult to learn than their spoken languages.

In each of these cases, we see the subtle power of nonverbal communication. The only language used throughout most of the history of humanity (in evolutionary terms, vocal communication is relatively recent), it is the first form of communication you learn. You use this preverbal language, consciously and unconsciously, every day to tell other people how you feel about yourself and them. This language includes your posture, gestures, facial expressions, costume, the way you walk, even your treatment of time and space and material things. All people communicate on several different levels at the same time, but are usually aware of only the verbal dialog and don't realize that they respond to nonverbal messages. But when a person says one thing and really believes something else, the discrepancy between the two can usually be sensed. Nonverbal communication systems are much less subject to the conscious deception that often occurs in verbal systems. When we find ourselves thinking, "I don't know what it is about him, but he doesn't seem sincere," it's usually this lack of congruity between a person's words and his behavior that makes us anxious and uncomfortable.

Few of us realize how much we all depend on body movement in our conversation or are aware of the hidden rules that govern listening behavior. But we know instantly whether or not the person we're talking to is "tuned in" and we're very sensitive to any breach in listening etiquette. In white middle-class American culture, when someone wants to show he is listening to someone else, he looks either at the other person's face or, specifically, at his eyes, shifting his gaze from one eye to the other.

If you observe a person conversing, you'll notice that he indicates he's listening by nodding his head. He also makes little "Hmm" noises. If he agrees with what's being said, he may give a vigorous nod. To show pleasure or affirmation, he smiles; if he has some reservations, he looks skeptical by raising an eyebrow or pulling down the corners of his mouth. If a participant wants to terminate the conversation, he may start shifting his body position, stretching his legs, crossing or uncrossing them, bobbing his foot or diverting his gaze from the speaker. The more he fidgets, the more the speaker becomes aware that he has lost his audience. As a last measure, the listener may look at his watch to indicate the imminent end of the conversation.

Talking and listening are so intricately intertwined that a person cannot do one without the other. Even when one is alone and talking to oneself, there is part of the brain that speaks while another part listens. In all conversations, the listener is positively or negatively reinforcing the speaker all the time. He may even guide the conversation without knowing it, by laughing or frowning or dismissing the argument with a wave of his hand.

The language of the eyes—another age-old way of exchanging feelings—is both subtle and complex. Not only do men and women use their eyes differently but there are class, generation, regional, ethnic, and national cultural differences. Americans often complain about the way foreigners stare at people or hold a glance too long. Most Americans look away from someone who is using his eyes in an unfamiliar way because it makes them self-conscious. If a man looks at another man's wife in a certain way, he's asking for trouble, as indicated earlier. But he might not be ill-mannered or seeking to challenge the husband. He might be a European in this country who hasn't learned our visual mores. Many American women visiting France or Italy are acutely embarrassed because, for the first time in their lives, men really look at them—their eyes, hair, nose, lips, breasts, hips, legs, thighs, knees, ankles, feet, clothes, hairdo, even their walk. These same women, once they have become used to being looked at, often return to the United States and are overcome with the feeling that "No one ever really looks at me anymore."

Analyzing the mass of data on the eyes, it is possible to sort out at least three ways in which the eyes are used to communicate: dominance vs. submission, involvement vs. detachment, and positive vs. negative attitude. In addition, there are three levels of consciousness and control, which can be categorized as follows: (1) conscious use of the eyes to communicate, such as the flirting blink and the intimate nose-wrinkling squint; (2) the very extensive category of unconscious but learned behavior governing where the eyes are directed and when (this unwritten set of rules dictates how and under what circumstances the sexes, as well as people of all status categories, look at each other); and (3) the response of the eye itself, which is completely outside both awareness and control—changes in the cast (the sparkle) of the eye and the pupillary reflex.

The eye is unlike any other organ of the body, for it is an extension of the brain. The unconscious pupillary reflex and the cast of the eye have been known by people of Middle Eastern origin for years—although most are unaware of their knowledge. Depending on the context, Arabs and others look either directly at the eyes or deeply *into* the eyes of their interlocutor. We became aware of this in the Middle East several years ago while looking at jewelry. The merchant suddenly started to push a particular bracelet at a customer and said, "You buy this one." What interested us was that the bracelet was not the one that had been consciously selected by the purchaser. But the merchant, watching the pupils of the eyes, knew what the purchaser really wanted to buy. Whether he specifically knew *how* he knew is debatable.

A psychologist at the University of Chicago, Eckhard Hess, was the first to conduct systematic studies of the pupillary reflex. His wife remarked one evening, while watching him reading in bed, that he must be very interested in the text because his pupils were dilated. Following up on this, Hess slipped some pictures of nudes into a stack of photographs that he gave to his male assistant. Not looking at the photographs but watching his assistant's pupils, Hess was able to tell precisely when the assistant came to the nudes. In further experiments, Hess retouched the eyes in a photograph of a woman. In one print, he made the pupils small, in another, large; nothing else was changed. Subjects who were given the photographs found the woman with the dilated pupils much more attractive. Any man who has had the experience of seeing a woman look at him as her pupils widen with reflex speed knows that she's flashing him a message.

The eye-sparkle phenomenon frequently turns up in our interviews of couples in love. It's apparently one of the first reliable clues in the other person that love is genuine. To date, there is no scientific data to explain eye sparkle; no investigation of the pupil, the cornea, or even the white sclera of the eye shows how the sparkle originates. Yet we all know it when we see it.

One common situation for most people involves the use of the eyes in the street and in public. Although eye behavior follows a definite set of rules, the rules vary according to the place, the needs and feelings of the people, and their ethnic background. For urban whites, once they're within definite recognition distance (16–32 feet for people with average eyesight), there is mutual avoidance of eye contact—unless they want something specific: a pickup, a handout, or information of some kind. In the West and in small towns generally, however, people are much more likely to look at and greet one another, even if they're strangers.

It's permissible to look at people if they're beyond recognition distance; but once inside this sacred zone, you can only steal a glance at strangers. You *must* greet friends, however; to fail to do so is insulting. Yet, to stare too fixedly even at them is considered rude and hostile. Of course, all of these rules are variable.

A great many blacks, for example, greet each other in public even if they don't know each other. To blacks, most eye behavior of whites has the effect of giving the impression that they aren't there, but this is due to white avoidance of eye contact with *anyone* in the street.

Another very basic difference between people of different ethnic backgrounds is their sense of territoriality and how they handle space. This is the silent communication, or miscommunication, that caused friction between Mr. Ybarra and Sir Edmund Jones in our earlier example. We know from research that everyone has around himself an invisible bubble of space that contracts and expands depending on several factors: his emotional state, the activity he's performing at the time and his cultural background. This bubble is a kind of mobile territory that he will defend against intrusion. If he is accustomed to close personal distance between himself and others, his bubble will be smaller than that of someone who's accustomed to greater personal distance. People of North European heritage—English, Scandinavian, Swiss, and German—tend to avoid contact. Those whose heritage is Italian, French, Spanish, Russian, Latin American, or Middle Eastern like close personal contact.

People are very sensitive to any intrusion into their spatial bubble. If someone stands too close to you, your first instinct is to back up. If that's not possible, you lean away and pull yourself in, tensing your muscles. If the intruder doesn't respond to these body signals, you may then try to protect yourself, using a briefcase, umbrella, or raincoat. Women—especially when traveling alone—often plant their pocketbook in such a way that no one can get very close to them. As a last resort, you may move to another spot and position yourself behind a desk or a chair that provides screening. Everyone tries to adjust the space around himself in a way that's comfortable for him; most often, he does this unconsciously.

Emotions also have a direct effect on the size of a person's territory. When you're angry or under stress, your bubble expands and you require more space. New York psychiatrist Augustus Kinzel found a difference in what he calls Body-Buffer Zones between violent and nonviolent prison inmates. Dr. Kinzel conducted experiments in which each prisoner was placed in the center of a small room and then Dr. Kinzel slowly walked toward him. Nonviolent prisoners allowed him to come quite close, while prisoners with a history of violent behavior couldn't tolerate his proximity and reacted with some vehemence.

Apparently, people under stress experience other people as looming larger and closer than they actually are. Studies of schizophrenic patients have indicated that they sometimes have a distorted perception of space, and several psychiatrists have reported patients who experience their body boundaries as filling up an entire room. For these patients, anyone who comes into the room is actually inside their body, and such an intrusion may trigger a violent outburst.

Unfortunately, there is little detailed information about normal people who live in highly congested urban areas. We do know, of course, that the noise, pollution, dirt, crowding, and confusion of our cities induce feelings of stress in most of us, and stress leads to a need for greater space. The man who's packed into a subway, jostled in the street, crowded into an elevator, and forced to work all day in a bull pen or in a small office without auditory or visual privacy is going to be very stressed at the end of his day. He needs places that provide relief from constant overstimulation of his nervous system. Stress from overcrowding is cumulative and people can tolerate more crowding early in the day than later; note the increased bad temper during the evening rush hour as compared with the morning melee. Certainly one factor in people's desire to commute by car is the need for privacy and relief from crowding (except, often, from other cars); it may be the only time of the day when nobody can intrude.

In crowded public places, we tense our muscles and hold ourselves stiff, and thereby communicate to others our desire not to intrude on their space and, above all, not to touch them. We also avoid eye contact, and the total effect is that of someone who has "tuned out." Walking along the street, our bubble expands slightly as we move in a stream of strangers, taking care not to bump into them. In the office, at meetings, in restaurants, our bubble keeps changing as it adjusts to the activity at hand.

Most white middle-class Americans use four main distances in their business and social relations: intimate, personal, social, and public. Each of these distances has a near and a far phase and is accompanied by changes in the volume of the voice. Intimate distance varies from direct physical contact with another person to a distance of six to eighteen inches and is used for our most private activities—caressing another person or making love. At this distance, you are overwhelmed by sensory inputs from the other person—heat from the body, tactile stimulation from the skin, the fragrance of perfume, even the sound of breathing—all of which literally envelop you. Even at the far phase, you're still within easy touching distance. In general, the use of intimate distance in public between adults is frowned on. It's also much too close for strangers, except under conditions of extreme crowding.

In the second zone—personal distance—the close phase is 1½ to 2½ feet; it's at this distance that wives usually stand from their husbands in public. If another woman moves into this zone, the wife will most likely be disturbed. The far phase—2½ to 4 feet—is the distance used to "keep someone at arm's length" and is the most common spacing used by people in conversation.

The third zone—social distance—is employed during business transactions or exchanges with a clerk or repairman. People who work together tend to use close social distance—4 to 7 feet. This is also the distance for conversation at social gatherings. To stand at this distance from someone who is seated has a dominating effect (for example, teacher to pupil, boss to secretary). The far phase of the third zone—7 to 12 feet—is where people stand when someone says, "Stand back so I can look at you." This distance lends a formal tone to business or social discourse. In an executive office, the desk serves to keep people at this distance.

The fourth zone—public distance—is used by teachers in classrooms or speakers at public gatherings. At it farthest phase—25 feet and beyond—it is used for important public figures. Violations of this distance can lead to serious complications. During his 1970 U.S. visit, the president of France, Georges Pompidou, was harassed by pickets in Chicago, who were permitted to get within touching distance. Since pickets in France are kept behind barricades a block or more away, the president was outraged by this insult to his person, and President Nixon was obliged to communicate his concern as well as offer his personal apologies.

It is interesting to note how American pitchmen and panhandlers exploit the unwritten, unspoken conventions of eye and distance. Both take advantage of the fact that once explicit eye contact is established, it is rude to look away, because to do so means to brusquely dismiss the other person and his needs. Once having caught the eye of his mark, the panhandler then locks on, not letting go until he moves through the public zone, the social zone, and, finally, into the intimate sphere, where people are most vulnerable.

Touch also is an important part of the constant stream of communication that takes place between people. A light touch, a firm touch, a blow, a caress, are all communications. In an effort to break down barriers among people, there's been a recent upsurge in group-encounter activities, in which strangers are encouraged to touch one another. In special situations such as these, the rules for not touching are broken with group approval and people gradually lose some of their inhibitions.

Although most people don't realize it, space is perceived and distances are set not by vision alone but with all the senses. Auditory space is perceived with the ears, thermal space with the skin, kinesthetic space with the muscles of the body, and olfactory space with the nose. And, once again, it's our culture that determines how our senses are programmed—which sensory information ranks highest and lowest. The important thing to remember is that culture is very persistent. In this country, we've noted the existence of cultural patterns that determine distance between people in the third and fourth generations of some families, despite their prolonged contact with people of very different cultural heritages.

Whenever there is great cultural distance between two people, there are bound to be problems arising from differences in behavior and expectations. An example is the American couple who consulted a psychiatrist about their marital problems. The husband was from New England and had been brought up by reserved parents who taught him to control his emotions and to respect the need for privacy. His wife was from an Italian family and had been brought up in close contact with all the members of her large family, who were extremely warm, volatile, and demonstrative.

When the husband came home after a hard day at the office, dragging his feet, and longing for peace and quiet, his wife would rush to him and smother him. Clasping his hands, rubbing his brow, crooning over his weary head, she never left him alone. But when his wife was upset or anxious about her day, the husband's response was to withdraw completely and leave her alone. No comforting, no affectionate embrace, no attention—just solitude. The woman became convinced her husband didn't love her and, in desperation, she consulted a psychiatrist. Their problem wasn't basically psychological but cultural.

Why have we developed all these different ways of communicating messages without words? One reason is that people don't like to spell out certain kinds of messages. We prefer to find other ways of showing our feelings. This is especially true in relationships as sensitive as courtship. Men don't like to be rejected and most women don't want to turn a man down bluntly. Instead, we work out subtle ways of encouraging or discouraging each other that save face and avoid confrontations.

How a person handles space in dating others is an obvious and very sensitive indicator of how he or she feels about the other person. On a first date, if a woman sits or stands so close to a man that he is acutely conscious of her physical presence—inside the intimate-distance zone—the man usually construes it to mean that she is encouraging him. However, before the man starts moving in on the woman, he should be sure what message she's really sending; otherwise, he risks bruising his ego. What is close to someone of North European background may be neutral or distant to someone of Italian heritage. Also, women sometimes use space as a way of misleading a man, and there are few things that put men off more than women who communicate contradictory messages—cuddling up and then acting insulted when a man takes the next step.

How does a woman communicate interest in a man? In addition to such familiar gambits as smiling at him, she may glance shyly at him, blush, and then look away. Or she may give him a real come-on look and move in very close when he approaches. She may touch his arm and ask for a light. As she leans forward to light her cigarette, she may brush him lightly, enveloping him in her perfume. She'll probably continue to smile at him and she may use what ethnologists call preening gestures—touching the back of her hair, thrusting her breasts forward, tilting her hips as she stands or crossing her legs if she's seated, perhaps even exposing one thigh or putting a hand on her thigh and stroking it. She may also stroke her wrists as she converses or show the palm of her hand as a way of gaining his attention. Her skin may be unusually flushed or quite pale, her eyes brighter, the pupils larger.

If a man sees a woman whom he wants to attract, he tries to present himself by his posture and stance as someone who is self-assured. He moves briskly and confidently. When he catches the eye of the woman, he may hold her glance a little longer than normal. If he gets an encouraging smile, he'll move in close and engage her in small talk. As they converse, his glance shifts over her face and body. He, too, may make preening gestures—straightening his tie, smoothing his hair, or shooting his cuffs.

How do people learn body language? The same way they learn spoken language—by observing and imitating people around them as they're growing up. Little girls imitate their mothers or an older female. Little boys imitate their fathers or a respected uncle or a character on television. In this way, they learn the gender signals appropriate for their sex. Regional, class, and ethnic patterns of body behavior are also learned in childhood and persist throughout life.

Such patterns of masculine and feminine body behavior vary widely from one culture to another. In America, for example, women stand with their thighs together. Many walk with their pelvis tipped slightly forward and their upper arms close to their body. When they sit, they cross their legs at the knee or, if they are well past middle age, they may cross their ankles. American men hold their arms away from their body, often swinging them as they walk. They stand with their legs apart (an extreme example is the cowboy, with legs apart and thumbs tucked into his belt). When they sit, they put their feet on the floor with legs apart and, in some parts of the country, they cross their legs by putting one ankle on the other knee.

Leg behavior indicates sex, status, and personality. It also indicates whether or not one is at ease or is showing respect or disrespect for the other person. Young Latin American males avoid crossing their legs. In their world of *machismo,* the preferred position for young males when with one another (if there is no older dominant male present to whom they must show respect) is to sit on the base of their spine with their leg muscles relaxed and their feet wide apart. Their respect position is like our military equivalent; spine straight, heels and ankles together—almost identical to that displayed by properly brought up young women in New England in the early part of this century.

American women who sit with their legs spread apart in the presence of males are *not* normally signaling a come-on—they are simply (and often unconsciously) sitting like men. Middle-class women in the presence of other women to whom they are very close may on occasion throw themselves down on a soft chair or sofa and let themselves go. This is a signal that nothing serious will be taken up. Males, on the other hand, lean back and prop their legs up on the nearest object.

The way we walk, similarly, indicates status, respect, mood, and ethnic or cultural affiliation. The many variants of the female walk are too well known to go into here, except to say that a man would have to be blind not to be turned on by the way some women walk—a fact that made Mae West rich before scientists ever studied these matters. To white Americans, some French middle-class males walk in a way that is both humorous and suspect. There is a bounce and looseness to the French walk, as though the parts of the body were somehow unrelated. Jacques Tati, the French movie actor, walks this way; so does the great mime, Marcel Marceau.

Blacks and whites in America—with the exception of middle- and upper-middle-class professionals of both groups—move and walk very differently from each other. To the blacks, whites often seem incredibly stiff, almost mechanical in their movements. Black males, on the other hand, have a looseness and coordination that frequently makes whites a little uneasy; it's too different, too integrated, too alive, too male. Norman Mailer has said that squares walk from the shoulders, like bears, but blacks and hippies walk from the hips, like cats.

All over the world, people walk not only in their own characteristic way but have walks that communicate the nature of their involvement with whatever it is they're doing. The purposeful walk of North Europeans is an important component of proper behavior on the job. Any male who has been in the military knows how essential it is to walk properly (which makes for a continuing source of tension between blacks and whites in the Service). The quick shuffle of servants in the Far East in the old days was a show of respect. On the island of Truk, when we last visited, the inhabitants even had a name for the respectful walk that one used when in the presence of a chief or when walking past a chief's house. The term was *sufan,* which meant to be humble and respectful.

The notion that people communicate volumes by their gestures, facial expressions, posture, and walk is not new; actors, dancers, writers, and psychiatrists have long been aware of it. Only in recent years, however, have scientists begun to make systematic observations of body motions. Ray L.

Birdwhistell of the University of Pennsylvania is one of the pioneers in body-motion research and coined the term *kinesics* to describe this field. He developed an elaborate notation system to record both facial and body movements, using an approach similar to that of the linguist, who studies the basic elements of speech. Birdwhistell and other kinesicists such as Albert Sheflen, Adam Kendon, and William Condon take movies of people interacting. They run the film over and over again, often at reduced speed for frame-by-frame analysis, so that they can observe even the slightest body movements not perceptible at normal interaction speeds. These movements are then recorded in notebooks for later analysis. . . .

The language of behavior is extremely complex. Most of us are lucky to have under control one subcultural system—the one that reflects our sex, class, generation, and geographic region within the United States. Because of its complexity, efforts to isolate bits of nonverbal communication and generalize from them are in vain; you don't become an instant expert on people's behavior by watching them at cocktail parties. Body language isn't something that's independent of the person, something that can be donned and doffed like a suit of clothes.

Our research and that of our colleagues have shown that, far from being a superficial form of communication that can be consciously manipulated, nonverbal communication systems are interwoven into the fabric of the personality and, as sociologist Erving Goffman has demonstrated, into society itself. They are the warp and woof of daily interactions with others and they influence how one expresses oneself, how one experiences oneself as a man or a woman.

Nonverbal communications signal to members of your own group what kind of person you are, how you feel about others, how you'll fit into and work in a group, whether you're assured or anxious, the degree to which you feel comfortable with the standards of your own culture, as well as deeply significant feelings about the self, including the state of your own psyche. For most of us, it's difficult to accept the reality of another's behavioral system. And, of course, none of us will ever become fully knowledgeable of the importance of every nonverbal signal. But as long as each of us realizes the power of these signals, this society's diversity can be a source of great strength rather than a further—and subtly powerful—source of division.

Review Questions

1. What are the ways people communicate with each other nonverbally, according to Edward and Mildred Hall?
2. What are the four culturally learned speaking distances used by Americans?
3. How does the nonverbal communication described by the Halls relate to the concept of tacit culture discussed in the last section?
4. Why is nonverbal communication so likely to be a source of cross-cultural misunderstanding?

6

Conversation Style: Talking on the Job

Deborah Tannen

In the last article, we looked at the important role played by nonverbal symbols in human communication. Speaking distances, gestures, smiles, and a host of other tacit signs make up this silent language. In this piece excerpted from her book about conversation in the workplace, Deborah Tannen discusses a second tacit dimension of communication, conversation style. Looking at the different ways men and women approach or avoid asking for help on the job, she argues that gender differences in conversation style are responsible for not only miscommunication but for misguided evaluations and moral judgments about the performance and character of co-workers.

People have different conversational styles, influenced by the part of the country they grew up in, their ethnic backgrounds and those of their parents, their age, class, and gender. But conversational style is invisi-

From the introduction and first chapter of *Talking from 9 to 5,* William Morrow & Company, 1994. Copyright © by Deborah Tannen, 1994. Reprinted by permission of the author.

ble. Unaware that these and other aspects of our backgrounds influence our ways of talking, we think we are simply saying what we mean. Because we don't realize that others' styles are different, we are often frustrated in conversations. Rather than seeing the culprit as differing styles, we attribute troubles to others' intentions (she doesn't like me), abilities (he's stupid), or character (she's rude, he's inconsiderate), our own failure (what's wrong with me?), or the failure of a relationship (we just can't communicate). . . .

Although I am aware of the many influences on conversational style and have spent most of my career studying and writing about them, . . . [here] . . . style differences influenced by gender receive particular attention. This is not only because these are the differences people most want to hear about (although this is so and is a factor), but also because there is something fundamental about our categorization by gender. When you spot a person walking down the street toward you, you immediately and automatically identify that person as male or female. You will not necessarily try to determine which state they are from, what their class background is, or what country their grandparents came from. A secondary identification, in some places and times, may be about race. But, while we may envision a day when a director will be able to cast actors for a play without reference to race, can we imagine a time when actors can be cast without reference to their sex?

Few elements of our identities come as close to our sense of who we are as gender. If you mistake people's cultural background—you thought they were Greek, but they turn out to be Italian; you assumed they'd grown up in Texas, but it turns out they're from Kentucky; you say "Merry Christmas" and they say, "we don't celebrate Christmas; we're Muslim"—it catches you off guard and you rearrange the mental frame through which you view them. But if someone you thought was male turns out to be female—like the jazz musician Billy Tipton, whose own adopted sons never suspected that their father was a woman until the coroner broke the news to them after his (her) death—the required adjustment is staggering. Even infants discriminate between males and females and react differently depending on which they confront.

Perhaps it is because our sense of gender is so deeply rooted that people are inclined to hear descriptions of gender patterns as statements about gender *identity*—in other words, as absolute differences rather than a matter of degree and percentages, and as universal rather than culturally mediated. The patterns I describe are based on observations of particular speakers in a particular place and time: mostly (but not exclusively) middle-class Americans of European background working in offices at the present time. Other cultures evince very different patterns of talk associated with gender—and correspondingly different assumptions about the "natures" of women and men. I don't put a lot of store in talk about "natures" or what is "natural." People in every culture will tell you that the behaviors common in their own culture are "natural." I also don't put a lot of store in people's explanations that their way of talking is a natural response to their environment, as there is always an equally natural and opposite way of responding to the same environment. We all tend to regard the way things are as the way things have to be—as only natural.

The reason ways of talking, like other ways of conducting our daily lives, come to seem natural is that the behaviors that make up our lives are ritualized. Indeed, the "ritual" character of interaction is at the heart of this book. Having grown up in a particular culture, we learn to do things as the people we encounter do them, so the vast majority of our decisions about how to speak become automatic. You see someone you know, you ask "How are you?," chat, then take your leave, never pausing to ponder the many ways you could handle this interaction differently—and would, if you lived in a different culture. Just as an American automatically extends a hand for a handshake while a Japanese automatically bows, what the American and Japanese find it natural to say is a matter of convention learned over a lifetime.

No one understood the ritual nature of everyday life better than sociologist Erving Goffman, who also understood the fundamental role played by gender in organizing our daily rituals. In his article "The Arrangement Between the Sexes," Goffman pointed out that we tend to say "sex-linked" when what we mean is "sex-class-linked." When hearing that a behavior is "sex-linked," people often conclude that the behavior is to be found in every individual of that group, and that it is somehow inherent in their sex, as if it came hooked to a chromosome. Goffman suggests the term "genderism" (on the model, I assume, of "mannerism," not of "sexism") for "a sex-class linked individual behavioral practice." This is the spirit in which I intend references to gendered patterns of behavior: not to imply that there is anything inherently male or female about particular ways of talking, nor to claim that every individual man or woman adheres to the pattern, but rather to observe that a larger percentage of women or men *as a group* talk in a particular way, or individual women and men *are more likely* to talk one way or the other.

That individuals do not always fit the pattern associated with their gender does not mean that the pattern is not typical. Because more women or men speak in a particular way, that way of speaking becomes associated with women or men—or, rather, it is the other way around: More women or men learn to speak particular ways *because* those ways are associated with their own gender. And individual men or women who speak in ways associated with the other gender will pay a price for departing from cultural expectations.

If my concept of how gender displays itself in everyday life has been influenced by Goffman, the focus of my research—talk—and my method for studying it grow directly out of my own discipline, linguistics. My understanding of what goes on when people talk to each other is based on observing and listening as well as tape-recording, transcribing, and analyzing conversation. In response to my book *You Just Don't Understand,* I was contacted by people at many companies who asked whether I could help them apply the insights in that book to the problem of "the glass ceiling": Why weren't women advancing as quickly as the men who were hired at the same time? And more generally, they wanted to understand how to integrate women as well as others who were historically not "typical" employees into the increasingly diverse workforce. I realized that in order to offer insight, I needed to observe what was really going on in the workplace. . . .

Women and Men Talking on the Job

Amy was a manager with a problem: She had just read a final report written by Donald, and she felt it was woefully inadequate. She faced the unsavory task of telling him to do it over. When she met with Donald, she made sure to soften the blow by beginning with praise, telling him everything about his report that was good. Then she went on to explain what was lacking and what needed to be done to make it acceptable. She was pleased with the diplomatic way she had managed to deliver the bad news. Thanks to her thoughtfulness in starting with praise, Donald was able to listen to the criticism and seemed to understand what was needed. But when the revised report appeared on her desk, Amy was shocked. Donald had made only minor, superficial changes, and none of the necessary ones. The next meeting with him did not go well. He was incensed that she was now telling him his report was not acceptable and accused her of having misled him. "You told me before it was fine," he protested.

Amy thought she had been diplomatic; Donald thought she had been dishonest. The praise she intended to soften the message "This is unacceptable" sounded to him like the message itself: "This is fine." So what she regarded as the main point—the needed changes—came across to him as optional suggestions, because he had already registered her praise as the main point. She felt he hadn't listened to her. He thought she had changed her mind and was making him pay the price.

Work days are filled with conversations about getting the job done. Most of these conversations succeed, but too many end in impasses like this. It could be that Amy is a capricious boss whose wishes are whims, and it could be that Donald is a temperamental employee who can't hear criticism no matter how it is phrased. But I don't think either was the case in this instance. I believe this was one of innumerable misunderstandings caused by differences in conversational style. Amy delivered the criticism in a way that seemed to her self-evidently considerate, a way she would have preferred to receive criticism herself: taking into account the other person's feelings, making sure he knew that her ultimate negative assessment of his report didn't mean she had no appreciation of his abilities. She offered the praise as a sweetener to help the nasty-tasting news go down. But Donald didn't expect criticism to be delivered in that way, so he mistook the praise as her overall assessment rather than a preamble to it.

This conversation could have taken place between two women or two men. But I do not think it is a coincidence that it occurred between a man and a woman. . . . Conversational rituals common among men often involve using opposition such as banter, joking, teasing, and playful put-downs, and expending effort to avoid the one-down position in the interaction. Conversational rituals common among women are often ways of maintaining an appearance of equality, taking into account the effect of the exchange on the other person, and expending effort to downplay the speakers' authority so they can get the job done without flexing their muscles in an obvious way.

When everyone present is familiar with these conventions, they work well. But when ways of speaking are not recognized as conventions, they are taken literally, with negative results on both sides. Men whose oppositional strategies are interpreted literally may be seen as hostile when they are not, and their efforts to ensure that they avoid appearing one-down may be taken as arrogance. When women use conversational strategies designed to avoid appearing boastful and to take the other person's feelings into account, they may be seen as less confident and competent than they really are. As a result, both women and men often feel they are not getting sufficient credit for what they have done, are not being listened to, are not getting ahead as fast as they should.

When I talk about women's and men's characteristic ways of speaking, I always emphasize that both styles make sense and are equally valid in themselves, though the difference in styles may cause trouble in interaction. In a sense, when two people form a private relationship of love or friendship, the bubble of their interaction is a world unto itself, even though they both come with the prior experience of their families, their community, and a lifetime of conversations. But someone who takes a job is entering a world that is already functioning, with its own characteristic style already in place. Although there are many influences such as regional background, the type of industry involved, whether it is a family business or a large corporation, in general, workplaces that have previously had men in positions of power have already established male-style interaction as the norm. In that sense, women, and others whose styles are different, are not starting out equal, but are at a disadvantage. Though talking at work is quite similar to talking in private, it is a very different enterprise in many ways.

When Not Asking Directions Is Dangerous to Your Health

If conversational-style differences lead to troublesome outcomes in work as well as private settings, there are some work settings where the outcomes of style are a matter of life and death. Healthcare professionals are often in such situations. So are airline pilots.

Of all the examples of women's and men's characteristic styles that I discussed in *You Just Don't Understand,* the one that (to my surprise) attracted the most attention was the question "Why don't men like to stop and ask for directions?" Again and again, in the responses of audiences, talk-show hosts, letter writers, journalists, and conversationalists, this question seemed to crystallize the frustration many people had experienced in their own lives. And my explanation seems to have rung true: that men are more likely to be aware that asking for directions, or for any kind of help, puts them in a one-down position.

With regard to asking directions, women and men are keenly aware of the advantages of their own style. Women frequently observe how much time they would save if their husbands simply stopped and asked someone instead of driving around trying in vain to find a destination themselves. But I have also been told by men that it makes sense not to ask directions because you learn a lot about a neighborhood, as well as about navigation, by driving around and finding your own way.

But some situations are more risky than others. A Hollywood talk-show producer told me that she had been flying with her father in his private airplane when he was running out of gas and uncertain about the precise location of the local landing strip he was heading for. Beginning to panic, the woman said, "Daddy! Why don't you radio the control tower and ask them where to land?" He answered, "I don't want them to think I'm lost." This story had a happy ending, else the woman would not have been alive to tell it to me.

Some time later, I repeated this anecdote to a man at a cocktail party—a man who had just told me that the bit about directions was his favorite part of my book, and who, it turned out, was also an amateur pilot. He then went on to tell me that he had had a similar experience. When learning to fly, he got lost on his first solo flight. He did not want to humiliate himself by tuning his radio to the FAA emergency frequency and asking for help, so he flew around looking for a place to land. He spotted an open area that looked like a landing field, headed for it—and found himself deplaning in what seemed like a deliberately hidden landing strip that was mercifully deserted at the time. Fearing he had stumbled upon an enterprise he was not supposed to be aware of, let alone poking around in, he climbed back into the plane, relieved that he had not gotten into trouble. He managed to find his way back to his home airport as well, before he ran out of gas. He maintained, however, that he was certain that more than a few small-plane crashes have occurred because other amateur pilots who did not want to admit they were lost were less lucky. In light of this, the amusing question of why men prefer not to stop and ask for directions stops being funny.

The moral of the story is not that men should immediately change and train themselves to ask directions when they're in doubt, any more than women should immediately stop asking directions and start honing their navigational skills by finding their way on their own. The moral is flexibility: Sticking to habit in the face of all challenges is not so smart if it ends up getting you killed. If we all understood our own styles and knew their limits and their alternatives, we'd be better off—especially at work, where the results of what we do have repercussions for co-workers and the company, as well as for our own futures.

To Ask or Not to Ask

An intern on duty at a hospital had a decision to make. A patient had been admitted with a condition he recognized, and he recalled the appropriate medication. But that medication was recommended for a number of conditions, in different dosages. He wasn't quite sure what dose was right for this condition. He had to make a quick decision: Would he interrupt the supervising resident during a meeting to check the dose, or would he make his best guess and go for it?

What was at stake? First and foremost, the welfare, and maybe even the life, of the patient. But something else was at stake too—the reputation, and eventually the career, of the intern. If he interrupted the resident to ask about the dosage, he was making a public statement about what he didn't know, as well as making himself something of a nuisance. In this case, he went with his guess, and there were no negative effects. But, as with small-plane crashes, one wonders how many medical errors have resulted from decisions to guess rather than ask.

It is clear that not asking questions can have disastrous consequences in medical settings, but asking questions can also have negative consequences. A physician wrote to me about a related experience that occurred during her medical training. She received a low grade from her supervising physician. It took her by surprise because she knew that she was one of the best interns in her group. She asked her supervisor for an explanation, and he replied that she didn't know as much as the others. She knew from her day-to-day dealings with her peers that she was one of the most knowledgeable, not the least. So she asked what evidence had led him to his conclusion. And he told her, "You ask more questions."

There is evidence that men are less likely to ask questions in a public situation, where asking will reveal their lack of knowledge. One such piece of evidence is a study done in a university classroom, where sociolinguist Kate Remlinger noticed that women students asked the professor more questions than men students did. As part of her study, Remlinger interviewed six students at length, three men and three women. All three men told her that they would not ask questions in class if there was something they did not understand. Instead, they said they would try to find the answer later by reading the textbook, asking a friend, or, as a last resort, asking the professor in private during office hours. As one young man put it, "If it's vague to me, I usually don't ask. I'd rather go home and look it up."

Of course, this does not mean that no men will ask questions when they are in doubt, nor that all women will; the differences, as always, are a matter of likelihood and degree. As always, cultural differences play a role too. It is not unusual for American professors to admit their own ignorance when they do not know the answer to a student's question, but there are many cultures in which professors would not, and students from those cultures may judge American professors by those standards. A student from the Middle East told a professor at a California university that she had just lost all respect for one of his colleagues. The reason: She had asked a question in class, and the offending professor had replied, "I don't know offhand, but I'll find out for you."

The physician who asked her supervisor why he gave her a negative evaluation may be unusual in having been told directly what behavior led to the misjudgment of her skill. But in talking to doctors and doctors-in-training around the country, I have learned that there is nothing exceptional about her experience, that it is common for interns and residents to conceal their ignorance by not asking questions, since those who do ask are judged less capable. Yet it seems that many women who are more likely than men to ask questions (just as women are more likely to stop and ask for directions when they're lost) are unaware that they may make a negative impression at the same time that they get information. Their antennae have not been attuned to making sure they don't appear one-down.

This pattern runs counter to two stereotypes about male and female styles: that men are more focused on information and that women are more sensitive. In regard to classroom behavior, it seems that the women who ask questions are more focused on information, whereas the men who refrain from doing so are more focused on interaction—the impression their asking will make on others. In this situation, it is the men who are more sensitive to the impression made on others by their behavior, although their concern is, ultimately, the effect on themselves rather than on others. And this sensitivity is likely to make them look better in the world of work. Realizing this puts the intern's decision in a troubling perspective. He had to choose between putting his career at risk and putting the patient's health at risk.

It is easy to see benefits of both styles: Someone willing to ask questions has ready access to a great deal of information—all that is known by the people she can ask. But just as men have told me that asking directions is useless since the person you ask may not know and may give you the wrong answer, some people feel they are more certain to get the right information if they read it in a book, and they are learning more by finding it themselves. On the other hand, energy may be wasted looking up information someone else has at hand, and I have heard complaints from people who feel they were sent on wild-goose chases by colleagues who didn't want to admit they really were not sure of what they pretended to know.

The reluctance to say "I don't know" can have serious consequences for an entire company—and did: On Friday, June 17, 1994, a computer problem prevented Fidelity Investments from calculating the value of 166 mutual funds. Rather than report that the values for these funds were not available, a manager decided to report to the National Association of Securities Dealers that the values of these funds had not changed from the day before. Unfortunately, June 17 turned out to be a bad day in the financial markets, so the values of Fidelity's funds that were published in newspapers around the country stood out as noticeably higher than those of other funds. Besides the cost and inconvenience to brokerage firms who had to re-compute their customers' accounts, and the injustice to investors who made decisions to buy or sell based on inaccurate information, the company was mightily embarrassed and forced to apologize publicly. Clearly this was an instance in which it would have been preferable to say, "We don't know."

Flexibility, again, is key. There are many situations in which it serves one well to be self-reliant and discreet about revealing doubt or ignorance, and others in which it is wise to admit what you don't know.

Review Questions

1. What does Tannen mean by conversational style?
2. What is the important style difference in the way men and women ask for directions or help, according to Tannen?
3. What is Tannen's hypothesis about why males avoid asking other people for directions?
4. In Tannen's perspective, what conclusions do men and women draw about each other when they display typically different approaches to asking directions?

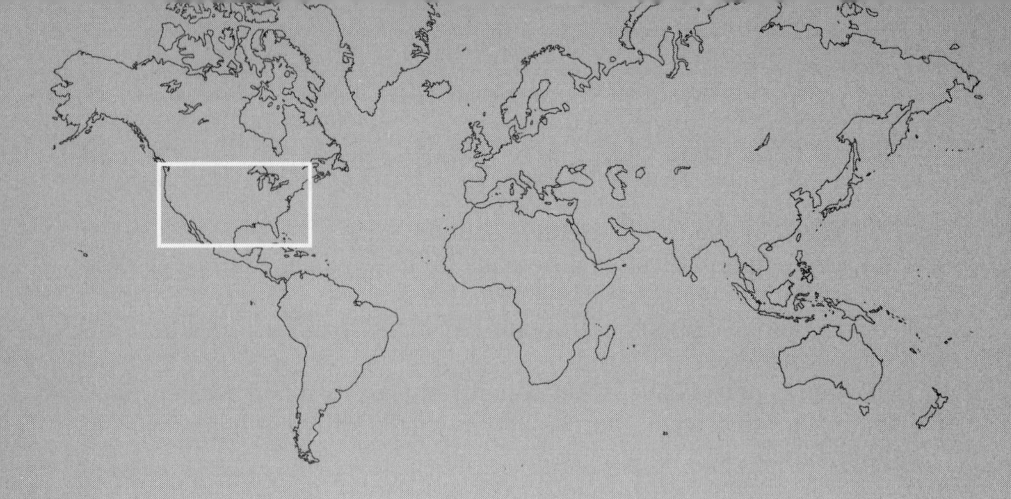

7

The Sapir-Whorf Hypothesis: Worlds Shaped by Words

David S. Thomson

For many people, language mirrors reality. Words are labels for what we sense; they record what is already there. This view, which is another manifestation of what we have called naive realism, *is clearly challenged by previous selections in this book. We have seen, for example, that members of different societies may not share cultural categories; words from one language often cannot be translated directly into another. In the 1930s, a young linguist named Benjamin Lee Whorf took the objection to the "words label reality" assertion one step further by arguing that words and grammatical structure actually shape reality. This piece by David Thomson describes Whorf's theory, shows how linguists have evaluated it, and applies it in modified form to the use of words, euphemisms, and doublespeak in the modern United States.*

The scene is the storage room at a chemical plant. The time is evening. A night watchman enters the room and notes that it is partially filled

From *Human Behavior: Language* by David S. Thomson and the editors of Time-Life Books (New York: Time-Life Books, 1975). Copyright © by Time-Life Books, Inc., 1975.

with gasoline drums. The drums are in a section of the room where a sign says "Empty Barrels." The watchman lights a cigarette and throws the still-hot match into one of the empty barrels.

The result: an explosion.

The immediate cause of the explosion, of course, was the gasoline fumes that remained in the barrels. But it could be argued that a second cause of the explosion was the English language. The barrels were empty of their original contents and so belonged under the empty sign. Yet they were not empty of everything—the fumes were still present. English has no word—no single term—that can convey such a situation. Containers in English are either empty or they are not; there is no word describing the ambiguous state of being empty and yet not empty. There is not term in the language for "empty but not quite" or "empty of original contents but with something left over." There being no word for such an in-between state, it did not occur to the watchman to think of the explosive fumes.

This incident is hypothetical, but the questions about language it raises are real. The example of the gasoline drums often was cited by Benjamin Lee Whorf to illustrate a revolutionary theory he had about language. Whorf was an unusual man who combined two careers, for he was both a successful insurance executive and a brilliant (and largely self-taught) linguistic scholar. Language, he claimed, may be shaped by the world, but it in turn shapes the world. He reasoned that people can think about only those things that their language can describe or express. Without the words or structures with which to articulate a concept, that concept will not occur. To turn the proposition around, if a language is rich in ways to express certain sorts of ideas, then the speakers of that language will habitually think along those linguistic paths. In short, the language that humans speak governs their view of reality; it determines their perception of the world. The picture of the universe shifts from tongue to tongue.

The originator of this startling notion came from an intellectually active New England family. Whorf's brother John became an artist of note and his brother Richard a consummately professional actor. Benjamin's early bent was not for drawing or acting but photography, especially the chemistry that was involved in developing pictures, and this interest may have influenced his choice of the Massachusetts Institute of Technology, where he majored in chemical engineering. After he was graduated from M.I.T. he became a specialist in fire prevention and in 1919 went to work for the Hartford Fire Insurance Company. His job was to inspect manufacturing plants, particularly chemical plants, that the Hartford insured to determine whether they were safe and thus good insurance risks. He quickly became highly skilled at his work. "In no time at all," wrote C. S. Kremer, then the Hartford's board chairman, "he became in my opinion as thorough and fast a fire prevention inspector as there ever has been."

Whorf was a particularly acute chemical engineer. On one occasion he was refused admittance to inspect a client's building because, a company official maintained, a secret process was in use here. "You are making such-

and-such a product?" asked Whorf. "Yes," said the official. Whorf pulled out a pad and scribbled the formula of the supposedly secret process, adding coolly, "You couldn't do it any other way." Needless to say, he was allowed to inspect the building. Whorf rose in the Hartford hierarchy to the post of assistant secretary of the company in 1940. But then in 1941 his health, never strong, gave way, and he died at the early age of forty-four.

While Whorf was becoming a successful insurance executive, he was also doing his revolutionary work in linguistics. He started by studying Hebrew but then switched to Aztec and other related languages of Mexico. Later he deciphered Maya inscriptions, and tried to reconstruct the long-lost language of the ancient Maya people of Mexico and Central America. Finally he tackled the complexities of the still-living language of the Hopi Indians of Arizona. He published his findings in respected anthropological and linguistic journals, earning the praise and respect of scholars in the two fields—all without formal training in linguistic science. As his fame as a linguist spread, the Hartford obligingly afforded him vacations and leaves to travel to the Southwest in pursuit of the structure and lexicon of the Hopi. He also put in countless hours in the Watkinson Library in Connecticut, a rich repository of Mexican and Indian lore.

It was primarily his study of Hopi that impelled Whorf toward his revolutionary ideas. He was encouraged and aided by the great cultural anthropologist and linguist of Yale, Edward Sapir, and the idea that language influences a person's view of the world is generally known as the Sapir-Whorf hypothesis. Whorf formulated it a number of times, but perhaps his clearest statement comes from his 1940 essay "Science and Linguistics": "The background linguistic system (in other words, the grammar) of each language is not merely a reproducing instrument for voicing ideas but rather is itself the shaper of ideas. . . . We dissect nature along lines laid down by our native language. The categories and types that we isolate from the world of phenomena we do not find there because they stare every observer in the face; on the contrary, the world is presented in a kaleidoscopic flux of impressions which has to be organized by our minds—and this means largely by the linguistic systems in our minds."

These ideas developed from Whorf's study of the Hopi language. He discovered that it differs dramatically from languages of the Indo-European family such as English or French, particularly in its expression of the concept of time. English and its related languages have three major tenses—past, present, and future ("it was," "it is," "it will be")—plus the fancier compound tenses such as "it will have been." Having these tenses, Whorf argued, encourages Europeans and Americans to think of time as so many ducks in a row. Time past is made up of uniform units of time—days, weeks, months, years—and the future is similarly measured out. This division of time is essentially artificial, Whorf said, since people can only experience the present. Past and future are only abstractions, but Westerners think of them as real because their language virtually forces them to do so. This view of time has given rise to the fondness in Western cultures for diaries, records, annals, histories, clocks, calendars, wages paid by the hour or day, and elaborate timetables for the use of future time. Time is continually quantified. If Westerners set out to build a house they establish a deadline; the work will be completed at a specified time in the future, such as May 5 or October 15.

Hopis do not behave this way; when they start to weave a mat they are not concerned about when it will be completed. They work on it desultorily, then quit, then begin again; the finished product may take weeks. This casual progress is not laziness but a result of the Hopi's view of time—one symptom of the fact that their language does not have the past, present, and future tenses. Instead it possesses two modes of thought: the objective, that is, things that exist now, and the subjective, things that can be thought about and therefore belong to a state of becoming. Things do not become in terms of a future measured off in days, weeks, months. Each thing that is becoming has its own individual life rhythms, growing or declining or changing in much the same manner as a plant grows, according to its inner nature. The essence of Hopi life, therefore, Whorf said, is preparing in the present so that those things that are capable of becoming can in fact come to pass. Thus weaving a mat is preparing a mat to become a mat; it will reach that state when its nature so ordains—whenever that will be.

This view of the future is understandable, Whorf noted, in an agricultural people whose welfare depends on the proper preparing of earth and seeds and plants for the hoped-for harvest. It also helps explain why the Hopi have such elaborate festivals, rituals, dances, and magic ceremonies: All are intended to aid in the mental preparation that is so necessary if the crops, which the Hopi believe to be influenced by human thought, are to grow properly. This preparing involves "much visible activity," Whorf said, "introductory formalities, preparing of special food . . . intensive sustained muscular activity like running, racing, dancing, which is thought to increase the intensity of development of events (such as growth of crops), mimetic and other magic preparations based on esoteric theory involving perhaps occult instruments like prayer sticks, prayer feathers, and prayer meal, and finally the great cyclic ceremonies and dances, which have the significance of preparing rain and crops." Whorf went on to note that the very noun for *crop* is derived from the verb that means "to prepare." *Crop* therefore is in the Hopi language literally "the prepared." Further, the Hopi prayer pipe, which is smoked as an aid in concentrating good thoughts on the growing fields of corn and wheat, is named *na'twanpi,* "instrument of preparing."

The past to the Hopi, Whorf believed, is also different from the chronological time sense of the speakers of Indo-European languages. The past is not a uniform row of days or weeks to the Hopi. It is rather an undifferentiated stream in which many deeds were done that have accumulated and prepared the present and will continue to prepare the becoming that is ahead. Everything is connected, everything accumulates. The past is not a series of events, separated and completed, but is present in the present.

To Whorf these striking differences in the Hopi language and sense of time implied that the Hopi live almost literally in another world from the speakers of Indo-European languages. The Hopi language grew out of its speakers' peculiar circumstances: As a geographically isolated agricultural people in a land where rainfall was scanty, they did the same things and prayed the same prayers year after year and thus did not need to have past and future tenses. But the language, once it had developed, perpetuated their particular and seemingly very different world view.

Many linguists and anthropologists who have worked with American Indians of the Southwest have been convinced that Whorf's theories are by and large correct. Other linguists are not convinced, however, and through the years since Whorf's death they have attacked his proposals. The controversy is unlikely to be settled soon, if ever. One of the problems is the difficulty of setting up an experiment that would either prove or disprove the existence of correlations between linguistic structure and nonlinguistic behavior. It would be fruitless to go about asking people of various cultures their opinions as to whether the language they spoke had determined the manner in which they thought, had dictated their view of the world. Nobody would be able to answer such a question, for a people's language is so completely embedded in their consciousness that they would be unable to conceive of any other way of interpreting the world.

Despite the near impossibility of proving or disproving Whorf's theory, it will not go away but keeps coming back, intriguing each succeeding generation of linguists. It is certainly one of the most fascinating theories created by the modern mind. It is comparable in some ways to Einstein's theory of relativity. Just as Einstein said that how people saw the phenomena of the universe was relative to their point of observation, so Whorf said that a people's world view was relative to the language they spoke.

And demonstrations of Whorf's ideas are not entirely lacking. They come mainly from studies of color—one of the very few aspects of reality that can be specified by objective scientific methods and also is rather precisely specified by people's naming of colors. In this instance it is possible to compare one person's language, expressing that person's view of the world, with another's language for exactly the same characteristic of the world. The comparison can thus reveal different views that are linked to different descriptions of the same reality. English-speakers view purple as a single relatively uniform color; only if pressed and then only with difficulty will they make any attempt to divide it into such shades as lavender and mauve. But no English-speaker would lump orange with purple; to the users of English, those colors are completely separate, for no single word includes both of them. If other languages made different distinctions in the naming of color—if lavender and mauve were always separate, never encompassed by a word for purple, or if orange and purple were not distinguished but were called by a name that covered both—then it would seem that the users of those languages interpreted those colors differently.

Such differences in color-naming, it turns out, are fairly widespread. Linguist H. A. Gleason compared the color spectrum as described by English-speaking persons to the way it was labeled by speakers of Bassa, a language spoken in Liberia, and by speakers of Shona, spoken in Rhodesia. English-speaking people, when seeing sunlight refracted through a prism, identify by name at least six colors—purple, blue, green, yellow, orange, and red. The speakers of Shona, however, have only three names for the colors of the spectrum. They group orange, red, and purple under one name. They also lump blue and green-blue under one of their other color terms and use their third word to identify yellow and the yellower hues of green. The speakers of Bassa are similarly restricted by a lack of handy terms for color, for they have only two words for the hues of the spectrum.

Gleason's observations prompted psychologists to perform an experiment that also showed the influence words can have on the way colors are handled intellectually and remembered. It was an ingenious and complex experiment with many checks and double checks of the results, but in essence it boiled down to something like this: English-speaking subjects were shown a series of color samples—rather like the little "chips" provided by a paint store to help customers decide what color to paint the living room. The subjects were then asked to pick out the colors they had seen from a far larger array of colors. It turned out that they could more accurately pick out the right colors from the larger selection when the color involved had a handy, ordinary name like "green." The subjects had difficulty with the ambiguous, in-between colors such as off-purples and misty blues. In other words, a person can remember a color better if that person's language offers a handy label for it, but has trouble when the language does not offer such a familiar term. Again the human ability to differentiate reality seemed to be affected by the resources offered by language.

Richness of linguistic resource undoubtedly helps people to cope with subtle gradations in the things they deal with every day. The Hanunóo people of the Philippine Islands have different names for ninety-two varieties of rice. They can easily distinguish differences in rice that would be all but invisible to English-speaking people, who lump all such grains under the single world *rice.* Of course, English-speakers can make distinctions by resorting to adjectives and perhaps differentiate long-grain, brown rice from small-grain, yellow rice, but surely no European or American would, lacking the terms, have a sufficiently practiced eye to distinguish ninety-two varieties of rice. Language is essentially a code that people use both to think and to communicate. As psychologist Roger Brown sums up the rice question: "Among the Hanunóo, who have names for ninety-two varieties of rice, any one of those varieties is highly codable in the array of ninety-one other varieties. The Hanunóo have a word for it and so can transmit it efficiently and presumably can recognize it easily. Among speakers of English one kind of rice among ninety-one other kinds would have very low codability."

Brown goes on to suppose that the Hanunóo set down in New York would be baffled by the reality around them partly because they would then be the ones lacking the needed words. "If the Hanunóo were to visit the annual Automobile Show in New York City, they would find it difficult to encode distinctively any particular automobile in that array. But an American having such lexical resources as *Chevrolet, Ford, Plymouth, Buick, Corvette, hard-top, convertible, four-door, station wagon,* and the like could easily encode ninety-two varieties."

The very existence of so many different languages, each linked to a distinctive culture, is itself support of a sort for Whorf's hypothesis. At least since the time of the Tower of Babel, no single tongue has been shared by all the people of the world. Many attempts have been made to invent an international language, one so simply structured and easy to learn it would be used by everyone around the globe as a handy adjunct to their native speech. Yet even the most successful of these world languages, Esperanto, has found but limited acceptance.

There are international languages, however, to serve international cultures. The intellectual disciplines of music, dance, and mathematics might be considered specialized cultures; each is shared by people around the world, and each has an international language, used as naturally in Peking as in Paris. English is a world language in certain activities that straddle national boundaries, such as international air travel; it serves for communications between international flights and the ground in every country—a Lufthansa pilot approaching Athens talks with the airport control tower neither in German nor in Greek but in English.

The trouble with most attempts to lend credence to the Sapir-Whorf hypothesis is that, while they indicate connections between culture and language, they do not really prove that a language shaped its users' view of the world. Just because the speakers of Shona have only three main distinctions of color does not mean that their "world view" is all that different from that of the English-speaker who has more convenient color terms. Shona speakers obviously see all the colors in the rainbow that English-speakers see. Their eyes are physiologically the same. Their comparative poverty of words for those colors merely means that it is harder for them to talk about color. Their "code" is not so handy; the colors' codability is lower.

Critics also point out that Whorf may have mistaken what are called dead metaphors for real differences in the Hopi language. All languages are loaded with dead metaphors—figures of speech that have lost all figurative value and are now just familiar words. The word "goodbye" is a dead metaphor. Once it meant "God be with you," but in its contracted form it conjures up no thought or picture of God. If a Whorfian linguist who was a native speaker of Hopi turned the tables and analyzed English he might conclude that English-speakers were perpetually thinking of religion since this everyday word incorporates a reference to God—a ridiculous misreading of a term that has lost all of its original religious significance. In like fashion, perhaps Whorf was reading too much into the Hopi lexicon and grammar, seeing significances where there were none.

The argument about how far Whorf's ideas can be stretched has gone on for several decades and promises to go on for several more. Most psychologists believe that all people see pretty much the same reality; their languages merely have different words and structures to approximate in various idiosyncratic ways a picture of that reality. And yet the experts accept what might be called modified Whorfism—a belief in the power of language to affect, if not to direct, the perception of reality. If a language is rich in terms for certain things or ideas—possesses extensive codability for them—then the people speaking that language can conceive of, and talk about, those things or ideas more conveniently. If different languages do not give their speakers entirely different world views, they certainly influence thinking to some degree.

Even within the Indo-European family of languages, some tongues have words for concepts that other tongues lack. German is especially rich in philosophical terms that have no exact counterparts in English, French, Italian—or any known language. One is *Weltschmerz,* which combines in itself meanings that it takes three English phrases to adequately convey—"weariness of life," "pessimistic outlook," and "romantic discontent." Another German word that has no direct translation is *Weltanschauung.* To approximate its meaning in English requires a number of different terms—"philosophy of life," "world outlook," "ideology"—for all of these elements are included in the German word. "Weltanschauung" is untranslatable into any single English term. It represents an idea for which only German has a word. Possessing the convenient term, German writers can develop this idea more easily than the users of other languages, and thus explore its ramifications further.

Even when a word from one language may seem to be easily translatable into another, it often is not really equivalent. The French term *distingué* would appear to translate easily enough into the English *distinguished.* But the French use their word in ways that no English-speaker would ever employ for *distinguished.* A Frenchman might reprimand his son by saying that his impolite behavior was not *distingué* or he might tell his wife that a scarf she has worn out to dinner is charmingly *distingué.* The word does not mean "distinguished" as English-speakers employ the term, but something more like "suitable," or "appropriate," or "in keeping with polite standards." It is simply not the same word in the two languages no matter how similar the spelling. It represents a different idea, connoting a subtle difference in mental style.

In some cases the existence of a word leads users of it down tortured logical paths toward dead ends. The common word nothing is one example. Since there is a word for the concept, points out philosopher George Pitcher, it tempts people to think that "nothing" is a real entity, that somehow it exists, a palpable realm of not-being. It has in fact led a number of philosophers, including the twentieth-century French thinker Jean-Paul Sartre, to spend a great deal of effort speculating about the nature of "nothing." The difficulty of this philosophic dilemma is indicated by a typical Sartre sentence on the subject: "The Being by which Nothingness arrives in the world must nihilate. Nothingness in its Being, and even so it still runs the risk of establishing Nothingness as a transcendent in the very heart of immanence unless it nihilates Nothingness in its being in connection with its own being." Sartre could hardly have gotten himself tangled up in such agonized prose had French lacked a noun for *le neant,* nothing, and the value to human welfare of his attempt to explain is open to question.

The power of language to influence the world can be seen not only in comparisons of one tongue to another, but also within a single language. The way in which people use their native tongue—choosing one term over another to express the same idea or action, varying structures or phrases for different situations—has a strong effect on their attitudes toward those situations. Distasteful ideas can be made to seem acceptable or even desirable by careful choices of words, and language can make actions or beliefs that might otherwise be considered correct appear to be obsolescent or naive. Value judgments of many kinds can be attached to seemingly simple statements. Shakespeare may have believed that "a rose by any other name would smell as sweet," but he was wrong, as other theatrical promoters have proved repeatedly. A young English vaudevillian known as Archibald Leach was a minor comedian until he was given the more romantic name of Cary Grant. The new name did not make him a star, but it did create an atmosphere in which he could demonstrate his talent, suggesting the type of character he came to exemplify.

If the power of a stage name to characterize personality seems of relatively minor consequence in human affairs, consider the effect of a different sort of appellation: "boy." It was—and sometimes still is—the form of address employed by whites in the American South in speaking to black males of any age. This word, many authorities believe, served as an instrument of subjugation. It implied that the black was not a man but a child, someone not mature enough to be entrusted with responsibility for himself, let alone authority over others. His inferior position was thus made to seem natural and justified, and it could be enforced without compunction.

Characterizing people by tagging them with a word label is a world-wide practice. Many peoples use a single word to designate both themselves and the human race. "The Carib Indians, for example, have stated with no equivocation, 'We alone are people,'" reported anthropologist Jack Conrad. "Similarly, the ancient Egyptians used the word *romet* (men) only among themselves and in no case for strangers. The Lapps of Scandinavia reserve term 'human being' for those of their own kind, while the Cherokee Indians call themselves *Ani-Yunwiya,* which means 'principal people.' The Kiowa Indians of the Southwest are willing to accept other peoples as human, but the very name, *Kiowa,* meaning 'real people,' shows their true feeling." The effect of reserving a term indicating "human" to one group is far-reaching. It alters the perception of anyone from outside that group. He is not called "human," and need not be treated as human. Like an animal, he can be entrapped, beaten, or even killed with more or less impunity. This use of a word to demote whole groups from the human class is often a wartime tactic—the enemy is referred to by a pejorative name to justify killing him.

While language can be twisted to make ordinarily good things seem bad, it can also be twisted in the opposite direction to make bad things seem good or run-of-the-mill things better than they really are. The technique depends on the employment of euphemisms, a term derived from the Greek for "words of good omen." A euphemism is roundabout language that is intended to conceal something embarrassing or unpleasant. Some classes of euphemism—little evasions that people use every day—are inoffensive enough. It is when such cloudy doubletalk invades the vital areas of politics and foreign affairs that it becomes perilous.

A large and commonly used—and relatively harmless—class of euphemism has to do with bodily functions. Many people shy away from frank talk about excretion or sex; in fact, many of the old, vivid terms—the four-letter words—are socially taboo. So people for centuries have skirted the edge of such matters, inventing a rich vocabulary of substitute terms. Americans offered turkey on Thanksgiving commonly say "white meat" or "dark meat" to announce their preference. These terms date back to the nineteenth century when it was considered indelicate to say "breast" or "leg." *Toilet,* itself a euphemism coined from the French *toilette* ("making oneself presentable to the outside world"), long ago became tainted and too graphic for the prudish. The list of euphemistic substitutes is almost endless, ranging from the commonplace *washroom, bathroom,* and *restroom* (whoever rests in a restroom?) to *john, head,* and *Chic Sale* in the United States, and in England *the loo. Loo* may be derived from a mistaken English pronunciation of the French *l'eau,* water. Or it may be a euphemism derived from a euphemism. The French, with Gallic delicacy, once commonly put the number 100 on bathroom doors in hotels. It is easy to see how an English person might have mistaken the number for the word *loo.* Meanwhile, ladies in restaurants have adopted "I'm going to powder my nose" or, in England, where it once cost a penny to use public toilets, "I'm going to spend a penny."

Another generally harmless use of euphemistic language is the practice, especially notable in the United States, of giving prestigious names to more-or-less ordinary trades. As H. L. Mencken pointed out in *The American Language,* his masterly examination of English as spoken in the United States, ratcatchers are fond of calling themselves "exterminating engineers" and hairdressers have long since showed a preference for "beautician." The *-ician* ending, in fact, has proved very popular, doubtless because it echoes "physician" and thus sounds both professional and scientific. In the late nineteenth century undertakers had already begun to call themselves "funeral directors," but starting in 1916 ennobled themselves even further by battening on the newer euphemistic coinage, "mortician." Meanwhile a tree trimmer became a "tree surgeon" (that love of medicine again) and a press agent became a "publicist" or, even more grandly, a "public relations counsel."

Americans (and the English, too) not only chose high-sounding euphemisms for their professions but also gave new and gaudy names to their places of business. Thus pawn shops became "loan offices," saloons became "cocktail rooms," pool halls became "billiard parlors," and barber shops "hair-styling salons."

Purists might say that such shading or blunting of the stark truth leads to moral decay, but it is difficult to see why anybody should be the worse for allowing women to excuse themselves by pleading that they must powder their noses. There are euphemisms, however, that are clearly anything but harmless. These are evasive, beclouding phraseologies that hide truths people must clearly perceive if they are to govern themselves intelligently and keep a check on those in positions of power. Slick phrases, slippery evasions—words deliberately designed to hide unpleasant truth rather than reveal it—can so becloud political processes and so easily hide mistaken policies that the entire health of a nation is imperiled.

The classic treatise on the political misuse of language in modern times is the 1946 essay "Politics and the English Language" by the British writer George Orwell. "In our time, political speech and writing are largely the defence of the indefensible," Orwell said. "Thus political language has to consist largely of euphemism, question-begging and sheer cloudy vagueness." He concluded, "Such phraseology is needed if one wants to name things without calling up mental pictures of them. . . . When there is a gap between one's real and one's declared aims, one turns as it were instinctively to long words and exhausted idioms, like a cuttlefish squirting out ink."

Orwell supplied numerous examples to buttress his charges. "Defenceless villages are bombarded from the air, the inhabitants driven out into the countryside, the cattle machine-gunned, the huts set on fire with incendiary bullets: this is called *pacification.*" He went on to observe that in Stalin's Russia people were "imprisoned for years without trial or shot in the back of the neck or sent to die of scurvy in Arctic lumber camps: this is called *elimination of unreliable elements.*"

Orwell, who died at the age of forty-six in 1950, did not live to collect even more deplorable distortions of language. The French clothed their brutal war in Algeria with a veil of euphemism; the North Koreans accused the South Koreans of "aggression" when the North invaded the South. The United States invented a whole lexicon of gobbledygook to disguise the horror of the war in Vietnam: "protective reaction strike" (the bombing of a Vietnamese village); "surgical bombing" (the same as protective reaction strike); "free-fire zone" (an area in which troops could shoot anything that moved, including helpless villagers); "new life hamlet" (a refugee camp for survivors of a surgical bombing).

Perhaps the most appalling use of this type of euphemism was the word employed by the Nazis for their program to exterminate all of Europe's Jews. The word is *Endlösung,* which means final solution. Behind that verbal façade the Nazis gassed, burned, shot, or worked to death some six million Jews from Germany, France, Poland, and other conquered parts of Europe. Hitler and Gestapo chief Himmler often employed the euphemism among themselves, and it was always used in official records—but not necessarily to preserve secrecy for purposes of state security. Apparently the euphemism shielded the Nazis from themselves. Openly brutal and murderous as they were, they could not face up to the horrible reality of what they were doing, and they had to hide it in innocuous language.

Such distortion of language can do more than disguise truth. It can turn truth around, so that the idea conveyed is the opposite of actuality. After the USSR savagely crushed the Hungarian rebellion in 1956 the Soviet aggression was made to seem, in the twisted language used by other Communist dictatorships, an expression of friendship. The Peking radio commented after the rebellion was put down: "The Hungarian people can see that Soviet policy toward the people's democracies is truly one of equality, friendship, and mutual assistance, not of conquest, aggression, and plunder."

The possibility that such topsy-turvy language might ultimately make the world topsy-turvy—an ironic demonstration of the fundamental truth of Benjamin Lee Whorf's insights—was raised in a dramatic way by George Orwell. His novel *1984,* a chilling and convincing description of life in a totalitarian society, shows how language might destroy reality. In the imaginary nation of Oceania the official language is Newspeak, which is intended to facilitate "doublethink," the ability to accept simultaneously ideas contradicting each other. The Oceania state apparatus includes a Ministry of Truth, its headquarters building emblazoned with three slogans: "WAR IS PEACE"; "FREEDOM IS SLAVERY"; "IGNORANCE IS STRENGTH." There are also other ministries, Orwell explained: "The Ministry of Peace, which concerned itself with war; the Ministry of Love, which maintained law and order." Anyone who would use language this way, Orwell made clear, denies the meaning of his or her words. He or she has lost touch with reality and substituted for it an emptiness concealed in sounds that once had meaning.

There is another threat to language besides the intentional twisting of words by demagogues and others who would control people's thoughts. It is less obvious, but a danger nevertheless: simple imprecision, slovenliness, mindlessness in the use of the language. It seems a small matter that English-speakers increasingly confuse *uninterested* with *disinterested,* for example. But these words do not mean the same thing. *Disinterested* means impartial, not taking sides. *Uninterested* means lacking in interest, bored. A judge should be *disinterested* but never *uninterested.* Many such changes result from the inevitable evolution of language as it changes over the years, but the change can be a loss. The slow erosion of distinctions, visible in much writing, audible in many conversations, makes language imprecise and thus clumsy and ineffective as communication.

Among the symptoms of such erosion are stock phrases that people mindlessly repeat, substituting noise for thought. Everyone has heard speechmakers use such clichés as "having regard to," "play into the hands of," "in the interest of," "no axe to grind." Although this brief list is drawn from Orwell's essay of 1946 these exhausted clichés are still heard. Such verbal dead limbs do not distort thought but rather tend to obliterate it in a cloud of meaninglessness. "The slovenliness of our language makes it easier for us to have foolish thoughts," wrote Orwell. And ultimately, as has been pointed out by commentator Edwin Newman in his book *Strictly Speaking,* "Those for whom words have lost their value are likely to find that ideas have also lost their value."

Review Questions

1. According to Thomson, what is the Sapir-Whorf hypothesis? Give some examples.
2. According to Whorf, how can grammar affect people's perceptions? Give examples.
3. The Sapir-Whorf hypothesis has been tested in several ways. What are some of the tests of the hypothesis described by Thomson, and how have these modified the theory?
4. What are some of the ways in which language affects or modifies perception in modern America? Can you add examples from your own experience to those presented by Thomson?

8

Teleconditioning and the Postmodern Classroom

Conrad Phillip Kottak

The previous articles in this part have dealt with ways and styles of communication and the manipulation of meaning. This selection by Conrad Kottak looks at one medium *of communication, television. Kottak notes that the repeated act of watching television has modified the cultural behavior of Americans in nontelevision settings. He focuses specifically on what he calls the postmodern classroom, a setting marked by a blurring and breakdown of traditional "cannons, categories, and boundaries." In large university classes, "teleconditioned" students are likely to treat instructors like TV sets, getting up for breaks, reading, talking, and occasionally turning off the "set" by leaving class early. In response, Kottak often roves among his student "audience" with a cordless mike, the academic version of a TV talk show host.*

From "Teaching in the Postmodern Classroom," *General Anthropology.* Copyright © by the American Anthropological Association, 1994. Reprinted by permission of the American Anthropological Association and the author.

New culture patterns related to television's penetration of the American home have emerged since the 1950s. As technology, television affects collective behavior, as people duplicate, in many areas of their lives, habits developed while watching TV. Television content also influences mass culture because it provides widely shared common knowledge, beliefs, and expectations. (Conrad Kottak, Prime-Time Society: An Anthropological Analysis of Television and Culture.)

As millennium approaches, linkages in the world system have both enlarged and erased old boundaries and distinctions. Arjun Appadurai[1] characterizes today's world as a "translocal" "interactive system" that is "strikingly new." Whether as refugees, migrants, tourists, pilgrims, proselytizers, laborers, business people, development agents, employees of nongovernmental organizations (NGOs), politicians, soldiers, sports figures, students, reporters, or media-borne images, people travel more than ever.

Postmodernity describes our time and situation—today's world in flux, these media-saturated people on-the-move who must manage new, shifting, and multiple identities depending on place and context. In its most general sense, *postmodern* refers to the blurring and breakdown of established rules, standards, categories, distinctions, and boundaries.[2] In multiple guises, postmodernity has invaded the classroom, as traditional roles, boundaries, and canons of behavior are contested, challenged, opened up, and broken down. The electronic mass media, especially television, have played a major role in this process. I shall draw on my own experience in showing how.

I have taught introductory anthropology at the University of Michigan since 1968. I teach the course, which enrolls 550–600 students, in a large auditorium. A microphone is necessary if the perennial instructor wants to avoid cancer of the larynx. Each fall, I stand on a platform in front of these massed undergraduates. In 13–14 weeks of lecturing I survey the subfields of general anthropology.

Among the first courses taken at the University of Michigan, Anthropology 101 carries social science distribution credit. It also satisfies our new Diversity requirement (a course dealing with race or ethnicity). Few of the students in it plan to major in anthropology, and many will never take another anthropology course. For these reasons, the lecturer must work hard to keep students' attention, and my evaluations usually give me good marks for making the course interesting. In this setting students perceive a suc-

---

[1] "Disjuncture and Difference in the Global Cultural Economy," *Public Culture,* vol. 2, no. 2, pp. 1–24, 1990.

[2] The word is taken from *postmodernism*—a style and movement in architecture that succeeded modernism, beginning in the 1970s. Postmodern architecture rejected the rules, geometric order, and austerity of modernism. Modernist buildings were expected to have a clear and functional design. Postmodern design is "messier" and more playful. It draws on a diversity of styles from different times and places—including popular, ethnic, and nonwestern cultures. Postmodernism extends "value" well beyond classic, elite, and western cultural forms. *Postmodern* is now used to describe comparable developments in music, literature, and visual art.

cessful lecturer not simply as a teacher, but as something of an entertainer. The combination of large auditorium, huddled masses, and electronic amplification transforms this assembly from a mere class into an audience. Although these conditions have remained fairly constant since I began teaching in 1968, there have been noticeable changes in student behavior, particularly in their less formal classroom comportment. Indeed, my observation of Anthropology 101 students helped turn my attention to the influence of the electronic mass media on human behavior (as elaborated in my 1990 book *Prime-Time Society: An Anthropological Analysis of Television and Culture*).

My students have never known a world without TV. The tube has been as much a fixture in their homes as mom or dad. Considering how common divorce has become, the TV even outlasts the father in many homes. American kids devote 22 to 30 hours to television each week. By the end of high school, they will have spent 22,000 hours in front of the set, versus only 11,000 in the classroom.[3] Such prolonged exposure must affect their behavior in observable ways.

I've discussed the behavior modification I see in my classroom with university colleagues; many report similar observations. The point I'm making here differs from familiar pronouncements about television's effects on human behavior. Other researchers have found, or asserted, links between exposure to media content (e.g., violence) and individual behavior (hyperactivity, aggression, "acting out"). Like them, I believe that content may affect behavior. But I make a more basic claim: The very habit of watching TV has modified the behavior of Americans who have grown up with television.

Anyone who has been to a movie house (or to an annual meeting of the American Anthropological Association) lately has seen examples of TV-conditioned behavior—*teleconditioning.* Audience members talk, babies gurgle and cry, people file out and in, getting snacks and going to the bathroom. Students act similarly in college courses. In the "golden age" before teleconditioning (the pre-postmodern world), there was always an isolated student who did such things. What is new is a behavior pattern characteristic of a group rather than an individual. This cultural pattern is becoming more pronounced, and I think it's linked to all those hours of "watching television." Stated simply, the pattern, which I call teleconditioning, is this: Televiewing causes people to duplicate in many areas of their lives styles of behavior developed while watching television, and this fuels the culture of postmodernity.

Remembering that *postmodern* refers to the blurring and breakdown of established canons, categories, and boundaries, some examples of teleconditioning in the postmodern classroom are in order. Almost nothing bothers a professor more than having someone read a newspaper in class. Lecturers are understandably perturbed when a student shows more interest in a sports

---

[3] "Too Much TV Time Linked to Obesity in Children, Teens," *Ann Arbor News,* May 6, 1985.

column or *Doonesbury* than in the lecture content. I don't often get newspapers in class, but one day I noticed a student sitting in the front row reading a paperback novel. Irritated by her audacity, I stopped lecturing and asked "Why are you reading a book in my class?" Her answer: "Oh, I'm not in your class. I just came in here to read my book."

How is this wildly improbable response to be explained? Why would someone take the trouble to migrate into a lecture hall to read? The answer, I think, is this: after years of televiewing (plus rock music), many young Americans have trouble reading unless they have background noise. Research confirms that most Americans do something else while watching television. Often they read. Even I do it. It's not unusual for me to get home, turn on the TV, sit down in a comfortable chair and go through the mail or read the newspaper.

Research on television's impact confirms that televiewing evolves through certain stages. The first stage, when sets are introduced, is rapt attention, gazes glued to the screen. Some of us can remember from the late 1940s or early 1950s sitting in front of our first TV, dumbly watching even test patterns. Later, as the novelty diminishes, viewers become less attentive. Televiewers in Brazil, whom I began studying systematically in 1983, had already moved past the first stage, but they were still much more attentive than Americans. A study done in São Paulo illustrates the contrast. The study shocked Rede Globo, Brazil's dominant network, when it revealed that half the viewers weren't paying full attention to commercials. Worried about losing advertising revenue, Rede Globo challenged the research. (American sponsors, by contrast, are so accustomed to inattention and, nowadays, remote control tune-outs, that it would delight them if even half the audience stayed put.)

The student who came to my class to read a novel was simply an extreme example of a culture pattern derived from exposure to the mass media. Because of her lifelong TV dependency, she had trouble reading without background noise. It didn't matter to her whether the hum came from a stereo, a TV set, or a live professor. Accustomed to machines that don't talk back, she probably was amazed I noticed her at all. My questioning may even have prompted her to check inside her set that night to see if someone real was lurking there.

Another effect of televiewing is students' increasing tendency to enter and leave classrooms at will. Of course, individual students do occasionally get sick or have a dentist's appointment. But here again I'm describing a group pattern rather than individual circumstances or idiosyncrasies. During the past few years I've regularly observed students getting up in mid-lecture, leaving the room for a few minutes, then returning. Sometimes they bring back a canned soft drink or coffee and doughnuts (which campus groups have started selling in classroom buildings).

I don't think these ambulatory students mean to be disrespectful; rather, the rules and boundaries they recognize differ from those of students past. They are transferring a home-grown pattern of informality, including snack and bathroom breaks, from family (TV) room to classroom. They perceive nothing unusual in acting the same way in front of a live speaker and fellow students as they do when they watch television. (A few students manage to remain seated for only 10–15 minutes, then get up and leave. They are exhibiting a less flattering pattern. Either they have diarrhea, as one student told me he did, or they have decided to turn off the "set" or "change channels.")

Nowadays, almost all Americans talk while watching TV. Talking is getting more common in the classroom, just as in the movie house, and this also illustrates television's effects on our collective behavior. Not only do my students bring food and drink to class, some lie down on the floor if they arrive too late to get a seat. I've even seen couples kissing and caressing just a few rows away. New examples of post-modern expectations and/or teleconditioning pop up all the time. In two recent semesters, students requested that I say, publicly, "Happy Birthday" to a friend in the class. They perceived me as a professorial analogue of Willard Scott, the NBC "Today Show" weather caster who offers birthday greetings (to people 100 and over). Long ago I put into my syllabus injunctions against reading newspapers and eating crunchy foods in class. Now I feel compelled to announce "I don't do birthdays."

In response to all this, I've modified my lecture style, trying to enhance students' attention, interest, and, I hope, learning. In search of ways of dealing with teleconditioning and post-modernity, I subscribed to a newsletter called *The Teaching Professor* (Magna Publications). I've heeded some of its advice for more effective teaching—"Don't stand passively at the front of the room and lecture." "Don't let yourself be chained to a chalkboard, lectern, podium, overhead projector, or microphone." "Move around and show your students you own the entire classroom."

These lessons led me to adopt the technology of the current television age to instruct students who have been teleconditioned. Now, like the TV talk-show host Phil Donahue, I use a remote microphone, which allows me to roam the lecture hall at will. A teaching assistant sits at the overhead projector in front and writes down terms and notes as I walk and talk. Unlike Phil, whose studio layout promotes his elicitation of comments from audience members (into whose faces Donahue regularly pushes his microphone), my mobility and personal encounters (student "feedback," "participation," or "empowerment") are constrained by an auditorium that is very wide and lacks a center aisle. Unlike Phil and Oprah (Winfrey), I can't rush up and down the center aisle asking probing questions like "What do you think of serial monogamy?" or "Should Americans adopt bifurcate collateral kinship terminology?" I have to confine my striding to the front, sides, and back of the auditorium, occasionally moving a few seats into a row (sometimes activating the Boundary Recognition and Response System of students who have failed to recognize the reciprocal implications of postmodernity).

Student attention shifts between me, the peripatetic lecturer, and the front of the auditorium, where my vigilant TA scribe works at the overhead and where loudspeakers broadcast my voice. Wandering from time to time to the rear of the room, I occasionally challenge the anonymity of a somnolent or notetaking young man in the last row (where only male students sit). Sometimes, I let a student ask a question into the microphone. Often, if I see someone about to leave during lecture, my remote mike allows me to head in that direction. I believe that my roaming, which permits me to mingle with students more than I used to, inhibits the teleconditioned behavior that used to bother me (and that increasingly perturbs my colleagues who teach the same class without circumambulating). If you can't lick it, join it.

My students grow accustomed to my style and generally pay attention, but the supply of postmodern manifestations seems endless. Thus, students "empowered" by campus email send me questions, comments, poems, stories, even pictures of MTV's Beavis and Butt-head. (The Dean of the College and the President of the University get some of the same mail.)

As Fall 1993 progressed, I started noticing a young male student who perpetually arrived late and greeted me with a friendly wave. One day he extended his hand and gave me what seemed to be a secret shake. Another day, as I began my lecture at the front of the auditorium, he and two friends walked up to me, shook hands, and sat down in the front row. My most memorable encounter with this, my most postmodern student, came one day on the University of Michigan "Diag." He approached me on a bike, stopped, stuck out his hand, and said "Gimme five, Connie, baby." Conditioned by my own teen-aged son to do that without pause, I matched him, high and low, and continued my trek across campus. If Franz Boas were alive today to witness such behavior, he would, as they say, turn over in his grave.

Review Questions

1. What does Conrad Kottak mean by the term *postmodernism?* How does this term apply to student behavior in the large university classroom?
2. What does Kottak mean by the term *teleconditioning?* What are some examples of teleconditioning?
3. According to Kottak, habitual televiewing results in a special form of cultural behavior. What is this behavior and, why does Kottak call it *cultural* rather than *personal?*
4. What is enculturation, and how does television contribute to the enculturation of American TV watchers?
5. What is Kottak's solution to teaching in the postmodern classroom?

4

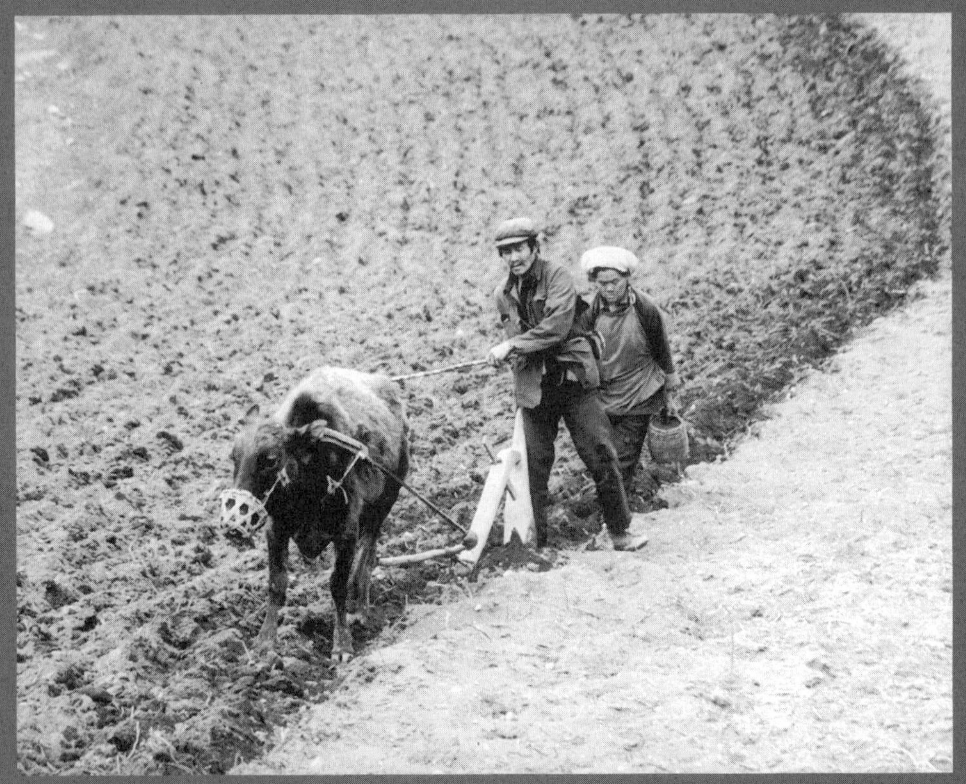

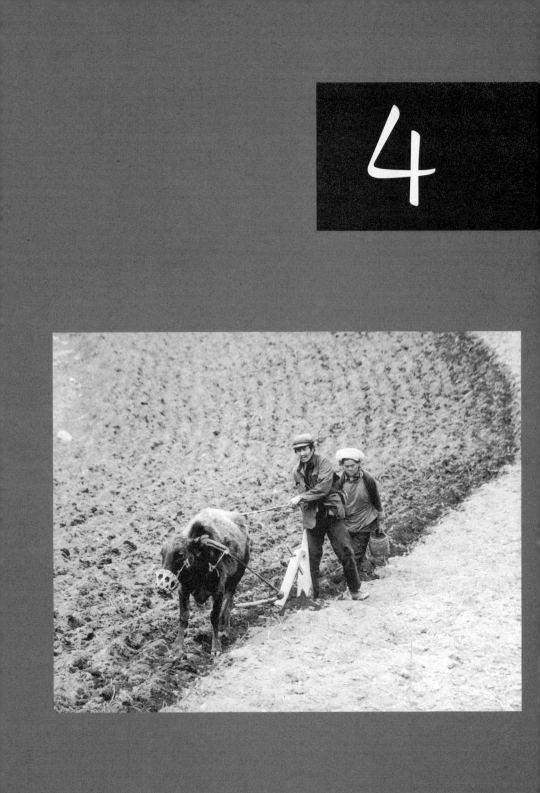

ECOLOGY AND SUBSISTENCE

Ecology is the relationship of an organism to other elements within its environmental sphere. Every species, no matter how simple or complex, fits into a larger complex ecological system; each adapts to its ecological niche unless rapid environmental alterations outstrip the organism's ability and potential to adapt successfully. An important aim of ecological studies is to show how organisms fit within particular environments. Such studies also look at the effect environments have on the shape and behavior of life forms.

Every species has adapted biologically through genetically produced variation and natural selection. For example, the bipedal (two-footed) locomotion characteristic of humans is one possible adaptation to walking on the ground. It also permitted our ancestors to carry food, tools, weapons, and almost anything else they desired, enabling them to range out from a home base and bring things back for others to share.

Biological processes have led to another important human characteristic, the development of a large and complex brain. The human brain is capable of holding an enormous inventory of information. With it, we can classify the parts of our environment and retain instructions for complex ways to deal with the things in our world. Because we can communicate our knowledge symbolically through language, we are able to teach one another. Instead of a genetic code that directs behavior automatically, we operate with a learned cultural code. Culture gives us the ability to behave in a much wider variety of ways and to change rapidly in new situations. With culture, people have been able to live successfully in almost every part of the world.

Cultural ecology is the way people use their culture to adapt to particular environments. All people live in a *physical environment,* the world they can experience through their senses, but they will conceive of it in terms that seem most important to their adaptive needs and cultural perspective. We call this perspective the *cultural environment.*

All human societies must provide for the material needs of their members. People everywhere have to eat, clothe themselves, provide shelter against the elements, and take care of social requirements such as hospitality, gift giving, and proper dress.

Societies employ several different strategies to meet their material needs, strategies that affect their complexity and internal organization as well as relationships to the natural environment and to other human groups. Anthropologists often use these *subsistence strategies* to classify different groups into five types: hunter-gatherers, horticulturalists, pastoralists, agriculturalists, and industrialists. Let us look briefly at each of these.

Hunter-gatherers depend on wild plants and animals for subsistence. They forage for food, moving to different parts of their territories as supplies of plants, animals, and water grow scarce. They live in small bands of from 10 to 50 people and are typically egalitarian, leading a life marked by sharing and cooperation. Because hunter-gatherer bands are so small, they tend to lack formal political, legal, and religious structure, although members have regular ways to make group decisions, settle disputes, and deal ritually with the questions of death, adversity, social value, and world identification.

Hunter-gatherers tend to see themselves as part of the environment, not masters of it. This view shapes a religious ritual aimed at the maintenance and restoration of environmental harmony. All people lived as hunter-gatherers until about ten thousand years ago, when the first human groups began to farm and dwell in more permanent settlements. Today few hunter-gatherers survive. Most have lost their habitats to more powerful groups bent on economic and political exploitation.

Horticulture represents the earliest farming strategy, one that continues on a diminishing basis among many groups today. Horticulturalists garden. They often use a technique called *slash-and-burn agriculture,* which requires them to clear and burn over wild land and, with the aid of a digging stick, sow seeds in the ashes. When fields lose their fertility after a few years, they are abandoned and new land is cleared. Although horticulturalists farm, they often continue to forage for wild foods and still feel closely related to the natural environment.

Horticulture requires a substantial amount of undeveloped land, so overall population densities must remain fairly low. But the strategy permits higher population densities than hunting and gathering, so horticulturalists tend to live in larger permanent settlements numbering from 50 to 250 individuals. (Some horticultural societies have produced chiefdomships with much larger administrative and religious town centers.) Although they are still small by our standards, horticultural communities are large enough to require more complex organizational strategies. They often display more elaborate kinship systems based on descent, political structures that include headmen or chiefs, political alliances, religions characterized by belief in a variety of supernatural beings, and the beginnings of social inequality. Many of today's so-called tribal peoples are horticulturalists.

Pastoralists follow a subsistence strategy based on the herding of domesticated animals such as cattle, goats, sheep, and camels. Although herding strategies vary from one environment to another, pastoralists share some general attributes. They move on a regular basis during the year to take advantage of fresh sources of water and fodder for their animals. They usually congregate in large encampments for part of the year when food and water are plentiful, then divide into smaller groups when these resources become scarce. Pastoralists often display a strong sense of group identity and pride, a fierce independence, and skill at war and raiding. Despite attempts by modern governments to place them in permanent settlements, many pastoral groups in Africa and Asia continue their nomadic lifestyle.

Agriculture is still a common subsistence strategy in many parts of the world. Agriculture refers to a kind of farming based on the intensive cultivation of permanent land holdings. Agriculturalists usually use plows and organic fertilizers and may irrigate their fields in dry conditions.

Agrarian societies are marked by a high degree of social complexity. They are often organized as nation-states with armies and bureaucracies, social stratification, markets, extended families and kin groups, and some occupational specialization. Religion takes on a formal structure and is organized as a separate institution.

The term *industrialism* labels the final kind of subsistence strategy. Ours is an industrial society, as is much of the Western, and more recently, the Asian world. Industrial nations are highly complex; they display an extensive variety of subgroups and social statuses. Industrial societies tend to be dominated by market economies in which goods and services are exchanged on the basis of price, supply, and demand. There is a high degree of economic specialization, and mass marketing may lead to a depersonalization of human relations. Religious, legal, political, and economic systems find expression as separate institutions in a way that might look disjointed to hunter-gatherers or others from smaller, more integrated societies.

The study of cultural ecology involves more than an understanding of people's basic subsistence strategies. Each society exists in a distinctive environment. Although a group may share many subsistence methods with other societies, there are always special environmental needs that shape productive techniques. Andean farmers, for example, have developed approximately three thousand varieties of potatoes to meet the demands of growing conditions at different elevations in their mountain habitat. Bhil farmers in India have learned to create fields by damming up small streams in their rugged Aravalli hill villages. Otherwise, they would find it difficult to cultivate there at all. American farmers learned to "contour-plow" parallel to slopes in response to water erosion and now increasingly use plowless farming to prevent the wind from carrying away precious topsoil.

No matter how successful are their microenvironmental adjustments, most groups in the world now face more serious adaptive challenges. One difficulty is the exploitation of their lands by outsiders, who are often unconstrained by adaptive necessity. A second is the need to overexploit the environment to meet market demand (see Part 5 for articles on market pressures). In either case, many local peoples find that their traditional subsistence techniques no longer work. They have lost control of their own environmental adjustment and must struggle to adapt to outsiders and what is left of their habitat.

The !Kung, described by Richard Lee in the first selection, provide an excellent example of a traditional foraging lifestyle. But today, the same bands of people who once lived on wild foods in the Kalahari find themselves confined to small government-mandated settlements. Cattle herders tend their animals on the desert lands once occupied by the !Kung. The second article, by Richard Reed, is a sobering reminder of what can happen to a horticultural people who once subsisted in harmony with their tropical forest habitat, but who now find themselves being displaced by colonists. These outsiders have stripped the forest bare. The third selection on India's sacred cattle by Marvin Harris demonstrates that even religious beliefs may be used to facilitate adaptation to a group's subsistence requirements. Finally, the fourth article by Jared Diamond describes the Fate of Easter Islanders who failed to conserve natural resources in their confined world.

Key Terms

- ecology
- cultural ecology
- physical environment
- cultural environment
- subsistence strategies
- hunting and gathering
- horticulture
- slash-and-burn agriculture
- pastoralism
- agriculture
- industrialism

Readings in This Section

The Hunters: Scarce Resources in the Kalahari *Richard Borshay Lee,* page 105

Cultivating the Tropical Forest *Richard K. Reed,* page 120

India's Sacred Cow *Marvin Harris,* page 130

Adaptive Failure: Easter's End *Jared Diamond,* page 141

9

The Hunters: Scarce Resources in the Kalahari

Richard Borshay Lee

Until about 10,000 years ago, everyone in the world survived by hunting and gathering wild foods. They lived in intimate association with their natural environments and employed a complex variety of strategies to forage for food and other necessities of life. Agriculture displaced foraging as the main subsistence technique over the next few thousand years, but some hunter-gatherers lived on in the more remote parts of the world. This study by Richard Lee was done in the early 1960s and describes the important features of one of the last foraging groups, the Ju/Hoansi-!Kung living in the Kalahari Desert. It argues against the idea, held by many anthropologists at that time, that hunter-gatherers live a precarious, hand-to-mouth existence. Instead, Lee found that the !Kung, depending more on vegetable foods than meat, actually spent little time collecting food

---

Reprinted by permission of Richard Lee and Irvin Devore, editors, *Man the Hunter* (Hawthorne, NY: Aldine Publishing Company). Copyright © by the Wenner-Gren Foundation for Anthropological Research, Inc, 1968. (Update by Richard Lee and Megan Biesele exerpted from *General Anthropology*, 1994.)

and managed to live long and fruitful lives in their difficult desert home. The update by Lee and Megan Biesele that appears at the end of the article details the events that have led the !Kung to settle down permanently to life as small-scale farmers and cattle raisers.

The current anthropological view of hunter-gatherer subsistence rests on two questionable assumptions. First is the notion that these people are primarily dependent on the hunting of game animals, and second is the assumption that their way of life is generally a precarious and arduous struggle for existence.

Recent data on living hunter-gatherers show a radically different picture. We have learned that in many societies, plant and marine resources are far more important than are game animals in the diet. More important, it is becoming clear that, with few conspicuous exceptions, the hunter-gatherer subsistence base is at least routine and reliable and at best surprisingly abundant. Anthropologists have consistently tended to underestimate the viability of even those "marginal isolates" of hunting peoples that have been available to ethnographers.

The purpose of this paper is to analyze the food-getting activities of one such "marginal" people, the !Kung Bushmen of the Kalahari Desert. Three related questions are posed: How do the Bushmen make a living? How easy or difficult is it for them to do this? What kinds of evidence are necessary to measure and evaluate the precariousness or security of a way of life? And after the relevant data are presented, two further questions are asked: What makes this security of life possible? To what extent are the Bushmen typical of hunter-gatherers in general?

Bushman Subsistence

The !Kung Bushmen of Botswana are an apt case for analysis. They inhabit the semi-arid northwest region of the Kalahari Desert. With only six to nine inches of rainfall per year, this is, by any account, a marginal environment for human habitation. In fact, it is precisely the unattractiveness of their homeland that has kept the !Kung isolated from extensive contact with their agricultural and pastoral neighbors.

Fieldwork was carried out in the Dobe area, a line of eight permanent waterholes near the South-West Africa border and 125 miles south of the Okavango River. The population of the Dobe area consists of 466 Bushmen, including 379 permanent residents living in independent camps or associated with Bantu cattle posts, as well as 87 seasonal visitors. The Bushmen share the area with some 340 Bantu pastoralists largely of the Herero and Tswana tribes. The ethnographic present refers to the period of fieldwork: October 1963 to January 1965.

The Bushmen living in independent camps lack firearms, livestock, and agriculture. Apart from occasional visits to the Herero for milk, these !Kung

Table 1 Numbers and Distribution of Resident Bushmen and Bantu by Waterhole*

Name of Waterhole	*No. of Camps*	*Population of Camps*	*Other Bushmen*	*Total Bushmen*	*Bantu*
Dobe	2	37	—	37	—
!angwa	1	16	23	39	84
Bate	2	30	12	42	21
!ubi	1	19	—	19	65
!gose	3	52	9	61	18
/ai/ai	5	94	13	107	67
!xabe	—	—	8	8	12
Mahopa	—	—	23	23	73
Total	14	248	88	336	340

*Figures do not include 130 Bushmen outside area on the date of census.

are entirely dependent upon hunting and gathering for their subsistence. Politically they are under the nominal authority of the Tswana headman, although they pay no taxes and receive very few government services. European presence amounts to one overnight government patrol every six to eight weeks. Although Dobe-area !Kung have had some contact with outsiders since the 1880s, the majority of them continue to hunt and gather because there is no viable alternative locally available to them.

Each of the fourteen independent camps is associated with one of the permanent waterholes. During the dry season (May–October) the entire population is clustered around these wells. Table 1 shows the numbers at each well at the end of the 1964 dry season. Two wells had no camp resident and one large well supported five camps. The number of camps at each well and the size of each camp changed frequently during the course of the year. The "camp" is an open aggregate of cooperating persons which changes in size and composition from day to day. Therefore, I have avoided the term "band" in describing the !Kung Bushman living groups.

Each waterhole has a hinterland lying within a six-mile radius that is regularly exploited for vegetable and animal foods. These areas are not territories in the zoological sense, since they are not defended against outsiders. Rather, they constitute the resources that lie within a convenient walking distance of a waterhole. The camp is a self-sufficient subsistence unit. The members move out each day to hunt and gather, and return in the evening to pool the collected foods in such a way that every person present receives an equitable share. Trade in foodstuffs between camps is minimal; personnel do move freely from camp to camp, however. The net effect is of a population constantly in motion. On the average, an individual spends a third of his time living only with close relatives, a third visiting other camps, and a third entertaining visitors from other camps.

Because of the strong emphasis on sharing, and the frequency of movement, surplus accumulation of storable plant foods and dried meat is kept to a minimum. There is rarely more than two or three days' supply of food on hand in a camp at any time. The result of this lack of surplus is that a constant subsistence effort must be maintained throughout the year. Unlike agriculturalists, who work hard during the planting and harvesting seasons and undergo "seasonal unemployment" for several months, the Bushmen hunter-gatherers collect food every third or fourth day throughout the year.

Vegetable foods comprise from 60 to 80 percent of the total diet by weight, and collecting involves two or three days of work per woman per week. The men also collect plants and small animals, but their major contribution to the diet is the hunting of medium and large game. The men are conscientious but not particularly successful hunters; although men's and women's work input is roughly equivalent in terms of man-day of effort, the women provide two to three times as much food by weight as the men.

Table 2 summarizes the seasonal activity cycle observed among the Dobe-area !Kung in 1964. For the greater part of the year, food is locally abundant and easily collected. It is only during the end of the dry season in September and October, when desirable foods have been eaten out in the immediate vicinity of the waterholes, that the people have to plan longer hikes of 10 to 15 miles and carry their own water to those areas where the mongongo nut is still available. The important point is that food is a constant, but distance required to reach food is a variable; it is short in the summer, fall, and early winter, and reaches its maximum in the spring.

This analysis attempts to provide quantitative measures of subsistence status, including data on the following topics: abundance and variety of resources, diet selectivity, range size and population density, the composition of the work force, the ratio of work to leisure time, and the caloric and protein levels in the diet. The value of quantitative data is that they can be used comparatively and also may be useful in archeological reconstruction. In addition, one can avoid the pitfalls of subjective and qualitative impressions; for example, statements about food "anxiety" have proven to be difficult to generalize across cultures.

Abundance and Variety of Resources

It is impossible to define "abundance" of resources absolutely. However, one index of *relative* abundance is whether or not a population exhausts all the food available from a given area. By this criterion, the habitat of the Dobe-area Bushmen is abundant in naturally occurring foods. By far the most important food is the mongongo (mangetti) nut (*Ricinodendron rautanenii* Schinz). Although tens of thousands of pounds of these nuts are harvested and eaten each year, thousands more rot on the ground each year for want of picking.

The mongongo nut, because of its abundance and reliability, alone accounts for 50 percent of the vegetable diet by weight. In this respect it resembles a cultivated staple crop such as maize or rice. Nutritionally it is even more remarkable, for it contains five times the calories and ten times the proteins per cooked unit of the cereal crops. The average daily per capita consumption of 300 nuts yields about 1,260 calories and 56 grams of protein. This modest por-

Table 2 The Bushman Annual Round

	Jan.	*Feb.*	*Mar.*	*April*	*May*	*June*	*July*	*Aug.*	*Sept.*	*Oct.*	*Nov.*	*Dec.*
Season	*Summer Rains*			*Autumn Dry*			*Winter Dry*			*Spring Dry*		*First Rains*
Availability of water	Temporary summer pools everywhere			Large summer pools			Permanent waterholes only					Summer pools developing
Group moves	Widely dispersed at summer pools			At large summer pools			All population restricted to permanent waterholes					Moving out to summer pools
Men's subsistence activities	1. Hunting with bow, arrows, and dogs (year-round) 2. Running down immatures 3. Some gathering (year-round)					Trapping small game in snares				Running down newborn animals		
Women's subsistence activities	1. Gathering of mongongo nuts (year-round) 2. Fruits, berries, melons					Roots, bulbs, resins				Roots, leafy greens		
Ritual activities	Dancing, trance performances, and ritual curing (year-round)				Boys' initiation*							†
Relative subsistence hardship			Water-food distance minimal			Increasing distance from water to food				Water-food distance minimal		

*Held once every five years; none in 1963–64.

†New Year's: Bushmen join the celebrations of their missionized Bantu neighbors.

tion, weighing only about 7.5 ounces, contains the caloric equivalent of 2.5 pounds of cooked rice and the protein equivalent of 14 ounces of lean beef.

Furthermore, the mongongo nut is drought resistant, and it will still be abundant in the dry years when cultivated crops may fail. The extremely hard outer shell protects the inner kernel from rot and allows the nuts to be harvested for up to twelve months after they have fallen to the ground. A diet based on mongongo nuts is in fact more reliable than one based on cultivated foods, and it is not surprising, therefore, that when a Bushman was asked why he hadn't taken to agriculture, he replied: "Why should we plant, when there are so many mongongo nuts in the world?"

Apart from the mongongo, the Bushmen have available eighty-four other species of edible food plants, including twenty-nine species of fruits, berries, and melons and thirty species of roots and bulbs. The existence of this variety allows for a wide range of alternatives in subsistence strategy. During the summer months the Bushmen have no problem other than to choose among the tastiest and most easily collected foods. Many species, which are quite edible but less attractive, are bypassed, so that gathering never exhausts *all* the available plant foods of an area. During the dry season the diet becomes much more eclectic and the many species of roots, bulbs, and edible resins make an important contribution. It is this broad base that provides an essential margin of safety during the end of the dry season, when the mongongo nut forests are difficult to reach. In addition, it is likely that these rarely utilized species provide important nutritional and mineral trace elements that may be lacking in the more popular foods.

Diet Selectivity

If the Bushmen were living close to the "starvation" level, then one would expect them to exploit every available source of nutrition. That their life is well above this level is indicated by the data in Table 3. Here all the edible plant species are arranged in classes according to the frequency with which they were observed to be eaten. It should be noted that although there are some eighty-five species available, about 90 percent of the vegetable diet by weight is drawn from only twenty-three species. In other words, 75 percent of the listed species provide only 10 percent of the food value.

In their meat-eating habits, the Bushmen show a similar selectivity. Of the 223 local species of animals known and named by the Bushmen, 54 species are classified as edible, and of these only 17 species were hunted on a regular basis. Only a handful of the dozens of edible species of small mammals, birds, reptiles, and insects that occur locally are regarded as food. Such animals as rodents, snakes, lizards, termites, and grasshoppers, which in the literature are included in the Bushman diet, are despised by the Bushmen of the Dobe area.

Range Size and Population Density

The necessity to travel long distances, the high frequency of moves, and the maintenance of populations at low densities are also features commonly as-

Table 3 !Kung Bushman Plant Foods

	Part Eaten									Totals (percentages)	
Food Class	*Fruit and Nut*	*Bean and Root*	*Fruit and Stalk*	*Root, Bulb*	*Fruit, Berry, Melon*	*Resin*	*Leaves*	*Seed, Bean*	*Total Number of Species in Class*	*Estimated Contribution by Weight to Vegetable Diet*	*Estimated Contribution of Each Species*
I. Primary Eaten daily throughout year (mongongo nut)	1	—	—	—	—	—	—	—	1	c.50	c.50*
II. Major Eaten daily in season	1	1	1	1	4	—	—	—	8	c.25	c.3†
III. Minor Eaten several times per week in season	—	—	—	7	3	2	2	—	14	c.15	c.1
IV. Supplementary Eaten when classes I–III locally unavailable	—	—	—	9	12	10	1	—	32	c.7	c.0.2
V. Rare Eaten several times per year	—	—	—	9	4	—	—	—	13	c.3	c.0.1‡
VI. Problematic Edible but not observed to be eaten	—	—	—	4	6	4	1	2	17	nil	nil
Total Species	2	1	1	30	29	16	4	2	85	100	—

*1 species constitutes 50 percent of the vegetable diet by weight.

†23 species constitute 90 percent of the vegetable diet by weight.

‡62 species constitute the remaining 10 percent of the diet.

sociated with the hunting and gathering way of life. Density estimates for hunters in western North America and Australia have ranged from 3 persons/square mile to as low as 1 person/100 square miles. In 1963–65, the resident and visiting Bushmen were observed to utilize an area of about 1,000 square miles during the course of the annual round for an effective population density of 41 person/100 square miles. Within this area, however, the amount of ground covered by members of an individual camp was surprisingly small. A day's round-trip of twelve miles serves to define a "core" area six miles in radius surrounding each water point. By fanning out in all directions from their well, the members of a camp can gain access to the food resources of well over 100 square miles of territory within a two-hour hike. Except for a few weeks each year, areas lying beyond this six-mile radius are rarely utilized, even though they are no less rich in plants and game than are the core areas.

Although the Bushmen move their camps frequently (five or six times a year), they do not move them very far. A rainy season camp in the nut forests is rarely more than ten or twelve miles from the home waterhole, and often new campsites are occupied only a few hundred yards away from the previous one. By these criteria, the Bushmen do not lead a free-ranging nomadic way of life. For example, they do not undertake long marches of 30 to 100 miles to get food, since this task can be readily fulfilled within a day's walk of home base. When such long marches do occur they are invariably for visiting, trading, and marriage arrangements, and should not be confused with the normal routine of subsistence.

Demographic Factors

Another indicator of the harshness of a way of life is the age at which people die. Ever since Hobbes characterized life in the state of nature as "nasty, brutish and short," the assumption has been that hunting and gathering is so rigorous that members of such societies are rapidly worn out and meet an early death. Silberbauer, for example, says of the Gwi Bushmen of the central Kalahari that "life expectancy . . . is difficult to calculate, but I do not believe that many live beyond 45." And Coon has said of hunters in general:

> The practice of abandoning the hopelessly ill and aged has been observed in many parts of the world. It is always done by people living in poor environments where it is necessary to move about frequently to obtain food, where food is scarce, and transportation difficult. . . . Among peoples who are forced to live in this way the oldest generation, the generation of individuals who have passed their physical peak, is reduced in numbers and influence. There is no body of elders to hand on tradition and control the affairs of younger men and women, and no formal system of age grading.

The !Kung Bushmen of the Dobe area flatly contradict this view. In a total population of 466, no fewer than 46 individuals (17 men and 29 women) were determined to be over sixty years of age, a proportion that compares favorably to the percentage of elderly in industrialized populations.

The aged hold a respected position in Bushmen society and are the effective leaders of the camps. Senilicide is extremely rare. Long after their productive years have passed, the old people are fed and cared for by their children and grandchildren. The blind, the senile, and the crippled are respected for the special ritual and technical skills they possess. For instance, the four elders at !gose waterhole were totally or partially blind, but this handicap did not prevent their active participation in decision making and ritual curing.

Another significant feature of the composition of the work force is the late assumption of adult responsibility by the adolescents. Young people are not expected to provide food regularly until they are married. Girls typically marry between the ages of fifteen and twenty, and boys about five years later, so that it is not unusual to find healthy, active teenagers visiting from camp to camp while their older relatives provide food for them.

As a result, the people in the twenty to sixty age group support a surprisingly large percentage of nonproductive young and old people. About 40 percent of the population in camps contributes little to the food supplies. This allocation of work to young and middle-aged adults allows for a relatively carefree childhood and adolescence and a relatively unstrenuous old age.

Leisure and Work

Another important index of ease or difficulty of subsistence is the amount of time devoted to the food quest. Hunting has usually been regarded by social scientists as a way of life in which merely keeping alive is so formidable a task that members of such societies lack the leisure time necessary to "build culture." The !Kung Bushmen would appear to conform to the rule, for as Lorna Marshall says:

> It is vividly apparent that among the !Kung Bushmen, ethos, or "the spirit which actuates manners and customs," is survival. Their time and energies are almost wholly given to this task, for life in their environment requires that they spend their days mainly in procuring food.

It is certainly true that getting food is the most important single activity in Bushman life. However, this statement would apply equally well to small-scale agricultural and pastoral societies too. How much time is *actually* devoted to the food quest is fortunately an empirical question. And an analysis of the work effort of the Dobe Bushmen shows some unexpected results. From July 6 to August 2, 1964, I recorded all the daily activities of the Bushmen living at the Dobe waterhole. Because of the coming and going of visitors, the camp population fluctuated in size day by day, from a low of 23 to a high of 40, with a mean of 31.8 persons. Each day some of the adult members of the camp went out to hunt and/or gather while others stayed home or went visiting. The daily recording of all personnel on hand made it possible to calculate the number of man-days of work as a percentage of total number of man-days of consumption.

Although the Bushmen do not organize their activities on the basis of a seven-day week, I have divided the data this way to make them more intelligible. The workweek was calculated to show how many days out of seven

Table 4 Summary of Dobe Work Diary

Week	(1) Mean Group Size	(2) Adult-Days	(3) Child-Days	(4) Total Man-Days of Consumption	(5) Man-Days of Work	(6) Meat (lbs.)	(7) Average Workweek /Adult	(8) Index of Subsistence Effort
I	25.6	114	65	179	37	104	2.3	.21
(July 6–12)	(23–29)							
II	28.3	125	73	198	22	80	1.2	.11
(July 13–19)	(23–27)							
III	34.3	156	84	240	42	177	1.9	.18
(July 20–26)	(29–40)							
IV	35.6	167	82	249	77	129	3.2	.31
(July 27–Aug. 2)	(32–40)							
4-wk. total	30.9	562	304	866	178	490	2.2	.21
Adjusted total*	31.8	437	231	668	156	410	2.5	.23

*See text

Key: Column 1: Mean group size = $\frac{\text{total man-days of consumption}}{7}$.

Column 7: Workweek = the number of workdays per adult per week.

Column 8: Index of subsistence effort = $\frac{\text{man-days of work}}{\text{man-days of consumption}}$ (e.g., in Week I, the value of "S" = 21, i.e., 21 days of work/100 days of consumption or 1 workday produces food for 5 consumption days).

each adult spent in subsistence activities (Table 4, Column 7). Week II has been eliminated from the totals since the investigator contributed food. In week I, the people spent an average of 2.3 days in subsistence activities, in week II, 1.9 days, and in week IV, 3.2 days. In all, the adults of the Dobe camp worked about two and a half days a week. Since the average working day was about six hours long, the fact emerges that !Kung Bushmen of Dobe, despite their harsh environment, devote from twelve to nineteen hours a week to getting food. Even the hardest-working individual in the camp, a man named ≠oma who went out hunting on sixteen of the twenty-eight days, spent a maximum of thirty-two hours a week in the food quest.

Because the Bushmen do not amass a surplus of foods, there are no seasons of exceptionally intensive activities such as planting and harvesting, and no seasons of unemployment. The level of work observed is an accurate reflection of the effort required to meet the immediate caloric needs of the group. This work diary covers the midwinter dry season, a period when food is neither at its most plentiful nor at its scarcest levels, and the diary documents the transition from better to worse conditions (see Table 2). During the fourth week the gatherers were making overnight trips to camps in the mongongo nut forests seven to ten miles distant from the waterhole. These longer trips account for the rise in the level of work, from twelve or thirteen to nineteen hours per week.

If food getting occupies such a small proportion of a Bushman's waking hours, then how *do* people allocate their time? A woman gathers on one day enough food to feed her family for three days, and spends the rest of her time resting in camp, doing embroidery, visiting other camps, or entertaining visitors from other camps. For each day at home, kitchen routines, such as cooking, nut cracking, collecting firewood, and fetching water, occupy one to three hours of her time. This rhythm of steady work and steady leisure is maintained throughout the year.

The hunters tend to work more frequently than the women, but their schedule is uneven. It is not unusual for a man to hunt avidly for a week and then do nothing at all for two or three weeks. Since hunting is an unpredictable business and subject to magical control, hunters sometimes experience a run of bad luck and stop hunting for a month or longer. During these periods, visiting, entertaining, and especially dancing are the primary activities of men. (Unlike the Hadza, gambling is only a minor leisure activity.)

The trance dance is the focus of Bushman ritual life; over 50 percent of the men have trained as trance-performers and regularly enter trance during the course of the all-night dances. At some camps, trance dances occur as frequently as two or three times a week, and those who have entered trances the night before rarely go out hunting the following day. . . . In a camp with five or more hunters, there are usually two or three who are actively hunting and several others who are inactive. The net effect is to phase the hunting and non-hunting so that a fairly steady supply of meat is brought into camp.

Caloric Returns

Is the modest work effort of the Bushmen sufficient to provide the calories necessary to maintain the health of the population? Or have the !Kung, in common with some agricultural peoples, adjusted to a permanently substandard nutritional level?

During my fieldwork I did not encounter any cases of kwashiorkor, the most common nutritional disease in the children of African agricultural societies. However, without medical examinations, it is impossible to exclude the possibility that subclinical signs of malnutrition existed.

Another measure of nutritional adequacy is the average consumption of calories and proteins per person per day. The estimate for the Bushmen is based on observations of the weights of foods of known composition that were brought into Dobe camp on each day of the study period. The per-capita figure is obtained by dividing the total weight of foodstuffs by the total number of persons in the camp. These results are set out in detail elsewhere and can only be summarized here. During the study period 410 pounds of meat were brought in by the hunters of the Dobe camp, for a daily share of nine ounces of meat per person. About 700 pounds of vegetables were gathered

Table 5 Caloric and Protein Levels in the !Kung Bushman Diet, July–August, 1964

	Per-Capita Consumption				
Class of Food	*Percentage Contribution to Diet by Weight*	*Weight in Grams*	*Protein in Grams*	*Calories per Person per Day*	*Percentage Caloric Contribution of Meat and Vegetables*
Meat	37	230	34.5	690	33
Mongongo nuts	33	210	56.7	1,260	67
Other vegetable foods	30	190	1.9	190	
Total all sources	100	630	93.1	2,140	100

and consumed during the same period. Table 5 sets out the calories and proteins available per capita in the !Kung Bushman diet from meat, mongongo nuts, and other vegetable sources.

This output of 2,140 calories and 93.1 grams of protein per person per day may be compared with the Recommended Daily Allowances (RDA) for persons of the small size and stature but vigorous activity regime of the !Kung Bushmen. The RDA for Bushmen can be estimated at 1,975 calories and 60 grams of protein per person per day. Thus it is apparent that food output exceeds energy requirements by 165 calories and 33 grams of protein. One can tentatively conclude that even a modest subsistence effort of two or three days' work per week is enough to provide an adequate diet for the !Kung Bushmen.

The Security of Bushman Life

I have attempted to evaluate the subsistence base of one contemporary hunter-gatherer society living in a marginal environment. The !Kung Bushmen have available to them some relatively abundant high-quality foods, and they do not have to walk very far or work very hard to get them. Furthermore, this modest work effort provides sufficient calories to support not only active adults, but also a large number of middle-aged and elderly people. The Bushmen do not have to press their youngsters into the service of the food quest, nor do they have to dispose of the oldsters after they have ceased to be productive.

The evidence presented assumes an added significance because this security of life was observed during the third year of one of the most severe droughts in South Africa's history. Most of the 576,000 people of Botswana are pastoralists and agriculturalists. After the crops had failed three years in succession and over 100,000 head of cattle had died on the range for lack of water, the World Food Program of the United Nations instituted a famine relief program which has grown to include 180,000 people, over 30 percent of the population. This program did not touch the Dobe area in the isolated northwest corner of the country, and the Herero and Tswana women there were able to feed their families only by joining the Bushman women to forage for wild foods. Thus the natural plant resources of the Dobe area were carrying a higher proportion of population than would be the case in years when the Bantu harvested crops. Yet this added pressure on the land did not seem to adversely affect the Bushmen.

In one sense it was unfortunate that the period of my fieldwork happened to coincide with the drought, since I was unable to witness a "typical" annual subsistence cycle. However, in another sense, the coincidence was a lucky one, for the drought put the Bushmen and their subsistence system to the acid test and, in terms of adaptation to scarce resources, they passed with flying colors. One can postulate that their subsistence base would be even more substantial during years of higher rainfall.

What are the crucial factors that make this way of life possible? I suggest that the primary factor is the Bushmen's strong emphasis on vegetable food sources. Although hunting involves a great deal of effort and prestige, plant foods provide from 60 to 80 percent of the annual diet by weight. Meat has come to be regarded as a special treat; when available, it is welcomed as a break from the routine of vegetable foods, but it is never depended upon as a staple. No one ever goes hungry when hunting fails.

The reason for this emphasis is not hard to find. Vegetable foods are abundant, sedentary, and predictable. They grow in the same place year after year, and the gatherer is guaranteed a day's return of food for a day's expenditure of energy. Game animals, by contrast, are scarce, mobile, unpredictable, and difficult to catch. A hunter has no guarantee of success and may in fact go for days or weeks without killing a large mammal. During the study period, there were eleven men in the Dobe camp, of whom four did no hunting at all. The seven active men spent a total of 78 mandays hunting, and this work input yielded eighteen animals killed, or one kill for every four man-days of hunting. The probability of any one hunter making a kill on a given day was 0.23. By contrast, the probability of a woman finding plant food on a given day was 1.00. In other words, hunting and gathering are not equally felicitous subsistence alternatives.

Consider the productivity per man-hour of the two kinds of subsistence activities. One man-hour of hunting produces about 100 edible calories, and of gathering, 240 calories. Gathering is thus seen to be 2.4 times more productive than hunting. In short, hunting is a *high-risk, low-return* subsistence activity, while gathering is a low-risk, high-return subsistence activity.

It is not at all contradictory that the hunting complex holds a central place in the Bushmen ethos and that meat is valued more highly than vegetable foods. Analogously, steak is valued more highly than potatoes in the food preferences of our own society. In both situations the meat is more "costly" than the vegetable food. In the Bushman case, the cost of food can be measured in terms of time and energy expended. By this standard, 1,000 calories of meat "costs" ten man-hours, while the "cost" of 1,000 calories of vegetable foods is only four man-hours. Further, it is to be expected that the less predictable, more expensive food source would have a greater accretion of myth and ritual built up around it than would the routine staples of life, which rarely if ever fail.

Conclusions

Three points ought to be stressed. First, life in the state of nature is not necessarily nasty, brutish, and short. The Dobe-area Bushmen live well today on wild plants and meat, in spite of the fact that they are confined to the least productive portion of the range in which Bushman peoples were formerly found. It is likely that an even more substantial subsistence would have been characteristic of these hunters and gatherers in the past, when they had the pick of African habitats to choose from.

Second, the basis of Bushman diet is derived from sources other than meat. This emphasis makes good ecological sense to the !Kung Bushmen and appears to be a common feature among hunters and gatherers in general. Since a 30 to 40 percent input of meat is such a consistent target for modern hunters in a variety of habitats, is it not reasonable to postulate a similar percentage for prehistoric hunters? Certainly the absence of plant remains on archeological sites is by itself not sufficient evidence for the absence of gathering. Recently abandoned Bushman campsites show a similar absence of vegetable remains, although this paper has clearly shown that plant foods comprise over 60 percent of the actual diet.

Finally, one gets the impression that hunting societies have been chosen by ethnologists to illustrate a dominant theme, such as the extreme importance of environment in the molding of certain cultures. Such a theme can best be exemplified by cases in which the technology is simple and/or the environment is harsh. This emphasis on the dramatic may have been pedagogically useful, but unfortunately it has led to the assumption that a precarious hunting subsistence base was characteristic of all cultures in the Pleistocene. This view of both modern and ancient hunters ought to be reconsidered. Specifically I am suggesting a shift in focus away from the dramatic and unusual cases, and toward a consideration of hunting and gathering as a persistent and well-adapted way of life.

Epilogue: The Ju/'Hoansi in 1994[1]

In 1963 perhaps three-quarters of the Dobe Ju/'hoansi were living in camps based primarily on hunting and gathering while the rest were attached to Black cattle posts. Back then there had been no trading stores, schools, or

[1] Excerpted from "A Local Culture in the Global System: The Ju/'Hoansi-!Kung Today," Richard B. Lee and Megan Biesele, *General Anthropology,* vol. 1, no. 1, fall, pp. 1, 3–5, 1994.

clinics, no government feeding programs, boreholes, or airstrips, and no resident civil servants (apart from the tribally-appointed headman, his clerk, and constable). By 1994 all these institutions and facilities were in place and the Dobe people were well into their third decade of rapid social change; they had been transformed in a generation from a society of foragers, some of whom herded and worked for others, to a society of small-holders who eked out a living by herding, farming, and craft production, along with some hunting and gathering.

Ju villages today look like others in Botswana. The beehive-shaped grass huts are gone, replaced by semi-permanent mud-walled houses behind makeshift stockades to keep out cattle. Villages ceased to be circular and tight-knit. Twenty-five people who lived in a space twenty by twenty meters now spread themselves out in a line village several hundred meters long. Instead of looking across the central open space at each other, the houses face the kraal where cattle and goats are kept, inscribing spatially a symbolic shift from reliance on each other to reliance on property in the form of herds.

Hunting and gathering, which provided Dobe Ju with over 85% of their subsistence as recently as 1964, now supplies perhaps 30% of their food. The rest is made up of milk and meat from domestic stock, store-bought mealie (corn) meal, and vast quantities of heavily-sugared tea whitened with powdered milk. Game meat and foraged foods and occasional produce from gardens makes up the rest of the diet. However, for most of the 1980s government and foreign drought relief provided the bulk of the diet. . . .

In the long run, Dobe area Ju/'Hoansi face serious difficulties. Since 1975, wealthy Tswana have formed borehole syndicates to stake out ranches in remote areas. With 99 year leases, which can be bought and sold, ownership is tantamount to private tenure. By the late 1980s borehole drilling was approaching the Dobe area. If the Dobe Ju do not form borehole syndicates soon, with overseas help, their traditional foraging areas may be permanently cut off from them by commercial ranching.

Review Questions

1. How does Lee assess the day-to-day quality of !Kung life when they lived as foragers? How does this view compare with that held by many anthropologists in the early 1960s?
2. What evidence does Lee give to support his view about the !Kung?
3. According to Lee, !Kung children are not expected to work until after they are married; old people are supported and respected. How does this arrangement differ from behavior in our own society, and what might explain the difference?
4. What was a key to successful subsistence for the !Kung and other hunter-gatherers, according to Lee?
5. In what ways has life changed for the !Kung since 1994? What has caused these changes?

10

Cultivating the Tropical Forest

Richard K. Reed

To most industrialized peoples, the practice of slash-and-burn agriculture seems especially wasteful. The horticulturalists who manifest such practices must often laboriously cut and burn thick forest cover, then plant in the ashes. Because clearing is difficult and fields are left fallow for many years to recover from agricultural use, most land lies dormant. For people used to thinking of agriculture as a source of income, horticultural practices seem to epitomize "under-development." In this article, Richard Reed challenges this simplistic notion. Describing the subsistence practices of the Guarani Indians living in the tropical forests of Paraguay, he shows that Indian slash-and-burn agriculture combined with foraging for wild game and plants represents the optimal use of the forest and a model for modern forest management programs.

The world's great tropical forests, which once seemed so forbidding and impenetrable, are now prime targets for economic exploitation. Devel-

This article was written especially for this book. Copyright © by Richard K. Reed, 1990. Reprinted by permission of the author. (Updated in 1996.)

opers and colonists, from Brazil to Indonesia, flock to the jungle frontiers armed with chain saws and bulldozers. They build roads, clear-cut timber, and denude the land of foliage, often burning the trees and brush as they go. The scope of this human invasion staggers the mind. Development destroys hundreds of square miles of virgin tropical forest each day. In the Amazon alone, an area the size of Louisiana is cleared every year. At this rate, authorities predict that the forests will be gone by the year 2000.

Damage to the forest has not gone unnoticed. Publicized by newscasters, environmentalists, rock stars, and a host of others, the plight of rain forests is now familiar to many Americans. Concern has centered most on the consequences of deforestation for the world ecosystem. Forests are the "lungs of the earth," producing crucial oxygen. Burning them not only reduces world oxygen production, it releases large amounts of carbon dioxide, a greenhouse gas, into the atmosphere. A warmer world is the likely result.

Many authorities have also warned about the impact of deforestation on the survival of wildlife. Tropical forests contain the world's richest variety of animals and plants. As the trees disappear, so do countless irreplaceable species.

Curiously, there is less said about the plight of people who are native to the forests. In South America, for example, up to six million Indians once lived scattered across the vast lowland forests. Only a tenth of that population remains today, the rest having fallen victim to the colonial advance over the past 400 years. Each year, these survivors find it increasingly difficult to maintain their populations and communities.

The damage being done to these Indian societies is particularly distressing because they are the only humans who have managed to subsist in the forest without causing permanent harm. By employing a subsistence strategy that combines horticulture, gathering, and hunting, these indigenous peoples have managed to live in harmony with the forest environment for centuries.

We may ask what accounts for this successful adaptation. Is there a special genius to the social organization of indigenous peoples? What subsistence strategies permit them to live amicably with the forest? What happens to them when they are overtaken by settlers and commercial development? Can such people provide a model for successful tropical forest management? Let's look at these questions in the context of one group living in the South American forest, the Guarani of eastern Paraguay.

The Guarani

The Guarani Indians provide an excellent example of a group well adapted to the forest environment. Like most horticulturalists, they live in small, widely scattered communities. Because their population densities are low, and because they practice a mixture of slash-and-burn agriculture and foraging, they place a light demand on forest resources. Small size also means a more personal social organization and an emphasis on cooperation and sharing. Although of greater size and complexity than hunter-gatherer bands, Guarani villages contain many of the cultural values found in these nomadic societies.

I have conducted ethnographic fieldwork among the Guarani for the past ten years, mostly in the village of Itanarami, located in eastern Paraguay. The residents of Itanarami are among the last of the Guarani Indians still living in the forests of southern South America. They are the remnants of an ethnic group that once dominated southern Brazil and Paraguay from the Atlantic Ocean to the Andes. The Guarani have suffered as their forests have fallen to development. Today, only 15,500 Guarani remain in Paraguay in isolated settlements where the tropical forest survives.

The forests surrounding Itanarami are characterized by high canopies that shade thick undergrowth and shelter both animal and human populations. From the air, the dense expanse of trees is broken only by streams and rivers that drain westward to the broad, marshy valley of the Parana River. Viewed from the ground, the density of the forest growth is matched only by the diversity of plant species.

Itanarami itself is built along a small stream that gives the settlement its name. To the uninformed observer, it is difficult to recognize the existence of a village at all. Homesteads, which consist of a clearing, a thatched hut, and one or two nearby fields, lie scattered in the forest, often out of sight of one another. Yet a closer look reveals the pathways through the deep forest that connect houses to each other and to a slightly larger homestead, that of the *tamoi* (literally grandfather), the group's religious leader. As in many small societies, households are tied together by kinship; people live only a short distance from close relatives. Kinship networks tie all members of the community together, weaving a tapestry of relations that organize social affairs and link Itanarami to other Guarani communities.

The Guarani emphasize sharing and cooperation. Sisters often share fieldwork and child care. Brothers usually hunt together. Food is distributed among members of the extended family, including cousins, aunts, and uncles. People emphasize the general welfare, not personal wealth.

The *tamoi,* although in no sense a leader with formal authority, commands considerable respect in the community. He settles disputes, chastises errant juniors, and leads the entire community in evening religious ceremonies where people drink *kanguijy* (fermented corn), dance, and sing to the gods.

The people of Itanarami not only live in the forest, they see themselves as part of it. The forest is basic to indigenous cosmology. The people refer to themselves as *ka'aguygua,* or "people of the forest." Villagers often name their children after the numerous varieties of forest song birds, symbolizing their close personal ties to the environment.

Subsistence

The Guarani have lived in their present locale for centuries and have dwelled throughout the tropical forests of lowland South America for thousands of years. During all this time, they have exploited flora, fauna, and soils of the forests without doing permanent harm. The secret of their success is in their production strategy. The Indians mix agriculture with gathering, hunting, and fishing in a way that permits environmental recovery. They even collect forest products for sale to outsiders, again without causing environmental damage.

Guarani farming is well-suited to forest maintenance. Using a form of shifting agriculture called slash-and-burn farming, the Indians permit the forest to recover from the damage of field clearing. The way Veraju, the *tamoi* of Itanarami, and his wife, Kitu, farm provides a typical example. When the family needs to prepare a new field, it is Veraju who does the heavy work. He cuts the trees and undergrowth to make a half-acre clearing near his house. Then he, Kitu, and some of their five children burn the fallen trees and brush, creating an ash that provides a natural fertilizer on top of the thin forest soils. When the field is prepared, Kitu uses a digging stick fashioned from a sapling to poke small holes in the ground, and plants the three staple Guarani crops, corn, beans, and manioc root (from which tapioca is made). When the crops mature, it is Kitu and her daughters who will harvest them.

The secret to successful slash-and-burn agriculture is field "shifting" or rotation. Crops flourish the first year and are plentiful the next, but the sun and rain soon take their toll on the exposed soil. The thin loam layer, so typical of tropical forests, degenerates rapidly to sand and clay. By the third year, the poor soils are thick with weeds and grow only a sparse corn crop and a few small manioc roots. Rather than replant a fourth time, Veraju and Kitu will clear a new field nearby where soils are naturally more fertile and the forest can be burned for additional ash fertilizer. The surrounding forest quickly reclaims the old field, reconstituting and strengthening the depleted soil. In this way, the forest produces a sustained yield without degrading the natural ecosystem.

The forest recovers sufficiently fast for the same plot to be cleared and planted within ten or fifteen years. This "swidden" agricultural system results in the cyclic use of a large area of forest, with a part under cultivation and a much larger portion lying fallow in various stages of decomposition.

If farming formed the only subsistence base, the Guarani would probably have to clear more land than the forest could rejuvenate. But they also turn to other forest resources—game, fish, and forest products—to meet their needs for food and material items. Guarani men often form small groups to hunt large animals, such as deer, tapir, and peccary, with guns purchased from outsiders or with the more traditional bows and arrows they make themselves. A successful hunt will provide enough meat to share liberally with kin and friends. Men also trap smaller mammals, such as armadillo and paca (a large rodent). They fashion snares and deadfall traps from saplings, tree trunks, and cactus fiber twine. These are set near homesteads, along stream banks, and at the edges of gardens. Traps not only catch small game for meat, they kill animals that would otherwise enter the fields to eat the crops.

Fish also supply protein in the Guarani diet and reduce dependence on agricultural produce. Many rivers and streams flow near Itanarami on flat bottom land. These water courses meander in broad loops that may be cut off when the river or stream changes course during a flood. Meanders, called oxbow lakes, make ideal fishing spots. In addition to hook and line, men capture the fish by using a poison extracted from the bark of a particular vine. Floated over the surface of the water, the poison stuns the fish and allows the men to catch them by hand.

The forest also supplies a variety of useful products for the Guarani. They make houses from tree trunks and bamboo stalks; rhododendron vines secure the thatched roofs. Villagers collect wild honey and fruit to add sweetness to their diets. Wild tubers replace manioc as a principal food source when crops fail in the gardens. Even several species of insect larva and ants are collected as tasty and nutritious supplements to the daily meal. Finally, the Indians know about a wide variety of medicinal plants. They process several different kinds of roots, leaves, flowers, and seeds to release powerful alkaloids and to make teas and poultices for the sick and injured.

White traders have entered the forests of the Guarani and give the Indians access to manufactured goods. The Guarani continue to produce for most of their needs, but items such as machetes, hooks, soap, and salt are more easily bought than manufactured or collected. As they do with farming and hunting, the Guarani turn to the forest to meet such economic needs. They regularly collect two forest products, *yerba mate* (a caffeinated tea) and oil extract from wild orange trees, used for flavorings and perfumes, to raise the necessary funds.

It is important to note the special Guarani knowledge and values associated with subsistence activities. Because they have lived in the forest for such a long time, and because they would have nowhere to turn if their own resources disappeared, they treat the rain forest with special respect. They can do so, however, only by using a special and complex knowledge of how the forest works and how it can be used.

For example, Guarani, such as Veraju, distinguish among a variety of "ecozones," each with a unique combination of soil, flora, and fauna. They recognize obvious differences, such as those among the high forests that grow on the hills, the deep swamps that cover the flood plains by the rivers, and the grassy savannahs of the high plains. But they make more subtle distinctions within these larger regions. For example, they call the low scrub bordering rivers, *ca'ati.* Flooded each year during the rainy season, this zone supports bamboo groves that harbor small animals for trapping and material for house construction. The forests immediately above the flood plain look like an extension of the *ca'ati,* but to the Guarani they differ in important ways. This ecozone supports varieties of bamboo that are useless for house construction but that attract larger animals, such as peccary and deer, that can be hunted. In all, the Guarani distinguish among nine resource zones, each with distinctive soils, flora, fauna, and uses. These subtle distinctions between ecozones enable the Guarani to use the forest to its greatest benefit. By shifting their subsistence efforts from one zone to another, just as they shift their fields from one spot to the next, the Guarani assure that their forest environment, with its rich variety of life, will always be able to renew itself.

The Impact of Development

In the last few years, intensive commercial development has come to the region in which Itanarami lies. The spectre of complete ecological destruction stalks the forest. White *colonos* (settlers), armed with chain saws and earth movers, attack the trees. They vandalize the land without concern for the carefully integrated ecozones. As the trees fall, the forest products, such as *yerba mate,* disappear. So do the mammals and fish, the bamboo and the rhododendron vines, the honey and the fruits, and the reconstituting fields. As these resources disappear, so does the economy of the once self-sufficient Guarani. Without their traditional mode of subsistence, their kin-organized society, the influence of the *tamoi,* and the willingness to share, their independence as a people becomes impossible. Indian communities are destroyed by poverty and disease, and the members who remain join the legions of poor laborers who form the lowest class of the national society.

Recent intensive development began near Itanarami with a road that *colonos* cut through the jungle located within two hours' walk of the village. Through this gash in the forest moved logging trucks, bulldozers, farm equipment, and buses. Accompanying the machinery of development were farmers, ranchers, and speculators, hoping to make a quick profit from the verdant land. They descended from their vehicles onto the muddy streets of a newly built frontier town. They cleared land for general stores and bars, which were soon filled with merchandise and warm beer. By day, the air in the town was fouled by truck noise and exhaust fumes; by night it was infused with the glare of electric lights and the noise of blaring tape players.

Soon the settlers began to fell the forest near the town and road, creating fields for cotton and soybeans, and pasture. Surveying teams demarcated boundaries and drew maps. Lumber companies invaded the forests, clear-cutting vast tracts of trees. Valuable timber was hauled off to newly established lumber mills; remaining brush was piled and burned. Heavy machinery created expanses of sunlight in the previously unbroken forest. Within months, grass, cotton, and soybeans sprouted in the exposed soils. Where once the land had been home for game, it now provided for cattle. Cattle herds often clogged the roads, blocking the path of trucks hauling cotton to market and chewing deep ruts in the soft forest soils. Settlers fenced in the fields and cut lanes through the forest to mark off portions that would be "private property," off-limits to Indians.

The road and clearing reached Itanarami in 1994. A cement bridge was built over the stream and the forests the Guarani once used for farming and hunting are now being assaulted by chain saws and bulldozers. The footpath that once carried Guarani to the tamoi's house now carries their timber to market in Brazil. The families are left with only their homesteads.

Moreover, by destroying the forest resources surrounding Indian villages, the *colonos* set in motion a process that destroyed the native culture and society. Guarani communities became small islands of forest surrounded by a sea of pastures and farm fields. Although the Indians retained some land for agriculture, they lost the forest resources needed to sustain their original mode of subsistence, which depended on hunting, fishing, and gathering in the forest as well as farming. These economic changes forced alterations in the Indian community.

First, without the forest to provide game, fish, and other products, the Guarani became dependent on farming alone for their survival. Without wild foods, they had to clear and farm fields three times larger than the original ones. Without the forest production of *yerba mate* leaves to collect for sale, they were forced to plant cash crops, such as cotton and tobacco. These two new crops demanded large, clean fields.

While the loss of the forest for hunting and gathering increased their dependence on agriculture, the fences and land titles of the new settlers reduced the land available to the Indians for cultivation. Families soon cleared the last of the remaining high forests that they controlled. Even the once forested stream banks were denuded.

After they had cleared their communities' remaining forest, Indian farmers were forced to replant fields without allowing sufficient fallow time for the soils to rejuvenate. Crops suffered from lack of nutrients and yields declined despite additional effort devoted to clearing and weeding. As production suffered, the Indians cleared and farmed even larger areas. The resulting spiral of poor harvests and enlarged farms outstripped the soil's capacity to produce and the Guarani's ability to care for the crops. Food in the Indian communities grew scarce. The Indian diet was increasingly restricted to nonnutritious manioc as a dietary staple, because it was the only plant that could survive in the exhausted soils.

The Guarani felt the decline in their subsistence base in other ways. The loss of game and poor crop yields exacerbated health problems. Settlers brought new diseases into the forest, such as colds and flu. The Guarani had no inherited resistance to these illnesses and poor nutrition reduced their defenses even further. Disease not only sapped the adults' energy for farming and child care, it increased death rates at all ages. Tuberculosis, which well-fed Guarani rarely contract, became the major killer in the community.

Deforestation also disrupted social institutions. Without their subsistence base, many Guarani needed additional cash to buy food and goods. Indian men were forced to seek work as farm hands, planting pasture and picking cotton on land where they once hunted. Women stayed at home to tend children and till the deteriorating soils of the family farms.

The search for wage labor eventually forced whole Guarani families to move. Many jobs were available on farms located over a day's walk from their villages. Entire families left home for hovels they constructed on the farms of their employers. From independent farmers and gatherers, they became tenants of *patrones* (landowners). *Patrones* prohibited the Guarani farmhands from planting gardens of their own, so the displaced Indians were forced to buy all their food, usually from the *patrones* themselves. Worse, *patrones* set their own inflated prices on the food and goods sold to Indians. Dependence on the white *patrones* displaced the mutual interdependence of traditional Guarani social organization.

As individuals and families left the Guarani villages in search of work on surrounding farms and ranches, *tamoi* leaders lost influence. It became impossible to gather relatives and friends together from disparate work places for religious ritual. The distances were too great for the elders' nieces and nephews to seek out counsel and medicines. Moreover, the diseases and problems suffered by the people were increasingly caused by people and powers outside the forest. The *tamoi* could neither control nor explain the changing world.

Finally, as the forest disappeared, so did its power to symbolize Guarani identity. No longer did young Indians see themselves as "people of the forest."

Today, many of the Guarani of eastern Paraguay remain in small but impoverished communities in the midst of a frontier society based on soybean farming and cattle ranching. The households that previously were isolated in individual plots are now concentrated in one small area without forest for fallow or privacy. The traditional *tamoi* continue to be the center of the social and religious life of the community, but no longer exert influence over village decisions, which are increasingly dominated by affairs external to the local community.

Development and Ecology

Some people might argue that the plight of the Guarani is inevitable and that in the long run, the Indians will be absorbed in a more modern, prosperous society. The forest, they claim, provides a rich, nearly unlimited resource for development. Its exploitation, although painful for a few indigenous Indians, will provide an unequaled opportunity for the poor of Latin America.

Unfortunately, this argument makes forest development appear to be socially responsible. Yet, the long-run implications of forest clearing are disastrous, not simply for the Guarani and other Indians, but for settlers and developers as well. The tropical forest ecosystem is extremely fragile. When the vegetable cover is destroyed, the soil quickly disappears. Erosion clogs rivers with silt, and the soils left behind are baked to a hardpan on which few plants can survive. Rainwater previously captured by foliage and soil is quickly lost to runoff, drying the winds that feed the regional rain systems. Although first harvests in frontier areas seem bountiful, long-term farming and ranching are unprofitable as the soils, deprived of moisture and the rejuvenating forces of the original forest, are reduced to a "red desert." And even worse, leaving the cleared land fallow does not restore it. Once destroyed, the forest cannot reclaim the hardpan left by modern development.

Nor have developers been interested in husbanding the land. The *colonos* who clear the forests are concerned with short-term profit. Entrepreneurs and peasant farmers maximize immediate returns on their labor and investment. When the trees and soils of one area are exhausted, the farmers, ranchers, and loggers move farther into the virgin forest in search of new resources. The process creates a development frontier that moves through fertile forest leaving destruction in its wake. Unlike the Guarani, developers are not forced to contend with the environmental destruction caused by their activities.

Conservation

International agencies and national governments have begun to recognize the damage caused by uncontrolled rain forest development. Although deforestation continues unchecked in many regions of the Amazon Basin, forest conservation programs are being established in some areas, based on the experience of indigenous Indians and often formulated with the help of anthropologists. In one innovative approach, biosphere reserves are being created, which restrict development but permit Indians to practice their traditional subsistence activities.

Such is the case in eastern Paraguay where a program is now being implemented to preserve the remaining tropical forests. Itanarami, so recently threatened by encroaching development, stands to benefit from this plan. The natural forests near the community are the last remaining undisturbed subtropical forest in eastern Paraguay. Although small, this area of 280 square miles is being set aside as a biosphere reserve. The Nature Conservancy, an international conservation agency, is working with the World Bank and the Paraguayan government to preserve the forest.

If the project is successful, Itanarami and its way of life will be preserved. Veraju, Kitu, and their compatriots will be able to continue trapping, hunting, fishing, and gathering on the land. Recognizing that Indian production does not destroy the land, planners are providing the Indians with the right to continue indigenous production, enabling the Guarani to maintain their traditional social organization and ethnic identity.

Furthermore, aided by anthropologists who have made detailed studies of Indian subsistence techniques, planners are integrating the Indians' own models of agro-forestry into an alternative design for tropical forest use. Guarani techniques of commercial extraction have been of special interest, particularly the harvest of *yerba mate* and fragrant oils. Guarani collect these products by trimming the foliage. They allow the trees to regrow so they will produce again. Planners believe that this use of the forest will economically outperform the proceeds gained from destructive farming in the long run, and they have adopted the Guarani model for implementation in other forested areas. Far from being backward and inefficient, the mixed horticultural subsistence strategies of indigenous forest groups have turned out to be the most practical way to manage the fragile tropical forest environment.

Review Questions

1. Anthropologists claim that subsistence strategies affect a society's social organization and ideology. Evaluate this assertion in light of reading about the way the Guarani live in their rain forest environment.
2. Why is horticulture more environmentally sensible than intensive agricultural and pastoral exploitation of the Amazonian rain forest?
3. Guarani Indians are largely subsistence farmers and foragers. How do they use their forest environment without destroying it?
4. How have *colonos* disrupted the lives of Guarani villagers? What does this tell us about the relationship between subsistence and social structure?
5. How can the Guarani use their rain forest habitat to make money, and what does their experience suggest as a way to integrate forest exploitation into a market economy without environmental destruction?

11

India's Sacred Cow

Marvin Harris

Other people's religious practices and beliefs may often appear to be wasteful. They seem to involve a large expenditure of scarce resources on ritual; they contain taboos that restrict the use of apparently useful materials. Their existence seems irrational in the face of ecological needs. One example that many cite in support of this viewpoint is the religious proscription on the slaughter of cattle in India. How can people permit millions of cattle to roam about eating, but uneaten, in a land so continuously threatened by food shortages and starvation? In this article, Marvin Harris challenges the view that religious value is ecologically irrational. Dealing with the Indian case, he argues that Indian cattle, far from being useless, are an essential part of Indian's productive base. Religious restrictions on killing cattle are ecologically sensible; they have developed and persisted to ensure a continuous supply of these valuable animals.

News photographs that came out of India during the famine of the late 1960s showed starving people stretching out bony hands to beg for food while sacred cattle strolled behind them undisturbed. The Hindu, it

From *Human Nature,* February 1978. Copyright © by Human Nature, Inc., 1978. Reprinted by permission of the publisher.

seems, would rather starve to death than eat his cow or even deprive it of food. The cattle appear to browse unhindered through urban markets eating an orange here, a mango there, competing with people for meager supplies of food.

By Western standards, spiritual values seem more important to Indians than life itself. Specialists in food habits around the world like Fred Simoons at the University of California at Davis consider Hinduism an irrational ideology that compels people to overlook abundant, nutritious foods for scarcer, less healthful foods.

What seems to be an absurd devotion to the mother cow pervades Indian life. Indian wall calendars portray beautiful young women with bodies of fat white cows, often with milk jetting from their teats into sacred shrines.

Cow worship even carries over into politics. In 1966 a crowd of 120,000 people, led by holy men, demonstrated in front of the Indian House of Parliament in support of the All-Party Cow Protection Campaign Committee. In Nepal, the only contemporary Hindu kingdom, cow slaughter is severely punished. As one story goes, the car driven by an official of a United States agency struck and killed a cow. In order to avoid the international incident that would have occurred when the official was arrested for murder, the Nepalese magistrate concluded that the cow had committed suicide.

Many Indians agree with Western assessments of the Hindu reverence for their cattle, the zebu, or *Bos indicus,* a large-humped species prevalent in Asia and Africa. M. N. Srinivas, an Indian anthropologist states: "Orthodox Hindu opinion regards the killing of cattle with abhorrence, even though the refusal to kill the vast number of useless cattle which exists in India today is detrimental to the nation." Even the Indian Ministry of Information formerly maintained that "the large animal population is more a liability than an asset in view of our land resources." Accounts from many different sources point to the same conclusion: India, one of the world's great civilizations, is being strangled by its love for the cow.

The easy explanation for India's devotion to the cow, the one most Westerners and Indians would offer, is that cow worship is an integral part of Hinduism. Religion is somehow good for the soul, even if it sometimes fails the body. Religion orders the cosmos and explains our place in the universe. Religious beliefs, many would claim, have existed for thousands of years and have a life of their own. They are not understandable in scientific terms.

But all this ignores history. There is more to be said for cow worship than is immediately apparent. The earliest Vedas, the Hindu sacred texts from the Second Millennium B.C., do not prohibit the slaughter of cattle. Instead, they ordain it as a part of sacrificial rites. The early Hindus did not avoid the flesh of cows and bulls; they ate it at ceremonial feasts presided over by Brahman priests. Cow worship is a relatively recent development in India; it evolved as the Hindu religion developed and changed.

This evolution is recorded in royal edicts and religious texts written during the last 3,000 years of Indian history. The Vedas from the First Millennium

B.C. contain contradictory passages, some referring to ritual slaughter and others to a strict taboo on beef consumption. A. N. Bose, in *Social and Rural Economy of Northern India, 600 B.C.–200 A.D.,* concludes that many of the sacred-cow passages were incorporated into the texts by priests of a later period.

By 200 A.D. the status of Indian cattle had undergone a spiritual transformation. The Brahman priesthood exhorted the population to venerate the cow and forbade them to abuse it or to feed on it. Religious feasts involving the ritual slaughter and consumption of livestock were eliminated, and meat eating was restricted to the nobility.

By 1000 A.D., all Hindus were forbidden to eat beef. Ahimsa, the Hindu belief in the unity of all life, was the spiritual justification for this restriction. But it is difficult to ascertain exactly when this change occurred. An important event that helped to shape the modern complex was the Islamic invasion, which took place in the Eighth Century A.D. Hindus may have found it politically expedient to set themselves off from the invaders, who were beefeaters, by emphasizing the need to prevent the slaughter of their sacred animals. Thereafter, the cow taboo assumed its modern form and began to function much as it does today.

The place of the cow in modern India is every place—on posters, in the movies, in brass figures, in stone and wood carvings, on the streets, in the fields. The cow is a symbol of health and abundance. It provides the milk that Indians consume in the form of yogurt and ghee (clarified butter), which contribute subtle flavors to much spicy Indian food.

This, perhaps, is the practical role of the cow, but cows provide less than half the milk produced in India. Most cows in India are not dairy breeds. In most regions, when an Indian farmer wants a steady, high-quality source of milk he usually invests in a female water buffalo. In India the water buffalo is the specialized dairy breed because its milk has a higher butterfat content than zebu milk. Although the farmer milks his zebu cows, the milk is merely a by-product.

More vital than zebu milk to South Asian farmers are zebu calves. Male calves are especially valued because from bulls come oxen, which are the mainstay of the Indian agricultural system.

Small, fast oxen drag wooden plows through late-spring fields when monsoons have dampened the dry, cracked earth. After harvest, the oxen break the grain from the stalk by stomping through mounds of cut wheat and rice. For rice cultivation in irrigated fields, the male water buffalo is preferred (it pulls better in deep mud), but for most other crops, including rainfall rice, wheat, sorghum, and millet, and for transporting goods and people to and from town, a team of oxen is preferred. The ox is the Indian peasant's tractor, thresher, and family car combined; the cow is the factory that produces the ox.

If draft animals instead of cows are counted, India appears to have too few domesticated ruminants, not too many. Since each of the 70 million farms in India requires a draft team, it follows that Indian peasants should use 140 million animals in the fields. But there are only 83 million oxen and male water buffalo on the subcontinent, a shortage of 30 million draft teams.

In other regions of the world, joint ownership of draft animals might overcome a shortage, but Indian agriculture is closely tied to the monsoon rains of late spring and summer. Field preparation and planting must coincide with the rain, and a farmer must have his animals ready to plow when the weather is right. When the farmer without a draft team needs bullocks most, his neighbors are all using theirs. Any delay in turning the soil drastically lowers production.

Because of this dependence on draft animals, loss of the family oxen is devastating. If a beast dies, the farmer must borrow money to buy or rent an ox at interest rates so high that he ultimately loses his land. Every year foreclosures force thousands of poverty-stricken peasants to abandon the countryside for the overcrowded cities.

If a family is fortunate enough to own a fertile cow, it will be able to rear replacements for a lost team and thus survive until life returns to normal. If, as sometimes happens, famine leads a family to sell its cow and ox team, all ties to agriculture are cut. Even if the family survives, it has no way to farm the land, no oxen to work the land, and no cows to produce oxen.

The prohibition against eating meat applies to the flesh of cows, bulls, and oxen, but the cow is the most sacred because it can produce the other two. The peasant whose cow dies is not only crying over a spiritual loss but over the loss of his farm as well.

Religious laws that forbid the slaughter of cattle promote the recovery of the agricultural system from the dry Indian winter and from periods of drought. The monsoon, on which all agriculture depends, is erratic. Sometimes it arrives early, sometimes late, sometimes not at all. Drought has struck large portions of India time and again in this century, and Indian farmers and the zebus are accustomed to these natural disasters. Zebus can pass weeks on end with little or no food and water. Like camels, they store both in their humps and recuperate quickly with only a little nourishment.

During droughts the cows often stop lactating and become barren. In some cases the condition is permanent but often it is only temporary. If barren animals were summarily eliminated, as Western experts in animal husbandry have suggested, cows capable of recovery would be lost along with those entirely debilitated. By keeping alive the cows that can later produce oxen, religious laws against cow slaughter assure the recovery of the agricultural system from the greatest challenge it faces—the failure of the monsoon.

The local Indian governments aid the process of recovery by maintaining homes for barren cows. Farmers reclaim any animal that calves or begins to lactate. One police station in Madras collects strays and pastures them in a field adjacent to the station. After a small fine is paid, a cow is returned to its rightful owner when the owner thinks the cow shows signs of being able to reproduce.

During the hot, dry spring months most of India is like a desert. Indian farmers often complain they cannot feed their livestock during this period. They maintain the cattle by letting them scavenge on the sparse grass along the roads. In the cities cattle are encouraged to scavenge near food stalls to supplement their scant diet. These are the wandering cattle tourists report seeing throughout India.

Westerners expect shopkeepers to respond to these intrusions with the deference due a sacred animal; instead, their response is a string of curses and the crack of a long bamboo pole across the beast's back or a poke at its genitals. Mahatma Gandhi was well aware of the treatment sacred cows (and bulls and oxen) received in India. "How we bleed her to take the last drop of milk from her. How we starve her to emaciation, how we ill-treat the calves, how we deprive them of their portion of milk, how cruelly we treat the oxen, how we castrate them, how we beat them, how we overload them."

Oxen generally receive better treatment than cows. When food is in short supply, thrifty Indian peasants feed their working bullocks and ignore their cows, but rarely do they abandon the cows to die. When cows are sick, farmers worry over them as they would over members of the family and nurse them as if they were children. When the rains return and when the fields are harvested, the farmers again feed their cows regularly and reclaim their abandoned animals. The prohibition against beef consumption is a form of disaster insurance for all India.

Western agronomists and economists are quick to protest that all the functions of the zebu cattle can be improved with organized breeding programs, cultivated pastures, and silage. Because stronger oxen would pull the plow faster, they could work multiple plots of land, allowing farmers to share their animals. Fewer healthy, well-fed cows could provide Indians with more milk. But pastures and silage require arable land, land needed to produce wheat and rice.

A look at Western cattle farming makes plain the cost of adopting advanced technology in Indian agriculture. In a study of livestock production in the United States, David Pimentel of the College of Agriculture and Life Sciences at Cornell University found that 91 percent of the cereal, legume, and vegetable protein suitable for human consumption is consumed by livestock. Approximately three quarters of the arable land in the United States is devoted to growing food for livestock. In the production of meat and milk, American ranchers use enough fossil fuel to equal more than 82 million barrels of oil annually. (See Figure 1.)

Indian cattle do not drain the system in the same way. In a 1971 study of livestock in West Bengal, Stewart Odend'hal of the University of Missouri found that Bengalese cattle ate only the inedible remains of subsistence crops—rice straw, rice hulls, the tops of sugar cane, and mustard-oil cake. Cattle graze in the fields after harvest and eat the remains of crops left on the ground; they forage for grass and weeds on the roadsides. The food for zebu cattle costs the human population virtually nothing. "Basically," Odend'hal says, "the cattle convert items of little direct human value into products of immediate utility." (See Figure 2.)

In addition to plowing the fields and producing milk, the zebus produce dung, which fires the hearths and fertilizes the fields of India. Much of the estimated 800 million tons of manure produced annually is collected by the

Figure 1
American cattle: Energy consumption and production

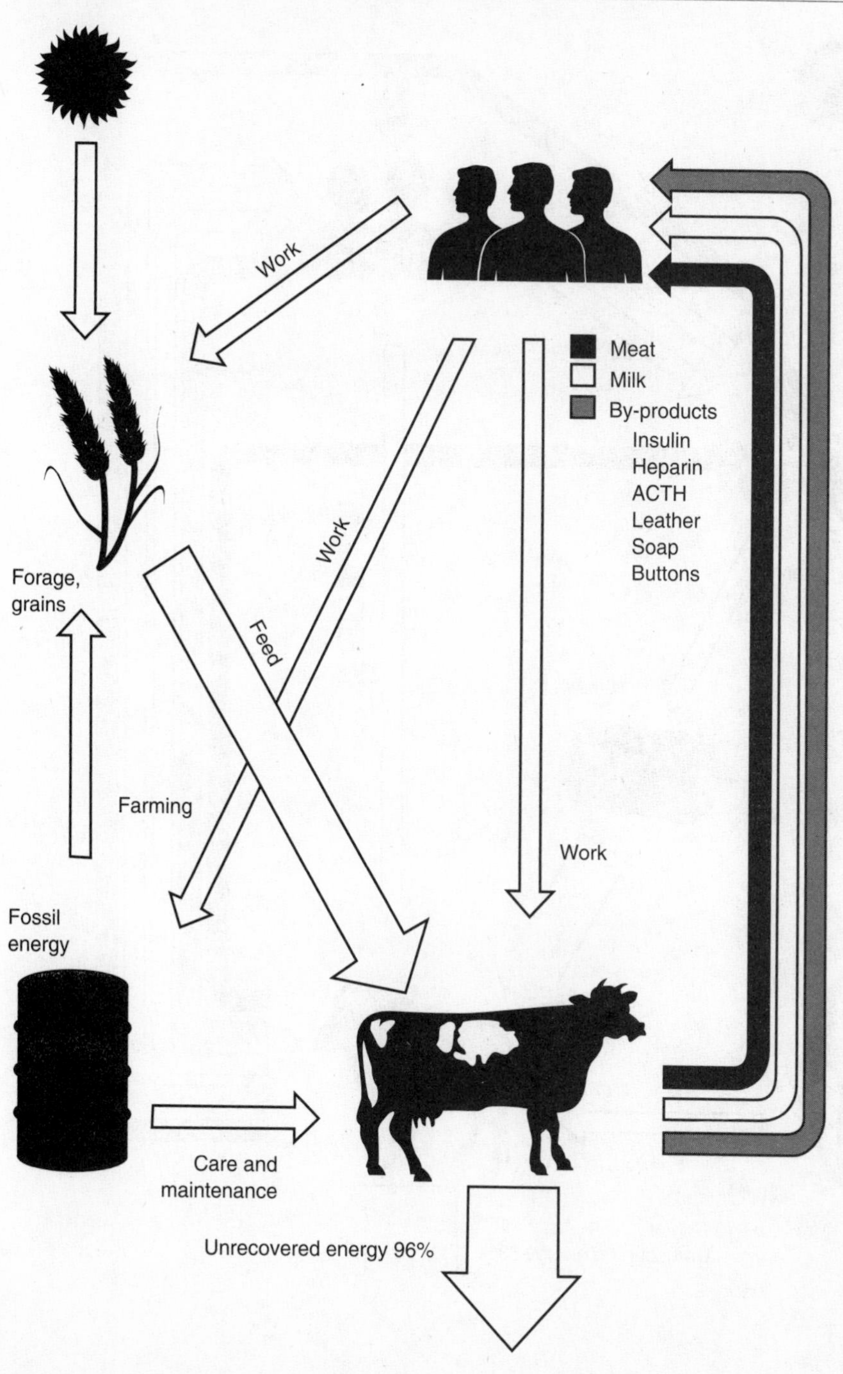

Figure 2
American cattle: Energy consumption and production.

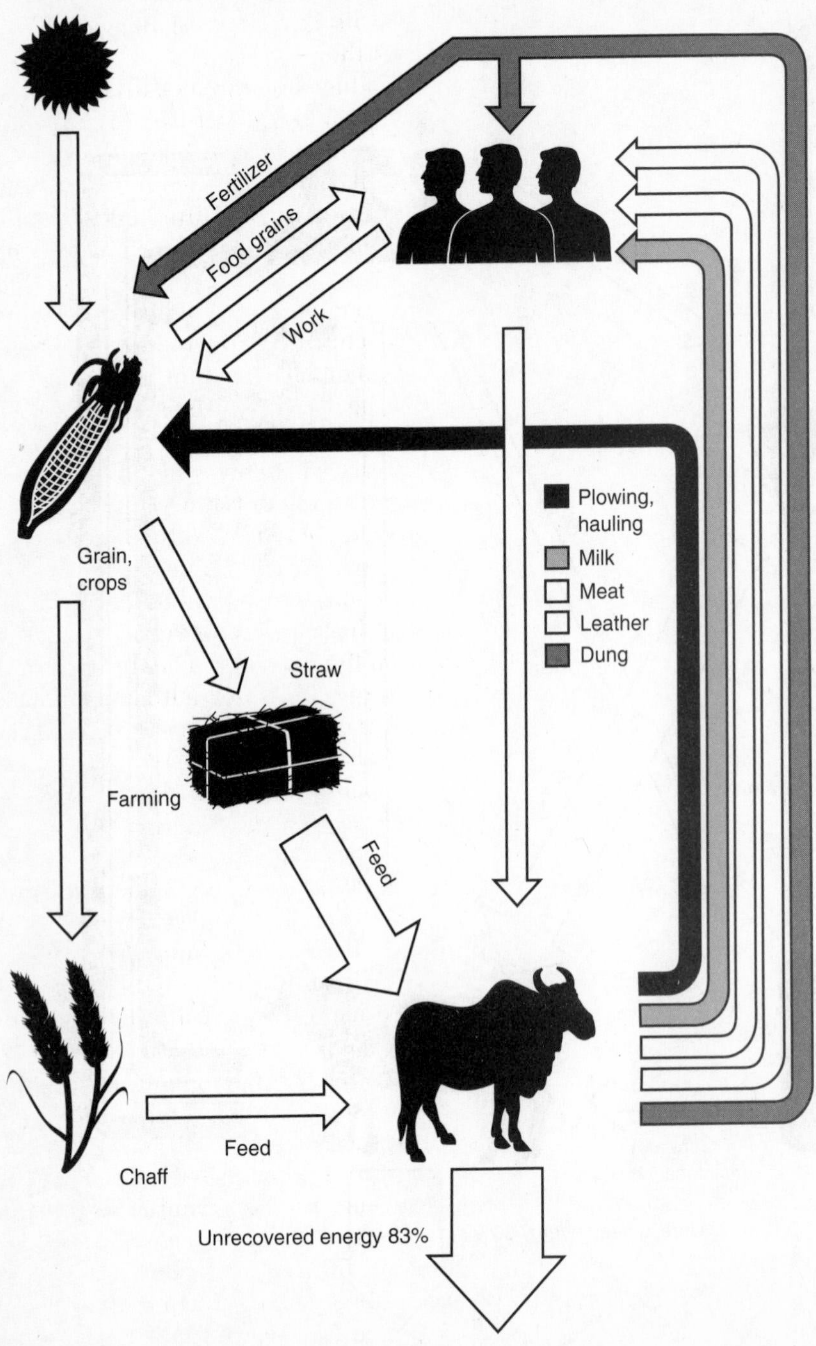

farmers' children as they follow the family cows and bullocks from place to place. And when the children see the droppings of another farmer's cattle along the road, they pick those up also. Odend'hal reports that the system operates with such high efficiency that the children of West Bengal recover nearly 100 percent of the dung produced by their livestock.

From 40 to 70 percent of all manure produced by Indian cattle is used as fuel for cooking; the rest is returned to the fields as fertilizer. Dried dung burns slowly, cleanly, and with low heat—characteristics that satisfy the household needs of Indian women. Staples like curry and rice can simmer for hours. While the meal slowly cooks over an unattended fire, the women of the household can do other chores. Cow chips, unlike firewood, do not scorch as they burn.

It is estimated that the dung used for cooking fuel provides the energy-equivalent of 43 million tons of coal. At current prices, it would cost India an extra 1.5 billion dollars in foreign exchange to replace the dung with coal. And if the 350 million tons of manure that are being used as fertilizer were replaced with commercial fertilizers, the expense would be even greater. Roger Revelle of the University of California at San Diego has calculated that 89 percent of the energy used in Indian agriculture (the equivalent of about 140 million tons of coal) is provided by local sources. Even if foreign loans were to provide the money, the capital outlay necessary to replace the Indian cow with tractors and fertilizers for the fields, coal for the fires, and transportation for the family would probably warp international financial institutions for years.

Instead of asking the Indians to learn from the American model of industrial agriculture, American farmers might learn energy conservation from the Indians. Every step in an energy cycle results in a loss of energy to the system. Like a pendulum that slows a bit with each swing, each transfer of energy from sun to plants, plants to animals, and animals to human beings involves energy losses. Some systems are more efficient than others; they provide a higher percentage of the energy inputs in a final, useful form. Seventeen percent of all energy zebus consume is returned in the form of milk, traction, and dung. American cattle raised on Western range land return only 4 percent of the energy they consume.

But the American system is improving. Based on techniques pioneered by Indian scientists, at least one commercial firm in the United States is reported to be building plants that will turn manure from cattle feedlots into combustible gas. When organic matter is broken down by anaerobic bacteria, methane gas and carbon dioxide are produced. After the methane is cleansed of the carbon dioxide, it is available for the same purposes as natural gas—cooking, heating, electricity generation. The company constructing the biogasification plant plans to sell its product to a gas-supply company, to be piped through the existing distribution system. Schemes similar to this one could make cattle ranches almost independent of utility and gasoline companies, for methane can be used to run trucks, tractors, and cars as well as to supply heat and electricity. The relative energy self-sufficiency that the Indian peasant has achieved is a goal American farmers and industry are now striving for.

Studies like Odend'hal's understate the efficiency of the Indian cow, because dead cows are used for purposes that Hindus prefer not to acknowledge. When a cow dies, an Untouchable, a member of one of the lowest ranking castes in India, is summoned to haul away the carcass. Higher castes consider the body of the dead cow polluting; if they do handle it, they must go through a rite of purification.

Untouchables first skin the dead animal and either tan the skin themselves or sell it to a leather factory. In the privacy of their homes, contrary to the teachings of Hinduism, untouchable castes cook the meat and eat it. Indians of all castes rarely acknowledge the existence of these practices to non-Hindus, but more are aware that beefeating takes place. The prohibition against beefeating restricts consumption by the higher castes and helps distribute animal protein to the poorest sectors of the population that otherwise would have no source of these vital nutrients.

Untouchables are not the only Indians who consume beef. Indian Muslims and Christians are under no restriction that forbids them beef, and its consumption is legal in many places. The Indian ban on cow slaughter is state, not national, law and not all states restrict it. In many cities, such as New Delhi, Calcutta, and Bombay, legal slaughterhouses sell beef to retail customers and to the restaurants that serve steak.

If the caloric value of beef and the energy costs involved in the manufacture of synthetic leather were included in the estimates of energy, the calculated efficiency of Indian livestock would rise considerably.

As well as the system works, experts often claim that its efficiency can be further improved. Alan Heston, an economist at the University of Pennsylvania, believes that Indians suffer from an overabundance of cows simply because they refuse to slaughter the excess cattle. India could produce at least the same number of oxen and the same quantities of milk and manure with 30 million fewer cows. Heston calculates that only 40 cows are necessary to maintain a population of 100 bulls and oxen. Since India averages 70 cows for every 100 bullocks, the difference, 30 million cows, is expendable.

What Heston fails to note is that sex ratios among cattle in different regions of India vary tremendously, indicating that adjustments in the cow population do take place. Along the Ganges River, one of the holiest shrines of Hinduism, the ratio drops to 47 cows for every 100 male animals. This ratio reflects the preference for dairy buffalo in the irrigated sectors of the Gangetic Plains. In nearby Pakistan, in contrast, where cow slaughter is permitted, the sex ratio is 60 cows to 100 oxen.

Since the sex ratios among cattle differ greatly from region to region and do not even approximate the balance that would be expected if no females were killed, we can assume that some culling of herds does take place; Indians do adjust their religious restrictions to accommodate ecological realities.

They cannot kill a cow but they can tether an old or unhealthy animal until it has starved to death. They cannot slaughter a calf but they can yoke it with a large wooden triangle so that when it nurses it irritates the mother's udder and gets kicked to death. They cannot ship their animals to the slaughterhouse but they can sell them to Muslims, closing their eyes to the fact that the Muslims will take the cattle to the slaughterhouse.

These violations of the prohibition against cattle slaughter strengthen the premise that cow worship is a vital part of Indian culture. The practice arose to prevent the population from consuming the animal on which Indian agriculture depends. During the First Millennium B.C., the Ganges Valley became one of the most densely populated regions of the world.

Where previously there had been only scattered villages, many towns and cities arose and peasants farmed every available acre of land. Kingsley Davis, a population expert at the University of California at Berkeley, estimates that by 300 B.C. between 50 million and 100 million people were living in India. The forested Ganges Valley became a windswept semidesert and signs of ecological collapse appeared; droughts and floods became commonplace, erosion took away the rich topsoil, farms shrank as population increased, and domesticated animals became harder and harder to maintain.

It is probable that the elimination of meat eating came about in a slow, practical manner. The farmers who decided not to eat their cows, who saved them for procreation to produce oxen, were the ones who survived the natural disasters. Those who ate beef lost the tools with which to farm. Over a period of centuries, more and more farmers probably avoided beef until an unwritten taboo came into existence.

Only later was the practice codified by the priesthood. While Indian peasants were probably aware of the role of cattle in their society, strong sanctions were necessary to protect zebus from a population faced with starvation. To remove temptation, the flesh of cattle became taboo and the cow became sacred.

The sacredness of the cow is not just an ignorant belief that stands in the way of progress. Like all concepts of the sacred and the profane, this one affects the physical world; it defines the relationships that are important for the maintenance of Indian society.

Indians have the sacred cow; we have the "sacred" car and the "sacred" dog. It would not occur to us to propose the elimination of automobiles and dogs from our society without carefully considering the consequences, and we should not propose the elimination of zebu cattle without first understanding their place in the social order of India.

Human society is neither random nor capricious. The regularities of thought and behavior called culture are the principal mechanisms by which we human beings adapt to the world around us. Practices and beliefs can be rational or irrational, but a society that fails to adapt to its environment is doomed to extinction. Only those societies that draw the necessities of life from their surroundings, without destroying those surroundings, inherit the earth. The West has much to learn from the great antiquity of Indian civilization, and the sacred cow is an important part of that lesson.

Review Questions

1. A friend asks, "Why don't Indians eat the millions of cattle that roam loose over their country?" Based on the information in this article, how would you answer?
2. What are the main uses and products of cattle in India? What is most important about cattle for continued human material welfare?
3. How does Harris explain the rise of cattle protection in India?
4. Clearly Indians need bulls and bullocks to plow, but why can't they limit the number of cows to a level just sufficient for breeding?
5. Some anthropologists argue that the sacredness of Indian cattle evolved as part of the religious system, apart from practical considerations. How would Harris respond to this assertion?

12

Adaptive Failure: Easter's End

Jared Diamond

In the last article, Marvin Harris argued that the existence of customs can often be explained as human responses to material necessity. But people may not always adapt successfully, as Jared Diamond shows in this discussion of the rise and fall of Easter Island civilization. Basing his conclusions on recent archaeological excavations, he notes that in 400 A.D., when the Polynesian ancestors of today's Easter Island population arrived on the Island, they found a heavily forested and fertile land. Within a few hundred years the islanders numbered between 7,000 to 20,000 and lived in a politically complex, prosperous society. By the 1400s, however, the forest was destroyed, making it impossible for people to build ocean-going canoes or continue the manufacture of stone heads, for which the island later became famous. Bird and sea mammal populations, once a major source of food, had also been decimated. Political chaos ensued and islanders turned to cannibalism as a dietary supplement. Diamond concludes that Easter Island civilization declined because environmental

From "Easter's End," *Discover*, August 1995. Copyright © by *Discover*, 1995. Reprinted by permission of the publisher.

destruction occurred slowly and because social concerns took precedence over conservation. In this sense, the island's fate serves as a warning about humanity's future in a highly stressed world environment.

Among the most riveting mysteries of human history are those posed by vanished civilizations. Everyone who has seen the abandoned buildings of the Khmer, the Maya, or the Anasazi is immediately moved to ask the same question: Why did the societies that erected those structures disappear?

Their vanishing touches us as the disappearance of other animals, even the dinosaurs, never can. No matter how exotic those lost civilizations seem, their framers were humans like us. Who is to say we won't succumb to the same fate? Perhaps someday New York's skyscrapers will stand derelict and overgrown with vegetation, like the temples at Angkor Wat and Tikal.

Among all such vanished civilizations, that of the former Polynesian society on Easter Island remains unsurpassed in mystery and isolation. The mystery stems especially from the island's gigantic stone statues and its impoverished landscape, but it is enhanced by our associations with the specific people involved: Polynesians represent for us the ultimate in exotic romance, the background for many a child's, and an adult's, vision of paradise. My own interest in Easter was kindled over 30 years ago when I read Thor Heyerdahl's fabulous accounts of his *Kon-Tiki* voyage.

But my interest has been revived recently by a much more exciting account, one not of heroic voyages but of painstaking research and analysis. My friend David Steadman, a paleontologist, has been working with a number of other researchers who are carrying out the first systematic excavations on Easter intended to identify the animals and plants that once lived there. Their work is contributing to a new interpretation of the island's history that makes it a tale not only of wonder but of warning as well.

Easter Island, with an area of only 64 square miles, is the world's most isolated scrap of habitable land. It lies in the Pacific Ocean more than 2,000 miles west of the nearest continent (South America), 1,400 miles from even the nearest habitable island (Pitcairn). Its subtropical location and latitude—at 27 degrees south, it is approximately as far below the equator as Houston is north of it—help give it a rather mild climate, while its volcanic origins make its soil fertile. In theory, this combination of blessings should have made Easter a miniature paradise, remote from problems that beset the rest of the world.

The island derives its name from its "discovery" by the Dutch explorer Jacob Roggeveen, on Easter (April 5) in 1722. Roggeveen's first impression was not of a paradise but of a wasteland: "We originally, from a further distance, have considered the said Easter Island as sandy; the reason for that is this, that we counted as sand the withered grass, hay, or other scorched and burnt vegetation, because its wasted appearance could give no other impression than of a singular poverty and barrenness."

The island Roggeveen saw was a grassland without a single tree or bush over ten feet high. Modern botanists have identified only 47 species of higher plants native to Easter, most of them grasses, sedges, and ferns. The list includes just two species of small trees and two of woody shrubs. With such flora, the islanders Roggeveen encountered had no source of real firewood to warm themselves during Easter's cool, wet, windy winters. Their native animals included nothing larger than insects, not even a single species of native bat, land bird, land snail, or lizard. For domestic animals, they had only chickens.

European visitors throughout the eighteenth and early nineteenth centuries estimated Easter's human population at about 2,000, a modest number considering the island's fertility. As Captain James Cook recognized during his brief visit in 1774, the islanders were Polynesians (a Tahitian man accompanying Cook was able to converse with them). Yet despite the Polynesians' well-deserved fame as a great seafaring people, the Easter Islanders who came out to Roggeveen's and Cook's ships did so by swimming or paddling canoes that Roggeveen described as "bad and frail." Their craft, he wrote, were "put together with manifold small planks and light inner timbers, which they cleverly stitched together with very fine twisted threads. . . . But as they lack the knowledge and particularly the materials for caulking and making tight the great number of seams of the canoes, these are accordingly very leaky, for which reason they are compelled to spend half the time in bailing." The canoes, only ten feet long, held at most two people, and only three or four canoes were observed on the entire island.

With such flimsy craft, Polynesians could never have colonized Easter from even the nearest island, nor could they have traveled far offshore to fish. The islanders Roggeveen met were totally isolated, unaware that other people existed. Investigators in all the years since his visit have discovered no trace of the islanders' having any outside contacts: not a single Easter Island rock or product has turned up elsewhere, nor has anything been found on the island that could have been brought by anyone other than the original settlers or the Europeans. Yet the people living on Easter claimed memories of visiting the uninhabited Sala y Gomez reef 260 miles away, far beyond the range of the leaky canoes seen by Roggeveen. How did the islanders' ancestors reach that reef from Easter, or reach Easter from anywhere else?

Easter Island's most famous feature is its huge stone statues, more than 200 of which once stood on massive stone platforms lining the coast. At least 700 more, in all stages of completion, were abandoned in quarries or on ancient roads between the quarries and the coast, as if the carvers and moving crews had thrown down their tools and walked off the job. Most of the erected statues were carved in a single quarry and then somehow transported as far as six miles—despite heights as great as 33 feet and weights up to 82 tons. The abandoned statues, meanwhile, were as much as 65 feet tall and weighed up to 270 tons. The stone platforms were equally gigantic: up to 500 feet long and 10 feet high, with facing slabs weighing up to 10 tons.

Roggeveen himself quickly recognized the problem the statues posed: "The stone images at first caused us to be struck with astonishment," he wrote, "because we could not comprehend how it was possible that these people, who are devoid of heavy thick timber for making any machines, as well as strong ropes, nevertheless had been able to erect such images." Roggeveen might have added that the islanders had no wheels, no draft animals, and no source of power except their own muscles. How did they transport the giant statues for miles, even before erecting them? To deepen the mystery, the statues were still standing in 1770, but by 1864 all of them had been pulled down, by the islanders themselves. Why then did they carve them in the first place? And why did they stop?

The statues imply a society very different from the one Roggeveen saw in 1722. Their sheer number and size suggest a population much larger than 2,000 people. What became of everyone? Furthermore, that society must have been highly organized. Easter's resources were scattered across the island: the best stone for the statues was quarried at Rano Raraku near Easter's northeast end; red stone, used for large crowns adorning some of the statues, was quarried at Puna Pau, inland in the southwest; stone carving tools came mostly from Aroi in the northwest. Meanwhile, the best farmland lay in the south and east, and the best fishing grounds on the north and west coasts. Extracting and redistributing all those goods required complex political organization. What happened to that organization, and how could it ever have arisen in such a barren landscape?

Easter Island's mysteries have spawned volumes of speculation for more than two and a half centuries. Many Europeans were incredulous that Polynesians—commonly characterized as "mere savages"—could have created the statues or the beautifully constructed stone platforms. In the 1950s, Heyerdahl argued that Polynesia must have been settled by advanced societies of American Indians, who in turn must have received civilization across the Atlantic from more advanced societies of the Old World. Heyerdahl's raft voyages aimed to prove the feasibility of such prehistoric transoceanic contacts. In the 1960s the Swiss writer Erich von Däniken, an ardent believer in Earth visits by extraterrestrial astronauts, went further, claiming that Easter's statues were the work of intelligent beings who owned ultramodern tools, became stranded on Easter, and were finally rescued.

Heyerdahl and Von Däniken both brushed aside overwhelming evidence that the Easter Islanders were typical Polynesians derived from Asia rather than from the Americas and that their culture (including their statues) grew out of Polynesian culture. Their language was Polynesian, as Cook had already concluded. Specifically, they spoke an eastern Polynesian dialect related to Hawaiian and Marquesan, a dialect isolated since about A.D. 400, as estimated from slight differences in vocabulary. Their fishhooks and stone adzes resembled early Marquesan models. Last year DNA extracted from 12 Easter Island skeletons was also shown to be Polynesian. The islanders grew bananas, taro, sweet potatoes, sugarcane, and paper mulberry—typical Polynesian crops, mostly of Southeast Asian origin. Their sole domestic animal, the chicken, was also typically Polynesian and ultimately Asian, as were the rats that arrived as stowaways in the canoes of the first settlers.

What happened to those settlers? The fanciful theories of the past must give way to evidence gathered by hardworking practitioners in three fields: archeology, pollen analysis, and paleontology.

Modern archeological excavations on Easter have continued since Heyerdahl's 1955 expedition. The earliest radiocarbon dates associated with human activities are around A.D. 400 to 700, in reasonable agreement with the approximate settlement date of 400 estimated by linguists. The period of statue construction peaked around 1200 to 1500, with few if any statues erected thereafter. Densities of archeological sites suggest a large population; an estimate of 7,000 people is widely quoted by archeologists, but other estimates range up to 20,000, which does not seem implausible for an island of Easter's area and fertility.

Archeologists have also enlisted surviving islanders in experiments aimed at figuring out how the statues might have been carved and erected. Twenty people, using only stone chisels, could have carved even the largest completed statue within a year. Given enough timber and fiber for making ropes, teams of at most a few hundred people could have loaded the statues onto wooden sleds, dragged them over lubricated wooden tracks or rollers, and used logs as levers to maneuver them into a standing position. Rope could have been made from the fiber of a small native tree, related to the linden, called the hauhau. However, that tree is now extremely scarce on Easter, and hauling one statue would have required hundreds of yards of rope. Did Easter's now barren landscape once support the necessary trees?

That question can be answered by the technique of pollen analysis, which involves boring out a column of sediment from a swamp or pond, with the most recent deposits at the top and relatively more ancient deposits at the bottom. The absolute age of each layer can be dated by radiocarbon methods. Then begins the hard work: examining tens of thousands of pollen grains under a microscope, counting them, and identifying the plant species that produced each one by comparing the grains with modern pollen from known plant species. For Easter Island, the bleary-eyed scientists who performed that task were John Flenley, now at Massey University in New Zealand, and Sarah King of the University of Hull in England.

Flenley and King's heroic efforts were rewarded by the striking new picture that emerged of Easter's prehistoric landscape. For at least 30,000 years before human arrival and during the early years of Polynesian settlement, Easter was not a wasteland at all. Instead, a subtropical forest of trees and woody bushes towered over a ground layer of shrubs, herbs, ferns, and grasses. In the forest grew tree daisies, the rope-yielding hauhau tree, and the toromiro tree, which furnishes a dense, mesquite-like firewood. The most common tree in the forest was a species of palm now absent on Easter but formerly so abundant that the bottom strata of the sediment column were packed with its pollen. The Easter Island palm was closely related to the still-surviving Chilean wine palm, which grows up to 82 feet tall and 6 feet in diameter. The tall, unbranched trunks of the Easter Island palm would have been ideal for transporting and erecting statues and constructing large canoes. The palm would also have been a valuable food source, since its Chilean relative yields edible nuts as well as sap from which Chileans make sugar, syrup, honey, and wine.

What did the first settlers of Easter Island eat when they were not glutting themselves on the local equivalent of maple syrup? Recent excavations by David Steadman, of the New York State Museum at Albany, have yielded a picture of Easter's original animal world as surprising as Flenley and King's picture of its plant world. Steadman's expectations for Easter were conditioned by his experiences elsewhere in Polynesia, where fish are overwhelmingly the main food at archeological sites, typically accounting for more than 90 percent of the bones in ancient Polynesian garbage heaps. Easter, though, is too cool for the coral reefs beloved by fish, and its cliffgirded coastline permits shallow-water fishing in only a few places. Less than a quarter of the bones in its early garbage heaps (from the period 900 to 1300) belonged to fish; instead, nearly one-third of all bones came from porpoises.

Nowhere else in Polynesia do porpoises account for even 1 percent of discarded food bones. But most other Polynesian islands offered animal food in the form of birds and mammals, such as New Zealand's now extinct giant moas and Hawaii's now extinct flightless geese. Most other islanders also had domestic pigs and dogs. On Easter, porpoises would have been the largest animal available—other than humans. The porpoise species identified at Easter, the common dolphin, weighs up to 165 pounds. It generally lives out at sea, so it could not have been hunted by line fishing or spearfishing from shore. Instead, it must have been harpooned far offshore, in big seaworthy canoes built from the extinct palm tree.

In addition to porpoise meat, Steadman found, the early Polynesian settlers were feasting on seabirds. For those birds, Easter's remoteness and lack of predators made it an ideal haven as a breeding site, at least until humans arrived. Among the prodigious numbers of seabirds that bred on Easter were albatross, boobies, frigate birds, fulmars, petrels, prions, shearwaters, storm petrels, terns, and tropic birds. With at least 25 nesting species, Easter was the richest seabird breeding site in Polynesia and probably in the whole Pacific.

Land birds as well went into early Easter Island cooking pots. Steadman identified bones of at least six species, including barn owls, herons, parrots, and rail. Bird stew would have been seasoned with meat from large numbers of rats, which the Polynesian colonists inadvertently brought with them; Easter Island is the sole known Polynesian island where rat bones outnumber fish bones at archeological sites. (In case you're squeamish and consider rats inedible, I still recall recipes for creamed laboratory rat that my British biologist friends used to supplement their diet during their years of wartime food rationing.)

Porpoises, seabirds, land birds, and rats did not complete the list of meat sources formerly available on Easter. A few bones hint at the possibility of breeding seal colonies as well. All these delicacies were cooked in ovens fired by wood from the island's forests.

Such evidence lets us imagine the island onto which Easter's first Polynesian colonists stepped ashore some 1,600 years ago, after a long canoe voyage from eastern Polynesia. They found themselves in a pristine paradise. What then happened to it? The pollen grains and the bones yield a grim answer.

Pollen records show that destruction of Easter's forests was well under way by the year 800, just a few centuries after the start of human settlement. Then charcoal from wood fires came to fill the sediment cores, while pollen of palms and other trees and woody shrubs decreased or disappeared, and pollen of the grasses that replaced the forest became more abundant. Not long after 1400 the palm finally became extinct, not only as a result of being chopped down but also because the now ubiquitous rats prevented its regeneration: of the dozens of preserved palm nuts discovered in caves on Easter, all had been chewed by rats and could no longer germinate. While the hauhau tree did not become extinct in Polynesian times, its numbers declined drastically until there weren't enough left to make ropes from. By the time Heyerdahl visited Easter, only a single, nearly dead toromiro tree remained on the island, and even that lone survivor has now disappeared. (Fortunately, the toromiro still grows in botanical gardens elsewhere.)

The fifteenth century marked the end not only for Easter's palm but for the forest itself. Its doom had been approaching as people cleared land to plant gardens; as they felled trees to build canoes, to transport and erect statues, and to burn; as rats devoured seeds; and probably as the native birds died out that had pollinated the trees' flowers and dispersed their fruit. The overall picture is among the most extreme examples of forest destruction anywhere in the world: the whole forest gone, and most of its tree species extinct.

The destruction of the island's animals was as extreme as that of the forest: without exception, every species of native land bird became extinct. Even shellfish were overexploited, until people had to settle for small sea snails instead of larger cowries. Porpoise bones disappeared abruptly from garbage heaps around 1500; no one could harpoon porpoises anymore, since the trees used for constructing the big seagoing canoes no longer existed. The colonies of more than half of the seabird species breeding on Easter or on its offshore islets were wiped out.

In place of these meat supplies, the Easter Islanders intensified their production of chickens, which had been only an occasional food item. They also turned to the largest remaining meat source available: humans, whose bones became common in late Easter Island garbage heaps. Oral traditions of the islanders are rife with cannibalism; the most inflammatory taunt that could be snarled at an enemy was "The flesh of your mother sticks between my teeth." With no wood available to cook these new goodies, the islanders resorted to sugarcane scraps, grass, and sedges to fuel their fires.

All these strands of evidence can be wound into a coherent narrative of a society's decline and fall. The first Polynesian colonists found themselves on an island with fertile soil, abundant food, bountiful building materials, ample lebensraum, and all the prerequisites for comfortable living. They prospered and multiplied.

After a few centuries, they began erecting stone statues on platforms, like the ones their Polynesian forebears had carved. With passing years, the statues and platforms became larger and larger, and the statues began sporting ten-ton red crowns—probably in an escalating spiral of one-upmanship, as rival clans tried to surpass each other with shows of wealth and power. (In the same way, successive Egyptian pharaohs built ever-larger pyramids. Today Hollywood movie moguls near my home in Los Angeles are displaying their wealth and power by building ever more ostentatious mansions. Tycoon Marvin Davis topped previous moguls with plans for a 50,000-square-foot house, so now Aaron Spelling has topped Davis with a 56,000-square-foot house. All that those buildings lack to make the message explicit are ten-ton red crowns.) On Easter, as in modern America, society was held together by a complex political system to redistribute locally available resources and to integrate the economies of different areas.

Eventually Easter's growing population was cutting the forest more rapidly than the forest was regenerating. The people used the land for gardens and the wood for fuel, canoes, and houses—and, of course, for lugging statues. As forest disappeared, the islanders ran out of timber and rope to transport and erect their statues. Life became more uncomfortable—springs and streams dried up, and wood was no longer available for fires.

People also found it harder to fill their stomachs, as land birds, large sea snails, and many seabirds disappeared. Because timber for building seagoing canoes vanished, fish catches declined and porpoises disappeared from the table. Crop yields also declined, since deforestation allowed the soil to be eroded by rain and wind, dried by the sun, and its nutrients to be leeched from it. Intensified chicken production and cannibalism replaced only part of all those lost foods. Preserved statuettes with sunken cheeks and visible ribs suggest that people were starving.

With the disappearance of food surpluses, Easter Island could no longer feed the chiefs, bureaucrats, and priests who had kept a complex society running. Surviving islanders described to early European visitors how local chaos replaced centralized government and a warrior class took over from the hereditary chiefs. The stone points of spears and daggers, made by the warriors during their heyday in the 1600s and 1700s, still litter the ground of Easter today. By around 1700, the population began to crash toward between one-quarter and one-tenth of its former number. People took to living in caves for protection against their enemies. Around 1770 rival clans started to topple each other's statues, breaking the heads off. By 1864 the last statue had been thrown down and desecrated.

As we try to imagine the decline of Easter's civilization, we ask ourselves, "Why didn't they look around, realize what they were doing, and stop before it was too late? What were they thinking when they cut down the last palm tree?"

I suspect, though, that the disaster happened not with a bang but with a whimper. After all, there are those hundreds of abandoned statues to consider. The forest the islanders depended on for rollers and rope didn't simply disappear one day—it vanished slowly, over decades. Perhaps war interrupted the moving teams; perhaps by the time the carvers had finished their work, the last rope snapped. In the meantime, any islander who tried to warn about the dangers of progressive deforestation would have been overridden by vested interests of carvers, bureaucrats, and chiefs, whose jobs depended on continued deforestation. Our Pacific Northwest loggers are only the latest in a long line of loggers to cry, "Jobs over trees!" The changes in forest cover from year to year would have been hard to detect: yes, this year we cleared those woods over there, but trees are starting to grow back again on this abandoned garden site here. Only older people, recollecting their childhoods decades earlier, could have recognized a difference. Their children could no more have comprehended their parents' tales than my eight-year-old sons today can comprehend my wife's and my tales of what Los Angeles was like 30 years ago.

Gradually trees became fewer, smaller, and less important. By the time the last fruit-bearing adult palm tree was cut, palms had long since ceased to be of economic significance. That left only smaller and smaller palm saplings to clear each year, along with other bushes and treelets. No one would have noticed the felling of the last small palm.

By now the meaning of Easter Island for us should be chillingly obvious. Easter Island is Earth writ small. Today, again, a rising population confronts shrinking resources. We too have no emigration valve, because all human societies are linked by international transport, and we can no more escape into space than the Easter Islanders could flee into the ocean. If we continue to follow our present course, we shall have exhausted the world's major fisheries, tropical rain forests, fossil fuels, and much of our soil by the time my sons reach my current age.

Every day newspapers report details of famished countries—Afghanistan, Liberia, Rwanda, Sierra Leone, Somalia, the former Yugoslavia, Zaire—where soldiers have appropriated the wealth or where central government is yielding to local gangs of thugs. With the risk of nuclear war receding, the threat of our ending with a bang no longer has a chance of galvanizing us to halt our course. Our risk now is of winding down, slowly, in a whimper. Corrective action is blocked by vested interests, by well-intentioned political and business leaders, and by their electorates, all of whom are perfectly correct in not noticing big changes from year to year. Instead, each year there are just somewhat more people, and somewhat fewer resources, on Earth.

It would be easy to close our eyes or to give up in despair. If mere thousands of Easter Islanders with only stone tools and their own muscle power sufficed to destroy their society, how can billions of people with metal tools and machine power fail to do worse? But there is one crucial difference. The Easter Islanders had no books and no histories of other doomed societies. Unlike the Easter Islanders, we have histories of the past—information that can save us. My main hope for my sons' generation is that we may now choose to learn from the fates of societies like Easter's.

Review Questions

1. What was the ecology of Easter Island when Polynesians first arrived on the island about 400 A.D., according to Jared Diamond?
2. What were the main sources of food eaten by Easter Islanders in the early years of island habitation?
3. What changes occurred in the Easter Island environment due to human exploitation? How did these changes affect the life and social organization of the islanders?
4. How does Diamond explain the inability of Easter Islanders to see the effect they were having on their island's habitat?
5. How does the Easter Island case apply to what is happening in the world today?

5

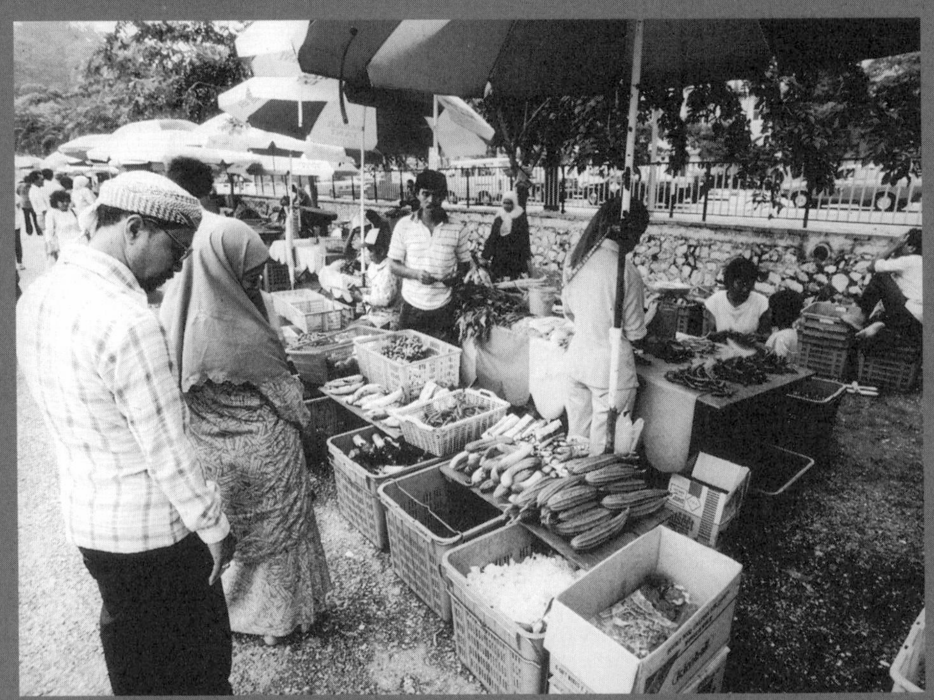

ECONOMIC SYSTEMS

People everywhere experience wants that can be satisfied only by the acquisition and use of material goods and the services of others. To meet such wants, humans rely on an aspect of their cultural inventory, the *economic system,* which we will define as the provision of goods and services to meet biological and social wants.

The meaning of the term *want* can be confusing. It can refer to what humans *need* for their survival. We must eat, drink, maintain a constant body temperature, defend ourselves, and deal with injury and illness. The economic system meets these needs by providing food, water, clothing, shelter, weapons, medicines, and the cooperative services of others.

But material goods serve more than just our survival needs: they meet our culturally defined *wants* as well. We need clothes to stay warm, but we want garments of a particular style, cut, and fabric to signal our status, rank, or anything else we wish to communicate socially. We need food to sustain life, but we want particular foods prepared in special ways to fill our aesthetic and social desires. Services and goods may also be exchanged to strengthen ties between people or groups. Birthday presents may not always meet physical needs, but they clearly function to strengthen the ties between the parties to the exchange.

Part of the economic system is concerned with *production,* which means rendering material items useful and available for human consumption. Production systems must designate ways to allocate resources. The *allocation of resources* refers to the cultural rules people use to assign rights to the ownership and use of resources. Production systems must also include technologies. Americans usually associate technology with the tools and machines used for manufacturing, rather than with the knowledge for doing it. But many anthropologists link the concept directly to culture. Here we will define *technology* as the cultural knowledge for making and using tools and extracting and refining raw materials.

Production systems also include a *division of labor,* which refers to the rules that govern the assignment of jobs to people. In hunting and gathering societies, labor is most often divided along the lines of gender, and sometimes age. In these societies, almost everyone knows how to produce, use, and collect the necessary material goods. In industrial society, however, jobs are highly specialized, and labor is divided, at least ideally, on the basis of skill and experience. It is rarely that we know how to do someone else's job in our complex society.

The *unit of production,* meaning the persons or groups responsible for producing goods, follows a pattern similar to the way labor is divided in various societies. Among hunter-gatherers, there is little specialization; individuals, families, groups of friends, or sometimes bands form the units of production. But in our own complex society, we are surrounded by groups specially organized to manufacture, transport, and sell goods.

Another part of the economic system is *distribution.* There are three basic modes of distribution: market exchange, reciprocal exchange, and redistribution.

We are most conscious of market exchange because it lies at the heart of our capitalist system. *Market exchange* is the transfer of goods and services based on price, supply, and demand. Every time we enter a store and pay for something, we engage in market exchange. The price of an item may change with the supply. For example, a discount store may lower the price of a television set because it has too many of the appliances on hand. Prices may go up, however, if everyone wants the sets when there are few to sell. Money is often used in market systems; it enables people to exchange a large variety of items easily. Barter involves the trading of goods, not money, but it, too, is a form of market exchange because the number of items exchanged may also vary with supply and demand. Market exchange appears in human history when societies become larger and more complex. It is well suited for exchange between the strangers who make up these larger groups.

Although we are not so aware of it, we also engage in reciprocal exchange. *Reciprocal exchange* involves the transfer of goods and services between two people or groups based on role obligations. Birthday and holiday gift giving is a fine example of reciprocity. On these occasions we exchange goods not because we necessarily need or want them, but because we are expected to do so as part of our status and role. Parents should give gifts to their children, for example; children should reciprocate. If we fail in our reciprocal obligations, we signal an unwillingness to continue the relationship. Small, simply organized societies, such as the !Kung described earlier, base their exchange systems on reciprocity. Complex ones like ours, although largely organized around the market or redistribution, still manifest reciprocity between kin and close friends.

Finally, there is *redistribution,* the transfer of goods and services between a central collecting source and a group of individuals. Like reciprocity, redistribution is based on role obligation. Taxes typify this sort of exchange in the United States. We must pay our taxes because we are citizens, not because we are buying something. We receive goods and services back—education, transportation, roads, defense—but not necessarily in proportion to the amount we contribute. Redistribution may be the predominant mode of exchange in socialist societies.

Anthropologists also frequently talk about two kinds of economies. In the past, many of the world's societies had *subsistence economies* organized around the need to meet material necessities and social obligations. Subsistence economies are typically associated with smaller groups. They occur at a local level. Such economies depend most on the non-market-exchange mechanisms: reciprocity and redistribution. Their members are occupational generalists. Most people can do most jobs, although there may be distinctions on the basis of gender and age. The !Kung described by Richard Lee in Parts II and IV of this book had subsistence economies as do most horticulturalists.

Market economies differ from subsistence economies in their size and motive for production. Although reciprocity and redistribution exist in market economies, market exchange drives production and consumption. Market economies are larger (indeed, there is a growing world market economy that includes almost everyone) and are characterized by high economic specialization, as well as impersonality. The American economy is market-driven as are most national systems. If they have not been already, most subsistence economies will, in the near future, be absorbed into national market systems.

The selections in this part illustrate several of the concepts discussed above. In the first article, Lee Cronk looks at gift giving, a classic example of reciprocity. He finds that gifts can cement relationships, confer prestige, and obligate subordinates. Sara Mitter describes a kind of market-oriented work in the second selection. She details how poor, low-caste women work as "self-employed" cleaners in the shadow economy of Bombay. Uneducated and lacking special skills, these women labor for low wages without opportunity to acquire higher-paying work. In the third article, Philippe Bourgois writes about why Latino African Americans work in the inner-city shadow economy of New York drug selling. Limited to services jobs, which degrade them, they continue to perform the unpleasant work available in their own neighborhoods. The fourth article, by Bernard Nietschmann, details the impact of the international market system on a local subsistence economy. Motivated by money, Miskito Indians came to be dependent on outsiders for food and found themselves unable to meet their traditional reciprocal obligations. Readers should note that most Miskito Indians were displaced from their traditional communities and occupations by the Sandanista government of Nicaragua after this article was written. Many have not returned to their former homes.

Key Terms

economic system
production
allocation of resources
technology
division of labor
unit of production
distribution
market exchange
reciprocal exchange
redistribution
subsistence economies
market economies

Readings in This Section

Reciprocity and the Power of Giving *Lee Cronk*, page *157*

The Shadow Economy: Cleaners in Bombay *Sara S. Mitter*, page *164*

Workaday World—Crack Economy *Philippe Bourgois*, page *171*

Subsistence and Market: When the Turtle Collapses *Bernard Nietschmann*, page *180*

13

Reciprocity and the Power of Giving

Lee Cronk

As we saw in the introduction to Part 5, reciprocity constitutes an important exchange system in every society. At the heart of reciprocal exchange is the idea of giving. In this article, Lee Cronk explores the functions of giving using a variety of examples from societies around the world. Giving may be benevolent. It may be used to strengthen existing relationships or to form new ones. Gifts may also be used aggressively to "fight" people, to "flatten" them with generosity. Givers often gain position and prestige in this way. Gifts may also be used to place others in debt so that one can control them and require their loyalty. Cronk shows that, in every society, from !Kung hxaro *exchange to American foreign aid, there are "strings attached" to giving that affect how people and groups relate to each other.*

During a trek through the Rockies in the 1830s, Captain Benjamin Louis E. de Bonneville received a gift of a fine young horse from a Nez Percé

From "Strings Attached," *The Sciences*, May/June 1989. Copyright © *The Sciences*, 1989. Reprinted by permission of the publisher.

chief. According to Washington Irving's account of the incident, the American explorer was aware that "a parting pledge was necessary on his own part, to prove that this friendship was reciprocated." Accordingly, he "placed a handsome rifle in the hands of the venerable chief; whose benevolent heart was evidently touched and gratified by this outward and visible sign of amity."

Even the earliest white settlers in New England understood that presents from natives required reciprocity, and by 1764, "Indian gift" was so common a phrase that the Massachusetts colonial historian Thomas Hutchinson identified it as "a proverbial expression, signifying a present for which an equivalent return is expected." Then, over time, the custom's meaning was lost. Indeed, the phrase now is used derisively, to refer to one who demands the return of a gift. How this cross-cultural misunderstanding occurred is unclear, but the poet Lewis Hyde, in his book *The Gift,* has imagined a scenario that probably approaches the truth.

Say that an Englishman newly arrived in America is welcomed to an Indian lodge with the present of a pipe. Thinking the pipe a wonderful artifact, he takes it home and sets it on his mantelpiece. When he later learns that the Indians expect to have the pipe back, as a gesture of goodwill, he is shocked by what he views as their short-lived generosity. The newcomer did not realize that, to the natives, the point of the gift was not to provide an interesting trinket but to inaugurate a friendly relationship that would be maintained through a series of mutual exchanges. Thus, his failure to reciprocate appeared not only rude and thoughtless but downright hostile. "White man keeping" was as offensive to native Americans as "Indian giving" was to settlers.

In fact, the Indians' tradition of gift giving is much more common than our own. Like our European ancestors, we think that presents ought to be offered freely, without strings attached. But through most of the world, the strings themselves are the main consideration. In some societies, gift giving is a tie between friends, a way of maintaining good relationships, whereas in others it has developed into an elaborate, expensive, and antagonistic ritual designed to humiliate rivals by showering them with wealth and obligating them to give more in return.

In truth, the dichotomy between the two traditions of gift giving is less behavioral than rhetorical: our generosity is not as unconditional as we would like to believe. Like European colonists, most modern Westerners are blind to the purpose of reciprocal gift giving, not only in non-Western societies but also, to some extent, in our own. Public declarations to the contrary, we, too, use gifts to nurture long-term relationships of mutual obligation, as well as to embarrass our rivals and to foster feelings of indebtedness. And this ethic touches all aspects of contemporary life, from the behavior of scientists in research networks to superpower diplomacy. Failing to acknowledge this fact, especially as we give money, machines, and technical advice to peoples around the world, we run the risk of being misinterpreted and, worse, of causing harm.

Much of what we know about the ethics of gift giving comes from the attempts of anthropologists to give things to the people they are studying.

Richard Lee, of the University of Toronto, learned a difficult lesson from the !Kung hunter-gatherers, of the Kalahari desert, when, as a token of goodwill, he gave them an ox to slaughter at Christmas. Expecting gratitude, he was shocked when the !Kung complained about having to make do with such a scrawny "bag of bones." Only later did Lee learn, with relief, that the !Kung belittle all gifts. In their eyes, no act is completely generous, or free of calculation; ridiculing gifts is their way of diminishing the expected return and of enforcing humility on those who would use gifts to raise their own status within the group.

Rada Dyson-Hudson, of Cornell University, had a similar experience among the Turkana, a pastoral people of northwestern Kenya. To compensate her informants for their help, Dyson-Hudson gave away pots, maize meal, tobacco, and other items. The Turkana reaction was less than heartwarming. A typical response to a gift of a pot, for example, might be, "Where is the maize meal to go in this pot?" or, "Don't you have a bigger one to give me?" To the Turkana, these are legitimate and expected questions.

The Mukogodo, another group of Kenyan natives, responded in a similar way to gifts Beth Leech and I presented to them during our fieldwork in 1986. Clothing was never nice enough, containers never big enough, tobacco and candies never plentiful enough. Every gift horse was examined carefully, in the mouth and elsewhere. Like the !Kung, the Mukogodo believe that all gifts have an element of calculation, and they were right to think that ours were no exception. We needed their help, and their efforts to diminish our expectations and lessen their obligations to repay were as fair as our attempts to get on their good side.

The idea that gifts carry obligations is instilled early in life. When we gave Mukogodo children candies after visiting their villages, their mothers reminded them of the tie: "Remember these white people? They are the ones who gave you candy." They also reinforced the notion that gifts are meant to circulate, by asking their children to part with their precious candies, already in their mouths. Most of the youngsters reluctantly surrendered their sweets, only to have them immediately returned. A mother might take, at most, a symbolic nibble from her child's candy, just to drive home the lesson.

The way food, utensils, and other goods are received in many societies is only the first stage of the behavior surrounding gift giving. Although repayment is expected, it is crucial that it be deferred. To reciprocate at once indicates a desire to end the relationship, to cut the strings; delayed repayment makes the strings longer and stronger. This is especially clear on the Truk Islands, of Micronesia, where a special word—*niffag*—is used to designate objects moving through the island's exchange network. From the Trukese viewpoint, to return niffag on the same day it is received alters its nature from that of a gift to that of a sale, in which all that matters is material gain.

After deciding the proper time for response, a recipient must consider how to make repayment, and that is dictated largely by the motive behind the gift. Some exchange customs are designed solely to preserve a relationship. The !Kung have a system, called *hxaro,* in which little attention is paid to whether the items exchanged are equivalent. Richard Lee's informant !Xoma explained to him that "Hxaro is when I take a thing of value and give it to you. Later, much later, when you find some good thing, you give it back to me. When I find something good I will give it to you, and so we will pass the years together." When Lee tried to determine the exact exchange values of various items (Is a spear worth three strings of beads, two strings, or one?), !Xoma explained that any return would be all right: "You see, we don't trade with things, we trade with people!"

One of the most elaborate systems of reciprocal gift giving, known as *kula,* exists in a ring of islands off New Guinea. Kula gifts are limited largely to shell necklaces, called *soulava,* and armbands, called *mwali.* A necklace given at one time is answered months or years later with an armband, the necklaces usually circulating clockwise, and the armbands counterclockwise, through the archipelago. Kula shells vary in quality and value, and men gain fame and prestige by having their names associated with noteworthy necklaces or armbands. The shells also gain value from their association with famous and successful kula partners.

Although the act of giving gifts seems intrinsically benevolent, a gift's power to embarrass the recipient and to force repayment has, in some societies, made it attractive as a weapon. Such antagonistic generosity reached its most elaborate expression, during the late nineteenth century, among the Kwakiutl, of British Columbia.

The Kwakiutl were acutely conscious of status, and every tribal division, clan, and individual had a specific rank. Disputes about status were resolved by means of enormous ceremonies (which outsiders usually refer to by the Chinook Indian term *potlatch*), at which rivals competed for the honor and prestige of giving away the greatest amount of property. Although nearly everything of value was fair game—blankets, canoes, food, pots, and, until the mid-nineteenth century, even slaves—the most highly prized items were decorated sheets of beaten copper, shaped like shields and etched with designs in the distinctive style of the Northwest Coast Indians.

As with the kula necklaces and armbands, the value of a copper sheet was determined by its history—by where it had been and who had owned it—and a single sheet could be worth thousands of blankets, a fact often reflected in its name. One was called "Drawing All Property from the House," and another, "About Whose Possession All Are Quarreling." After the Kwakiutl began to acquire trade goods from the Hudson's Bay Company's Fort Rupert post, in 1849, the potlatches underwent a period of extreme inflation, and by the 1920s, when items of exchange included sewing machines and pool tables, tens of thousands of Hudson's Bay blankets might be given away during a single ceremony.

In the 1880s, after the Canadian government began to suppress warfare between tribes, potlatching also became a substitute for battle. As a Kwakiutl man once said to the anthropologist Franz Boas, "The time of fighting is past. . . . We do not fight now with weapons: we fight with property." The usual

Kwakiutl word for potlatch was *p!Esa,* meaning to flatten (as when one flattens a rival under a pile of blankets), and the prospect of being given a large gift engendered real fear. Still, the Kwakiutl seemed to prefer the new "war of wealth" to the old "war of blood."

Gift giving has served as a substitute for war in other societies, as well. Among the Siuai, of the Solomon Islands, guests at feasts are referred to as attackers, while hosts are defenders, and invitations to feasts are given on short notice in the manner of "surprise attacks." And like the Kwakiutl of British Columbia, the Mount Hagen tribes of New Guinea use a system of gift giving called *moka* as a way of gaining prestige and shaming rivals. The goal is to become a tribal leader, a "big-man." One moka gift in the 1970s consisted of several hundred pigs, thousands of dollars in cash, some cows and wild birds, a truck, and a motorbike. The donor, quite pleased with himself, said to the recipient, "I have won. I have knocked you down by giving so much."

Although we tend not to recognize it as such, the ethic of reciprocal gift giving manifests itself throughout our own society, as well. We, too, often expect something, even if only gratitude and a sense of indebtedness, in exchange for gifts, and we use gifts to establish friendships and to manipulate our positions in society. As in non-Western societies, gift giving in America sometimes takes a benevolent and helpful form; at other times, the power of gifts to create obligations is used in a hostile way.

The Duke University anthropologist Carol Stack found a robust tradition of benevolent exchange in an Illinois ghetto known as the Flats, where poor blacks engage in a practice called swapping. Among residents of the Flats, wealth comes in spurts; hard times are frequent and unpredictable. Swapping, of clothes, food, furniture, and the like, is a way of guaranteeing security, of making sure that someone will be there to help out when one is in need and that one will get a share of any windfalls that come along.

Such networks of exchange are not limited to the poor, nor do they always involve objects. Just as the exchange of clothes creates a gift community in the Flats, so the swapping of knowledge may create one among scientists. Warren Hagstrom, a sociologist at the University of Wisconsin, in Madison, has pointed out that papers submitted to scientific journals often are called contributions, and, because no payment is received for them, they truly are gifts. In contrast, articles written for profit—such as this one—often are held in low esteem: scientific status can be achieved only through *giving* gifts of knowledge.

Recognition also can be traded upon, with scientists building up their gift-giving networks by paying careful attention to citations and acknowledgments. Like participants in kula exchange, they try to associate themselves with renowned and prestigious articles, books, and institutions. A desire for recognition, however, cannot be openly acknowledged as a motivation for research, and it is a rare scientist who is able to discuss such desires candidly. Hagstrom was able to find just one mathematician (whom he described as "something of a social isolate") to confirm that "junior mathematicians want recognition from big shots and, consequently, work in areas prized by them."

Hagstrom also points out that the inability of scientists to acknowledge a desire for recognition does not mean that such recognition is not expected by those who offer gifts of knowledge, any more than a kula trader believes it is all right if his trading partner does not answer his gift of a necklace with an armband. While failure to reciprocate in New Guinean society might once have meant warfare, among scientists it may cause factionalism and the creation of rivalries.

Whether in the Flats of Illinois or in the halls of academia, swapping is, for the most part, benign. But manipulative gift giving exists in modern societies, too—particularly in paternalistic government practices. The technique is to offer a present that cannot be repaid, coupled with a claim of beneficence and omniscience. The Johns Hopkins University anthropologist Grace Goodell documented one example in Iran's Khūzestān Province, which, because it contains most of the country's oil fields and is next door to Iraq, is a strategically sensitive area. Goodell focused on the World Bank-funded Dez irrigation project, a showpiece of the shah's ambitious "white revolution" development plan. The scheme involved the irrigation of tens of thousands of acres and the forced relocation of people from their villages to new, model towns. According to Goodell, the purpose behind dismantling local institutions was to enhance central government control of the region. Before development, each Khūzestāni village had been a miniature city-state, managing its own internal affairs and determining its own relations with outsiders. In the new settlements, decisions were made by government bureaucrats, not townsmen, whose autonomy was crushed under the weight of a large and strategically placed gift.

On a global scale, both the benevolent and aggressive dimensions of gift giving are at work in superpower diplomacy. Just as the Kwakiutl were left only with blankets with which to fight after warfare was banned, the United States and the Soviet Union now find, with war out of the question, that they are left only with gifts—called concessions—with which to do battle. Offers of military cutbacks are easy ways to score points in the public arena of international opinion and to shame rivals, and failure either to accept such offers or to respond with even more extreme proposals may be seen as cowardice or as bellicosity. Mikhail Gorbachev is a virtuoso, a master potlatcher, in this new kind of competition, and, predictably, Americans often see his offers of disarmament and openness as gifts with long strings attached. One reason U.S. officials were buoyed last December, when, for the first time since the Second World War, the Soviet Union accepted American assistance, in the aftermath of the Armenian earthquake, is that it seemed to signal a wish for reciprocity rather than dominance—an unspoken understanding of the power of gifts to bind people together.

Japan, faced with a similar desire to expand its influence, also has begun to exploit gift giving in its international relations. In 1989, it will spend more than ten billion dollars on foreign aid, putting it ahead of the United States for the second consecutive year as the world's greatest donor nation. Although this move was publicly welcomed in the United States as the sharing of a burden, fears, too, were expressed that the resultant blow to American prestige might cause a further slip in our international status. Third World leaders also have complained that too much Japanese aid is targeted at countries in which Japan has an economic stake and that too much is restricted to the purchase of Japanese goods—that Japan's generosity has less to do with addressing the problems of underdeveloped countries than with exploiting those problems to its own advantage.

The danger in all of this is that wealthy nations may be competing for the prestige that comes from giving gifts at the expense of Third World nations. With assistance sometimes being given with more regard to the donors' status than to the recipients' welfare, it is no surprise that, in recent years, development aid often has been more effective in creating relationships of dependency, as in the case of Iran's Khūzestān irrigation scheme, than in producing real development. Nor that, given the fine line between donation and domination, offers of help are sometimes met with resistance, apprehension and, in extreme cases, such as the Iranian revolution, even violence.

The Indians understood a gift's ambivalent power to unify, antagonize, or subjugate. We, too, would do well to remember that a present can be a surprisingly potent thing, as dangerous in the hands of the ignorant as it is useful in the hands of the wise.

Review Questions

1. What does Cronk mean by *reciprocity?* What is the social outcome of reciprocal gift giving?
2. According to Cronk, what are some examples of benevolent gift giving?
3. How can giving be used to intimidate other people or groups? Give some examples cited by Cronk and think of some from your own experience.
4. How does Cronk classify gift-giving strategies such as government foreign aid? Can you think of other examples of the use of exchange as a political device?

14

The Shadow Economy: Cleaners in Bombay

Sara S. Mitter

Market economies (usually linked to the global economy) seem to be a standard feature of most countries in today's world. Almost everywhere, there is a formal market economy *identified by visible, legal, organized economic structures and activities, which economists attempt to measure and governments can tax and regulate. Banks, factories, corporations, retail outlets—these and other publicly organized economic units are usually part of the formal economy. But underneath the formal economy lies an informal market system often called the* shadow economy, *which plays an important role in larger economic systems. The shadow economy is usually small-scale, personal, and at times, illegal. It involves transactions too small or illicit to observe. Governments find it difficult to measure and control the shadow economy. Yet it is the shadow economy that provides a living for hundreds of millions of largely poor people, many of them women, around the world today. In this selection, Sara Mit-*

From "Cleaners and Handicrafters," Chapter 4, *Dharmas Daughters,* Rutgers University Press. Copyright © by Sara S. Mitter, 1991. Reprinted by permission of the author.

ter describes the lives of one group that works in the shadow economy, the low-caste Bombay women who clean the apartments of more affluent urban dwellers. Lacking the education to do higher-paying work, and often accompanied by their children, these women manage to live and support their families in shanty towns that have sprung up all over Bombay. Mitter argues that the life of these women is beset by an inability to move into the higher-paying formal economy and a lack of power to achieve better pay for the work they do.

"When I'm not working I'm sleeping."

—Delhi slum woman

Shreemati, who cleaned our apartment every morning, lived in the seaside shantytown that was visible from the upper-story windows of our building. A brackish pond, due to be reclaimed and densely developed, lay between our two settlements. On the morning after the first night of pelting monsoon rain, Shreemati turned up late. She slipped off her plastic sandals at the door and wished us good day. She was wearing her usual blue printed cotton sari in the inelegant but functional Marathi style, pulled up between the legs and tucked at the waist.

We exchanged a word about the weather, and I asked her how her roof was holding. The week before, she had requested an advance on her salary and a morning off to buy and oversee the installation of several meters of bright blue plastic sheeting over the cardboard and woven palm-frond roof of her family's hut. She had to make her home secure before the rains began and the new school year started for her son, the youngest of her five children. "The roof is good," she told me, smiling, "But the floor is wet: water comes in through the doorway. Cooking very difficult," she said matter-of-factly, took up the straw whisk, and went to the bedroom to sweep.

Shreemati had been working for us for several months. Occasionally I, the foreign *memsahib,* would ask her questions about her situation. She would answer fully and at length—when asked. But she never initiated conversation, offered an opinion, or voiced the slightest complaint. Shreemati knew her place. Her reference to the cooking problem was not lost on me. I pictured the creeping water, the sodden earth floor, and the coal fire in the corner smokier than ever, threatening to sputter out.

Shreemati's seventeen-year-old daughter Gouri had cleaned house for us until her marriage three months earlier. We had followed the progress of the marriage preparations, through the increased giggliness of the daughter and the anxiety, then relief of the mother. Shreemati then took over Gouri's work by adding a fifth apartment to the daily four she already "did." She had had to borrow five thousand rupees to make a respectable wedding in their native village. One status-enhancing extravagance had been formal wedding invitations professionally printed in English, for distribution to employers and well-wishers like ourselves.

Like tens of thousands of illiterate working women in Bombay, Shreemati was born and grew up in a village a few hours' bus ride away. Schooling was not available to her. She was married in the 1960s, and her husband decided they would try their luck in the Big City. His brother and his cousin had already migrated and were "settled"—that is, squatting on undeveloped government-owned land at the southern tip of Bombay. The land bordered the huge military reservation where several thousand Navy officers' and enlisted men's families were housed. There was a steady market for shoemaking, the hereditary vocation of the men, and for the one kind of work Shreemati knew, household labor.

She was hired as a domestic in a junior officer's family. Her job was to do everything: cook, wash utensils, launder clothes, scrub the floors, do errands. In return, she had room and board: a mat and blanket on the kitchen floor and a diet of coarse rice, wheat chapatis, and table leftovers. Once in a while, there would be a five-rupee tip or the *largesse* of eighty centimeters of cloth for a new blouse on one of the Hindu holidays when higher status folk give gifts to their inferiors.

The arrangement became difficult after Shreemati had her first child, and with the coming of the second, impossible. She received no money for her work, and payment in kind did not feed her babies. Her husband had not had the initiative to establish his cobbler's trade in the fast-growing high-rise business district of Nariman Point or in the busy shopping streets of Colaba. Others from their shanty settlement had staked out a pavement plot, set up a large black umbrella against sun or rain, and laid out their needles and awls. They'd borrowed or scrounged for the initial investment in shoe polish, synthetic rubber heels, scrap leather, and nails. They were doing business, bringing in twenty-five rupees a day. Not that their wives saw much of it, aside from the few rupees they could wheedle for food rations. Living away from their native village, in refugee-camp conditions, among unfamiliar languages and different religions; subject to the caprices of the cops and petty racketeers, the men suffered what we would term alienation. Many sought solace in country liquor, easy to come by. The slums breed two-legged as well as four-legged predators.

By the time Shreemati had produced a son, after two daughters, she knew she needed to earn money. She became *bai,* the daily who comes to one apartment at eight a.m., to the next at nine-thirty, to X Memsahib at eleven, and to Y Memsahib in the late afternoon. In each apartment, she sweeps the floor with the traditional short-handled brush one has to bend or crouch to use effectively. Then on all fours she swabs the stone-amalgam floors with a damp rag, changing the dirty water in the bucket if you remind her—or if, like Shreemati, she is experienced, conscientious, and eager to please. Then she washes the clothes, and there are always a lot in a hot, humid climate: school uniforms, gym shorts drenched with mud, sweaty undershirts, long petticoats—everything to be got white and clean. She squats or kneels on the cement floor of the washing area, attacking the stains with a stiff brush, beating the garments exactly as her mother had, on a flat stone in the river or by the village pump. After she hangs the washing to dry, she sets about scouring pots and pans under the cold water tap. Her duties may also include pounding spices, ironing, polishing—whatever the memsahib may require.

Four households per day is about the limit, given that before sunrise such women sweep their own huts and cook the day's food for school-going or job-hunting children and for working or idling husbands. At noon, the women go home to eat something and see to the lunch of preschoolers or old folks and perhaps lie down for an hour before the afternoon stint. Shreemati has a good reputation and commands top wages: in 1986, one hundred rupees, today one hundred seventy rupees (ten dollars) per month per household. What else her employers might give—a daily cup of tea, a used sari, a tip at festival time—is *dan,* a gift she may expect, but never suggest.

Women like Shreemati who contrive some kind of work for themselves are referred to as the "unorganized sector" or the "self-employed." They are cleaners, piece-workers, petty producers, traders and vendors, and cottage artisans. They grind and bag spices, roll incense sticks, stitch garments; they turn rag remnants into quilts and waste paper into objects of papier-mâché. They represent 94 percent of nonagricultural employed women in India. These women do gruelling, repetitive work in primitive conditions at derisory pay. They have no wage protection, no organization, little visibility. Some of these occupations, like *zardozi* needlework, demand high concentration and skills passed on from mother to daughter, for generations. Zardozi, the intricate gold and silver embroidery and ornamental stitching on what will be very costly saris and evening wear, is a traditional female occupation in low-income Muslim households so orthodox that the married women rarely set foot outside their own door. Piecework contracts are short-term and brutally ill-paid; materials must be purchased from the same contractor who comes to the door to collect the finished work. . . .

In Bombay, most high-rise apartment complexes are skirted by shanty colonies. The maids come and go, jaunty teenagers to toughened grandmothers. Many are balancing heavy brass water jars on their heads. Access to running water, which they tote home twice a day, can be an unofficial perquisite of their work.

Some employers take a personal interest in the welfare of their maidservant and her children. Still, "lazy," "unreliable," "never keeps timings" are staple conversational bits of the memsahibs, many of whom have jobs and fixed schedules of their own. "Chicken is so expensive"; "butcher weighs too many bones in with the mutton"; "my maid didn't turn up, *again.*" It's such a standard tale that a newspaper advertisement introducing the squeeze-sponge floor mop—a piece of intermediate technology designed for the "modern woman" to operate herself—relies upon the following message of complicity with the target housewife.

> I took a SuperMop home [says a pretty, smiling face] and my husband said, "Phazool Kharch" [money down the drain]. Now he's changed his mind. No more jhaddus [broom whisks], no more swabs. No more dependence on the lazy, ever late maid. Just squeeze and sweep . . .

A while ago, in one residence where Shreemati works, someone decided that there was too much exploitation. The pay rate was unrealistic for the amount of work and time expected, given the high cost of living in Bombay. The woman who concluded that it was time for the maids to make a stand was from the Other Side—a young married doctoral student and active feminist. Roused by various atrocities committed against women elsewhere in the city, she had helped organize protest marches, form delegations, and distribute tracts. Now close to home she saw a chronic injustice to take up.

Sujata went down to the shanties and talked to the maids. A few days later, the maids entered the compound in a body and sat outside on the steps. No one went to work. "All very well for her," the homemakers complained. "Sujata is a radical, she lives in one room, she takes all her meals in a canteen, she has no children. Let her live the way she wants. But we have husbands to feed, classes to teach, diapers to be boiled."

Again the next day, the maids sat on the stairs. They said they wanted to talk money, hours, mutual obligations. What they wanted amounted to job descriptions and commensurate pay. For their strike to be taken seriously, it was crucial that no individual housemaid negotiate separately with her employers. But perceiving and asserting a common class interest, rather than bow to traditional allegiances, were not so evident, especially for the older women. These long-time housemaids were loyal to a memsahib who had always helped out when there was a medical emergency, who was generous with children's school supplies, who had arranged for math tutoring for the slum family's first tenth-grade graduate, and who could be relied upon for small loans, advice, kindness.

It is not easy to challenge such habits of devotion and self-denial. The less militant protesters were no doubt relieved when, on the third day of the strike, one of the most fair-minded and respected of the homemakers came forward to propose herself as negotiator.

The maids' *morcha* (protest demonstration) would not have taken place were it not for an outside instigator (who was, however, not a stranger) and the fact that the women all worked in one mini-community, rather than in isolated homes. Its outcome was not spectacular. Wages improved a bit, but no spark of shared sisterhood was kindled between the memsahibs and the maids. Rather, whatever sympathy developed for the maids resulted from a new appreciation of their domestic problems, and these were seen as functions of their lower-class status. For instance, the homemakers learned that many of these women were the sole, or sole reliable, contributor to their family's income.

It is commonly believed—and not only in India—that men have a right to strike for decent pay because they have families to support, while women, who are "self-employed" can afford to work for less. This is doubly erroneous in the lower sectors of Indian society. The first misconception is that women are primarily housewives who occasionally participate in the labor market. The second resides in the term "self-employed," implying ownership or control of the means and conditions of her employment. This is rarely the case.

The self-employed woman is neither working for herself nor spending her earnings on herself. Working to maintain the family, she puts her earnings into family subsistence, while the man generally keeps back some part of his. A female worker in the unorganized sector has a good chance of having a husband who is out of work, irregularly employed, or simply no'count. A survey done in 1988 in Ahmedabad, of four hundred women who make their living grinding chilis and spices, found that nearly one-fourth had unemployed husbands, more than one-third were solely dependent on their own income, and more than one-half did not know how much their husbands earned. And many have no husband at all. Analysis of the 1971 census figures in the three southern states of Andhra Pradesh, Karnataka, and Kerala showed that between 12 and 17 percent of households were headed by deserted, divorced, or widowed women. More recent, smaller-scale studies indicate a much higher figure, which would be consistent with both the emigration of male workers to industrial Indian cities or oil-rich Gulf states and the rising rates of desertion and divorce.

But subtler and more tenacious than the misnomer, self-employed, is the confusion about the actual nature of women's productive work. In the family hut or compound, it is difficult to differentiate between domestic chores, contribution to subsistence needs, and cash-earning activity. Where home is also the workplace, income-generating occupations like grinding and bagging spices, tending hens for eggs, or weaving baskets, overlap with housework and seem only extensions of the three C's—cooking, cleaning, and childcare. Nowhere more than in India is the truth of the old saw so evident: women's work is *never* done.

In 1987, the first national Commission on Self-Employed Women was appointed to document the condition of female workers of the informal sector and recommend ways of organizing and improving the status of these workers. Long overdue, this was the first official recognition of the productive labor of millions of women. The report, submitted to the prime minister in 1988, received considerable attention; to date, however, no major policy initiatives have emerged.

Whatever the concrete benefits might eventually be, they will not change anything for Shreemati's generation. Nor is Gouri likely to turn them to her advantage. Gouri has attended school too irregularly to learn much. Her father saw no point in her going, and neither did she. Pert and quick-witted, she knows the words of dozens of Hindi film songs. She croons them as she squats to wash clothes. Gouri's marriage did not suit her. The young man was making a steady living back in the village, but village life won't do for a Bombay girl. A few months after the wedding, she reappeared in her mother's hut and took up the old work—demeaning work, to my eyes. I assumed it was a comedown for her to be separated from her husband and back to duckwalking along the floor, swabbing under people's half-lifted feet.

Gouri does not see it that way. Being married gives her status—frees her from head-wagging and social pressure. She hasn't definitively quit her husband, of course: at seventeen, she is keeping her options open. Back in town, under her mother's roof, she can work as many hours as she needs to earn her keep and have money for cosmetics or the cinema. She values the fact that she has ready access to fine apartments and higher society.

Mother and daughter now turn up as a housework team. Shreemati is as always efficient and discreet. Gouri prefers to flip on the radio while she works. She manages to show herself often at the window, putting her head out to make disobliging remarks to lesser beings down below, the hawkers and headload carriers who can never dream of passing the threshold.

Review Questions

1. What is meant by the shadow economy, and how does the work done by Shreemati and Gouri described by Mitter illustrate this concept?
2. According to Mitter, why are women more likely to enter and be locked into the informal economy?
3. What are the conditions that lead people such as Shreemati to take up work in the shadow economy? What makes it difficult for them to organize for higher pay or to move their work as cleaners into the formal economy?
4. Is there an informal economy in the United States? Does it fit the model described by Mitter in this selection? Can you give examples?

15

Workaday World—Crack Economy

Philippe Bourgois

In the last article, we saw how low-caste Indian women supported themselves and their children through work as domestics in the shadow economy of Bombay. In this article, Philippe Bourgois focuses on the shadow economy found in inner-city New York. There, Latino/a African Americans work for little money under appalling conditions to sell drugs, even though they would prefer to do legal work. Caught in a legal economy dominated by service jobs in New York's finance, real estate, and insurance companies, these inner-city men cannot do legal work and keep their dignity. Work selling drugs, no matter how unpleasant, is the only answer.

I was forced into crack against my will. When I first moved to East Harlem—"El Barrio"—as a newlywed in the spring of 1985, I was looking for an inexpensive New York City apartment from which I could write

From "Workaday World—Crack Economy," *The Nation,* December 4, 1995, pp. 706–711.
Copyright © by *The Nation,* 1995. Reprinted by permission of the publisher.

about the experience of poverty and ethnic segregation in the heart of one of the most expensive cities in the world. I was interested in the political economy of inner-city street culture. I wanted to probe the Achilles' heel of the richest industrialized nation in the world by documenting how it imposes racial segregation and economic marginalization on so many of its Latino/a and African-American citizens.

My original subject was the entire underground (untaxed) economy, from curbside car repairing and baby-sitting to unlicensed off-track betting and drug dealing. I had never even heard of crack when I first arrived in the neighborhood—no one knew about this particular substance yet, because this brittle compound of cocaine and baking soda processed into efficiently smokable pellets was not yet available as a mass-marketed product. By the end of the year, however, most of my friends, neighbors and acquaintances had been swept into the multibillion-dollar crack cyclone: selling it, smoking it, fretting over it. I followed them, and I watched the murder rate in the projects opposite my crumbling tenement apartment spiral into one of the highest in Manhattan.

But this essay is not about crack, or drugs, per se. Substance abuse in the inner city is merely a symptom—and a vivid symbol—of deeper dynamics of social marginalization and alienation. Of course, on an immediately visible personal level, addiction and substance abuse are among the most immediate, brutal facts shaping daily life on the street. Most important, however, the two dozen street dealers and their families that I befriended were not interested in talking primarily about drugs. On the contrary, they wanted me to learn all about their daily struggles for subsistence and dignity at the poverty line.

Through the 1980s and 1990s, slightly more than one in three families in El Barrio have received public assistance. Female heads of these impoverished households have to supplement their meager checks in order to keep their children alive. Many are mothers who make extra money by baby-sitting their neighbors' children, or by housekeeping for a paying boarder. Others may bartend at one of the half-dozen social clubs and after-hours dancing spots scattered throughout the neighborhood. Some work "off the books" in their living rooms as seamstresses for garment contractors. Finally, many also find themselves obliged to establish amorous relationships with men who are willing to make cash contributions to their household expenses.

Male income-generating strategies in the underground economy are more publicly visible. Some men repair cars on the curb; others wait on stoops for unlicensed construction subcontractors to pick them up for fly-by-night demolition jobs or window renovation projects. Many sell "numbers"—the street's version of off-track betting. The most visible cohorts hawk "nickels and dimes" of one illegal drug or another. They are part of the most robust, multibillion-dollar sector of the booming underground economy. Cocaine and crack, in particular during the mid–1980s and through the early 1990s, followed by heroin in the mid–1990s, have become the fastest-growing—if not the only—equal-opportunity employers of men in Harlem. Retail drug sales easily outcompete other income-generating opportunities, whether legal or illegal.

Why should these young men and women take the subway to work minimum-wage jobs—or even double-minimum-wage jobs—in downtown offices when they can usually earn more, at least in the short run, by selling drugs on the street corner in front of their apartment or schoolyard? In fact, I am always surprised that so many inner-city men and women remain in the legal economy and work nine-to-five plus overtime, barely making ends meet. According to the 1990 Census of East Harlem, 48 percent of all males and 35 percent of females over 16 were employed in officially reported jobs, compared with a citywide average of 64 percent for men and 49 percent for women. In the census tracts surrounding my apartment, 53 percent of all men over 16 years of age (1,923 out of 3,647) and 28 percent of all women over 16 (1,307 out of 4,626) were working legally in officially censused jobs. An additional 17 percent of the civilian labor force was unemployed but actively looking for work, compared with 16 percent for El Barrio as a whole, and 9 percent for all of New York City.

'If I Was Working Legal . . .'

Street dealers tend to brag to outsiders and to themselves about how much money they make each night. In fact, their income is almost never as consistently high as they report it to be. Most street sellers, like my friend Primo (who, along with other friends and co-workers, allowed me to tape hundreds of hours of conversation with him over five years), are paid on a piece-rate commission basis. When converted into an hourly wage, this is often a relatively paltry sum. According to my calculations, the workers in the Game Room crackhouse, for example, averaged slightly less than double the legal minimum wage—between 7 and 8 dollars an hour. There were plenty of exceptional nights, however, when they made up to ten times minimum wage—and these are the nights they remember when they reminisce. They forget about all the other shifts when they were unable to work because of police raids, and they certainly do not count as forfeited working hours the nights they spent in jail.

This was brought home to me symbolically one night as Primo and his co-worker Caesar were shutting down the Game Room. Caesar unscrewed the fuses in the electrical box to disconnect the video games. Primo had finished stashing the left-over bundles of crack vials inside a hollowed-out live electrical socket and was counting the night's thick wad of receipts. I was struck by how thin the handful of bills was that he separated out and folded neatly into his personal billfold. Primo and Caesar then eagerly lowered the iron riot gates over the Game Room's windows and snapped shut the heavy Yale padlocks. They were moving with the smooth, hurried gestures of workers preparing to go home after an honest day's hard labor. Marveling at the universality in the body language of workers rushing at closing time, I felt an urge to compare the wages paid by this alternative economy. I grabbed Primo's wallet out of his back pocket, carefully giving a wide berth to the fatter wad in his front pocket that represented Ray's share of the night's income—and that could cost Primo his life if it were waylaid. Unexpectedly, I pulled out fifteen dollars' worth of food stamps along with two $20 bills. After an embarrassed giggle, Primo stammered that his mother had added him to her food-stamp allotment.

PRIMO: I gave my girl, Maria, half of it. I said, "Here, take it, use it if you need it for whatever." And then the other half I still got it in my wallet for emergencies.

Like that, we always got a couple of dollars here and there, to survive with. Because tonight, straight cash, I only got garbage. Forty dollars! Do you believe that?

At the same time that wages can be relatively low in the crack economy, working conditions are often inferior to those in the legal economy. Aside from the obvious dangers of being shot, or of going to prison, the physical work space of most crackhouses is usually unpleasant. The infrastructure of the Game Room, for example, was much worse than that of any legal retail outfit in East Harlem: There was no bathroom, no running water, no telephone, no heat in the winter and no air conditioning in the summer. Primo occasionally complained:

> Everything that you see here [sweeping his arm at the scratched and dented video games, the walls with peeling paint, the floor slippery with litter, the filthy windows pasted over with ripped movie posters] is fucked up. It sucks, man [pointing at the red 40-watt bare bulb hanging from an exposed fixture in the middle of the room and exuding a sickly twilight].

Indeed, the only furnishings besides the video games were a few grimy milk crates and bent aluminum stools. Worse yet, a smell of urine and vomit usually permeated the locale. For a few months Primo was able to maintain a rudimentary sound system, but it was eventually beaten to a pulp during one of Caesar's drunken rages. Of course, the deficient infrastructure was only one part of the depressing working conditions.

PRIMO: Plus I don't like to see people fucked up [handing over three vials to a nervously pacing customer]. This is fucked-up shit. I don't like this crack dealing. Word up.

[gunshots in the distance] Hear that?

In private, especially in the last few years of my residence, Primo admitted that he wanted to go back to the legal economy.

PRIMO: I just fuck up the money here. I rather be legal.

PHILIPPE: But you wouldn't be the head man on the block with so many girlfriends.

PRIMO: I might have women on my dick right now, but I would be much cooler if I was working legal. I wouldn't be drinking and the coke wouldn't be there every night.

Plus if I was working legally I would have women on my dick too, be cause I would have money.

PHILIPPE: But you make more money here than you could ever make working legit.

PRIMO: O.K. So you want the money but you really don't want to do the job.

> I really hate it, man. Hate it! I hate the people! I hate the environment! I hate the whole shit, man! But it's like you get caught up with it. You do it, and you say, "Ay, fuck it today!" Another day, another dollar. [pointing at an emaciated customer who was just entering] But I don't really, really think that I would have hoped that I can say I'm gonna be richer one day. I can't say that. I think about it, but I'm just living day to day.
>
> If I was working legal, I wouldn't be hanging out so much. I wouldn't be treating you. [pointing to the 16-ounce can of Colt 45 in my hand] In a job, you know, my environment would change . . . totally. 'Cause I'd have different friends. Right after work I'd go out with a co-worker, for lunch, for dinner. After work I may go home; I'm too tired for hanging out—I know I gotta work tomorrow.
>
> After working a legal job, I'm pretty sure I'd be good.

Burned in the FIRE Economy

The problem is that Primo's good intentions do not lead anywhere when the only legal jobs he can compete for fail to provide him with a livable wage. None of the crack dealers were explicitly conscious of the links between their limited options in the legal economy, their addiction to drugs and their dependence on the crack economy for economic survival and personal dignity. Nevertheless, all of Primo's colleagues and employees told stories of rejecting what they considered to be intolerable working conditions at entry-level jobs.

Most entered the legal labor market at exceptionally young ages. By the time they were 12, they were bagging and delivering groceries at the supermarket for tips, stocking beer off the books in local bodegas or running errands. Before reaching 21, however, virtually none had fulfilled their early childhood dreams of finding stable, well-paid legal work.

The problem is structural: From the 1950s through the 1980s second-generation inner-city Puerto Ricans were trapped in the most vulnerable niche of a factory-based economy that was rapidly being replaced by service industries. Between 1950 and 1990, the proportion of factory jobs in New York City decreased approximately threefold at the same time that service-sector jobs doubled. The Department of City Planning calculates that more than 800,000 industrial jobs were lost from the 1960s through the early 1990s, while the total number of jobs of all categories remained more or less constant at 3.5 million.

Few scholars have noted the cultural dislocations of the new service economy. These cultural clashes have been most pronounced in the office-work service jobs that have multiplied because of the dramatic expansion of the finance, real estate and insurance (FIRE) sector in New York City. Service work in professional offices is the most dynamic place for ambitious inner-city youths to find entry-level jobs if they aspire to upward mobility. Employment as mailroom clerks, photocopiers and messengers in the highrise office corridors of the financial district propels many into a wrenching cultural confrontation with the upper-middle-class white world. Obedience to the norms of highrise, office-corridor culture is in direct contradiction to street culture's definitions of personal dignity—especially for males who are socialized not to accept public subordination.

Most of the dealers have not completely withdrawn from the legal economy. On the contrary—they are precariously perched on its edge. Their poverty remains their only constant as they alternate between street-level crack dealing and just-above-minimum-wage legal employment. The working-class jobs they manage to find are objectively recognized to be among the least desirable in U.S. society; hence the following list of just a few of the jobs held by some of the Game Room regulars during the years I knew them: unlicensed asbestos remover, home attendant, street-corner flier distributor, deep-fat fry cook and night-shift security guard on the violent ward at the municipal hospital for the criminally insane.

The stable factory-worker incomes that might have allowed Caesar and Primo to support families have largely disappeared from the inner city. Perhaps if their social network had not been confined to the weakest sector of manufacturing in a period of rapid job loss, their teenage working-class dreams might have stabilized them for long enough to enable them to adapt to the restructuring of the local economy. Instead, they find themselves propelled headlong into an explosive confrontation between their sense of cultural dignity versus the humiliating interpersonal subordination of service work.

Workers like Caesar and Primo appear inarticulate to their professional supervisors when they try to imitate the language of power in the workplace; they stumble pathetically over the enunciation of unfamiliar words. They cannot decipher the hastily scribbled instructions—rife with mysterious abbreviations—that are left for them by harried office managers on diminutive Post-its. The "common sense" of white-collar work is foreign to them; they do not, for example, understand the logic in filing triplicate copies of memos or for postdating invoices. When they attempt to improvise or show initiative, they fail miserably and instead appear inefficient—or even hostile—for failing to follow "clearly specified" instructions.

In the highrise office buildings of midtown Manhattan or Wall Street, newly employed inner-city high school dropouts suddenly realize they look like idiotic buffoons to the men and women for whom they work. But people like Primo and Caesar have not passively accepted their structural victimization. On the contrary, by embroiling themselves in the underground economy and proudly embracing street culture, they are seeking an alternative to their social marginalization. In the process, on a daily level, they become the actual agents administering their own destruction and their community's suffering.

Both Primo and Caesar experienced deep humiliation and insecurity in their attempts to penetrate the foreign, hostile world of highrise office corridors. Primo had bitter memories of being the mailroom clerk and errand boy at a now-defunct professional trade magazine. The only time he explicitly admitted to having experienced racism was when he described how he was treated at that particular work setting.

PRIMO: I had a prejudiced boss. . . . When she was talking to people she would say, "He's illiterate," as if I was really that stupid that I couldn't understand what she was talking about.

So what I did one day—you see they had this big dictionary right there on the desk, a big heavy motherfucker—so what I just did was open up the dictionary, and I just looked up the word, "illiterate." And that's when I saw what she was calling me.

So she's saying that I'm stupid or something. I'm stupid! [pointing to himself with both thumbs and making a hulking face] "He doesn't know shit."

In contrast, in the underground economy Primo never had to risk this kind of threat to his self-worth.

PRIMO: Ray would never disrespect me that way; he wouldn't tell me that because he's illiterate too, plus I've got more education than him. I almost got a G.E.D.

The contemporary street sensitivity to being dissed immediately emerges in these memories of office humiliation. The machismo of street culture exacerbates the sense of insult experienced by men because the majority of office supervisors at the entry level are women. In the lowest recesses of New York City's FIRE sector, tens of thousands of messengers, photocopy machine operators and security guards serving the Fortune 500 companies are brusquely ordered about by young white executives—often female—who sometimes make bimonthly salaries superior to their underlings' yearly wages. The extraordinary wealth of Manhattan's financial district exacerbates the sense of sexist-racist insult associated with performing just-above-minimum-wage labor.

'I Don't Even Got a Dress Shirt'

Several months earlier, I had watched Primo drop out of a "motivational training" employment program in the basement of his mother's housing project, run by former heroin addicts who had just received a multimillion-dollar private sector grant for their innovative approach to training the "unemployable." Primo felt profoundly disrespected by the program, and he focused his discontent on the humiliation he faced because of his inappropriate wardrobe. The fundamental philosophy of such motivational job-training programs is that "these people have an attitude problem." They take a boot-camp approach to their unemployed clients, ripping their self-esteem apart during the first week in order to build them back up with an epiphanic realization that they want to find jobs as security guards, messengers and data-input clerks in just-above-minimum-wage service-sector positions. The program's highest success rate had been with middle-aged African-American women who wanted to terminate their relationship to welfare once their children leave home.

I originally had a "bad attitude" toward the premise of psychologically motivating and manipulating people to accept boring, poorly paid jobs. At the same time, however, the violence and self-destruction I was witnessing at the Game Room was convincing me that it is better to be exploited at work than to be outside the legal labor market. In any case, I persuaded Primo and a half-dozen of his Game Room associates to sign up for the program. Even Caesar was tempted to join.

None of the crack dealers lasted for more than three sessions. Primo was the first to drop out, after the first day. For several weeks he avoided talking about the experience. I repeatedly pressed him to explain why he "just didn't show up" at the sessions. Only after repeated badgering on my part did he finally express the deep sense of shame and vulnerability he experienced whenever he attempted to venture into the legal labor market.

PHILIPPE: Yo Primo, listen to me. I worry that there's something taking place that you're not aware of, in terms of yourself. Like the coke that you be sniffing all the time; it's like every night.

PRIMO: What do you mean?

PHILIPPE: Like not showing up at the job training. You say it's just procrastination, but I'm scared that it's something deeper that you're not dealing with. . . .

PRIMO: The truth though—listen Felipe—my biggest worry was the dress code, 'cause my gear is limited. I don't even got a dress shirt, I only got one pair of shoes, and you can't wear sneakers at that program. They wear ties too—don't they? Well, I ain't even got ties—I only got the one you lent me.

I would've been there three weeks in the same gear: T-shirt and jeans. *Estoy jodido como un bón!* [I'm all fucked up like a bum!]

PHILIPPE: What the fuck kinda bullshit excuse are you talking about? Don't tell me you were thinking that shit. No one notices how people are dressed.

PRIMO: Yo, Felipe, this is for real! Listen to me! I was thinking about that shit hard. Hell yeah!

Hell, yes, they would notice if somebody's wearing a fucked-up tie and shirt.

I don't want to be in a program all *abochornado* [bumlike]. I probably won't even concentrate, getting dished, like . . . and being looked at like a sucker. Dirty jeans . . . or like old jeans, because I would have to wear jeans, 'cause I only got one slack. Word though! I only got two dress shirts and one of them is missing buttons.

I didn't want to tell you about that because it's like a poor excuse, but that was the only shit I was really thinking about. At the time I just said, "Well, I just don't show up."

And Felipe, I'm a stupid [very] skinny nigga'. So I have to be careful how I dress, otherwise people will think I be on the stem [a crack addict who smokes out of a glass-stem pipe].

PHILIPPE: [nervously] Oh shit. I'm even skinnier than you. People must think I'm a total drug addict.

PRIMO: Don't worry. You're white.

Review Questions

1. What kinds of jobs, both legal and "shadow," can Latino African-American men work at in East Harlem, New York City, according to Bourgois?
2. Why do so many poor Latino/a African-American men and women hold legal jobs in New York?
3. What are the structural changes that have occurred in New York City's economy over the past 40 years? How do these limit the work that is available to African-American men and women?
4. How are Latino African Americans treated in the "FIRE" service economy?
5. Why did Bourgois' African-American informants drop out of the motivational program some of them entered, and how did their response to this program resemble their reaction to work in the legal service economy?

16

Subsistence and Market: When the Turtle Collapses

Bernard Nietschmann

Subsistence economies were once common in the world. People hunted and gathered or farmed largely for their own needs. But the world market economy has penetrated even the most remote areas and has brought with it a change from subsistence economies to production for money. In this article, Bernard Nietschmann traces the disturbing effect of the international market for green sea turtles on the Miskito Indians, who once harpooned the large sea reptiles only for food. Trapped in a vicious circle, Indians began to catch the turtles to sell rather than to eat. With no turtle meat to eat came a need for money to buy food. Money came only from catching and selling more turtles. The need for cash also reduced the Indians' ability to perform reciprocal economic obligations. In the end, the new economy began to disappear because of the diminished catch of overexploited turtles, leaving the Miskito without even their original means of subsistence.

Originally published as "When the Turtle Collapses, the World Ends." With permission from *Natural History*, June–July 1974. Copyright © by the American Museum of Natural History, 1974.

In the half-light of dawn, a sailing canoe approaches a shoal where nets have been set the day before. A Miskito turtleman stands in the bow and points to a distant splash that breaks the gray sheen of the Caribbean waters. Even from a hundred yards, he can tell that a green turtle has been caught in one of the nets. His two companions quickly bring the craft alongside the turtle, and as they pull it from the sea, its glistening shell reflects the first rays of the rising sun. As two men work to remove the heavy reptile from the net, the third keeps the canoe headed into the swells and beside the anchored net. After its fins have been pierced and lashed with bark fiber cord, the 250-pound turtle is placed on its back in the bottom of the canoe. The turtlemen are happy. Perhaps their luck will be good today and their other nets will also yield many turtles.

These green turtles, caught by Miskito Indian turtlemen off the eastern coast of Nicaragua, are destined for distant markets. Their butchered bodies will pass through many hands, local and foreign, eventually ending up in tins, bottles, and freezers far away. Their meat, leather, shell, oil, and calipee, a gelatinous substance that is the base for turtle soup, will be used to produce goods consumed in more affluent parts of the world.

The coastal Miskito Indians are very dependent on green turtles. Their culture has long been adapted to utilizing the once vast populations that inhabited the largest sea turtle feeding grounds in the Western Hemisphere. As the most important link between livelihood, social interaction, and environment, green turtles were the pivotal resource around which traditional Miskito Indian society revolved. These large reptiles also provided the major source of protein for Miskito subsistence. Now this priceless and limited resource has become a prized commodity that is being exploited almost entirely for economic reasons.

In the past, turtles fulfilled the nutritional needs as well as the social responsibilities of Miskito society. Today, however, the Miskito depend mainly on the sale of turtles to provide them with the money they need to purchase household goods and other necessities. But turtles are a declining resource; overdependence on them is leading the Miskito into an ecological blind alley. The cultural control mechanisms that once adapted the Miskito to their environment and faunal resources are now circumvented or inoperative, and they are caught up in a system of continued intensification of turtle fishing, which threatens to provide neither cash nor subsistence.

I have been studying this situation for several years, unraveling its historical context and piecing together its past and future effect on Miskito society, economy, and diet, and on the turtle population.

The coastal Miskito Indians are among the world's most adept smallcraft seamen and turtlemen. Their traditional subsistence system provided dependable yields from the judicious scheduling of resource procurement activities. Agriculture, hunting, fishing, and gathering were organized in accordance with seasonal fluctuations in weather and resource availability and provided adequate amounts of food and materials without overexploiting any one species or site. Women cultivated the crops while men hunted and fished. Turtle fishing was the backbone of subsistence, providing meat throughout the year.

Miskito society and economy were interdependent. There was no economic activity without a social context and every social act had a reciprocal economic aspect. To the Miskito, meat, especially turtle meat, was the most esteemed and valuable resource, for it was not only a mainstay of subsistence, it was the item most commonly distributed to relatives and friends. Meat shared in this way satisfied mutual obligations and responsibilities and smoothed out daily and seasonal differences in the acquisition of animal protein. In this way, those too young, old, sick, or otherwise unable to secure meat received their share, and a certain balance in the village was achieved: minimal food requirements were met, meat surplus was disposed of to others, and social responsibilities were satisfied.

Today, the older Miskito recall that when meat was scarce in the village, a few turtlemen would put out to sea in their dugout canoes for a day's harpooning on the turtle feeding grounds. In the afternoon, the men would return, sailing before the northeast trade wind, bringing meat for all. Gathered on the beach, the villagers helped drag the canoes into thatched storage sheds. After the turtles were butchered and the meat distributed, everyone returned home to the cooking fires.

Historical circumstances and a series of boom-bust economic cycles disrupted the Miskito's society and environment. In the seventeenth and eighteenth centuries, intermittent trade with English and French buccaneers—based on the exchange of forest and marine resources for metal tools and utensils, rum, and firearms—prompted the Miskito to extend hunting, fishing, and gathering beyond subsistence needs to exploitative enterprises.

During the nineteenth and early twentieth centuries, foreign-owned companies operating in eastern Nicaragua exported rubber, lumber, and gold, and initiated commercial banana production. As alien economic and ecological influences were intensified, contract wage labor replaced seasonal, short-term economic relationships; company commissaries replaced limited trade goods; and large-scale exploitation of natural resources replaced sporadic, selective extraction. During economic boom periods the relationship between resources, subsistence, and environment was drastically altered for the Miskito. Resources became a commodity with a price tag, market exploitation a livelihood, and foreign wages and goods a necessity.

For more than two hundred years, relations between the coastal Miskito and the English were based on sea turtles. It was from the Miskito that the English learned the art of turtling, which they then organized into intensive commercial exploitation of Caribbean turtle grounds and nesting beaches. Sea turtles were among the first resources involved in trade relations and foreign commerce in the Caribbean. Zoologist Archie Carr, an authority on sea turtles, has remarked that "more than any other dietary factor, the green turtle supported the opening up of the Caribbean." The once abundant turtle populations provided sustenance to ships' crews and to the new settlers and plantation laborers.

The Cayman Islands, settled by the English, became in the seventeenth and eighteenth centuries the center of commercial turtle fishing in the Caribbean. By the early nineteenth century, pressure on the Cayman turtle grounds and nesting beaches to supply meat to Caribbean and European markets became so great that the turtle population was decimated. The Cayman Islanders were forced to shift to other turtle areas off Cuba, the Gulf of Honduras, and the coast of eastern Nicaragua. They made annual expeditions, lasting four to seven weeks, to the Miskito turtle grounds to net green turtles, occasionally purchasing live ones, dried calipee, and the shells of hawksbill turtles *(Eretmochelys imbricata)* from the Miskito Indians. Reported catches of green turtles by the Cayman turtlers generally ranged between two thousand and three thousand a year up to the early 1960s, when the Nicaraguan government failed to renew the islanders' fishing privileges.

Intensive resource extraction by foreign companies led to seriously depleted and altered environments. By the 1940s, many of the economic booms had turned to busts. As the resources ran out and operating costs mounted, companies shut down production and moved to other areas in Central America. Thus, the economic mainstays that had helped provide the Miskito with jobs, currency, markets, and foreign goods were gone. The company supply ships and commissaries disappeared, money became scarce, and store-bought items expensive.

In the backwater of the passing golden boom period, the Miskito were left with an ethic of poverty, but they still had the subsistence skills that had maintained their culture for hundreds of years. Their land and water environment was still capable of providing reliable resources for local consumption. As it had been in the past, turtle fishing became a way of life, a provider of life itself. But traditional subsistence culture could no longer integrate Miskito society and environment in a state of equilibrium. Resources were now viewed as having a value and labor a price tag. All that was needed was a market.

Recently, two foreign turtle companies began operations along the east coast of Nicaragua. One was built in Puerto Cabezas in late 1968, and another was completed in Bluefields in 1969. Both companies were capable of processing and shipping large amounts of green turtle meat and byproducts to markets in North America and Europe. Turtles were acquired by purchase from the Miskito. Each week company boats visited coastal Miskito communities and offshore island turtle camps to buy green turtles. The "company" was back, money was again available, and the Miskito were expert in securing the desired commodity. Another economic boom period was at hand. But the significant difference between this boom and previous ones was that the Miskito were now selling a subsistence resource.

As a result, the last large surviving green turtle population in the Caribbean was opened to intensive, almost year-round exploitation. Paradoxically, it would be the Miskito Indians, who once caught only what they needed for food, who would conduct the assault on the remaining turtle population. . . .

Green turtles, *Chelonia mydas,* are large, air-breathing, herbivorous marine reptiles. They congregate in large populations and graze on underwater beds of vegetation in relatively clear, shallow, tropical waters. A mature turtle can weigh two hundred fifty pounds or more and when caught, can live indefinitely in a saltwater enclosure or for a couple of weeks if kept in shade on land. Green turtles have at least six behavioral characteristics that are important in their exploitation: they occur in large numbers in localized areas; they are air breathing, so they have to surface; they are mass social nesters; they have an acute location-finding ability; when mature, they migrate seasonally on an overlapping two- or three-year cycle for mating and nesting; and they exhibit predictable local distributional patterns.

The extensive shallow shelf off eastern Nicaragua is dotted with numerous small coral islands, thousands of reefs, and vast underwater pastures of marine vegetation called "turtle banks." During the day, a large group of turtles may be found feeding at one of the many turtle banks, while adjacent marine pastures may have only a few turtles. They graze on the vegetation, rising periodically to the surface for air and to float for a while before diving again. In the late afternoon, groups of turtles will leave the feeding areas and swim to shoals, some up to four or five miles away, to spend the night. By five the next morning, they gather to depart again for the banks. The turtles' precise, commuterlike behavior between sleeping and feeding areas is well known to the Miskito and helps insure good turtling.

Each coastal turtling village exploits an immense sea area, containing many turtle banks and shoals. For example, the Miskito of Tasbapauni utilize a marine area of approximately six hundred square miles, with twenty major turtle banks and almost forty important shoals.

Having rather predictable patterns of movement and habitat preference, green turtles are commonly caught by the Miskito in three ways: on the turtle banks with harpoons; along the shoal-to-feeding area route with harpoons; and on the shoals using nets, which entangle the turtles when they surface for air.

The Miskito's traditional means of taking turtles was by harpoon—an eight- to ten-foot shaft fitted with a detachable short point tied to a strong line. The simple technology pitted two turtlemen in a small, seagoing canoe against the elusive turtles. Successful turtling with harpoons requires an extensive knowledge of turtle behavior and habits and tremendous skill and experience in handling a small canoe in what can be very rough seas. Turtlemen work in partnerships: a "strikerman" in the bow; the "captain" in the stern. Together, they make a single unit engaged in the delicate and almost silent pursuit of a wary prey, their movements coordinated by experience and rewarded by proficiency. Turtlemen have mental maps of all the banks and shoals in their area, each one named and located through a complex system of celestial navigation, distance reckoning, wind and current direction, and the individual surface-swell motion over each site. Traditionally, not all Miskito were sufficiently expert in seamanship and turtle lore to become respected "strikermen," capable of securing turtles even during hazardous sea conditions. Theirs was a very specialized calling. Harpooning restrained possible overexploitation since turtles were taken one at a time by two men directly involved in the chase, and there were only a limited number of really proficient "strikermen" in each village.

Those who still use harpoons must leave early to take advantage of the land breeze and to have enough time to reach the distant offshore turtle grounds by first light. Turtlemen who are going for the day, or for several days, will meet on the beach by 2:00 A.M. They drag the canoes on bamboo rollers from beachfront sheds to the water's edge. There, in the swash of spent breakers, food, water, paddles, lines, harpoons, and sails are loaded and secured. Using a long pole, the standing bowman propels the canoe through the foaming surf while the captain in the stern keeps the craft running straight with a six-foot mahogany paddle. Once past the inside break, the men count the dark rolling seas building outside until there is a momentary pause in the sets; then with paddles digging deep, they drive the narrow, twenty-foot canoe over the cresting swells, rising precipitously on each wave face and then plunging down the far side as the sea and sky seesaw into view. Once past the breakers, they rig the sail and, running with the land breeze, point the canoe toward a star in the eastern sky.

A course is set by star fix and by backsight on a prominent coconut palm on the mainland horizon. Course alterations are made to correct for the direction and intensity of winds and currents. After two or three hours of sailing the men reach a distant spot located between a turtle sleeping shoal and feeding bank. There they intercept and follow the turtles as they leave for specific banks.

On the banks the turtlemen paddle quietly, listening for the sound of a "blowing" turtle. When a turtle surfaces for air it emits a hissing sound audible for fifty yards or more on a calm day. Since a turtle will stay near the surface for only a minute or two before diving to feed, the men must approach quickly and silently, maneuvering the canoe directly in front of or behind the turtle. These are its blind spots. Once harpooned, a turtle explodes into a frenzy of action, pulling the canoe along at high speeds in its hopeless, underwater dash for escape until it tires and can be pulled alongside the canoe.

But turtle harpooning is a dying art. The dominant method of turtling today is the use of nets. Since their introduction, the widespread use of turtle nets has drastically altered turtling strategy and productivity. Originally brought to the Miskito by the Cayman Islanders, nets are now extensively distributed on credit by the turtle companies. This simple technological change, along with a market demand for turtles, has resulted in intensified pressure on green turtle populations.

Buoyed by wooden floats and anchored to the bottom by a single line, the fifty-foot-long by fourteen-foot-wide nets hang from the surface like underwater flags, shifting direction with the current. Nets are set in place during midday when the turtlemen can see the dark shoal areas. Two Miskito will set five to thirty nets from one canoe, often completely saturating a small shoal. In the late afternoon, green turtles return to their shoals to spend the night. There they will sleep beside or beneath a coral outcrop, periodically surfacing for air where a canopy of nets awaits them.

Catching turtles with nets requires little skill; anyone with a canoe can now be a turtleman. The Miskito set thousands of nets daily, providing continuous coverage in densely populated nocturnal habitats. Younger Miskito can become turtlemen almost overnight simply by following more experienced men to the shoal areas, thus circumventing the need for years of accumulated skill and knowledge that once were the domain of the "strikermen." All one has to do is learn where to set the nets, retire for the night, remove the entangled turtles the next morning, and reset the nets. The outcome is predictable: more turtlemen, using more effective methods, catch more turtles.

With an assured market for turtles, the Miskito devote more time to catching turtles, traveling farther and staying at sea longer. Increased dependence on turtles as a source of income and greater time inputs have meant disruption of subsistence agriculture and hunting and fishing. The Miskito no longer produce foodstuffs for themselves; they buy imported foods with money gained from the sale of turtles. Caught between contradictory priorities—their traditional subsistence system and the market economy—the Miskito are opting for cash.

The Miskito are now enveloped in a positive feedback system where change spawns change. Coastal villages rely on turtles for a livelihood. Decline of subsistence provisioning has led to the need to secure food from local shopkeepers on credit to feed the families in the villages and the men during their turtling expeditions. Initial high catches of turtles encouraged more Miskito to participate, and by 1972 the per-person and per-day catch began to decline noticeably.

In late 1972, several months after I had returned to Michigan, I received a letter from an old turtleman, who wrote: "Turtle is getting scarce, Mr. Barney. You said it would happen in five or ten years but it is happening now."

Burdened by an overdependence on an endangered species and with accumulating debts for food and nets, the Miskito are finding it increasingly difficult to break even, much less secure a profit. With few other economic alternatives, the inevitable step is to use more nets and stay out at sea longer.

The turtle companies encourage the Miskito to expand turtling activities by providing them with building materials so that they can construct houses on offshore cays, thereby eliminating the need to return to the mainland during rough weather. On their weekly runs up and down the coast, company boats bring food, turtle gear, and cash for turtles to fishing camps from the

Miskito Cays to the Set Net Cays. Frequent visits keep the Miskito from becoming discouraged and returning to their villages with the turtles. On Saturdays, villagers look to sea, watching for returning canoes. A few men will bring turtle for their families; the majority will bring only money. Many return with neither.

Most Miskito prefer to be home on Sunday to visit with friends and for religious reasons. (There are Moravian, Anglican, and Catholic mission churches in many of the villages.) But more and more, turtlemen are staying out for two to four weeks. The church may promise salvation, but only the turtle companies can provide money.

Returning to their villages, turtlemen are confronted with a complex dilemma: how to satisfy both social and economic demands with a limited resource. Traditional Miskito social rules stipulate that turtle meat should be shared among kin, but the new economic system requires that turtles be sold for personal economic gain. Kin expect gifts of meat, and friends expect to be sold meat. Turtlemen are besieged with requests forcing them to decide between who will or will not receive meat. This is contrary to the traditional Miskito ethic, which is based on generosity and mutual concern for the well-being of others. The older Miskito ask why the turtlemen should have to allocate a food that was once abundant and available to all. Turtlemen sell and give to other turtlemen, thereby ensuring reciprocal treatment for themselves, but there simply are not enough turtles to accommodate other economic and social requirements. In order to have enough turtles to sell, fewer are butchered in the villages. This means that less meat is being consumed than before the turtle companies began operations. The Miskito presently sell 70 to 90 percent of the turtles they catch; in the near future they will sell even more and eat less. . . .

Social tension and friction are growing in the villages. Kinship relationships are being strained by what some villagers interpret as preferential and stingy meat distribution. Rather than endure the trauma caused by having to ration a limited item to fellow villagers, many turtlemen prefer to sell all their turtles to the company and return with money, which does not have to be shared. However, if a Miskito sells out to the company, he will probably be unable to acquire meat for himself in the village, regardless of kinship or purchasing power. I overheard an elderly turtleman muttering to himself as he butchered a turtle: "I no going to sell, neither give dem meat. Let dem eat de money."

The situation is bad and getting worse. Individuals too old or sick to provide for themselves often receive little meat or money from relatives. Families without turtlemen are families without money or access to meat. The trend is toward the individualization of nuclear families, operating for their own economic ends. Miskito villages are becoming neighborhoods rather than communities.

The Miskito diet has suffered in quality and quantity. Less protein and fewer diverse vegetables and fruits are consumed. Present dietary staples—

rice, white flour, beans, sugar, and coffee—come from the store. In one Miskito village, 65 percent of all food eaten in a year was purchased.

Besides the nutritional significance of what is becoming a largely carbohydrate diet, dependence on purchased foods has also had major economic reverberations. Generated by national and international scarcities, inflationary fallout has hit the Miskito. Most of their purchased foods are imported, much coming from the United States. In the last five years prices for staples have increased 100 to 150 percent. This has had an overwhelming impact on the Miskito, who spend 50 to 75 percent of their income for food. Consequently, their entry into the market by selling a subsistence resource, diverting labor from agriculture, and intensifying exploitation of a vanishing species has resulted in their living off poorer-quality, higher-priced foods.

The Miskito now depend on outside systems to supply them with money and materials that are subject to world market fluctuations. They have lost their autonomy and their adaptive relationship with their environment. Life is no longer socially rewarding, nor is their diet satisfying. The coastal Miskito have become a specialized and highly vulnerable sector of the global market economy.

Loss of turtle markets would be a serious economic blow to the Miskito, who have almost no other means of securing cash for what have now become necessities. Nevertheless, continued exploitation will surely reduce the turtle population to a critical level.

National and international legislation is urgently needed. At the very least, commercial turtle fishing must be curtailed for several years until the *Chelonia* population can rebound and exploitation quotas can be set. While turtle fishing for subsistence should be permitted, exportation of sea turtle products used in the gourmet, cosmetic, or jewelry trade should be banned.

Restrictive environmental legislation, however, is not a popular subject in Nicaragua, a country that has recently been torn by earthquakes, volcanic eruption, and hurricanes. A program for sea turtle conservation submitted to the Nicaraguan government for consideration ended up in a pile of rubble during the earthquake that devastated Managua in December 1972, adding a sad footnote to the Miskito-sea turtle situation. With other problems to face, the government has not yet reviewed what is happening on the distant east coast, separated from the capital by more than two hundred miles of rain forest—and years of neglect.

As it is now, the turtles are going down and, along with them, the Miskito—seemingly a small problem in terms of the scale of ongoing ecological and cultural change in the world. But each localized situation involves species and societies with long histories and, perhaps, short futures. They are weathervanes in the conflicting winds of economic and environmental priorities. As Bob Dylan sang: "You don't need a weatherman to tell which way the wind blows."

Review Questions

1. What does Nietschmann mean by *subsistence economy?*
2. How has the Miskito Indians' exploitation of the green sea turtle affected their economy?
3. What does Nietschmann mean when he says that the Miskito Indian economy is "enveloped in a positive feedback system"?
4. How has the world market affected the Miskito economy?

6

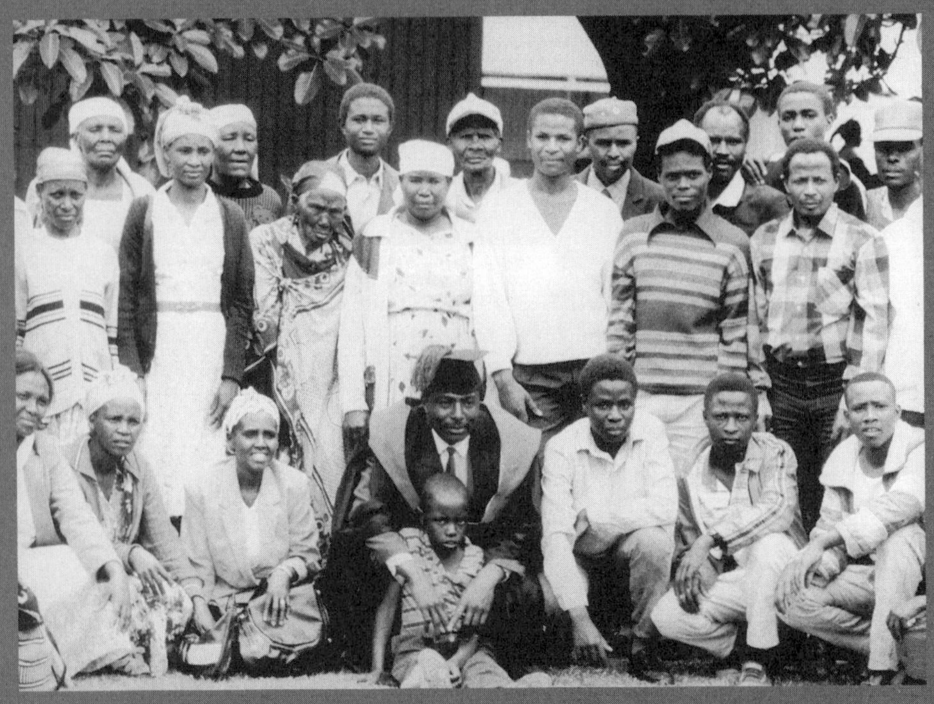

KINSHIP AND FAMILY

Social life is essential to human existence. We remain in the company of other people from the day we are born to the time of our death. People teach us to speak. They show us how to relate to our surroundings. They give us the help and the support we need to achieve personal security and mental well-being. Alone, we are relatively frail, defenseless primates; in groups we are astonishingly adaptive and powerful. Yet despite these advantages, well-organized human societies are difficult to achieve. Some species manage to produce social organization genetically. But people are not like bees or ants. We lack the genetically coded directions for behavior that make these insects successful social animals. Although we seem to inherit a general need for social approval, we also harbor individual interests and ambitions that can block or destroy close social ties. To overcome these divisive tendencies, human groups organize around several principles designed to foster cooperation and group loyalty. Kinship is among the strongest of these.

We may define *kinship* as the complex system of culturally defined social relationships based on marriage (the principle of *affinity*) and birth (the principle of *consanguinity*). The study of kinship involves consideration of such principles as descent, kinship status and roles, family and other kinship groups, marriage, and residence. In fact, kinship has been such an important organizing factor in many of the societies studied by anthropologists that it is one of the most elaborate areas of the discipline. What are some of the important concepts?

First is descent. *Descent* is based on the notion of a common heritage. It is a cultural rule tying together people on the basis of reputed common ancestry. Descent functions to guide inheritance, group loyalty, and, above all, the formation of families and extended kinship groups.

There are three main rules of descent. One is *patrilineal descent,* which links relatives through males only. In patrilineal systems, females are part of their father's line, but their children descend from the husbands. *Matrilineal descent* links relatives through females only. Males belong to their mother's line; the children of males descend from the wives. *Bilateral descent* links a person to kin through both males and females simultaneously. We Americans are said to have bilateral descent, whereas most of the people in India, Japan, and China are patrilineal. Such groups as the Apache and Trobriand Islanders are matrilineal.

Descent often defines groups called, not surprisingly, *descent groups.* One of these is the *lineage,* a localized group that is based on unilineal (patrilineal or matrilineal) descent and that usually has some corporate powers. In the Marshall Islands, for example, the matriline holds rights to land, which, in turn, it allots to its members. Lineages in India sometimes hold rights to land but are a more important arena for other kinds of decisions such as marriage. Lineage mates must be consulted about the advisability, timing, and arrangements for weddings. (See article 18.)

Clans are composed of lineages. Clan members believe they are all descended from a common ancestor, but because clans are larger, members cannot trace their genealogical relationships to everyone in the group. In some societies, clans may be linked together in even larger groups called *phratries.* Because phratries are usually large, the feeling of common descent they offer is weaker.

Ramages, or cognatic kin groups, are based on bilateral descent. They often resemble lineages in size and function but provide more recruiting flexibility. An individual can choose membership from among several ramages where he or she has relatives.

Another important kinship group is the family. This unit is more difficult to define than we may think, because people have found so many different ways to organize "familylike" groups. Here we will follow anthropologist George P. Murdock's approach and define the *family* as a kin group consisting of at least one married couple sharing the same residence with their children and performing sexual, reproductive, economic, and educational functions. A *nuclear family* consists of a single married couple and their children. An *extended family* consists of two or more married couples and their children. Extended families have a quality all their own and are often found in societies where family performance and honor are paramount to the reputation of individual family members. Extended families are most commonly based on patrilineal descent. Women marry into such families and must establish themselves among the line members and other women who live there.

Marriage, the socially approved union of a man and a woman, is a second major principle of kinship. The regulation of marriage takes elaborate forms from one society to the next. Marriage may be *exogamous,* meaning marriage outside any particular named group, or *endogamous,* indicating the opposite. Bhil tribals of India, for example, are clan and village exogamous (they should marry outside these groups), but tribal endogamous (they should marry other Bhils).

Marriage may also be *monogamous,* where it is preferred that only one woman should be married to one man at a time, or *polygamous,* meaning that one person may be married to more than one person simultaneously. There are two kinds of polygamy, *polygyny,* the marriage of one man with more than one woman simultaneously, and *polyandry,* the marriage of one woman with more than one man.

Many anthropologists view marriage as a system of alliances between families and descent lines. Viewed in these terms, rules such as endogamy and exogamy can be explained as devices to link or internally strengthen various kinship groups. The *incest taboo,* a legal rule that prohibits sexual intercourse or marriage between particular classes of kin, is often explained as a way to extend alliances between kin groups.

Finally, the regulation of marriage falls to the parents and close relatives of eligible young people in many societies. These elders concern themselves with more than wedding preparations; they must also see to it that young people marry appropriately, which means they consider the reputation of prospective spouses and their families' economic strength and social rank.

The selections in Part 6 illustrate several aspects of kinship systems. In the first article, Nancy Scheper-Hughes looks at the relationship that poor Brazilian mothers have with their infants. Because babies die so often, mothers must delay forming attachments to them until their children show that they can survive. The second article, by David McCurdy, looks at the way kinship organizes life for the inhabitants of a Rajasthani Bhil village. Arranging a marriage requires use and consideration of clans, lineages, families, and weddings. Despite its origin in peasant society, the Indian kinship system is proving useful as people try to cope with a modernizing society. The third article, by Melvyn Goldstein, describes a rare form of marriage—polyandry—and shows why, despite other choices, Tibetan brothers often choose to share a single wife among them. Finally, Margery Wolf looks at the structure of the Taiwanese extended family from the point of view of the women who constitute it. It is only by establishing her own uterine family that a woman can gain power with the patrilineal group.

Key Terms

kinship
affinity
consanguinity
descent
patrilineal descent
matrilineal descent
bilateral descent
descent groups
lineage
clan
phratry
ramage
family
nuclear family
extended family
marriage
exogamy
endogamy
monogamy
polygamy
polygyny
polyandry
incest taboo

Readings in This Section

Mother's Love: Death Without Weeping *Nancy Scheper-Hughes,* page *195*

Family and Kinship in Village India *David W. McCurdy,* page *205*

Polyandry: When Brothers Take a Wife *Melvyn C. Goldstein,* page *214*

Uterine Families and the Women's Community *Margery Wolf,* page *222*

17

Mother's Love: Death Without Weeping

Nancy Scheper-Hughes

Kinship systems are based on marriage and birth. Both, anthropologists assume, create ties that can link kin into close, cooperative, enduring structures. What happens to such ties, however, in the face of severe hardship imposed by grinding poverty and urban migration? Can we continue to assume, for example, that there will be a close bond between mother and child? This is the question pursued by Nancy Scheper-Hughes in the following article about the mother-infant relationship among poor women in a Brazilian shantytown. The author became interested in the question following a "baby die-off" in the town of Bom Jesus in 1965. She noticed that mothers seemed to take these events casually. After 25 years of research in the Alto do Cruzeiro shantytown there, she has come to see such indifference as a cultural response to high rates of infant death due to poverty and malnutrition. Mothers, and surrounding social institutions such as the Catholic Church, expect babies to die eas-

From "Death Without Weeping," *Natural History,* October 1989. Copyright © by the American Museum of Natural History, 1989. Reprinted by permission of the publisher.

ily. Mothers concentrate their support on babies who are "fighters" and let themselves grow attached to their children only when they are reasonably sure that the offspring will survive. The article also provides an excellent illustration of what happens to kinship systems in the face of poverty and social dislocation. Such conditions may easily result in the formation of woman-headed families, and in a lack of the extended kinship networks so often found in more stable, rural societies.

I have seen death without weeping
The destiny of the Northeast is death
Cattle they kill
To the people they do something worse

—Anonymous Brazilian singer (1965)

"Why do the church bells ring so often?" I asked Nailza de Arruda soon after I moved into a corner of her tiny mud-walled hut near the top of the shantytown called the Alto do Cruzeiro (Crucifix Hill). I was then a Peace Corps volunteer and a community development/health worker. It was the dry and blazing hot summer of 1965, the months following the military coup in Brazil, and save for the rusty, clanging bells of N.S. das Dores Church, an eerie quiet had settled over the market town that I call Bom Jesus da Mata. Beneath the quiet, however, there was chaos and panic. "It's nothing," replied Nailza, "just another little angel gone to heaven."

Nailza had sent more than her share of little angels to heaven, and sometimes at night I could hear her engaged in a muffled but passionate discourse with one of them, two-year-old Joana. Joana's photograph, taken as she lay propped up in her tiny cardboard coffin, her eyes open, hung on a wall next to one of Nailza and Ze Antonio taken on the day they eloped.

Nailza could barely remember the other infants and babies who came and went in close succession. Most had died unnamed and were hastily baptized in their coffins. Few lived more than a month or two. Only Joana, properly baptized in church at the close of her first year and placed under the protection of a powerful saint, Joan of Arc, had been expected to live. And Nailza had dangerously allowed herself to love the little girl.

In addressing the dead child, Nailza's voice would range from tearful imploring to angry recrimination: "Why did you leave me? Was your patron saint so greedy that she could not allow me one child on this earth?" Ze Antonio advised me to ignore Nailza's odd behavior, which he understood as a kind of madness that, like the birth and death of children, came and went. Indeed, the premature birth of a stillborn son some months later "cured" Nailza of her "inappropriate" grief, and the day came when she removed Joana's photo and carefully packed it away.

More than fifteen years elapsed before I returned to the Alto do Cruzeiro, and it was anthropology that provided the vehicle of my return. Since 1982 I have returned several times in order to pursue a problem that first attracted my attention in the 1960s. My involvement with the people of the Alto do Cruzeiro now spans a quarter of a century and three generations of parenting in a community where mothers and daughters are often simultaneously pregnant.

The Alto do Cruzeiro is one of three shantytowns surrounding the large market town of Bom Jesus in the sugar plantation zone of Pernambuco in Northeast Brazil, one of the many zones of neglect that have emerged in the shadow of the now tarnished economic miracle of Brazil. For the women and children of the Alto do Cruzeiro the only miracle is that some of them have managed to stay alive at all.

The Northeast is a region of vast proportions (approximately twice the size of Texas) and of equally vast social and developmental problems. The nine states that make up the region are the poorest in the country and are representative of the Third World within a dynamic and rapidly industrializing nation. Despite waves of migrations from the interior to the teeming shantytowns of coastal cities, the majority still live in rural areas on farms and ranches, sugar plantations and mills.

Life expectancy in the Northeast is only forty years, largely because of the appallingly high rate of infant and child mortality. Approximately one million children in Brazil under the age of five die each year. The children of the Northeast, especially those born in shantytowns on the periphery of urban life, are at a very high risk of death. In these areas, children are born without the traditional protection of breast-feeding, subsistence gardens, stable marriages, and multiple adult caretakers that exists in the interior. In the hillside shantytowns that spring up around cities or, in this case, interior market towns, marriages are brittle, single parenting is the norm, and women are frequently forced into the shadow economy of domestic work in the homes of the rich or into unprotected and oftentimes "scab" wage labor on the surrounding sugar plantations, where they clear land for planting and weed for a pittance, sometimes less than a dollar a day. The women of the Alto may not bring their babies with them into the homes of the wealthy, where the often-sick infants are considered sources of contamination, and they cannot carry the little ones to the riverbanks where they wash clothes because the river is heavily infested with schistosomes and other deadly parasites. Nor can they carry their young children to the plantations, which are often several miles away. At wages of a dollar a day, the women of the Alto cannot hire baby sitters. Older children who are not in school will sometimes serve as somewhat indifferent caretakers. But any child not in school is also expected to find wage work. In most cases, babies are simply left at home alone, the door securely fastened. And so many also die alone and unattended.

Bom Jesus da Mata, centrally located in the plantation zone of Pernambuco, is within commuting distance of several sugar plantations and mills. Consequently, Bom Jesus has been a magnet for rural workers forced off their small subsistence plots by large landowners wanting to use every available piece of land for sugar cultivation. Initially, the rural migrants to Bom Jesus were squatters who were given tacit approval by the mayor to put up temporary straw huts on each of the three hills overlooking the town. The Alto do Cruzeiro is the oldest, the largest, and the poorest of the shantytowns. Over the past three decades many of the original migrants have become permanent residents, and the primitive and temporary straw huts have been replaced by small homes (usually of two rooms) made of wattle and daub, sometimes covered with plaster. The more affluent residents use bricks and tiles. In most Alto homes, dangerous kerosene lamps have been replaced by light bulbs. The once tattered rural garb, often fashioned from used sugar sacking, has likewise been replaced by store-bought clothes, often castoffs from a wealthy *patrão* (boss). The trappings are modern, but the hunger, sickness, and death that they conceal are traditional, deeply rooted in a history of feudalism, exploitation, and institutionalized dependency.

My research agenda never wavered. The questions I addressed first crystallized during a veritable "die-off" of Alto babies during a severe drought in 1965. The food and water shortages and the political and economic chaos occasioned by the military coup were reflected in the handwritten entries of births and deaths in the dusty, yellowed pages of the ledger books kept at the public registry office in Bom Jesus. More than 350 babies died in the Alto during 1965 alone—this from a shantytown population of little more than 5,000. But that wasn't what surprised me. There were reasons enough for the deaths in the miserable conditions of shantytown life. What puzzled me was the seeming indifference of Alto women to the death of their infants, and their willingness to attribute to their own tiny offspring an aversion to life that made their death seem wholly natural, indeed all but anticipated.

Although I found that it was possible, and hardly difficult, to rescue infants and toddlers from death by diarrhea and dehydration with a simple sugar, salt, and water solution (even bottled Coca-Cola worked fine), it was more difficult to enlist a mother herself in the rescue of a child she perceived as ill-fated for life or better off dead, or to convince her to take back into her threatened and besieged home a baby she had already come to think of as an angel rather than as a son or daughter.

I learned that the high expectancy of death, and the ability to face child death with stoicism and equanimity, produced patterns of nurturing that differentiated between those infants thought of as thrivers and survivors and those thought of as born already "wanting to die." The survivors were nurtured, while stigmatized, doomed infants were left to die, as mothers say, *a mingua*, "of neglect." Mothers stepped back and allowed nature to take its course. This pattern, which I call mortal selective neglect, is called passive infanticide by anthropologist Marvin Harris. The Alto situation, although culturally specific in the form that it takes, is not unique to Third World shantytown communities and may have its correlates in our own impoverished urban communities in some cases of "failure to thrive" infants.

I use as an example the story of Zezinho, the thirteen-month-old toddler of one of my neighbors, Lourdes. I became involved with Zezinho when I was called in to help Lourdes in the delivery of another child, this one a fair and robust little tyke with a lusty cry. I noted that while Lourdes showed great interest in the newborn, she totally ignored Zezinho who, wasted and severely malnourished, was curled up in a fetal position on a piece of urine- and feces-soaked cardboard placed under his mother's hammock. Eyes open and vacant, mouth slack, the little boy seemed doomed.

When I carried Zezinho up to the community day-care center at the top of the hill, the Alto women who took turns caring for one another's children (in order to free themselves for part-time work in the cane fields or washing clothes) laughed at my efforts to save Ze, agreeing with Lourdes that here was a baby without a ghost of a chance. Leave him alone, they cautioned. It makes no sense to fight with death. But I did do battle with Ze, and after several weeks of force-feeding (malnourished babies lose their interest in food), Ze began to succumb to my ministrations. He acquired some flesh across his taut chest bones, learned to sit up, and even tried to smile. When he seemed well enough, I returned him to Lourdes in her miserable scrap-material lean-to, but not without guilt about what I had done. I wondered whether returning Ze was at all fair to Lourdes and to his little brother. But I was busy and washed my hands of the matter. And Lourdes did seem more interested in Ze now that he was looking more human.

When I returned in 1982, there was Lourdes among the women who formed my sample of Alto mothers—still struggling to put together some semblance of life for a now grown Ze and her five other surviving children. Much was made of my reunion with Ze in 1982, and everyone enjoyed retelling the story of Ze's rescue and of how his mother had given him up for dead. Ze would laugh the loudest when told how I had had to force-feed him like a fiesta turkey. There was no hint of guilt on the part of Lourdes and no resentment on the part of Ze. In fact, when questioned in private as to who was the best friend he ever had in life, Ze took a long drag on his cigarette and answered without a trace of irony, "Why my mother, of course!" "But of course," I replied.

Part of learning how to mother in the Alto do Cruzeiro is learning when to let go of a child who shows that it "wants" to die or that it has no "knack" or no "taste" for life. Another part is learning when it is safe to let oneself love a child. Frequent child death remains a powerful shaper of maternal thinking and practice. In the absence of firm expectation that a child will survive, mother love as we conceptualize it (whether in popular terms or in the psychobiological notion of maternal bonding) is attenuated and delayed with consequences for infant survival. In an environment already precarious to young life, the emotional detachment of mothers toward some of their babies contributes even further to the spiral of high mortality—high fertility in a kind of macabre lock-step dance of death.

The average woman of the Alto experiences 9.5 pregnancies, 3.5 child deaths, and 1.5 stillbirths. Seventy percent of all child deaths in the Alto occur in the first six months of life, and 82 percent by the end of the first year. Of all deaths in the community each year, about 45 percent are of children under the age of five.

Women of the Alto distinguish between child deaths understood as natural (caused by diarrhea and communicable diseases) and those resulting from sorcery, the evil eye, or other magical or supernatural afflictions. They also recognize a large category of infant deaths seen as fated and inevitable. These hopeless cases are classified by mothers under the folk terminology "child sickness" or "child attack." Women say that there are at least fourteen different types of hopeless child sickness, but most can be subsumed under two categories—chronic and acute. The chronic cases refer to infants who are born small and wasted. They are deathly pale, mothers say, as well as weak and passive. They demonstrate no vital force, no liveliness. They do not suck vigorously; they hardly cry. Such babies can be this way at birth or they can be born sound but soon show no resistance, no "fight" against the common crises of infancy: diarrhea, respiratory infections, tropical fevers.

The acute cases are those doomed infants who die suddenly and violently. They are taken by stealth overnight, often following convulsions that bring on head banging, shaking, grimacing, and shrieking. Women say it is horrible to look at such a baby. If the infant begins to foam at the mouth or gnash its teeth or go rigid with its eyes turned back inside its head, there is absolutely no hope. The infant is "put aside"—left alone—often on the floor in a back room, and allowed to die. These symptoms (which accompany high fevers, dehydration, third-stage malnutrition, and encephalitis) are equated by Alto women with madness, epilepsy, and worst of all, rabies, which is greatly feared and highly stigmatized.

Most of the infants presented to me as suffering from chronic child sickness were tiny, wasted famine victims, while those labeled as victims of acute child attack seemed to be infants suffering from the deliriums of high fever or the convulsions that can accompany electrolyte imbalance in dehydrated babies.

Local midwives and traditional healers, praying women, as they are called, advise Alto women on when to allow a baby to die. One midwife explained: "If I can see that a baby was born unfortuitously, I tell the mother that she need not wash the infant or give it a cleansing tea. I tell her just to dust the infant with baby powder and wait for it to die." Allowing nature to take its course is not seen as sinful by these often very devout Catholic women. Rather, it is understood as cooperating with God's plan.

Often I have been asked how consciously women of the Alto behave in this regard. I would have to say that consciousness is always shifting between allowed and disallowed levels of awareness. For example, I was awakened early one morning in 1987 by two neighborhood children who had been sent to fetch me to a hastily organized wake for a two-month-old infant whose mother I had unsuccessfully urged to breast-feed. The infant was being sustained on sugar water, which the mother referred to as *soro* (serum), using a medical term for the infant's starvation regime in light of his chronic diarrhea. I had cautioned the mother that an infant could not live on *soro* forever.

The two girls urged me to console the young mother by telling her that it was "too bad" that her infant was so weak that Jesus had to take him. They were coaching me in proper Alto etiquette. I agreed, of course, but asked, "And what do *you* think?" Xoxa, the eleven-year-old, looked down at her dusty flip-flops and blurted out, "Oh, Dona Nanci, that baby never got enough to eat, but you must never say that!" And so the death of hungry babies remains one of the best kept secrets of life in Bom Jesus da Mata.

Most victims are waked quickly and with a minimum of ceremony. No tears are shed, and the neighborhood children form a tiny procession, carrying the baby to the town graveyard where it will join a multitude of others. Although a few fresh flowers may be scattered over the tiny grave, no stone or wooden cross will mark the place, and the same spot will be reused within a few months' time. The mother will never visit the grave, which soon becomes an anonymous one.

What, then, can be said of these women? What emotions, what sentiments motivate them? How are they able to do what, in fact, must be done? What does mother love mean in this inhospitable context? Are grief, mourning, and melancholia present, although deeply repressed? If so, where shall we look for them? And if not, how are we to understand the moral visions and moral sensibilities that guide their actions?

I have been criticized more than once for presenting an unflattering portrait of poor Brazilian women, women who are, after all, themselves the victims of severe social and institutional neglect. I have described these women as allowing some of their children to die, as if this were an unnatural and inhuman act rather than, as I would assert, the way any one of us might act, reasonably and rationally, under similarly desperate conditions. Perhaps I have not emphasized enough the real pathogens in this environment of high risk: poverty, deprivation, sexism, chronic hunger, and economic exploitation. If mother love is, as many psychologists and some feminists believe, a seemingly natural and universal maternal script, what does it mean to women for whom scarcity, loss, sickness, and deprivation have made that love frantic and robbed them of their grief, seeming to turn their hearts to stone?

Throughout much of human history—as in a great deal of the impoverished Third World today—women have had to give birth and to nurture children under ecological conditions and social arrangements hostile to child survival, as well as to their own well-being. Under circumstances of high childhood mortality, patterns of selective neglect and passive infanticide may be seen as active survival strategies.

They also seem to be fairly common practices historically and across cultures. In societies characterized by high childhood mortality and by a correspondingly high (replacement) fertility, cultural practices of infant and child care tend to be organized primarily around survival goals. But what this means is a pragmatic recognition that not all of one's children can be expected to live. The nervousness about child survival in areas of northeast Brazil, northern India, or Bangladesh, where a 30 percent or 40 percent mortality rate in the first years of life is common, can lead to forms of delayed attachment and a casual or benign neglect that serves to weed out the worst bets so as to enhance the life chances of healthier siblings, including those yet to be born. Practices similar to those that I am describing have been recorded for parts of Africa, India, and Central America.

Life in the Alto do Cruzeiro resembles nothing so much as a battlefield or an emergency room in an overcrowded inner-city public hospital. Consequently, morality is guided by a kind of "lifeboat ethics," the morality of triage. The seemingly studied indifference toward the suffering of some of their infants, conveyed in such sayings as "little critters have no feelings," is understandable in light of these women's obligation to carry on with their reproductive and nurturing lives.

In their slowness to anthropomorphize and personalize their infants, everything is mobilized so as to prevent maternal overattachment and, therefore, grief at death. The bereaved mother is told not to cry, that her tears will dampen the wings of her little angel so that she cannot fly up to her heavenly home. Grief at the death of an angel is not only inappropriate, it is a symptom of madness and of a profound lack of faith.

Infant death becomes routine in an environment in which death is anticipated and bets are hedged. While the routinization of death in the context of shantytown life is not hard to understand, and quite possible to empathize with, its routinization in the formal institutions of public life in Bom Jesus is not as easy to accept uncritically. Here the social production of indifference takes on a different, even a malevolent, cast.

In a society where triplicates of every form are required for the most banal events (registering a car, for example), the registration of infant and child death is informal, incomplete, and rapid. It requires no documentation, takes less than five minutes, and demands no witnesses other than office clerks. No questions are asked concerning the circumstances of the death, and the cause of death is left blank, unquestioned and unexamined. A neighbor, grandmother, older sibling, or common-law husband may register the death. Since most infants die at home, there is no question of a medical record.

From the registry office, the parent proceeds to the town hall, where the mayor will give him or her a voucher for a free baby coffin. The fulltime municipal coffinmaker cannot tell you exactly how many baby coffins are dispatched each week. It varies, he says, with the seasons. There are more needed during the drought months and during the big festivals of Carnaval and Christmas and São Joao's Day because people are too busy, he supposes, to take their babies to the clinic. Record keeping is sloppy.

Similarly, there is a failure on the part of city-employed doctors working at two free clinics to recognize the malnutrition of babies who are weighed, measured, and immunized without comment and as if they were not, in fact, anemic, stunted, fussy, and irritated starvation babies. At best the mothers are told to pick up free vitamins or a health "tonic" at the municipal chambers. At worst, clinic personnel will give tranquilizers and sleeping pills to quiet the hungry cries of "sick-to-death" Alto babies.

The church, too, contributes to the routinization of, and indifference toward, child death. Traditionally, the local Catholic church taught patience and resignation to domestic tragedies that were said to reveal the imponderable workings of God's will. If an infant died suddenly, it was because a particular saint had claimed the child. The infant would be an angel in the service of his or her heavenly patron. It would be wrong, a sign of a lack of faith, to weep for a child with such good fortune. The infant funeral was, in the past, an event celebrated with joy. Today, however, under the new regime of "liberation theology," the bells of N. S. das Dores parish church no longer peal for the death of Alto babies, and no priest accompanies the procession of angels to the cemetery where their bodies are disposed of casually and without ceremony. Children bury children in Bom Jesus da Mata. In this most Catholic of communities, the coffin is handed to the disabled and irritable municipal gravedigger, who often chides the children for one reason or another. It may be that the coffin is larger than expected and the gravedigger can find no appropriate space. The children do not wait for the gravedigger to complete his task. No prayers are recited and no sign of the cross made as the tiny coffin goes into its shallow grave.

When I asked the local priest, Padre Marcos, about the lack of church ceremony surrounding infant and childhood death today in Bom Jesus, he replied: "In the old days, child death was richly celebrated. But those were the baroque customs of a conservative church that wallowed in death and misery. The new church is a church of hope and joy. We no longer celebrate the death of child angels. We try to tell mothers that Jesus doesn't want all the dead babies they send him." Similarly, the new church has changed its baptismal customs, now often refusing to baptize dying babies brought to the back door of a church or rectory. The mothers are scolded by the church attendants and told to go home and take care of their sick babies. Baptism, they are told, is for the living; it is not to be confused with the sacrament of extreme unction, which is the anointing of the dying. And so it appears to the women of the Alto that even the church has turned away from them, denying the traditional comfort of folk Catholicism.

The contemporary Catholic church is caught in the clutches of a double bind. The new theology of liberation imagines a kingdom of God on earth based on justice and equality, a world without hunger, sickness, or childhood mortality. At the same time, the church has not changed its official position on sexuality and reproduction, including its sanctions against birth control, abortion, and sterilization. The padre of Bom Jesus da Mata recognizes this contradiction intuitively, although he shies away from discussions on the topic, saying that he prefers to leave questions of family planning to the discretion and the "good consciences" of his impoverished parishioners. But this, of course, sidesteps the extent to which those good consciences have been shaped by traditional church teachings in Bom Jesus, especially by his recent predecessors. Hence, we can begin to see that the seeming indifference of Alto mothers toward the death of some of their infants is but a pale reflection of the official indifference of church and state to the plight of poor women and children.

Nonetheless, the women of Bom Jesus are survivors. One woman, Biu, told me her life history, returning again and again to the themes of child death, her first husband's suicide, abandonment by her father and later by her second husband, and all the other losses and disappointments she had suffered in her long forty-five years. She concluded with great force, reflecting on the days of Carnaval '88 that were fast approaching:

> No, Dona Nanci, I won't cry, and I won't waste my life thinking about it from morning to night. . . . Can I argue with God for the state that I'm in? No! And so I'll dance and I'll jump and I'll play Carnaval! And yes, I'll laugh and people will wonder at a *pobre* like me who can have such a good time.

And no one did blame Biu for dancing in the streets during the four days of Carnaval—not even on Ash Wednesday, the day following Carnaval '88 when we all assembled hurriedly to assist in the burial of Mercea, Biu's beloved *casula,* her last-born daughter who had died at home of pneumonia during the festivities. The rest of the family barely had time to change out of their costumes. Severino, the child's uncle and godfather, sprinkled holy water over the little angle while he prayed: "Mercea, I don't know whether you were called, taken, or thrown out of this world. But look down at us from your heavenly home with tenderness, with pity, and with mercy." So be it.

Review Questions

1. What did Scheper-Hughes notice about mother's reactions during the baby die-off of 1965 in Bom Jesus, Brazil?
2. How do poor Brazilian mothers react to their infants' illnesses and death? How do other institutions, such as the church, clinic, and civil authorities respond? Give examples.
3. How does Scheper-Hughes explain the apparent indifference of mothers to the death of their infants?
4. What does the indifference of mothers to the deaths of their children say about basic human nature, especially the mother–child bond?

18

Family and Kinship in Village India

David W. McCurdy

Anyone who reads older ethnographic accounts of different cultures will inevitably run across terms such as clan, lineage, avunculocal, levirate, extended family, polyandry, cross-cousin, *and* Crow *terminology. All these terms and many more were created by anthropologists to describe categories, groups, social arrangements, and roles associated with the complex kinship systems that characterized so many of the groups they studied. The importance of kinship for one of these societies, that found in an Indian village, is the topic of this article by David McCurdy. He argues that kinship forms the core social groups and associations in rural India in a system well adapted to family-centered land-holding and small-scale farming. He concludes by pointing out that Indians have used their close family ties to adapt to life in cash-labor-oriented modernizing world.*

This article was written for *Conformity and Conflict.* Copyright © by David W. McCurdy, 1997.

On a hot afternoon in May, 1962, I sat talking with three Bhil men in the village of Ratakote, located in southern Rajasthan, India.[1] We spoke about the results of recent national elections, their worry over a cattle disease that was afflicting the village herds, and predictions about when the monsoon rains would start. But our longest discussion concerned kin—the terms used to refer to them, the responsibilities they had toward one another, and the importance of marrying them off properly. It was toward the end of this conversation that one of the men, Kanji, said, "Now sāb (Bhili for sāhīb), you are finally asking about a good thing. This is what we want you tell people about us when you go back to America."

As I thought about it later, I was struck by how different this social outlook was from mine. I doubt that I or any of my friends in the United States would say something like this. Americans do have kin. We have parents, although our parents may not always live together, and we often know other relatives, some of whom are likely to play important parts in our lives. We grow up in families and we often create new ones if we have children. But we also live in a social network of other people whom we meet at work or encounter in various "outside" social settings, and these people can be of equal or even greater importance to us than kin. Our social worlds include such non-kin stuctures as companies and other work organizations, schools, neighborhoods, churches and other religious groups, and voluntary associations, including recreational groups and social clubs. We are not likely to worry much about our obligations to relatives with the notable exceptions of our children and grandchildren (middle-class American parents are notoriously child-centered), and more grudgingly, our aging parents. We are not supposed to "live off" relatives or lean too heavily on them.

Not so in Ratakote. Ratakote's society, like many agrarian villages around the world, is kinship-centered. Villagers anchor themselves in their families. They spend great energy on creating and maintaining their kinship system. This actually is not so surprising. Elaborate kinship systems work well in agrarian societies where families tend to be corporate units and where peoples' social horizons are often limited to the distance they can walk in a day. For the same reasons, families in the United States were also stronger in the past when more of them owned farms and neighborhood businesses.

What may come as a surprise, however, is how resilient and strong Indian kinship systems such as Ratakote's have been in the face of recent economic changes, especially the growth of wage labor. Let us look more closely at the Bhil kinship system, especially at arranged marriage, to illustrate these ideas.

---

[1] Ratakote is a Bhil tribal village located 21 miles southwest of Udaipur, Rajasthan, in the Aravalli hills. I did ethnographic research in the village from 1961 to 1963, and again in 1985, 1991, and 1993 for shorter periods of time.

Arranging a Marriage

If there is anything that my American students have trouble understanding about India, it is arranged marriage. They can not imagine sitting passively by while their parents advertise their charms and evaluate emerging nuptial candidates. The thought of living—to say nothing of have sex with—a total stranger seems out of the question to them. In our country, personal independence takes precedence over loyalty to family.

Not so in India. There, arranged marriage is the norm, and most young people, as well as their elders, accept and support the custom. (They often find it sexually exciting, too.) There are many reasons why this is so, but one stands out for discussion here. Marriage constructs alliances between families, lineages, and clans. The resulting kinship network is a pivotal structure in Indian society. It confers social strength and security. People's personal reputations depend on the quality and number of their allied kin. There is little question in their minds about who should arrange marriages. The decision is too important to leave up to inexperienced and impressionable young people.

As an aside I should note that young Indians play a greater part in the process than they used to. Middle class boys often visit the families of prospective brides, where they manage to briefly "interview" them. They also tap into their kinship network to find out personal information about prospects. Young women also seek out information about perspective grooms. Bhils are no exception. They often conspire to meet those to whom they have been betrothed, usually at a fair or other public event where their contact is likely to go unnoticed. If they don't like each other, they will begin to pressure their parents to back out of the arrangement.

The importance of arranging a marriage was brought home to me several times during fieldwork in Ratakote, but one instance stands out most clearly. When I arrived in the village for a short stay in 1985, Kanji had just concluded marriage arrangements for his daughter, Rupani.[2] What he told me about the process underscored the important role kinship plays in the life of the village.

Kanji started by saying that he and his wife first discussed Rupani's marriage the previous year when the girl first menstruated. She seemed too young for such a union then so they had waited nine months before committing to the marriage process. Even then, Rupani was still only 15 years old. Kanji explained that everyone preferred early marriage for their children because young people were likely to become sexually active as they grew older and might fall in love and elope, preempting the arrangement process altogether. Now they figured that the time had come, and they began a series of steps to find a suitable spouse that would eventually involve most of their kin.

---

[2] Kanji and Rupani are not real people. Their experiences are a composite of several life histories.

The first step was to consult the members of Kanji's *lineage*. Lineage is an anthropological term, not one used by Bhils. But Bhils share membership in local groups of relatives that meet the anthropological definition. Lineages (in this case, (patrilineages) include closely related men who are all descended from a known ancestor. Kanji's lineage consists of his two married brothers, three married sons of his deceased father's brother (his father is also dead), and his own married son when the latter is home. All are the descendants of his grandfather who had migrated to Ratakote many years earlier. He had talked with all of them informally about the possibility of his daughter's marriage before this. Now he called them together for formal approval.

The approval of lineage mates is necessary because they are essential to the marriage process. Each one of them will help spread the word to other villages that Rupani is available for marriage. They will loan money to Kanji for wedding expenses, and when it comes time for the wedding ceremony, they will provide much of the labor needed to prepare food and arrange required activities. Each family belonging to the lineage will host a special meal for the bride (the groom is similarly entertained in his village) during the wedding period, and one or two will help her make offerings to their lineal ancestors. The groom will also experience this ritual.

The lineage also has functions not directly related to marriage. It has the right to redistribute the land of deceased childless, male members, and it provides its members with political support. It sees to memorial feasts for deceased members. Its members may cooperatively plow and sow fields together and combine their animals for herding.

With lineage approval in hand, Kanji announced Rupani's eligibility in other villages. (Bhils are village exogamous, meaning they prefer to marry spouses from other communities.) Kanji and his lineage mates went about this by paying visits to feminal relatives in other villages. These are kin of the women, now living in Ratakote, who have married into his family. They also include the daughters of his family line who have married and gone to live in other villages, along with their husbands and husbands' kin.

Once the word has been spread, news of prospective candidates begins to filter in. It may arrive with feminal kin from other villages when they visit Ratakote. Or it may come from neighbors who are acting as go-betweens in Ratakote for kin who live in other villages and who seek partners for their children. Either way, a process of evaluation starts. Does the family of the suggested boy or girl have a good reputation? Are they hospitable to their in-laws? Do they meet their obligations to others? What is the reputation of the boy or girl they are offering in marriage? Is he or she tall or short, light or dark, robust or frail, cheerful or complaining, hard-working or lazy? What about their level of education? Does the family have sufficient land and animals? Have they treated other sons- and daughters-in-law well?

The most fundamental question to ask, however, is whether the prospective spouse is from the right clan. In anthropology, the term *clan* refers to an aggregate of people who all believe they are descended from a common ancestor. In Ratakote this group is called an *arak*. Araks are named and the names are used as surnames when Bhils identify themselves. Kanji comes from the pargi arak and is thus known as Kanji Pargi. There is Lalu Bodar, Naraji Katara, Dita Hiravat, Nathu Airi—all men named for one of the 36 araks found in Ratakote. Women also belong to their father's clan, but unlike many American women who adopt their husband's surname at marriage, they keep their arak name all their lives.

Araks are based on a rule of patrilineal descent. This means that their members trace ancestry though males, only. (Matrilineal descent traces the line through females only, and bilateral descent, which is found in U.S. society, includes both sexes.) Patrilineal descent not only defines arak membership, it governs inheritance. (Sons inherit equally from their fathers in Ratakote; daughters do not inherit despite a national law giving them that right.) It says that the children of divorced parents stay with the father's family. It bolsters the authority of men over their wives and children. It supports the rule of patrilocality. It even defines the village view of conception. Men plant the "seeds" that grow into children; women provide the fields in which the seeds germinate and grow.

The arak symbolizes patrilineal descent. It is not an organized group, although the members of an arak worship the same mother goddess no matter where they live. Instead it is an identity, an indicator that tells people who their lineal blood relatives are. There are pargis in hundreds of other Bhil villages. Most are strangers to Kanji but if he meets pargis elsewhere, he knows they share a common blood heritage with him.

It is this sense of common heritage that affects marriage. Bhils, like most Indians, believe that clan (arak) mates are close relatives even thought they may be strangers. Marriage with them is forbidden. To make sure incest is impossible, it is also forbidden to marry anyone from your mother's arak or your father's mother's arak, to say nothing of anyone else you know you are related to.

This point was driven home to me on another occasion when a neighbor of Kanji's, Kamalaji Kharadi, who was sitting smoking with several other men, asked me which *arak* I belonged to. Instead of letting it go at "McCurdy," I said that I didn't have an *arak*. I explained that Americans didn't have a kinship group similar to this, and that was why I had to ask questions about kinship.

My listeners didn't believe me. After all, I must have a father and you get your arak automatically from him. It is a matter of birth and all people are born. They looked at each other as if to say, "We wonder why he won't tell us what his *arak* is?", then tried again to get me to answer. My second denial led them to ask, "OK, then what is your wife's *arak?*" (If you can't get at it one way, then try another.) I answered that she didn't have an *arak* either. This caused a mild sensation. "Then how do you know if you have not married your own relative?", they asked, secretly (I think) delighting by the scandalous prospect.

The third step that occurred during the arrangement of Rupani's marriage came after the family had settled on a prospective groom. This step is the betrothal, and it took place when the groom's father and some of his lineage mates and neighbors paid a formal visit to Kanji's house. When they arrive,

Kanji must offer his guests a formal meal, usually slaughtering a goat and distilling some liquor for the occasion. The bride, her face covered by her sari, will be brought out for a brief viewing, as well. But most of the time will be spent making arrangements—when will the actual wedding take place?; who will check the couple's horoscopes for fit?; how much will the bride price (also called bride wealth by many anthropologists) be?

Bride price (*dapa*) deserves special comment. It is usually a standard sum of money (about 700 rupees in 1985), although it may also include silver ornaments or other valuables. The dapa is given by the groom's father and his line to the parents of the bride. Bhils view this exchange as a compensation for the loss of the bride's services to her family. It also pays for a shift in her loyalty.

The exchange points up an important strain on families in patrilineal societies, the transfer of a woman from her natal family and line to those of her husband. This transfer includes not only her person, but her loyalty, labor, and children. Although she always will belong to her father's arak, she is now part of her husband's family, not his.

This problem is especially troublesome in India because of the close ties formed there by a girl and her parents. Parents know their daughter will leave when she marries, and they know that in her husband's house and village, she will be at a disadvantage. She will be alone, and out of respect for his parents her husband may not favor her wishes, at least in public. Because of this, they tend to give her extra freedom and support. In addition, they recognize the strain she will be under when she first goes to live with her new husband and his family. To ease her transition, they permit her to visit her parents frequently for a year or two. They also may try to marry her into a village where other women from Ratakote have married, so that she has some kin or at least supporters.

After her marriage, a woman's parents and especially her brothers find it hard not to care about her welfare. Their potential interest presents a built-in structural conflict that could strain relations between the two families if nothing were done about it.

A solution to this problem is to make the marriage into an exchange, and bride price is one result. Bride price also helps to dramatize the change in loyalty and obligation accompanying the bride's entrance into her new family.

Bhils have also devised a number of wedding rituals to dramatize the bride's shift in family membership. The bride must cry to symbolize that she is leaving her home. The groom ritually storms the bride's house at the beginning of the final ceremony. He does so like a conquering hero, drawing his sword to strike a ceremonial arch placed over the entrance while simultaneously stepping on a small fire (he wears a slipper to protect his foot), ritually violating the household's sacred hearth. At the end of the wedding, the groom, with some friends, engages in a mock battle with the bride's brothers and other young men, and symbolically abducts her. The meaning of this ritual is a dramatic equivalent of a father "giving away the bride" at American weddings.

One additional way of managing possible tension between in-laws is the application of respect behavior. The parents of the bride must always treat those of the groom and their relatives with respect. They must not joke in their presence, and they must use respectful language and defer to the groom's parents in normal conversation. In keeping with the strong patrilineal system, a groom may not accept important gifts from his wife's family except on ritual occasions, such as weddings, when exchange is expected. A groom may help support his own father, but he should not do so with his in-laws. That is up to their sons.

Bride price exchange also sets in motion a life-long process of mutual hospitality between the two families. Once the marriage has taken place, the families will become part of each other's feminal kin. They will exchange gifts on some ritual occasions, open their houses to each other, and, of course, help one another make future marriages.

The Future of Indian Kinship

On our last trip to India in 1994, my wife and I learned that Rupani had delivered three children since her wedding. Kanji had visited them a few months before we arrived, and he said that Rupani was happy and that he had wonderful grandchildren. But he also mentioned that her husband now spent most of his time in the nearby city of Udaipur working in construction there. He sent money home, but his absence left Rupani to run the house and raise the children by herself, although she did so with the assistance of his parents and lineage mates.

Rupani's case is not unusual. Every morning 70 or 80 men board one of the 20 or so busses that travel the road, now paved, that runs through Ratakote to the city. There they wait to be recruited by contractors for day labor at a low wage. If they are successful, gain special skills, or make good connections, they may get more permanent, better-paying jobs and live for weeks at a time in the city.

The reason they have to take this kind of work is simple. Ratakote has more than doubled in population since 1962. (The village had a population of 1,184 in 1963. By 1994 an estimate put the number at about 2,600.) There is not enough land for everyone to farm nor can the land produce enough to feed the growing population, even in abundant years. Work in the city is the answer, especially for householders whose land is not irrigated like Kanji's.

Cash labor has a potential to break down the kinship system that Bhils value so highly. It frees men and women from economic dependence on the family (since they make their own money working for someone else). It takes up time, too, making it difficult for them to attend the leisurely eleven-day weddings of relatives or meet other obligations to kin that require their presence. With cash labor, one's reputation is likely to hinge less on family than on work. For some, work means moving the family altogether. Devaji Katara, one of Kanji's neighbors, has a son who has moved with his wife and children to the Central Indian city of Indore. He has a good factory job there, and the move has kept them together. By doing so, however, he and they are largely removed from the kinship loop.

Despite these structural changes, kinship in Ratakote and for India as a whole remains exceptionally strong. Even though they may live farther away, Bhil sons and daughters still visit their families regularly. They send money home, and they try to attend weddings. They talk about their kin, too, and surprisingly, they continue the long process of arranging marriage for their children.

Perhaps one reason for kinship's vitality is the use to which kinship is put by many Indians. The people of Ratakote and other Indians have never given up teaching their children to respect their elders and subordinate their interests to those of the family. Family loyalty is still a paramount value. They use this loyalty to help each other economically. Family members hire each other in business. They take one another in during hard times. They offer hospitality to each other. Unlike Americans who feel guilty about accepting one-sided help from relatives, Indians look to the future. Giving aid now may pay off with a job or a favor later. Even if it doesn't, it is the proper thing to do.

Instead of breaking up the kinship network, work that takes men and families away from the village has simply stretched it out. An Indian student I know has found relatives in every American city he has visited. He knows of kin in Europe and southeast Asia too. Anywhere he goes he is likely to have relatives to stay with and to help him. When he settles down he will be expected to return the favor. Another Indian acquaintance, who went to graduate school in the United States and who continues to work here, has sent his father thousands of dollars to help with the building of a house. This act, which would surprise many Americans, seems perfectly normal to him.

Kanji is not disturbed by the economic changes that are overtaking the quiet agricultural pace of Ratakote. I last left him standing in front of his house with a grandson in his arms. His son, who had left the village in 1982 to be a "wiper" on a truck, returned to run the farm. He will be able to meet the family's obligation to lineage and feminal kin. For Kanji, traditional rules of inheritance have pulled a son and, for the moment at least, a grandson, back into the bosom of the family where they belong.

Review Questions

1. What are the main ways that kinship organizes Bhil society in Ratakote, according to McCurdy?
2. What is meant by the terms *clan, lineage, family, patrilineal descent, patrilocal residence, alliance,* and *feminal kin group?* Give examples of each.
3. Why do Bhil parents feel that marriage is too important a matter to be left up to their children?

4. What attributes do Bhil parents look for in a prospective bride or groom? How do young people try to influence the marriage partner their parents choose for them?
5. Although the American kinship system seems limited by comparison to India's, many argue that it is more important than most of us think? Can you think of ways this might be true?

19

Polyandry: When Brothers Take a Wife

Melvyn C. Goldstein

Many of the world's societies permit polygamy, the marriage of an individual to more than one spouse. The most common form of polygamy is polygyny, an arrangement in which a man marries more than one wife. Polygyny may exist for many reasons, not the least of which is its relationship to the substantial economic contributions of women. But there is a second kind of polygamy called polyandry, organized around the marriage of a woman to more than one husband, and its causes may seem less clear. In this article, Melvyn Goldstein describes the fraternal polyandry practiced by Tibetans living in Northern Nepal and seeks to explain why, despite having a choice of marriage forms including monogamy and polygyny, men and women often choose this rare form of marriage. He argues that, by marrying a single wife, a group of brothers can more easily preserve their family resources, whereas monogamous or polygynous marriage usually costs a man his inheritance and requires him to make a fresh start.

Originally published as "When Brothers Take a Wife." With permission from *Natural History*, March 1987. Copyright © by the American Museum of Natural History, 1987.

Eager to reach home. Dorje drives his yaks hard over the seventeen-thousand-foot mountain pass, stopping only once to rest. He and his two older brothers, Pema and Sonam, are jointly marrying a woman from the next village in a few weeks, and he has to help with the preparations.

Dorje, Pema, and Sonam are Tibetans living in Limi, a two-hundred-square-mile area in the northwest corner of Nepal, across the border from Tibet. The form of marriage they are about to enter—fraternal polyandry in anthropological parlance—is one of the world's rarest forms of marriage but is not uncommon in Tibetan society, where it has been practiced from time immemorial. For many Tibetan social strata, it traditionally represented the ideal form of marriage and family.

The mechanics of fraternal polyandry are simple. Two, three, four, or more brothers jointly take a wife, who leaves her home to come and live with them. Traditionally, marriage was arranged by parents, with children, particularly females, having little or no say. This is changing somewhat nowadays, but it is still unusual for children to marry without their parents' consent. Marriage ceremonies vary by income and region and range from all the brothers sitting together as grooms to only the eldest one formally doing so. The age of the brothers plays an important role in determining this: very young brothers almost never participate in actual marriage ceremonies, although they typically join the marriage when they reach their midteens.

The eldest brother is normally dominant in terms of authority, that is, in managing the household, but all the brothers share the work and participate as sexual partners. Tibetan males and females do not find the sexual aspect of sharing a spouse the least bit unusual, repulsive, or scandalous, and the norm is for the wife to treat all the brothers the same.

Offspring are treated similarly. There is no attempt to link children biologically to particular brothers, and a brother shows no favoritism toward his child even if he knows he is the real father because, for example, his other brothers were away at the time the wife became pregnant. The children, in turn, consider all of the brothers as their fathers and treat them equally, even if they also know who is their real father. In some regions children use the term "father" for the eldest brother and "father's brother" for the others, while in other areas they call all the brothers by one term, modifying this by the use of "elder" and "younger."

Unlike our own society, where monogamy is the only form of marriage permitted, Tibetan society allows a variety of marriage types, including monogamy, fraternal polyandry, and polygyny. Fraternal polyandry and monogamy are the most common forms of marriage, while polygyny typically occurs in cases where the first wife is barren. The widespread practice of fraternal polyandry, therefore, is not the outcome of a law requiring brothers to marry jointly. There is choice, and in fact, divorce traditionally was relatively simple in Tibetan society. If a brother in a polyandrous marriage became dissatisfied and wanted to separate, he simply left the main house and set up his own household. In such cases, all the children stayed in the main household with the remaining brother(s), even if the departing brother was known to be the real father of one or more of the children.

The Tibetans' own explanation for choosing fraternal polyandry is materialistic. For example, when I asked Dorje why he decided to marry with his two brothers rather than take his own wife, he thought for a moment, then said it prevented the division of his family's farm (and animals) and thus facilitated all of them achieving a higher standard of living. And when I later asked Dorje's bride whether it wasn't difficult for her to cope with three brothers as husbands, she laughed and echoed the rationale of avoiding fragmentation of the family and land, adding that she expected to be better off economically, since she would have three husbands working for her and her children.

Exotic as it may seem to Westerners, Tibetan fraternal polyandry is thus in many ways analogous to the way primogeniture functioned in nineteenth-century England. Primogeniture dictated that the eldest son inherited the family estate, while younger sons had to leave home and seek their own employment—for example, in the military or the clergy. Primogeniture maintained family estates intact over generations by permitting only one heir per generation. Fraternal polyandry also accomplishes this but does so by keeping all the brothers together with just one wife so that there is only one *set* of heirs per generation.

While Tibetans believe that in this way fraternal polyandry reduces the risk of family fission, monogamous marriages among brothers need not necessarily precipitate the division of the family estate: brothers could continue to live together, and the family land could continue to be worked jointly. When I asked Tibetans about this, however, they invariably responded that such joint families are unstable because each wife is primarily oriented to her own children and interested in their success and well-being over that of the children of the other wives. For example, if the youngest brother's wife had three sons while the eldest brother's wife had only one daughter, the wife of the youngest brother might begin to demand more resources for her children since, as males, they represent the future of the family. Thus the children from different wives in the same generation are competing sets of heirs, and this makes such families inherently unstable. Tibetans perceive that conflict will spread from the wives to their husbands and consider this likely to cause family fission. Consequently, it is almost never done.

Although Tibetans see an economic advantage to fraternal polyandry, they do not value the sharing of a wife as an end in itself. On the contrary, they articulate a number of problems inherent in the practice. For example, because authority is customarily exercised by the eldest brother, his younger male siblings have to subordinate themselves with little hope of changing their status within the family. When these younger brothers are aggressive and individualistic, tensions and difficulties often occur despite there being only one set of heirs.

In addition, tension and conflict may arise in polyandrous families because of sexual favoritism. The bride normally sleeps with the eldest brother, and the two have the responsibility to see to it that the other males have opportunities for sexual access. Since the Tibetan subsistence economy requires males to travel a lot, the temporary absence of one or more brothers facilitates this, but there are also other rotation practices. The cultural ideal unambiguously calls for the wife to show equal affection and sexuality to each of the brothers (and vice versa), but deviations from this ideal occur, especially when there is a sizable difference in age between the partners in the marriage.

Dorje's family represents just such a potential situation. He is fifteen years old and his two older brothers are twenty-five and twenty-two years old. The new bride is twenty-three years old, eight years Dorje's senior. Sometimes such a bride finds the youngest husband immature and adolescent and does not treat him with equal affection; alternatively, she may find his youth attractive and lavish special attention on him. Apart from that consideration, when a younger male like Dorje grows up, he may consider his wife "ancient" and prefer the company of a woman his own age or younger. Consequently, although men and women do not find the idea of sharing a bride or a bridegroom repulsive, individual likes and dislikes can cause familial discord.

Two reasons have commonly been offered for the perpetuation of fraternal polyandry in Tibet: that Tibetans practice female infanticide and therefore have to marry polyandrously, owing to a shortage of females; and that Tibet, lying at extremely high altitudes, is so barren and bleak that Tibetans would starve without resort to this mechanism. A Jesuit who lived in Tibet during the eighteenth century articulated this second view: "One reason for this most odious custom is the sterility of the soil, and the small amount of land that can be cultivated owing to the lack of water. The crops may suffice if the brothers all live together, but if they form separate families they would be reduced to beggary."

Both explanations are wrong, however. Not only has there never been institutionalized female infanticide in Tibet, but Tibetan society gives females considerable rights, including inheriting the family estate in the absence of brothers. In such cases, the woman takes a bridegroom who comes to live in her family and adopts her family's name and identity. Moreover, there is no demographic evidence of a shortage of females. In Limi, for example, there were (in 1974) sixty females and fifty-three males in the fifteen- to thirty-five-year age category, and many adult females were unmarried.

The second reason is incorrect because the climate in Tibet is extremely harsh, and ecological factors do play a major role in perpetuating polyandry, but polyandry is not a means of preventing starvation. It is characteristic, not of the poorest segments of the society, but rather of the peasant landowning families.

In the old society, the landless poor could not realistically aspire to prosperity, but they did not fear starvation. There was a persistent labor shortage throughout Tibet, and very poor families with little or no land and few animals could subsist through agricultural labor, tenant farming, craft occupations such as carpentry, or by working as servants. Although the per-person family income could increase somewhat if brothers married polyandrously and pooled their wages, in the absence of inheritable land, the advantage of fraternal polyandry was not generally sufficient to prevent them from setting up their own households. A more skilled or energetic younger brother could do as well or better alone, since he would completely control his income and would not have to share it with his siblings. Consequently, while there was and is some polyandry among the poor, it is much less frequent and more prone to result in divorce and family fission.

An alternative reason for the persistence of fraternal polyandry is that it reduces population growth (and thereby reduces the pressure on resources) by relegating some females to lifetime spinsterhood (see Figure 1). Fraternal polyandrous marriages in Limi (in 1974) averaged 2.35 men per woman, and not surprisingly, 31 percent of the females of child-bearing age (twenty to forty-nine) were unmarried. These spinsters either continued to live at home, set up their own households, or worked as servants for other families. They could also become Buddhist nuns. Being unmarried is not synonymous with exclusion from the reproductive pool. Discreet extramarital relationships are tolerated, and actually half of the adult unmarried women in Limi had one or more children. They raised these children as single mothers, working for wages or weaving cloth and blankets for sale. As a group, however, the unmarried women had far fewer offspring than the married women, averaging only 0.7 children per woman, compared with 3.3 for married women, whether polyandrous, monogamous, or polygynous. When polyandry helps regulate population, this function of polyandry is not consciously perceived by Tibetans and is not the reason they consistently choose it.

If neither a shortage of females nor the fear of starvation perpetuates fraternal polyandry, what motivates brothers, particularly younger brothers, to opt for this system of marriage? From the perspective of the younger brother in a landholding family, the main incentive is the attainment or maintenance of the good life. With polyandry, he can expect a more secure and higher standard of living, with access not only to his family's land and animals but also to its inherited collection of clothes, jewelry, rugs, saddles, and horses. In addition, he will experience less work pressure and much greater security because all responsibility does not fall on one "father." For Tibetan brothers, the question is whether to trade off the greater personal freedom inherent in monogamy for the real or potential economic security, affluence, and social prestige associated with life in a larger, labor-rich polyandrous family.

A brother thinking of separating from his polyandrous marriage and taking his own wife would face various disadvantages. Although in the majority of Tibetan regions all brothers theoretically have rights to their family's estate, in reality Tibetans are reluctant to divide their land into small fragments. Generally, a younger brother who insists on leaving the family will receive only a small plot of land, if that. Because of its power and wealth, the rest of the family usually can block any attempt of the younger brother to increase his share of land through litigation. Moreover, a younger brother may not even get a house and cannot expect to receive much above the minimum in terms of movable possessions, such as furniture, pots, and pans. Thus a

Figure 1
Family planning in Tibet

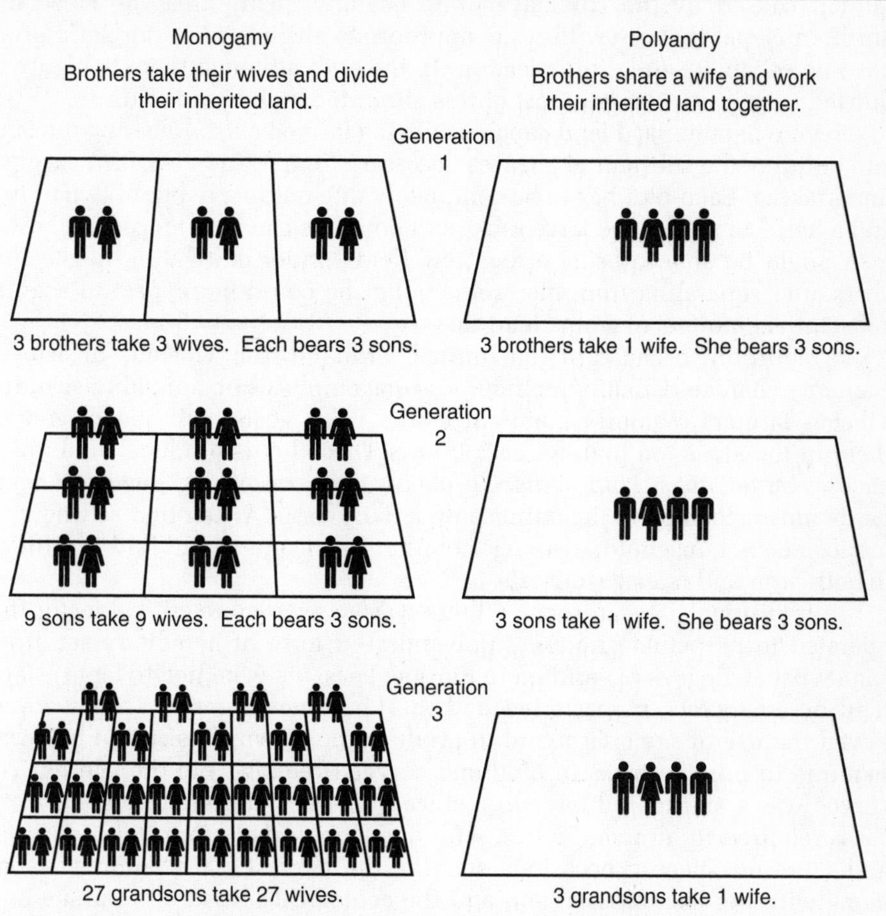

An economic rationale for fraternal polyandry is outlined in the diagram above, which emphasizes only the male offspring in each generation. If every wife is assumed to bear three sons, a family splitting up into monogamous households would rapidly multiply and fragment the family land. In this case, a rule of inheritance, such as primogeniture, could retain the family land intact, but only at the cost of creating many landless male offspring. In contrast, the family practicing fraternal polyandry maintains a steady ratio of persons to land.

brother contemplating going it on his own must plan on achieving economic security and the good life not through inheritance but through his own work.

The obvious solution for younger brothers—creating new fields from virgin land—is generally not a feasible option. Most Tibetan populations live at high altitudes (above 12,000 feet), where arable land is extremely scarce. For example, in Dorje's village, agriculture ranges only from about 12,900 feet, the lowest point in the area, to 13,300 feet. Above that altitude, early frost and snow destroy the staple barley crop. Furthermore, because of the low rainfall caused by the Himalayan rain shadow, many areas in Tibet and northern Nepal that are within the appropriate altitude range for agriculture have no reliable sources of irrigation. In the end, although there is plenty of unused land in such areas, most of it is either too high or too arid.

Even where unused land capable of being farmed exists, clearing the land and building the substantial terraces necessary for irrigation constitute a great undertaking. Each plot has to be completely dug out to a depth of two to two and a half feet so that the large rocks and boulders can be removed. At best, a man might be able to bring a few new fields under cultivation in the first years after separating from his brothers, but he could not expect to acquire substantial amounts of arable land this way.

In addition, because of the limited farmland, the Tibetan subsistence economy characteristically includes a strong emphasis on animal husbandry. Tibetan farmers regularly maintain cattle, yaks, goats, and sheep, grazing them in the areas too high for agriculture. These herds produce wool, milk, cheese, butter, meat, and skins. To obtain these resources, however, shepherds must accompany the animals on a daily basis. When first setting up a monogamous household, a younger brother like Dorje would find it difficult to both farm and manage animals.

In traditional Tibetan society, there was an even more critical factor that operated to perpetuate fraternal polyandry—a form of hereditary servitude somewhat analogous to serfdom in Europe. Peasants were tied to large estates held by aristocrats, monasteries, and the Lhasa government. They were allowed the use of some farmland to produce their own subsistence but were required to provide taxes in kind and corvée (free labor) to their lords. The corvée was a substantial hardship, since a peasant household was in many cases required to furnish the lord with one laborer daily for most of the year and more on specific occasions such as the harvest. This enforced labor, along with the lack of new land and the ecological pressure to pursue both agriculture and animal husbandry, made polyandrous families particularly beneficial. The polyandrous family allowed an internal division of adult labor, maximizing economic advantage. For example, while the wife worked the family fields, one brother could perform the lord's corvée, another could look after the animals, and a third could engage in trade.

Although social scientists often discount other people's explanations of why they do things, in the case of Tibetan fraternal polyandry, such explanations are very close to the truth. The custom, however, is very sensitive to changes in its political and economic milieu and, not surprisingly, is in decline in most Tibetan areas. Made less important by the elimination of the traditional serf-based economy, it is disparaged by the dominant non-Tibetan leaders of India, China, and Nepal. New opportunities for economic and social mobility in these countries, such as the tourist trade and government employment, are also eroding the rationale for polyandry, and so it may vanish within the next generation.

Review Questions

1. What is fraternal polyandry, and how does this form of marriage manage potential conflict over sex, children, and inheritance?
2. Why do many Tibetans choose polyandry over monogamous or polygynous marriage?
3. According to Tibetans, what are some of the disadvantages of polyandry?
4. What is wrong with the theory that Tibetan polyandry is caused either by a shortage of women due to infanticide or is a way to prevent famine by limiting population and land pressure?
5. Why might Tibetan polyandry disappear under modern conditions?

20

Uterine Families and the Women's Community

Margery Wolf

The size and organization of extended families vary from one society to the next, but extended families often share some important attributes. They are most often based on a rule of patrilineal descent. For men, the patrilineal family extends in an unbroken line of ancestors and descendants. Membership is permanent; loyalty assured. For women, the patrilineal family is temporary. Born into one family and married into another, women discover that their happiness and interests depend on bearing children to create their own uterine family. This and the importance of a local women's group are the subjects of this article by Margery Wolf in her discussion of Taiwanese family life.

Few women in China experience the continuity that is typical of the lives of the menfolk. A woman can and, if she is ever to have any eco-

Reprinted from *Women and the Family in Rural Taiwan* by Margery Wolf with the permission of the publishers, Stanford University Press. Copyright © by the Board of Trustees of the Leland Stanford Junior University, 1972.

nomic security, must provide the links in the male chain of descent, but she will never appear in anyone's genealogy as that all-important name connecting the past to the future. If she dies before she is married, her tablet will not appear on her father's altar; although she was a temporary member of his household, she was not a member of his family. A man is born into his family and remains a member of it throughout his life and even after his death. He is identified with the family from birth, and every action concerning him, up to and including his death, is in the context of that group. Whatever other uncertainties may trouble his life, his place in the line of ancestors provides a permanent setting. There is no such secure setting for a woman. She will abruptly leave the household into which she is born, either as an infant or as an adult bride, and enter another whose members treat her with suspicion or even hostility.

A man defines his family as a large group that includes the dead, and not-yet-born, and the living members of his household. But how does a woman define her family? This is not a question that China specialists often consider, but from their treatment of the family in general, it would seem that a woman's family is identical with that of the senior male in the household in which she lives. Although I have never asked, I imagine a Taiwanese man would define a woman's family in very much those same terms. Women, I think, would give quite a different answer. They do not have an unchanging place, assigned at birth, in any group, and their view of the family reflects this.

When she is a child, a woman's family is defined for her by her mother and to some extent by her grandmother. No matter how fond of his daughter the father may be, she is only a temporary member of his household and useless to his family—he cannot even marry her to one of his sons as he could an adopted daughter. Her irrelevance to her father's family in turn affects the daughter's attitude toward it. It is of no particular interest to her, and the need to maintain its continuity has little meaning for her beyond the fact that this continuity matters a great deal to some of the people she loves. As a child she probably accepts to some degree her grandmother's orientation toward the family: the household, that is, those people who live together and eat together, including perhaps one or more of her father's married brothers and their children. But the group that has the most meaning for her and with which she will have the most lasting ties is the smaller, more cohesive unit centering on her mother, that is, the uterine family—her mother and her mother's children. Father is important to the group, just as grandmother is important to some of the children, but he is not quite a member of it, and for some uterine families he may even be "the enemy." As the girl grows up and her grandmother dies and a brother or two marries, she discovers that her mother's definition of the family is becoming less exclusive and may even include such outsiders as her brother's new wife. Without knowing precisely when it happened, she finds that her brother's interests and goals have shifted in a direction she cannot follow. Her mother does not push her aside, but when the mother speaks of the future, she speaks in terms of her son's future. Although the mother sees her uterine family as adding new members and another generation, her daughter sees it as dissolving, leaving her with strong particular relationships, but with no group to which she has permanent loyalties and obligations.

When a young woman marries, her formal ties with the household of her father are severed. In one of the rituals of the wedding ceremony the bride's father or brothers symbolically inform her by means of spilt water that she, like the water, may never return, and when her wedding sedan chair passes over the threshold of her father's house, the doors are slammed shut behind her. If she is ill-treated by her husband's family, her father's family may intervene, but unless her parents are willing to bring her home and support her for the rest of her life (and most parents are not), there is little they can do beyond shaming the other family. This is usually enough.

As long as her mother is alive, the daughter will continue her contacts with her father's household by as many visits as her new situation allows. If she lives nearby she may visit every few days, and no matter where she lives she must at least be allowed to return at New Year. After her mother dies her visits may become perfunctory, but her relations with at least one member of her uterine family, the group that centered on her mother, remain strong. Her brother plays an important ritual role throughout her life. She may gradually lose contact with her sisters as she and they become more involved with their own children, but her relations with her brother continue. When her sons marry, he is the guest of honor at the wedding feasts, and when her daughters marry he must give a small banquet in their honor. If her sons wish to divide their father's estate, it is their mother's brother who is called on to supervise. And when she dies, the coffin cannot be closed until her brother determines to his own satisfaction that she died a natural death and that her husband's family did everything possible to prevent it.

With the ritual slam of her father's door on her wedding day, a young woman finds herself quite literally without a family. She enters the household of her husband—a man who in an earlier time, say fifty years ago, she would never have met and who even today, in modern rural Taiwan, she is unlikely to know very well. She is an outsider, and for Chinese an outsider is always an object of deep suspicion. Her husband and her father-in-law do not see her as a member of their family. But they do see her as essential to it; they have gone to great expense to bring her into their household for the purpose of bearing a new generation for their family. Her mother-in-law, who was mainly responsible for negotiating the terms of her entry, may harbor some resentment over the hard bargaining, but she is nonetheless eager to see another generation added to *her* uterine family. A mother-in-law often has the same kind of ambivalence toward her daughter-in-law as she has toward her husband—the younger woman seems a member of her family at times and merely a member of the household at others. The new bride may find that her husband's sister is hostile or at best condescending, both attitudes reflecting the daughter's distress at an outsider who seems to be making her way right into the heart of the family.

Chinese children are taught by proverb, by example, and by experience that the family is the source of their security, and relatives the only people who can be depended on. Ostracism from the family is one of the harshest sanctions that can be imposed on erring youth. One of the reasons mainlanders as individuals are considered so untrustworthy on Taiwan is the fact that they are not subject to the controls of (and therefore have no fear of ostracism from) their families. If a timid new bride is considered an object of suspicion and potentially dangerous because she is a stranger, think how uneasy her own first few months must be surrounded by strangers. Her irrelevance to her father's family may result in her having little reverence for descent lines, but she has warm memories of the security of the family her mother created. If she is ever to return to this certainty and sense of belonging, a woman must create her own uterine family by bearing children, a goal that happily corresponds to the goals of the family into which she has married. She may gradually create a tolerable niche for herself in the household of her mother-in-law, but her family will not be formed until she herself forms it of her own children and grandchildren. In most cases, by the time she adds grandchildren, the uterine family and the household will almost completely overlap, and there will be another daughter-in-law struggling with loneliness and beginning a new uterine family.

The ambiguity of a man's position in relation to the uterine families accounts for much of the hostility between mother-in-law and daughter-in-law. There is no question in the mind of the older woman but that her son *is* her family. The daughter-in-law might be content with this situation once her sons are old enough to represent her interests in the household and in areas strictly under men's control, but until then, she is dependent on her husband. If she were to be completely absorbed into her mother-in-law's family—a rare occurrence unless she is a *simpua*—there would be little or no conflict; but under most circumstances she must rely on her husband, her mother-in-law's son, as her spokesman, and here is where the trouble begins. Since it is usually events within the household that she wishes to affect, and the household more or less overlaps with her mother-in-law's uterine family, even a minor foray by the younger woman suggests to the older one an all-out attack on everything she has worked so hard to build in the years of her own loneliness and insecurity. The birth of grandchildren further complicates their relations, for the one sees them as new members for her family and the other as desperately needed recruits to her own small circle of security.

In summary, my thesis contends . . . that because we have heretofore focused on men when examining the Chinese family—a reasonable approach to a patrilineal system—we have missed not only some of the system's subtleties but also its near-fatal weaknesses. With a male focus we see the Chinese family as a line of descent, bulging to encompass all the members of a man's household and spreading out through his descendants. With a female focus, however, we see the Chinese family not as a continuous line stretching between the vague horizons of past and future, but as a contemporary group that comes into existence out of one woman's need and is held together insofar as she has the strength to do so, or, for that matter, the need to do so. After her death the uterine family survives only in the mind of her son and is symbolized by the special attention he gives her earthly remains and her ancestral tablet. The rites themselves are demanded by the ideology of the patriliny, but the meaning they hold for most sons is formed in the uterine family. The uterine family has no ideology, no formal structure, and no public existence. It is built out of sentiments and loyalties that die with its members, but it is no less real for all that. The descent lines of men are born and nourished in the uterine families of women, and it is here that a male ideology that excludes women makes its accommodations with reality.

Women in rural Taiwan do not live their lives in the walled courtyards of their husband's households. If they did, they might be as powerless as their stereotype. It is in their relations in the outside world (and for women in rural Taiwan that world consists almost entirely of the village) that women develop sufficient backing to maintain some independence under their powerful mothers-in-law and even occasionally to bring the men's world to terms. A successful venture into the men's world is no small feat when one recalls that the men of a village were born there and are often related to one another, whereas the women are unlikely to have either the ties of childhood or the ties of kinship to unite them. All the same, the needs, shared interests, and common problems of women are reflected in every village in a loosely knit society that can when needed be called on to exercise considerable influence.

Women carry on as many of their activities as possible outside the house. They wash clothes on the riverbank, clean and pare vegetables at a communal pump, mend under a tree that is a known meetingplace, and stop to rest on a bench or group of stones with other women. There is a continual moving back and forth between kitchens, and conversations are carried on from open doorways through the long, hot afternoons of summer. The shy young girl who enters the village as a bride is examined as frankly and suspiciously by the women as an animal that is up for sale. If she is deferential to her elders, does not criticize or compare her new world unfavorably with the one she has left, the older residents will gradually accept her presence on the edge of their conversations and stop changing the topic to general subjects when she brings the family laundry to scrub on the rocks near them. As the young bride meets other girls in her position, she makes allies for the future, but she must also develop relationships with the older women. She learns to use considerable discretion in making and receiving confidences, for a girl who gossips freely about the affairs of her husband's household may find herself labeled a troublemaker. On the other hand, a girl who is too reticent may find herself always on the outside of the group, or worse yet, accused of snobbery. I described in *The House of Lim* the plight of Lim Chui-ieng, who had little village backing in her troubles with her husband and his family as the result of her arrogance toward the women's community. In Peihotien the young wife of the storekeeper's son suffered a similar lack of support. Warned by her husband's parents not to be too "easy" with the other villagers lest they try to buy things on credit, she obeyed to the point of being considered unfriendly by the women of the village. When she began to have serious troubles with her husband and eventually his family, there was no one in the village she could turn to for solace, advice, and, most important, peacemaking.

Once a young bride has established herself as a member of the women's community, she has also established for herself a certain amount of protection. If the members of her husband's family step beyond the limits of propriety in their treatment of her—such as refusing to allow her to return to her natal home for her brother's wedding or beating her without serious justification—she can complain to a woman friend, preferably older, while they are washing vegetables at the communal pump. The story will quickly spread to the other women, and one of them will take it on herself to check the facts with another member of the girl's household. For a few days the matter will be thoroughly discussed whenever a few women gather. In a young wife's first few years in the community, she can expect to have her mother-in-law's side of any disagreement given fuller weight than her own—her mother-in-law has, after all, been a part of the community a lot longer. However, the discussion itself will serve to curb many offenses. Even if the older woman knows that public opinion is falling to her side, she will still be somewhat more judicious about refusing her daughter-in-law's next request. Still, the daughter-in-law who hopes to make use of the village forum to depose her mother-in-law or at least gain herself special privilege will discover just how important the prerogatives of age and length of residence are. Although the women can serve as a powerful protective force for their defenseless younger members, they are also a very conservative force in the village.

Taiwanese women can and do make use of their collective power to lose face for their menfolk in order to influence decisions that are ostensibly not theirs to make. Although young women may have little or no influence over their husbands and would not dare express an unsolicited opinion (and perhaps not even a solicited one) to their fathers-in-law, older women who have raised their sons properly retain considerable influence over their sons' actions, even in activities exclusive to men. Further, older women who have displayed years of good judgment are regularly consulted by their husbands about major as well as minor economic and social projects. But even men who think themselves free to ignore the opinions of their women are never free of their own concept, face. It is much easier to lose face than to have face. We once asked a male friend in Peihotien just what "having face" amounted to. He replied, "When no one is talking about a family, you can say it has face." This is precisely where women wield their power. When a man behaves in a way that they consider wrong, they talk about him—not only among themselves, but to their sons and husbands. No one "tells him how to mind his own business," but it becomes abundantly clear that he is losing face and by continuing in this manner may bring shame to the family of his ancestors and descendants. Few men will risk that.

The rules that a Taiwanese man must learn and obey to be a successful member of his society are well developed, clear, and relatively easy to stay within. A Taiwanese woman must also learn the rules, but if she is to be a successful woman, she must learn not to stay within them, but to *appear* to stay within them; to manipulate them, but not to appear to be manipulating them; to teach them to her children, but not to depend on her children for her protection. A truly successful Taiwanese woman is a rugged individualist who has learned to depend largely on herself while appearing to lean on her father, her husband, and her son. The contrast between the terrified young bride and the loud, confident, often lewd old woman who has outlived her mother-in-law and her husband reflects the tests met and passed by not strictly following the rules and by making purposeful use of those who must. The Chinese male's conception of women as "narrow-hearted" and socially inept may well be his vague recognition of this facet of women's power and technique.

The women's subculture in rural Taiwan is, I believe, below the level of consciousness. Mothers do not tell their about-to-be-married daughters how to establish themselves in village society so that they may have some protection from an oppressive family situation, nor do they warn them to gather their children into an exclusive circle under their own control. But girls grow up in village society and see their mothers and sisters-in-law settling their differences to keep them from a public airing or presenting them for the women's community to judge. Their mothers have created around them the meaningful unit in their father's households, and when they are desperately lonely and unhappy in the households of their husbands, what they long for is what they have lost. . . . [Some] areas in the subculture of women . . . mesh perfectly into the main culture of the society. The two cultures are not symbiotic because they are not sufficiently independent of one another, but neither do they share identical goals or necessarily use the same means to reach the goals they do share. Outside the village the women's subculture seems not to exist. The uterine family also has no public existence, and appears almost as a response to the traditional family organized in terms of a male ideology.

Review Questions

1. According to Wolf, what is a uterine family, and what relatives are likely to be members?
2. Why is the uterine family important to Chinese women who live in their husband's patrilineal extended families?
3. What is the relationship between a woman's uterine family and her power within her husband's family?
4. Why might the existence of the uterine family contribute to the division of extended families into smaller constituent parts?
5. How do you think a Chinese woman's desire to have a uterine family affects attempts to limit the Chinese population?

7

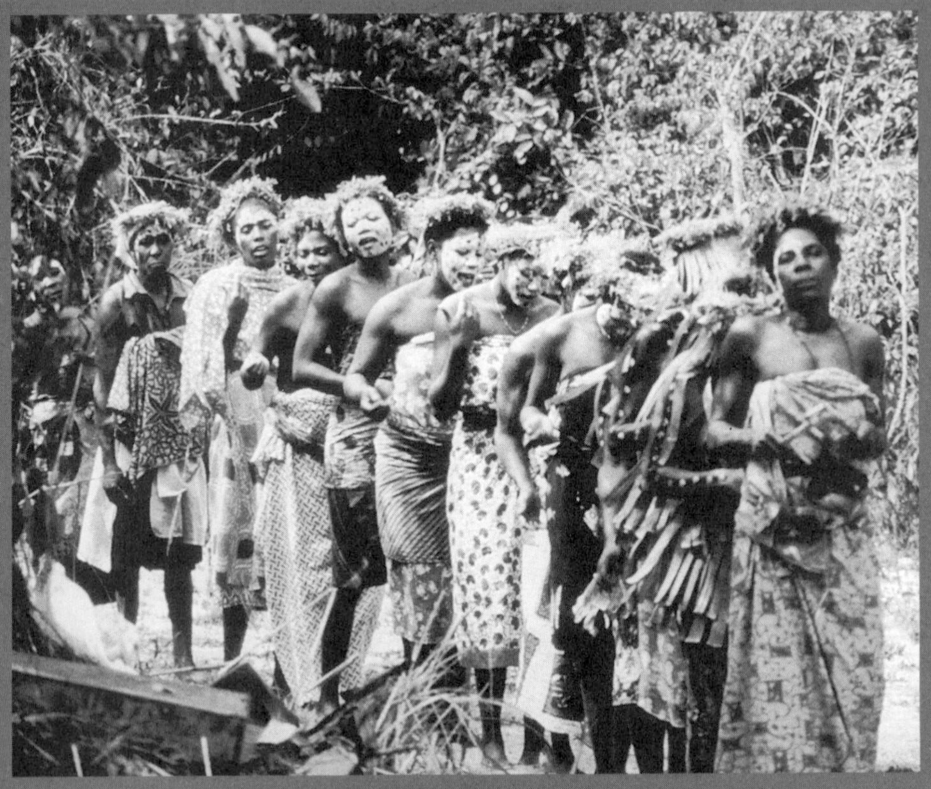

ROLES AND INEQUALITY

For most of us, social interaction is unconscious and automatic. We associate with other people from the time we are born. Of course we experience moments when we feel socially awkward and out of place, but generally we learn to act toward others with confidence. Yet our unconscious ease masks an enormously complex process. When we enter a social situation, how do we know what to do? What should we say? How are we supposed to act? Are we dressed appropriately? Are we talking to the right person? Without knowing it, we have learned a complex set of cultural categories for social interaction that enables us to estimate the social situation, identify the people in it, act appropriately, and recognize larger groups of people.

Status and role are basic to social intercourse. *Status* refers to the categories of different kinds of people who interact. The old saying, "You can't tell the players without a program," goes for our daily associations as well. Instead of a program, however, we identify the actors by a range of signs, from the way they dress to the claims they make about themselves. Most statuses are named, so we may be heard to say things like, "That's President Gavin," or "She's a lawyer," when we explain social situations to others. This identification of actors is a prerequisite for appropriate social interaction.

Roles are the rules for action associated with particular statuses. We use them to interpret and generate social behavior. For example, a professor plays a role in the classroom. Although often not conscious of this role, the professor will stand, use the blackboard, look at notes, and speak with a slightly more formal air than usual. The professor does not wear blue jeans and a T-shirt, chew gum, sit cross-legged on the podium, or sing. These actions might be appropriate for this person when assuming the identity of "friend" at a party, but they are out of place in the classroom.

People also always relate to each other in *social situations,* the settings in which social interaction takes place. Social situations consist of a combination of times, places, objects, and events. For example, if we see a stranger carrying a television set across campus at four o'clock in the afternoon, we will probably ignore the activity. Most likely someone is simply moving. But if we see the same person carrying the set at four in the morning, we may suspect a theft. Only the time has changed, but it is a significant marker of the social situation. Similarly, we expect classrooms to be associated with lectures, and stethoscopes to be part of medical exams. Such places and objects mark the social situations of which they are part.

Some degree of *inequality* is part of most human interaction. One spouse may dominate another; a child may receive more attention than his or her siblings; the boss's friends may be promoted faster than other employees. But inequality becomes most noticeable when it systematically affects whole classes of people. In its most obvious form, inequality emerges as *social stratification,* which is characterized by regularly experienced unequal access to valued economic resources and prestige.

Anthropologists recognize at least two kinds of social stratification: class and caste. *Class* stratification restricts individuals' access to valued resources and prestige within a partially flexible system. Although it is often a difficult process, individuals may change rank in a class system if they manage to acquire the necessary prerequisites.

Many sociologists and anthropologists believe that there is an American class system and use terms such as *lower class, working class, middle class,* and *upper class* to designate the unequal positions within it. Americans born into poverty lack access to goods and prestige in this system but can change class standing if they acquire wealth and symbols of higher standing on a continuing basis. Upward mobility is difficult to achieve, however, and few people at the bottom of the system manage to change rank significantly. Indeed, many social scientists feel there is now a permanent underclass in the United States.

Caste defines a second kind of social stratification, one based on permanent membership. People are born into castes and cannot change membership, no matter what they do. In India, for example, caste is a pervasive feature of social organization. South Asians are born into castes and remain members for life; intercaste marriage is forbidden. In the past, castes formed the building blocks of rural Indian society. They were governed by strict rules of deference and served to allocate access to jobs, land, wealth, and power. Cash labor and new industrial jobs have eroded the economic aspect of the system today, but caste persists as a form of rank throughout most of the Indian subcontinent.

Several anthropologists and sociologists have argued that American racial groups are the equivalent of Indian castes. Black and white Americans keep their racial identity for life; nothing can change one's race. Racial identity clearly affects chances for the acquisition of prestige and economic success.

Caste identity, whether Indian or American, tends to preserve and create cultural difference. There is noticeable cultural variation among members of castes in most Indian villages, just as cultural variation occurs among black and white people in the United States.

Using the idea of social stratification, anthropologists have constructed a rough classification of societies into three types: egalitarian, rank, and stratified. *Egalitarian societies* lack formal social stratification. They may display inequality in personal relations based on age, gender, or personal ability, but no category of persons within the same sex or age group has special privilege. Hunter-gatherer societies are most likely to be egalitarian.

Rank societies contain unequal access to prestige, but not to valued economic resources. In such societies there may be chiefs or other persons with authority and prestige, and they may gain access to rank by birth, but their positions give them no substantial economic advantage. Horticultural societies, including some chiefdomships, fit this category.

Stratified societies organize around formal modes of social stratification, as their name suggests. Members of stratified societies are likely to form classes or castes, and inequality affects access to both prestige and economic resources. Most complex societies, including agrarian and industrialized states, fit into this type.

Inequality may also be based on other human attributes, such as age and gender. In many societies, including our own, age and gender affect access to prestige, power, and resources. It is common for men to publicly outrank women along these dimensions, particularly in societies threatened by war or other adversity that requires male intervention.

The articles in this part explore the nature of status, role, and inequality. The first, by Elizabeth and Robert Fernea, describes the importance of the veil as a symbol defining the role and rank of women in the Middle East. The second selection, by Ernestine Friedl, explores the reasons behind difference in power experienced by women in hunting and gathering societies. Friedl concludes that women's power is governed by access to control over public resources. The third article, by Mark Cohen, looks at the way Americans have used the concept of IQ and IQ test results to explain why poor people and some racial groups are less successful in American society. He argues that IQ tests ignore deep cultural differences even when they are claimed to be culture neutral and cross-culturally applicable. In the final selection, Lincoln Keiser, whose original study of the Vice Lords, a Chicago gang, is an anthropological classic and explains why gangs persist or reappear in America today despite official attempts to stamp them out. Linking them to inner city poverty and the difficult conditions found in penitentiaries where many poor men end up, he points out that gangs serve positive functions for their members.

Key Terms

status	class
role	caste
social situation	egalitarian societies
inequality	rank societies
social stratification	stratified societies

Readings in This Section

Symbolizing Roles: Behind the Veil *Elizabeth W. Fernea and Robert A. Fernea,* page *235*

Society and Sex Roles *Ernestine Friedl,* page *243*

Culture, Rank, and IQ: The Bell Curve Phenomenon *Mark Nathan Cohen,* page *252*

The Vice Lord Phoenix *Lincoln Keiser,* page *259*

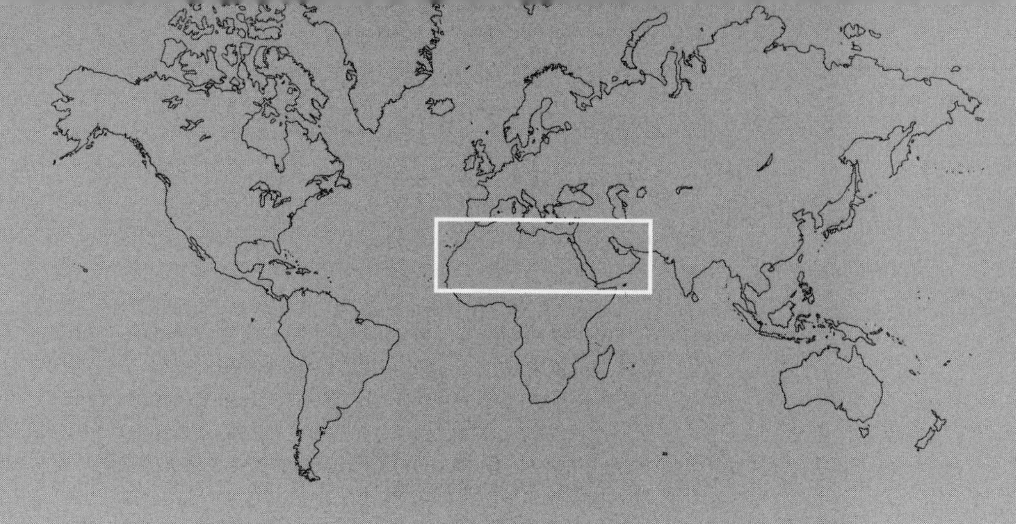

21

Symbolizing Roles: Behind the Veil

Elizabeth W. Fernea and Robert A. Fernea

Most societies have some things that serve as key symbols. The flag of the United States, for example, stands not only for the nation, but for a variety of important values that guide American behavior and perception. In this article, Elizabeth and Robert Fernea trace the meaning of another key symbol: the veil worn by women in the Middle East. Instead of reference to a national group, the veil codes many of the values surrounding the role of women. Often viewed by Westerners as a symbol of female restriction and inequality, for the women who wear it the veil signals honor, personal protection, the sanctity and privacy of the family, wealth and high status, and city life.

Blue jeans have come to mean America all over the world; three-piece wool suits signal businessmen; and in the 1980s pink or green air said "punk." What do we notice, however, in societies other than our own? Ishi,

This article was written for this book. Copyright © by Elizabeth Fernea and Robert Fernea, 1986. Reprinted by permission of the authors.

the last of a "lost" tribe of North American Indians who stumbled into twentieth-century California in 1911, is reported to have said that the truly interesting objects in the white culture were pockets and matches. Rifa'ah Tahtawi, one of the first young Egyptians to be sent to Europe to study in 1826, wrote an account of French society in which he noted that Parisians used many unusual objects of dress, among them something called a belt. Women wore belts, he said, apparently to keep their bosoms erect, and to show off the slimness of their waists and the fullness of their hips. Europeans are still fascinated by the Stetson hats worn by American cowboys; an elderly Dutch woman of our acquaintance recently carried six enormous Stetsons back to the Hague as presents for the male members of her family.

Like languages (Inca, French) or food (tacos, hamburgers), clothing has special meaning for people who wear it that strangers may not understand. But some objects become charged with meaning to other cultures. The veil is one article of clothing used in Middle Eastern societies that stirs strong emotions in the West. "The feminine veil has become a symbol: that of the slavery of one portion of humanity," wrote French ethnologist Germaine Tillion in 1966. A hundred years earlier, Sir Richard Burton, British traveler, explorer, and translator of the *Arabian Nights,* recorded a different view. "Europeans inveigh against this article [the face veil] . . . for its hideousness and jealous concealment of charms made to be admired," he wrote in 1855. "It is, on the contrary, the most coquettish article of women's attire . . . it conceals coarse skins, fleshy noses, wide mouths and vanishing chins, whilst it sets off to best advantage what in these lands is most lustrous and liquid—the eye. Who has not remarked this at a masquerade ball?"

In the present generation, the veil has become a focus of attention for Western writers, both popular and academic, who take a measure of Burton's irony and Tillion's anger to equate modernization of the Middle East with the discarding of the veil and to look at its return in Iran and in a number of Arab countries as a sure sign of retrogression. "Iran's 16 million women have come a long way since their floor-length cotton veil officially was abolished in 1935," an article noted in the 1970s, just before the Shah was toppled. Today [1986], with Ayatollah Khomeini in power, those 16 million Iranian women have put their veils back on again, as if to say that the long way they have come is not in the direction of the West.

The thousands of words written about the appearance and disappearance of the veil and of *purdah* (the seclusion of women) do little to help us understand the Middle East or the cultures that grew out of the same Judeo-Christian roots as our own. The veil and the all-enveloping garments that inevitably accompany it (the *milayah* in Egypt, the *abbayah* in Iraq, the *chadoor* in Iran, the *yashmak* in Turkey, the *burga'* in Afghanistan, and the *djellabah* and the *haik* in North Africa) are only the outward manifestations of cultural practices and meanings that are rooted deep in the history of Mediterranean and Southwest Asian society and are now finding expression once again. Today, with the resurgence of Islam, the veil has become a statement of difference between the Middle East and the Western world, a boundary no easier to cross now than it was during the Crusades or during the nineteenth century, when Western colonial powers ruled the area.

In English, the world *veil* has many definitions, and some of them are religious, just as in the Middle East. In addition to a face cover, the term also means "a piece of material worn over the head and shoulders, a part of a nun's head dress." The Arabic word for veiling and secluding comes from the root word *hajaba,* meaning "barrier." A *hijab* is an amulet worn to keep away the evil eye; it also means a diaphragm used to prevent conception. The gatekeeper or doorkeeper who guards the entrance to a government minister's office is a *hijab,* and in a casual conversation a person might say, "I want to be more informal with my friend so-and-so, but she always puts a *hijab* [barrier] between us."

In Islam, the Koranic verse that sanctions a barrier between men and women is called the Sura of the *hijab* (curtain): "Prophet, enjoin your wives, your daughters and the wives of true believers to draw their garments close round them. That is more proper, so that they may be recognized and not molested. Allah is forgiving and merciful." Notice, however, that veils of the first true believers did not conceal but rather announced the religious status of the women who wore them, drawing attention to the fact that they were Muslims and therefore to be treated with respect. The special Islamic dress worn by increasing numbers of modern Muslim women has much the same effect; it also says, "Treat me with respect."

Certainly some form of seclusion and of veiling was practiced before the time of Muhammad, at least among the urban elites and ruling families, but it was his followers, the first converts to Islam, who used veiling to signal religious faith. According to historic traditions, the *hijab* was established after the wives of the Prophet Muhammad were insulted by people coming to the mosque in search of the Prophet. Muhammad's wives, they said, had been mistaken for slaves. The custom of the *hijab* was thus established, and in the words of historian Nabia Abbott, "Muhammad's women found themselves, on the one hand, deprived of personal liberty, and on the other hand, raised to a position of honor and dignity." It is true, nonetheless, that the forms and uses of veiling and seclusion have varied greatly in practice over the last thousand years since the time of the Prophet, and millions of Muslim women have never been veiled at all. It is a luxury poorer families cannot afford, since any form of arduous activity, such as working in the fields, makes its use impossible. Thus it is likely that the use of the veil was envied by those who could not afford it, for it signaled a style of life that was generally admired. Burton, commenting on the Muslims portrayed in the *Arabian Nights,* says, "The women, who delight in restrictions which tend to their honour, accepted it willingly and still affect it, they do not desire a liberty or rather a license which they have learned to regard as inconsistent with their time-honored notions of feminine decorum and delicacy. They would think very meanly of a husband who permitted them to be exposed, like hetairae, to the public gaze."

The veil bears many messages about its wearers and their society, and many men and women in Middle Eastern communities today would quickly denounce nineteenth-century Orientalists like Sir Richard Burton and deny its importance. Nouha al Hejelan, wife of the Saudi Arabian ambassador to London, told Sally Quinn of *The Washington Post,* "If I wanted to take it all off [the *abbayah* and veil], I would have long ago. It wouldn't mean as much to me as it does to you." Basima Bezirgan, a contemporary Iraqi feminist, says, "Compared to the real issues that are involved between men and women in the Middle East today, the veil itself is unimportant." A Moroccan linguist, who buys her clothes in Paris, laughs when asked about the veil. "My mother wears a *djellabah* and a veil. I have never worn them. But so what? I still cannot get divorced as easily as a man, and I am still a member of my family group and responsible to them for everything I do. What is the veil? A piece of cloth." However, early Middle Eastern feminists felt differently. Huda Sharawi, an early Egyptian activist who formed the first Women's Union, removed her veil in public in 1923, a dramatic gesture to demonstrate her dislike of society's attitude toward women and her defiance of the system.

"The seclusion of women has many purposes," states Egyptian anthropologist Nadia Abu Zahra. "It expresses men's status, power, wealth, and manliness. It also helps preserve men's image of virility and masculinity, but men do not admit this; on the contrary they claim that one of the purposes of the veil is to guard women's honor." The veil and *purdah* are symbols of restriction, in men's behavior as well as women's. A respectable woman wearing conservative Islamic dress today on a public street is signaling, "Hands off! Don't touch me or you'll be sorry." Cowboy Jim Sayre of Deadwood, South Dakota, says, "If you deform a cowboy's hat, he'll likely deform you." A man who approaches a veiled woman is asking for similar trouble; not only the woman but also her family is shamed, and serious problems may result. "It is clear," says Egyptian anthropologist Ahmed Abou Zeid, "that honor and shame which are usually attributed to a certain individual or a certain kinship group have in fact a bearing on the total social structure, since most acts involving honor or shame are likely to affect the existing social equilibrium."

Veiling and seclusion almost always can be related to the maintenance of social status. The extreme example of the way the rich could use this practice was found among the wealthy sultans of pre-revolutionary Turkey. Stories of their women, kept in harems and guarded by eunuchs, formed the basis for much of the Western folklore concerning the nature of male-female relationships in Middle Eastern society. The forbidden nature of seclusion inflamed the Western imagination, but the Westerners who created erotic fantasies in films and novels would not have been able to enter the sultans' palaces any more than they could have penetrated their harems! It was eroticism plus opulence and luxury, the signs of wealth, that captured the imagination of the Westerners—and still does, as witnessed by the popularity of "Dallas" and "Dynasty."

The meaning associated with veiling or a lack of veiling changes according to locality. Most village women in the Egyptian delta have not veiled, nor have the Berber women of North Africa, but no one criticizes them for this.

"In the village, no one veils, because everyone is considered a member of the same large family," explained Aisha Bint Muhammad, a working-class wife of Marrakesh. "But in the city, veiling is *sunnah,* required by our religion." Veiling has generally been found in towns and cities, among all classes, where families feel that it is necessary to distinguish themselves from strangers. Some women who must work without the veil in factories and hotels may put such garments on when they go out on holidays or even walk on the streets after work.

Veiling and *purdah* not only indicate status and wealth; they also have some religious sanction and protect women from the world outside the home. *Purdah* delineates private space and distinguishes between the public and private sectors of society, as does the traditional architecture of the area. Older Middle Eastern houses do not have picture windows facing on the street, nor do they have walks leading invitingly to front doors. Family life is hidden away from strangers; behind blank walls may lie courtyards and gardens, refuges from the heat, cold, and bustle of the outside world, the world of nonkin that is not to be trusted. Outsiders are pointedly excluded.

Even within the household, among her close relatives, a traditional Muslim woman may veil before those kinsmen whom she could legally marry. If her maternal or paternal cousins, her brothers-in-law, or her sons-in-law come to call, she covers her head, or perhaps her whole face. To do otherwise, to neglect such acts of respect and modesty, would be considered shameless.

The veil does more than protect its wearers from known and unknown intruders; it can also conceal identity. Behind the anonymity of the veil, women can go about a city unrecognized and uncriticized. Nadia Abu Zahra reports anecdotes of men donning women's veils in order to visit their lovers undetected; women may do the same. The veil is such an effective disguise that Nouri Al-Sa'id, the late prime minister of Iraq, attempted to escape death from revolutionary forces in 1958 by wearing the *abbayah* and veil of a woman; only his shoes gave him away. When houses of prostitution were closed in Baghdad in the early 1950s, the prostitutes donned the same clothing to cruise the streets. Flashing open their outer garments was an advertisement to potential customers.

Political dissidents in many countries have used the veil for their own ends. The women who marched, veiled, through Cairo during the Nationalist demonstrations against the British after World War I were counting on the strength of Western respect for the veil to protect them against British gunfire. At first they were right. Algerian women also used the protection of the veil to carry bombs through French army checkpoints during the Algerian revolution. But when the French discovered the ruse, Algerian women discarded the veil and dressed like Europeans to move about freely.

The multiple meanings and uses of *purdah* and the veil do not fully explain how such practices came to be so deeply embedded in Mediterranean society. However, their origins lie in the asymmetrical relationship between men and women and the resulting attitudes about men's and women's roles.

Women, according to Fatma Mernissi, a Moroccan sociologist, are seen by men in Islamic societies as in need of protection because they are unable to control their sexuality and hence are a danger to the social order. In other words, they need to be restrained and controlled so that men do not give way to the impassioned desire they inspire, and society can thus function in an orderly way.

The notion that women present a danger to the social order is scarcely limited to Muslim society. Anthropologist Julian Pitt-Rivers has pointed out that the supervision and seclusion of women was also found in Christian Europe, even though veiling was not usually practiced there. "The idea that women not subjected to male authority are a danger is a fundamental one in the writings of the moralists from the Archpriest of Talavera to Padre Haro, and it is echoed in the modern Andalusian *pueblo*. It is bound up with the fear of ungoverned female sexuality which had been an integral element of European folklore ever since prudent Odysseus lashed himself to the mast to escape the sirens."

Pitt-Rivers is writing about northern Mediterranean communities, which, like those of the Middle Eastern societies, have been greatly concerned with family honor and shame rather than with individual guilt. The honor of the Middle Eastern extended family, its ancestors and its descendants, is the highest social value. The misdeeds of the grandparents are indeed visited on their grandchildren, but so also grandparents may be disgraced by grandchildren. Men and women always remain members of their natal families. Marriage is a legal contract, but a fragile one that is often broken; the ties between brother and sister, mother and child, father and child are lifelong and enduring. The larger natal family is the group to which the individual man or woman belongs and to which the individual owes responsibility in exchange for the social and economic security that the family group provides. It is the group that is socially honored—or dishonored—by the behavior of the individual.

Both male honor and female honor are involved in the honor of the family, but each is expressed differently. The honor of a man, *sharaf,* is a public matter, involving bravery, hospitality, and piety. It may be lost, but it may also be regained. The honor of a woman, *'ard,* is a private matter involving only one thing, her sexual chastity. Once believed to be lost, it cannot be regained. If the loss of female honor remains only privately known, a rebuke may be all that takes place. But if the loss of female honor becomes public knowledge, the other members of the family may feel bound to cleanse the family name. In extreme cases, the cleansing may require the death of the offending female member. Although such killings are now criminal offenses in the Middle East, suspended sentences are often given, and the newspapers in Cairo and Baghdad frequently carry sad stories of runaway sisters "gone bad" in the city, and the revenge taken upon them in the name of family honor by their brothers or cousins.

This emphasis on female chastity, many say, originated in the patrilineal society's concern with the paternity of the child and the inheritance that follows the male line. How could the husband know that the child in his wife's womb was his son? He could not know unless his wife was a virgin at marriage. Marriages were arranged by parents, and keeping daughters secluded from men was the best way of seeing that a girl remained a virgin until her wedding night.

Middle Eastern women also look upon seclusion as practical protection. In the Iraqi village where we lived from 1956 to 1958, one of us (Elizabeth) wore the *abbayah* and found that it provided a great deal of protection from prying eyes, dust, heat, and flies. Parisian women visiting Istanbul in the sixteenth century were so impressed by the ability of the all-enveloping garment to keep dresses clean of mud and manure and to keep women from being attacked by importuning men that they tried to introduce it into French fashion. Many women have told us that they felt self-conscious, vulnerable, and even naked when they first walked on a public street without the veil and *abbayah*—as if they were making a display of themselves.

The veil, as it has returned in the last decade in a movement away from wearing Western dress, has been called a form of "portable seclusion," allowing women to maintain a modest appearance that indicates respectability and religious piety in the midst of modern Middle Eastern urban life. This new style of dress always includes long skirts, long sleeves, and a head covering (scarf or turban). Some outfits are belted, some are loose, and some include face veils and shapeless robes, as well as gloves so that no skin whatsoever is exposed to the public eye. However, these clothes are seldom black, like the older garments. The women wearing such clothes in Egypt may work in shops or offices or go to college; they are members of the growing middle class.

This new fashion has been described by some scholars as an attempt by men to reassert their Muslim identity and to reestablish their position as heads of families, even though both spouses often must work outside the home. According to this analysis, the presence of the veil is a sign that the males of the household are in control of their women and are more able to assume the responsibilities disturbed or usurped by foreign colonial powers, responsibilities which continue to be threatened by Western politics and materialism. Other scholars argue that it is not men who are choosing the garb today but women themselves, using modest dress as a way of communicating to the rest of the world that though they may work outside their homes, they are nonetheless pious Muslims and respectable women.

The veil is the outward sign of a complex reality. Observers are often deceived by the absence of that sign and fail to see that in Middle Eastern societies (and in many parts of Europe) where the garb no longer exists, basic attitudes are unchanged. Women who have taken off the veil continue to play the old roles within the family, and their chastity remains crucial. A woman's behavior is still the key to the honor and the reputation of her family, no matter what she wears.

In Middle Eastern societies, feminine and masculine continue to be strong poles of identification. This is in marked contrast to Western society, where for more than a generation greater equality between men and women has been reflected in the blurring of distinctions between male and female clothing. Western feminists continue to state that biology is not the basis of behavior and therefore should not be the basis for understanding men's and women's roles. But almost all Middle Eastern reformers, whether upper or middle class, intellectuals or clerics, argue from the assumption of a fundamental, God-given difference, social and psychological as well as physical, between men and women. There are important disagreements among these reformers today about what should be done, however.

Those Muslim reformers still strongly influenced by Western models call for equal access to divorce, child custody, and inheritance; equal opportunities for education and employment; abolition of female circumcision and "crimes of honor"; an end to polygamy; and a law regulating the age of marriage. But of growing importance are reformers of social practice who call for a return to the example set by the Prophet Muhammad and his early followers; they wish to begin by eliminating what they feel to be the licentious practices introduced by Western influence, such as sexual laxity and the consumption of alcohol. To them, change in the laws affecting women should be in strict accord with their view of Islamic law, and women should begin by expressing their modesty and piety by wearing the new forms of veiling in public life. Seclusion may be impossible in modern urban societies, but conservative dress, the new form of veiling, is an option for women that sets the faithful Muslim apart from the corrupt world of the nonbeliever as it was believed to do in the time of the Prophet.

A female English film director, after several months in Morocco, said in an interview, "This business about the veil is nonsense. We all have our veils, between ourselves and other people. The question is what the veils are used for, and by whom." Today the use of the veil continues to trigger Western reaction, for as Islamic dress, it is not only a statement about the honor of the family or the boundary between family and stranger. Just as the changes in the nun's dress in the United States tell us something about the woman who wears it and the society of which she is a part, the various forms of veiling today communicate attitudes and beliefs about politics and religious morality as well as the roles of men and women in the Middle East.

Review Questions

1. What is the meaning to Westerners of the veil worn by Middle Eastern women? How does this view reflect Western values?
2. List the symbolic meanings of the veil to Middle Eastern women. How do these meanings relate to the Muslim concept of *purdah* and to other important Middle Eastern values?
3. There has been a resurgence of the veil in several Middle Eastern societies over the past few years. How can you explain this change?
4. Using this article as a model, analyze the meaning of some American articles of clothing. How do these relate to core values in the country?

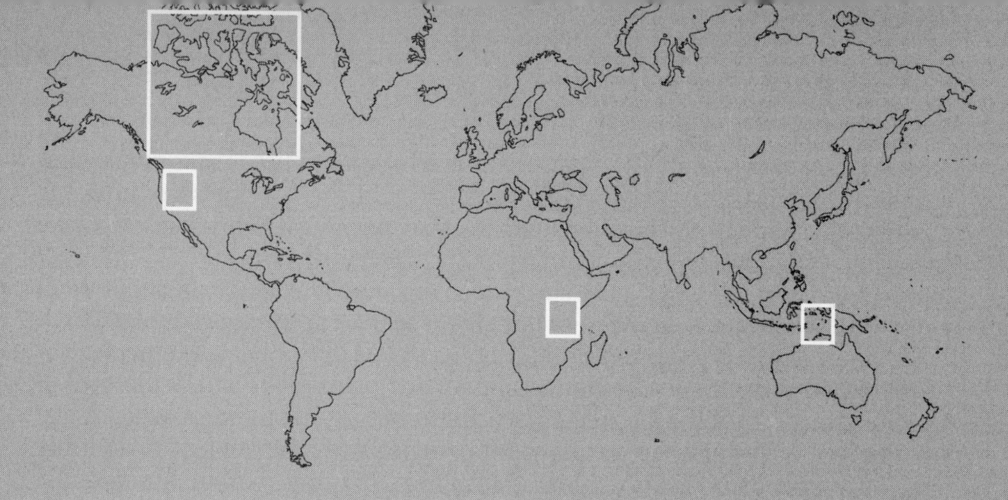

22

Society and Sex Roles

Ernestine Friedl

Many anthropologists claim that males hold formal authority over females in every society. Although the degree of masculine authority may vary from one group to the next, males always have more power. For some researchers, this unequal male-female relationship is the result of biological inheritance. As with other primates, they argue, male humans are naturally more aggressive, females more docile. Ernestine Friedl challenges this explanation in this selection. Comparing a variety of hunting and gathering groups, she concludes that relations between men and women are shaped by a culturally defined division of labor based on sex, not by inherited predisposition. Given access to resources that circulate publicly, women can attain equal or dominant status in any society, including our own.

"Women must respond quickly to the demands of their husbands," says anthropologist Napoleon Chagnon, describing the horticultural Yanomamö Indians of Venezuela. When a man returns from a hunting

"Society and Sex Roles" from *Human Nature Magazine,* April 1978, vol. 1, no. 4. Copyright © by Human Nature, Inc., 1978. Reprinted by permission of the publisher.

trip, "the woman, no matter what she is doing, hurries home and quietly but rapidly prepares a meal for her husband. Should the wife be slow in doing this, the husband is within his rights to beat her. Most reprimands . . . take the form of blows with the hand or with a piece of firewood. . . . Some of them chop their wives with the sharp edge of a machete or axe, or shoot them with a barbed arrow in some nonvital area, such as the buttocks or leg."

Among the Semai agriculturalists of central Malaya, when one person refuses the request of another, the offended party suffers *punan,* a mixture of emotional pain and frustration. "Enduring *punan* is commonest when a girl has refused the victim her sexual favors," reports Robert Dentan. "The jilted man's 'heart becomes sad.' He loses his energy and his appetite. Much of the time he sleeps, dreaming of his lost love. In this state he is in fact very likely to injure himself 'accidentally.'" The Semai are afraid of violence; a man would never strike a woman.

The social relationship between men and women has emerged as one of the principal disputes occupying the attention of scholars and the public in recent years. Although the discord is sharpest in the United States, the controversy has spread throughout the world. Numerous national and international conferences, including one in Mexico sponsored by the United Nations, have drawn together delegates from all walks of life to discuss such questions as the social and political rights of each sex and even the basic nature of males and females.

Whatever their position, partisans often invoke examples from other cultures to support their ideas about the proper role of each sex. Because women are clearly subservient to men in many societies, like the Yanomamö, some experts conclude that the natural pattern is for men to dominate. But among the Semai no one has the right to command others, and in West Africa women are often chiefs. The place of women in these societies supports the argument of those who believe that sex roles are not fixed, that if there is a natural order, it allows for many different arrangements.

The argument will never be settled as long as the opposing sides toss examples from the world's cultures at each other like intellectual stones. But the effect of biological differences on male and female behavior can be clarified by looking at known examples of the earliest forms of human society and examining the relationship between technology, social organization, environment, and sex roles. The problem is to determine the conditions in which different degrees of male dominance are found, to try to discover the social and cultural arrangements that give rise to equality or inequality between the sexes, and to attempt to apply this knowledge to our understanding of the changes taking place in modern industrial society.

As Western history and the anthropological record have told us, equality between the sexes is rare; in most known societies females are subordinate. Male dominance is so widespread that it is virtually a human universal; societies in which women are consistently dominant do not exist and have never existed.

Evidence of a society in which women control all strategic resources like food and water, and in which women's activities are the most prestigious, has never been found. The Iroquois of North America and the Lovedu of Africa came closest. Among the Iroquois, women raised food, controlled its distribution, and helped to choose male political leaders. Lovedu women ruled as queens, exchanged valuable cattle, led ceremonies, and controlled their own sex lives. But among both the Iroquois and Lovedu, men owned the land and held other positions of power and prestige. Women were equal to men; they did not have ultimate authority over them. Neither culture was a true matriarchy.

Patriarchies are prevalent, and they appear to be strongest in societies in which men control significant goods that are exchanged with people outside the family. Regardless of who produces food, the person who gives it to others creates the obligations and alliances that are at the center of all political relations. The greater the male monopoly on the distribution of scarce items, the stronger their control of women seems to be. This is most obvious in relatively simple hunter-gatherer societies.

Hunter-gatherers, or foragers, subsist on wild plants, small land animals, and small river or sea creatures gathered by hand; large land animals and sea mammals hunted with spears, bows and arrows, and blow guns; and fish caught with hooks and nets. The three hundred thousand hunter-gatherers alive in the world today include the Eskimos, the Australian aborigines, and the Pygmies of Central Africa.

Foraging has endured for two million years and was replaced by farming and animal husbandry only ten thousand years ago; it covers more than 99 percent of human history. Our foraging ancestry is not far behind us and provides a clue to our understanding of the human condition.

Hunter-gatherers are people whose ways of life are technologically simple and socially and politically egalitarian. They live in small groups of 50 to 200 and have neither kings, nor priests, nor social classes. These conditions permit anthropologists to observe the essential bases for inequalities between the sexes without the distortions induced by the complexities of contemporary industrial society.

The source of male power among hunter-gatherers lies in their control of a scarce, hard to acquire, but necessary nutrient—animal protein. When men in a hunter-gatherer society return to camp with game, they divide the meat in some customary way. Among the !Kung San of Africa, certain parts of the animal are given to the owner of the arrow that killed the beast, to the first hunter to sight the game, to the one who threw the first spear, and to all men in the hunting party. After the meat has been divided, each hunter distributes his share to his blood relatives and his in-laws, who in turn share it with others. If an animal is large enough, every member of the band will receive some meat.

Vegetable foods, in contrast, are not distributed beyond the immediate household. Women give food to their children, to their husbands, to other members of the household, and rarely, to the occasional visitor. No one outside the family regularly eats any of the wild fruits and vegetables that are gathered by the women.

The meat distributed by the men is a public gift. Its source is widely known, and the donor expects a reciprocal gift when other men return from a successful hunt. He gains honor as a supplier of a scarce item and simultaneously obligates others to him.

These obligations constitute a form of power or control over others, both men and women. The opinions of hunters play an important part in decisions to move the village; good hunters attract the most desirable women; people in other groups join camps with good hunters; and hunters, because they already participate in an internal system of exchange, control exchange with other groups for flint, salt, and steel axes. The male monopoly on hunting unites men in a system of exchange and gives them power; gathering vegetable food does not give women equal power even among foragers who live in the tropics, where the food collected by women provides more than half the hunter-gatherer diet.

If dominance arises from a monopoly on big-game hunting, why has the male monopoly remained unchallenged? Some women are strong enough to participate in the hunt and their endurance is certainly equal to that of men. Dobe San women of the Kalahari Desert in Africa walk an average of 10 miles a day carrying from 15 to 33 pounds of food plus a baby.

Women do not hunt, I believe, because of four interrelated factors: variability in the supply of game; the different skills required for hunting and gathering; the incompatibility between carrying burdens and hunting; and the small size of seminomadic foraging populations.

Because the meat supply is unstable, foragers must make frequent expeditions to provide the band with gathered food. Environmental factors such as seasonal and annual variation in rainfall often affect the size of the wildlife population. Hunters cannot always find game, and when they do encounter animals, they are not always successful in killing their prey. In northern latitudes, where meat is the primary food, periods of starvation are known in every generation. The irregularity of the game supply leads hunter-gatherers in areas where plant foods are available to depend on these predictable foods a good part of the time. Someone must gather the fruits, nuts, and roots and carry them back to camp to feed unsuccessful hunters, children, the elderly, and anyone who might not have gone foraging that day.

Foraging falls to the women because hunting and gathering cannot be combined on the same expedition. Although gatherers sometimes notice signs of game as they work, the skills required to track game are not the same as those required to find edible roots or plants. Hunters scan the horizon and the land for traces of large game; gatherers keep their eyes to the ground, studying the distribution of plants and the texture of the soil for hidden roots and animal holes. Even if a woman who was collecting plants came across the track of an antelope, she could not follow it; it is impossible to carry a load and hunt at the same time. Running with a heavy load is difficult, and should the animal be sighted, the hunter would be off balance and could neither shoot an arrow nor throw a spear accurately.

Pregnancy and child care would also present difficulties for a hunter. An unborn child affects a woman's body balance, as does a child in her arms, on her back, or slung at her side. Until they are two years old, many hunter-gatherer children are carried at all times, and until they are four, they are carried some of the time.

An observer might wonder why young women do not hunt until they become pregnant, or why mature women and men do not hunt and gather on alternate days, with some women staying in camp to act as wet nurses for the young. Apart from the effects hunting might have on a mother's milk production, there are two reasons. First, young girls begin to bear children as soon as they are physically mature and strong enough to hunt, and second, hunter-gatherer bands are so small that there are unlikely to be enough lactating women to serve as wet nurses. No hunter-gatherer group could afford to maintain a specialized female hunting force.

Because game is not always available, because hunting and gathering are specialized skills, because women carrying heavy loads cannot hunt, and because women in hunter-gatherer societies are usually either pregnant or caring for young children, for most of the last two million years of human history men have hunted and women have gathered.

If male dominance depends on controlling the supply of meat, then the degree of male dominance in a society should vary with the amount of meat available and the amount supplied by the men. Some regions, like the East African grasslands and the North American woodlands, abounded with species of large mammals; other zones, like tropical forests and semideserts, are thinly populated with prey. Many elements affect the supply of game, but theoretically, the less meat provided exclusively by the men, the more egalitarian the society.

All known hunter-gatherer societies fit into four basic types: those in which men and women work together in communal hunts and as teams gathering edible plants, as did the Washo Indians of North America; those in which men and women each collect their own plant foods although the men supply some meat to the group, as do the Hadza of Tanzania; those in which male hunters and female gatherers work apart but return to camp each evening to share their acquisitions, as do the Tiwi of North Australia; and those in which the men provide all the food by hunting large game, as do the Eskimo. In each case the extent of male dominance increases directly with the proportion of meat supplied by individual men and small hunting parties.

Among the most egalitarian of hunter-gatherer societies are the Washo Indians, who inhabited the valleys of the Sierra Nevada in what is now southern California and Nevada. In the spring they moved north to Lake Tahoe for the large fish runs of sucker and native trout. Everyone—men, women, and children—participated in the fishing. Women spent the summer gathering edible berries and seeds while the men continued to fish. In the fall some men hunted deer, but the most important source of animal protein was the jackrabbit, which was captured in communal hunts. Men and women together drove the rabbits into nets tied end to end. To provide food for the winter, husbands and wives worked as teams in the late fall to collect pine nuts.

Since everyone participated in most food-gathering activities, there were no individual distributors of food and relatively little difference in male and female rights. Men and women were not segregated from each other in daily activities; both were free to take lovers after marriage; both had the right to separate whenever they chose; menstruating women were not isolated from the rest of the group; and one of the two major Washo rituals celebrated hunting while the other celebrated gathering. Men were accorded more prestige if they had killed a deer, and men directed decisions about the seasonal movement of the group. But if no male leader stepped forward, women were permitted to lead. The distinctive feature of groups such as the Washo is the relative equality of the sexes.

The sexes are also relatively equal among the Hadza of Tanzania, but this near-equality arises because men and women tend to work alone to feed themselves. They exchange little food. The Hadza lead a leisurely life in the seemingly barren environment of the East African Rift Gorge, which is, in fact, rich in edible berries, roots, and small game. As a result of this abundance, from the time they are ten years old, Hadza men and women gather much of their own food. Women take their young children with them into the bush, eating as they forage, and collect only enough food for a light family meal in the evening. The men eat berries and roots as they hunt for small game, and should they bring down a rabbit or a hyrax, they eat the meat on the spot. Meat is carried back to the camp and shared with the rest of the group only on those rare occasions when a poisoned arrow brings down a large animal—an impala, a zebra, an eland, or a giraffe.

Because Hadza men distribute little meat, their status is only slightly higher than that of the women. People flock to the camp of a good hunter and the camp might take on his name because of his popularity, but he is in no sense a leader of the group. A Hadza man and a woman have an equal right to divorce, and each can repudiate a marriage simply by living apart for a few weeks. Couples tend to live in the same camp as the wife's mother, but they sometimes make long visits to the camp of the husband's mother. Although a man may take more than one wife, most Hadza males cannot afford to indulge in this luxury. In order to maintain a marriage, a man must supply both his wife and his mother-in-law with some meat and trade goods, such as beads and cloth, and the Hadza economy gives few men the wealth to provide for more than one wife and mother-in-law. Washo equality is based on cooperation; Hadza equality is based on independence.

In contrast to both these groups, among the Tiwi of Melville and Bathurst Islands off the northern coast of Australia, male hunters dominate female gatherers. The Tiwi are representative of the most common form of foraging society, in which the men supply large quantities of meat, although less than half the food consumed by the group. Each morning Tiwi women, most with babies on their backs, scatter in different directions in search of vegetables, grubs, worms, and small game such as bandicoots, lizards, and opossums. To track the game, they use hunting dogs. On most days women return to camp with some meat and with baskets full of *korka,* the nut of a native palm, which is soaked and mashed to make a porridge-like dish. The Tiwi men do not hunt small game and do not hunt every day, but when they do they often return with kangaroo, large lizards, fish, and game birds.

The porridge is cooked separately by each household and rarely shared outside the family, but the meat is prepared by a volunteer cook, who can be male or female. After the cook takes one of the parts of the animal traditionally reserved for him or her, the animal's "boss," the one who caught it, distributes the rest to all near kin and then to all others residing with the band. Although the small game supplied by the women is distributed in the same way as the big game supplied by the men, Tiwi men are dominant because the game they kill provides most of the meat.

The power of Tiwi men is clearest in their betrothal practices. Among the Tiwi, a woman must always be married. To ensure this, female infants are betrothed at birth and widows are remarried at the gravesides of their late husbands. Men form alliances by exchanging daughters, sisters, and mothers in marriage, and some collect as many as twenty-five wives. Tiwi men value the quantity and quality of the food many wives can collect and the many children they can produce.

The dominance of the men is offset somewhat by the influence of adult women in selecting their next husbands. Many women are active strategists in the political careers of their male relatives, but to the exasperation of some sons attempting to promote their own futures, widowed mothers sometimes insist on selecting their own partners. Women also influence the marriages of their daughters and granddaughters, especially when the selected husband dies before the bestowed child moves to his camp.

Among the Eskimo, representative of the rarest type of forager society, inequality between the sexes is matched by inequality in supplying the group with food. Inland Eskimo men hunt caribou throughout the year to provision the entire society, and maritime Eskimo men depend on whaling, fishing, and some hunting to feed their extended families. The women process the carcasses, cut and sew skins to make clothing, cook, and care for the young; but they collect no food of their own and depend on the men to supply all the raw materials for their work. Since men provide all the meat, they also control the trade in hides, whale oil, seal oil, and other items that move between the maritime and inland Eskimos.

Eskimo women are treated almost exclusively as objects to be used, abused, and traded by men. After puberty all Eskimo girls are fair game for any interested male. A man shows his intentions by grabbing the belt of a woman, and if she protests, he cuts off her trousers and forces himself upon her. These encounters are considered unimportant by the rest of the group. Men offer their wives' sexual services to establish alliances with trading partners and members of hunting and whaling parties.

Despite the consistent pattern of some degree of male dominance among foragers, most of these societies are egalitarian compared with agricultural and industrial societies. No forager has any significant opportunity for political leadership. Foragers, as a rule, do not like to give or take orders, and assume leadership only with reluctance. Shamans (those who are thought to be possessed by spirits) may be either male or female. Public rituals conducted by women in order to celebrate the first menstruation of girls are common, and the symbolism in these rituals is similar to that in the ceremonies that follow a boy's first kill.

In any society, status goes to those who control the distribution of valued goods and services outside the family. Equality arises when both sexes work side by side in food production, as do the Washo, and the products are simply distributed among the workers. In such circumstances, no person or sex has greater access to valued items than do others. But when women make no contribution to the food supply, as in the case of the Eskimo, they are completely subordinate.

When we attempt to apply these generalizations to contemporary industrial society, we can predict that as long as women spend their discretionary income from jobs on domestic needs, they will gain little social recognition and power. To be an effective source of power, money must be exchanged in ways that require returns and create obligations. In other words, it must be invested.

Jobs that do not give women control over valued resources will do little to advance their general status. Only as managers, executives, and professionals are women in a position to trade goods and services, to do others favors, and therefore to obligate others to them. Only as controllers of valued resources can women achieve prestige, power, and equality.

Within the household, women who bring in income from jobs are able to function on a more nearly equal basis with their husbands. Women who contribute services to their husbands and children without pay, as do some middle-class Western housewives, are especially vulnerable to dominance. Like Eskimo women, as long as their services are limited to domestic distribution they have little power relative to their husbands and none with respect to the outside world.

As for the limits imposed on women by their procreative functions in hunter-gatherer societies, childbearing and child care are organized around work as much as work is organized around reproduction. Some foraging groups space their children three to four years apart and have an average of only four to six children, far fewer than many women in other cultures. Hunter-gatherers nurse their infants for extended periods, sometimes for as long as four years. This custom suppresses ovulation and limits the size of their families. Sometimes, although rarely, they practice infanticide. By limiting reproduction, a woman who is gathering food has only one child to carry.

Different societies can and do adjust the frequency of birth and the care of children to accommodate whatever productive activities women customarily engage in. In horticultural societies, where women work long hours in gardens that may be far from home, infants get food to supplement their mothers' milk, older children take care of younger children, and pregnancies are widely spaced. Throughout the world, if a society requires a woman's labor, it finds ways to care for her children.

In the United States, as in some other industrial societies, the accelerated entry of women with preschool children into the labor force has resulted in the development of a variety of child-care arrangements. Individual women have called on friends, relatives, and neighbors. Public and private child-care centers are growing. We should realize that the declining birth rate, the increasing acceptance of childless or single-child families, and de-emphasis on motherhood are adaptations to a sexual division of labor reminiscent of the system of production found in hunter-gatherer societies.

In many countries where women no longer devote most of their productive years to childbearing, they are beginning to demand a change in the social relationship of the sexes. As women gain access to positions that control the exchange of resources, male dominance may become archaic, and industrial societies may one day become as egalitarian as the Washo.

Review Questions

1. According to Friedl, what factor accounts for the different degrees of dominance and power between males and females found in hunter-gatherer societies?
2. What are the four types of hunter-gatherer societies considered by Friedl in this article, and what is it about the structure of each that relates to the distribution of power and dominance between males and females?
3. Some anthropologists believe that male dominance is inherited. Comment on this assertion in light of Friedl's article.
4. Why does Friedl believe that women will gain equality with men in industrial society?

23

Culture, Rank, and IQ: The Bell Curve Phenomenon

Mark Nathan Cohen

To understand social stratification in complex societies, it is important to recognize how people explain why some individuals outrank others because such explanations perpetuate inequality. A case in point is a commonly held American view that mental capacity, often called IQ (intelligence quotient), is inherited and is a determinant of success. A parallel belief is that there are genetically determined groups called races. It is only a small logical step for people to propose that IQ levels can be inherited by poor groups and can be used to explain their differential rates of success in U.S. society. A book published in 1994, The Bell Curve, *by Charles Murray and Richard Herrnstein takes this point of view and attempts to provide supporting evidence. Anthropologists immeditely criticized* The Bell Curve *on a number of grounds, one of the most important being their assertion that IQ is not a single mental factor, and that IQ tests given across culturally different racial and ethnic groups cannot pro-*

Slightly edited from "Anthropology and Race: The Bell Curve Phenomenon," *General Anthropology*, 1995. Copyright © by the American Anthropological Association, 1995. Reprinted by permission of the American Anthropological Association and the author.

duce valid comparative results. This is the position argued by Mark Cohen in this article, which he wrote for anthropologists as a call to action. He points out that the IQ tests designed by psychologists to be culture neutral actually ignore many subtle cultural variations that lead to differences in group scores.

About six months ago, I organized a symposium to discuss the issues of Charles Murray and Richard Herrnstein's book *The Bell Curve* with the students on my campus. The book had burst on the scene without benefit of serious scholarly review, but with the benefit of enormous publicity including lead stories in the *New York Times Magazine and Book Review* and *Newsweek* as well as innumerable talk show appearances by Murray, its surviving author. It purported to demonstrate: (1) that what is commonly called "intelligence" was a single, real (transcultural) *thing* that could be measured on a single scale rather than being a complex amalgam of varied skills and abilities; (2) that IQ tests as constituted through the 20th century could measure it and did measure it fairly; (3) that IQ, the measure of this intelligence, was largely genetically determined; (4) that an individual's IQ could not be modified significantly in that individual's lifetime; (5) that the human "races" were differentially gifted with IQ (although individuals within any race might excel); (6) that IQ was associated as a cause, not as an effect, with economic success or poverty, with class status, with morality and criminality, and with adherence to middle class American, (Christian) "family values"; that the poor were deprived by virtue of their own shortcomings and already had as fair a slice of the country's wealth as their IQ merited; (7) that attempts to improve IQ by improvements in the learning environment were useless (for the poor/slow, although the authors called for more enriched education for the gifted); (8) that the genetic components of class stratification (via intelligence) were so significant that we were moving inexorably toward a society segregated by biologically determined intelligence; and (9) that government efforts to intercede educationally or economically on behalf of the poor were misguided and doomed to failure. (The authors professed to find the trend toward a society increasingly stratified by IQ distasteful but they did not simultaneously oppose any efforts to reverse the trend.)

The book was well received because it spoke perfectly to American prejudices against minority groups. It justified existing inequalities, and fed cherished beliefs such as the idea that access to success was based purely on merit and open to anyone with sufficient intelligence. It suggested that success, wealth, and high status were clearly deserved, through merit, and therefore easily defended; that failure was the result of individual inadequacy relieving us of social responsibility. It fueled the American dream that held that upward mobility was limited only by one's ability. It suggested that if the "melting pot" were failing, it could only be because some people (disproportionately in some races) were not capable; and by suggesting that efforts to help such individuals "make it" (whether through affirmative action, welfare, or Headstart) were misguided, it fueled conservative visions of government and reduced government expenditure. It helped fuel the current perception that affirmative action is the only barrier to true equality of opportunity. In short, cloaked in a veneer of objective science, it appealed (or even pandered) perfectly to what many Americans wanted to believe.

In response, my associates and I pointed out: (1) that the "races" Murray and Herrnstein relied on are not recognized by the overwhelming majority of anthropologists as almost any introductory textbook will affirm (They relied heavily on the racial vision of J. P. Rushton.); (2) that the individual traits that make up common racial stereotypes (not to mention myriad other human variations such as blood type) actually vary independently so that expecting a trait like IQ, even if genetic, to run in races, whether defined by color or defined differently by shape of nose or blood type, makes little sense; (3) that there is serious controversy about whether IQ, initially only a kind of average of various test scores, is in fact a "thing" at all rather than a collection of separate abilities or merely a reification of a number (as Stephen J. Gould has argued repeatedly); (4) that there are various reasons to question whether IQ tests measure intelligence fairly in any case as opposed to measuring a kind of cultural literacy (as discussed more fully below); (5) that Murray and Herrnstein's statements about whether IQ is "heritable" are in fact highly questionable on many grounds. They claim that IQ is 60% heritable by which they ultimately mean genetically determined and not modifiable by environmental factors, but they seem not to note that even by their figures, a very substantial environmental component is involved. The most essential point in this context is that measured "heritability" is only a statistical artifact of a given sample under specific conditions. It varies widely as the conditions change and is never a general, inherent property of IQ itself. Existing estimates are based heavily on twin studies that provide a badly skewed sample and in which the genetic and environmental components are badly confused.

Many of us raised such objections on campuses and in print. My sense is that we have won the battle but are losing the war. Outrage about the book has been so widespread that a great many people now know it is tainted. Murray himself (to judge by a recent performance at Harvard where he was very badly received) has taken to noting publicly that he has become something of a political pariah with whom even conservatives don't want to associate. So *The Bell Curve* itself may have been diffused.

But the overwhelming, "common sense knowledge" of all of this among the public, in which the book fits so well, is still there and it is clearly not getting better, although attempts to give it a scientific patina may have been slowed. People I talk to, including some of my closest non-anthropological friends, listen to me rebut *The Bell Curve* and then say, "yes-but . . . you can't deny that . . . ." (I have had the most trouble with the professional psychologists on my campus and their students who react as if this were simply a turf battle. IQ tests, it seems, are "their thing," to be protected at all costs, even if racist misuse of the tests must be protected as well. No psychologist on my campus has been willing to say forcefully that there are important values to

IQ tests but that Murray and Herrnstein abused them—or to help explain the limits of the tests or the distinctions between proper and improper use.)

The problem goes much deeper than Murray and Herrnstein and it is partly a failing of ours as anthropologists. We have not spread the message about what human variation actually consists of and what "multiculturalism" really means. I want to focus on the latter point because I think it is the less well understood issue. Well-meaning people around the country are busy celebrating ethnic differences in music, food, dance, and perhaps language under the banner of "multiculturalism," but even they don't get the deeper differences in cultures. It is our collective failure to teach and learn about the real meaning of culture that is at the heart of the problem and the shallow multicultural celebration only fuels it. It seems that no one except professional anthropologists understands the depth of cultural differences or, more important, the limits of our own cultural assumptions—and we are not getting those points across.

Perhaps the most telling point in *The Bell Curve* is Murray and Herrnstein's contention that the IQ tests are culturally fair (despite widespread criticism) because, they say, minorities don't disproportionately miss the questions with (the most obvious) cultural biases. According to the authors, minorities miss the questions with little cultural bias most closely associated with strict logic, "general intelligence" or "g," their concept of a central (transcultural) core of logical abilities. And therein lies the most important misunderstanding.

Some IQ tests, historically, have had egregious examples of overt cultural bias. To cite just three: a question given to South African Blacks in poor, segregated townships asking them to complete a drawing of a tennis court; a question to new immigrants and illiterate farm boys in the U.S. (in an era before widespread radio or television) asking them to identify famous baseball players; a question given to immigrants to the U.S. of varying ancestry asking them to identify a drawing of a Nordic looking man or woman as obviously more pleasing to the eye than a drawing of someone with more nondescript ethnic physiognomy (that in fact resembled many of the immigrants themselves!). (Murray and Herrnstein, although abhorring some of the errors of earlier tests, have no qualms about using those test results to help their case.)

Some more recent tests may have eliminated such obvious biases, *but they often fail to realize the degree and subtlety of cultural differences or the fact that one can live in the United States, Black or White, and still be a member of another culture.* Questions involving an acorn (see *Newsweek,* October 1994), a cow, or a single-family house missing its chimney may not seem culturally biased, and they still routinely appear on IQ and related tests. But I, for one, have worked with many inner-city children who have never seen any of these items. (Even taking my own college students on archaeological excavations has been a real eye-opener. When we got to Belize several years ago, most had never seen a palm tree, or a picture of one, and did not know what they were; some had never seen a pig before and didn't recognize one!) Moreover, we have to remember that mere exposure to such objects or their pictures is not sufficient to make the tests fair. If the objects have no salience to an individual's own life, they are less likely to be learned well. (Perhaps we could get rid of such culturally loaded items on the tests, although I doubt it. What items would be left?)

Questions involving drawings, of course, also have another layer of bias. It has been pointed out repeatedly that people in nonliterate cultures who know the items on which they are being tested may have difficulty interpreting two-dimensional drawings of those objects—a failure to understand our conventional representation, not ignorance of the objects of their own world. And we have to remember that drawing conventions vary from culture to culture even among literate groups and even within our own society. One IQ question still used involves noting the fact that a drawing of a cow with three legs is missing the fourth. It is supposed to be a straightforward question about cows. But we often draw a cow with only two or three legs *showing* depending on perspective and degree of stylization. (Line drawings are by definition very stylized.) So what is actually tested here is the knowledge that *in the drawing convention being employed,* a fourth leg would normally be depicted. But those are cultural rules, not simple logic or even natural knowledge.

But the real problem is much deeper and concerns the deeper meaning of cultural differences.

I recently had occasion to sit through a presentation by a psychologist of the very latest IQ questions offered in defense of IQ testing. Many of the errors above had been expunged and real efforts had been made to make the tests fair—*as long as cultural differences are understood to refer only to the cultural item content of the questions, not to the form of the questions or their underlying presentation, cultural "grammar," or logic.* It is as if we were studying French vocabulary but not grammar, French cuisine or art but not the logic of the thinking of French people. Once we begin looking at the structure of the questions as well as their content, every one can be dissected and layers of bias peeled away like the layers of an onion until nothing is left. We can do this dissection but have to bear in mind that most of us were reared with many of the same cultural biases and may not notice them because we take them for granted. I recommend that you dissect the following questions using these examples as a starting point.

Item. One question asks students to identify *either* of two famous, dead scientists, Albert Einstein or G. W. Carver. The question must be "fair" because it has both a Black and a White scientist! But I can think of at least two more levels of cultural bias (and I am sure there are more.) First, the category "scientist" is itself more salient in White American culture than in inner-city Black American culture (Carver is mostly a White person's Black hero) so a White is more likely to identify a scientist of either race. Second (I am not certain whether this applies to Black/White differences, but it surely applies more broadly), one culture, like ours, might focus more than another on the use of printed pictures as a way of "knowing" as opposed to, say, televised action images, oral traditions, or rap music. (In fact, "knowing" might be altogether less visual in some cultures than in others without implying that people were either less intelligent or even more ignorant of the subject.)

Item. Analogy problems of the type "*acorn* has the same relationship to *seed* as *oak* has to--?" (that appeared in *Newsweek,* October 1994) are supposed to measure logical ability, but in fact they are based on the way people put things in categories. All analogies, by definition, are based on categorizing. Any anthropologist familiar with Cole and Gay's work on Africa (or who has worked with Mesoamerican populations that employ the famous hot/cold classification) knows that different cultures classify things in different ways or at least focus initially on different (to them) salient properties. But IQ testers and the general public are apparently oblivious to this point. And we, ourselves, of course often classify things in different ways depending on the context. The answer to the acorn problem (*tree*) depends on whether one uses "seed" as an inclusive category containing acorns or whether acorns are "nuts" as opposed to seeds, as archaeologists often use the terms. (Remember that one need not be completely ignorant of a classifying principle to be penalized on an IQ test; one only has to be momentarily confused or slowed by the awareness of alternative possibilities. One's response only has to be less conditioned or automatic.)

Item. Using cartoon figures (that are supposed to be culture-free), students are asked to identify whether two figures viewed at separate times are the same or different. The correct answer in this case is that the two figures are different because the diagonal stripes on their tunics go in different directions. Most of the adults who attended the presentation where these questions were posed missed that one. A child—characterized by the psychologist on this basis as "extremely bright"—got it right. Anthropologists in the audience couldn't help thinking that anyone from a culture that marked gender or class by the direction of their stripes probably got it right. What was important was not mental ability(s) but cultural differences governing which visual distinctions, like phonemes, one is taught to identify and use, and which distinctions, like other phonetic distinctions, one is simply taught to ignore. (Most Americans probably pay no attention to whether a man's earring is in his right or left ear; but for some, that is important cultural information that they don't miss and that they remember. Most American men do notice on which finger a woman is wearing a ring, although in culture-free terms, it is a trivial thing.) The child got this question right not because she was "bright," but because she hadn't been socialized yet to ignore what our culture considers extraneous; but she was probably well trained to look for such details by the kind of common tests of sameness/difference that we give children in game books and comic strips.

Most Americans really can't comprehend that there are other systems of thought and they fail to recognize the "blinders" that our own culture imposes, blinders that keep us looking in a common direction and prevent us from seeing alternatives. The people who are trying to make IQ tests "fair"—

like the people who are teaching "international business"—apparently have no idea what it actually involves; nor do the people who are sick of affirmative action and who fail to realize the degree to which the status quo—reinforced by the tests is itself affirmative action for the in-group. They don't realize that by relying on tests of cultural literacy for so much of our social placement, we are not only discriminating, we are also straight jacketing our employees and limiting the richness we all might enjoy if we tolerated more cultural diversity in thinking and emotion, not just in food. Other aspects of our lives stand to be enriched as much as our cuisine or music. (Our medicine, for example, is now starting to react constructively to, and be enriched by, the knowledge of other groups.) Even efficiency might well increase through broader cultural tolerance after a period of adjustment. After all, in other areas, we tend to think that efficiency and quality improve as the variety of available options to select from increases.

This is what we must learn. Reasonable world order and understanding and cultural enrichment depend on it. We have to move public beyond the sense that "cultural relativism" means a kind of mindless blanket acceptance, abandoning judgment and simply equating all human behavior as the idea is portrayed by our critics. Instead, we need to focus on relativism's two major lessons: that we have to try to understand other people and their actions in context, and that we have to be willing to explore the limits and biases of our own cultural assumptions.

Review Questions

1. According to Cohen, what are the main points about IQ and race contained in Murray and Herrnstein's book, *The Bell Curve*?
2. What are some of the objections raised by anthropologists to the theory and evidence contained in *The Bell Curve*?
3. According to Cohen, how do cross-cultural differences invalidate IQ as a comparative measure of intelligence among groups? Identify three specific examples of this from the article.
4. Many anthropologists argue that as the term is used by Americans, *race* really designates culturally defined, not genetically determined, groups. What evidence supports or refutes this idea?

24

The Vice Lord Phoenix

Lincoln Keiser

Newspapers, TV news programs, and "specials" regularly report on the depredations of inner city gangs and their "alarming" spread to nearby suburbs. They also often trumpet the successes achieved by police actions and, less often, social programs designed to control or eliminate gangs. Yet gangs persist. Why this is the case is the topic of this article by Lincoln Keiser, whose pioneering ethnographic study of a Chicago gang, the Vice Lords, was originally published in 1969. Looking first at the way gangs are depicted by the media and people in authority, he continues by pointing out that gangs, despite official suppression, reappear and thrive because they prove highly adaptive to their members in the context of inner-city poverty and penitentiary control.

For the last twenty-five years I've played pick-up basketball every Monday, Wednesday, and Friday beginning at noon. Noon-ball, as it is called, has an interesting mix of players. Besides the students, some of the regulars work at the university where the game is played; some work in town

---

This article was written especially for *Conformity and Conflict.* Copyright © by Lincoln Keiser, 1997. Printed by permission of the author.

at various professional and non-professional jobs; and some are street people who work sporadically, if at all. Besides a good work-out, the best thing about noon-ball is the opportunity for me to make connections across race and class lines. But this paper is not about noon-ball, although that in itself would be a fascinating subject for the anthropological lens. Rather noon-ball began this paper for me.

A year ago last summer Joe, one of the guys from the African/American community in town, brought a copy of the *Examiner,* a supermarket tabloid, to the basketball court. Now Joe knew that the *Examiner* didn't exactly sit next to the *American Anthropologist* on my bookcase. Moreover, he knew as well of my previous work on gangs.[1] In this particular issue he had found an article called "Death of the Evil . . . Vice Lords" (with the sub-heading "America's most-feared and wanted drug gang goes out with just a whimper"),[2] and thought I might be interested. I was. For this piece relates to how poverty in the inner city is rooted in oppressive political and economic inequalities; to how popular culture creates meanings and understandings that obscure these roots; and to how these meanings and understandings are produced and maintained.[3]

But the piece does more than this. It also resonates, if ever so faintly, with something that should be just as important to anthropologists working in the inner city, specifically, understanding how, in various urban contexts, ". . . social actors organize themselves, relate to one another, acquire and use resources, (and) create order and meaning in their lives," to use the words of Michael Peletz.[4] In other words, this piece suggests ways to go beyond identifying the existence of oppression, as important as that might be, to analyzing how it works in shaping patterns of social relationships and the meanings and understandings that give them the degree of order and disorder they possess. When we do this, we find that oppression works in complex ways, with often unexpected and unintended consequences. This leads to my main focus—namely, using this framework to understand how groups like the Vice Lords, (started by a small group of friends in an Illinois juvenile detention facility some forty odd years ago) got to be cats with so many lives.

I should make clear that what I have to say is not based on recent fieldwork. This paper is a set of hypotheses, based on several sources of information. Its conclusions need to be tested, clarified, and modified by focused field research.

So, the *Examiner* has proclaimed the death of the Vice Lords, "Americas most feared and dreaded drug gang." But in the past forty years the Vice

---

1 R. Lincoln Keiser, *The Vice Lords: Warriors of the Streets* (New York: Holt, Rinehart, and Winston, 1969); "Some Thoughts on Generative Models in Urban Anthropology" *Ethnos* vol. 38: I–IV, 1974.

2 "Death of the Evil . . . Vice Lords" The *Examiner,* August 9, 1994.

3 Steven Gregory, "Time to Make the Doughnuts: On the Politics of Subjugation in the "Inner City,'" *PoLAR,* vol. 17, no. 1, 1994.

4 Michael G. Peletz, "Kinship Studies in Late 20th Century Anthropology," in William H. Durham, ed. *Annual Review of Anthropology* vol. 24, (Palo Alto: Annual Reviews Inc., 1995).

Lords and other similar groups in Chicago have been declared dead many times by powers of mainstream society, e.g., the Chicago police and the major daily newspapers. Yet, like phoenixes, they always rise from their ashes.

To understand why this is so let's begin by looking at the spin the media gives to the Vice Lords, and groups like the Black P-Stone Nation and the Gangster Disciples. The Examiner piece is particularly valuable in this respect because it's hyperbolic, alien-gives-birth-to-two-headed-monster-on-crowded-disco-floor approach to its subjects clarifies by its very exaggeration things often hidden by the more subtle approach of the traditional dailies.

The piece starts like this:

> In a stunning predawn raid, Chicago cops busted 21 top members of America's most powerful street gang—and broke their brutal hold on the city's crime-ravaged West Side. Their prize catch was kingpin Willie Lloyd, the arrogant, flamboyant boss of a multimillion-dollar crack cocaine dynasty that ruled the streets with an iron fist. When prosecutors finally convicted Lloyd on a weapons charge, it was a crushing blow to the 1,000-member Unknown Vice Lords, a savage criminal operation that forced kids and families into nightmare lives of coke, crime and degradation. "These people held a Chicago neighborhood hostage," says prosecutor Michael Smith. "They lived by none of society's rules. They lied, they cheated, they murdered and finally they turned on each other."

The piece goes on to tell how kingpin Lloyd "brazenly" spoke to his underlings by speaker phone while in jail, and even ran a snack shop and game room from his cell. (We'll come back to the snack shop later in the paper.) Finally, it tells with special relish how Lloyd was found having sex with his girlfriend in the jurors's bathroom during a court appearance.

The sub-narrative in the *Examiner* article is clear. The ills of the inner city, (people living lives of drugs, crime, and degradation) are caused by powerful criminal street gangs headed by evil tyrannical bosses that oppress entire urban communities. But if the guys in the white hats can smash these criminal organizations and put the evildoers away, they can no longer threaten the lives of everyday citizens. This will go a long way toward curing the sickness of the inner city.

This same narrative underlies news stories in more main stream newspapers, although the message there is more subtly told. Last summer the *Chicago Tribune* ran a series of articles about Larry Hoover and the Gangster Disciples, the group he heads.[5] Hoover, and other leaders of the Gangster Disciples, had just been indicted by the federal government on a variety of drug-related charges. Interestingly enough, the indictments came while Hoover was imprisoned in an Illinois correctional center.

These articles contain interesting ethnography, some of which I'll get to here. First, though, let's look at the way the *Tribune* portrayed Hoover.

---

[5] "U.S. Goes behind Bars to Indict 39 Gang Leaders," The *Chicago Tribune,* September 1, 1995; "Peace Can Have Its Price: Gang Leaders Often Keep Prisons in Tow," The *Chicago Tribune,* September 1, 1995; "Gang Indictments May Be Double-edged Sword," The *Chicago Tribune,* September 3, 1995.

Hoover is more difficult to demonize than Willie Lloyd, for he had captured the imagination of many people in Chicago through his attempts to use the Disciples as a force for political change, both in the Illinois prisons and the inner city. Hoover had played a key role in forging peace agreements with the Vice Lords, and, as the *Tribune* reported, he began a political action committee that registered many ghetto residents to vote, his organization sponsored public rap concerts, and his associates had even started a legitimate business, developing a line of clothing with designs created by Hoover himself. In prison he used his political power to maintain peace and to reduce the incidence of rape.

Yet, the article minimizes this side of Hoover by portraying it as a smoke screen designed to hide his real purpose, i.e., protecting and developing the Disciples's corner of the illegal drug trade. To quote the *Tribune,*

> The indictment of Hoover and 38 others, including a Chicago police officer, on federal drug conspiracy charges was portrayed as a crippling blow to the Midwest's largest and most violent street gang ... "I guess I would say, I told you so," said Jack Hynes, an assistant Cook County state's attorney who has vigorously opposed Hoover's efforts for parole from a murder conviction for which he has spent the last 21 years in prison. "This indictment has kind of torn down the facade and exposed the gang for what they are."

So the guys in the white hats have once again helped make the streets of the inner city safe by taking a guy who was behind bars, and well . . . putting him behind some more bars. It takes me back to Kohistan (a region of Pakistan where I have done research) and one old guy who threatened my research assistant with retribution if he ever told about the history of the village. "I'll find you in the after life and kill you!", he had said. The logic in protecting the public by jailing a person already in jail didn't seem to bother the federal prosecutors and state's attorneys any more than killing a person who was already dead bothered the old Kohistani.

But state's attorneys and federal prosecutors are not stupid. It seems clear to me that their actions, and the reporting of them in the newspapers, is not just about keeping the streets safe from urban predators. No. It's more about maintaining a political hierarchy in which the power of ghetto residents is minimized. In other words, it's oppression in action.

What interests me in this case, however, is not the existence of oppression. Nor is it even how oppression relates to hegemony and counter hegemony, to use jargon popular in contemporary anthropology. Rather what I find interesting is how the particular form oppression takes in this case affects patterns of social relationships and cultural forms in the inner city.

O.K., so politicians encourage the police to get the drug gangs off the streets by arresting and jailing their members, and instruct the courts to keep them in jail by passing laws requiring harsh, mandatory sentences. And all of this is supported in the media by giving our understanding of street gangs a particular spin. Not surprisingly, the police take their job very seriously, and, in the name of freeing the inner city from fear, arrest young ghetto males in gigantic numbers. The National Institute on Drug Abuse recently released figures showing that on any given day, one in three ghetto males between the ages of 20 and 29 is under the supervision of the criminal justice system, a figure vastly higher than accounted for either by their percentage of the population, or their rate of drug use.[6]

Undoubtedly this has many important consequences for ghetto men, but I have time to talk about only one here. Young men in the ghetto obviously see what's happening around them and know that in all probability the continuity in their lives will involve regular movements between prison and the streets. David Jacobson made this point about ghetto males in a piece entitled "Mobility, Continuity, and Urban Social Organization" back in 1971. He argued that for ghetto men,

> . . . the prospects were those of moving between street life and prison, a pattern of circulation which can be seen to underlie the persistence of their relationships, since they expect to see each other again and again both in and out of jail."[7]

By a rather circuitous route, this takes us back to Willie Lloyd and the snack shop he allegedly ran while in prison. Although some have criticized it, the best prison ethnography I have seen is R. T. Davidson's *Chicano Prisoners: The Key to San Quentin*. And what he had to say about underground prison shops (including snack shops) and how they operate in the underground prison economy is particularly illuminating. According to Davidson underground prison shops were sources of goods that made life more tolerable for the prisoners of San Quentin. Consequently, the control of their business was a major concern of the prisoner power structure.[8]

Obviously, San Quentin of the early 1970s does not equal the Illinois correctional facilities of today. Yet, material contained in the *Tribune* stories hints at a prison social/cultural system similar in many ways. Thus, according to the *Tribune,* "When inmates at Pontiac Correctional Center want a hot pizza, they can place an order and enjoy one fresh from the oven in the comfort of their cells, courtesy of a delivery man who also happens to be a fellow prisoner."

If these "Pizza Huts" (and the snack shop run by Willie Lloyd) do business like the underground shops described by Davidson, then it's not unlikely they are regulated by powers other than the prison authorities. And we know this must be the case with the production and circulation of illegal drugs and weapons in the Illinois prisons.

Like San Quentin, it seems clear that much of the political and economic power in underground prison society in Illinois lies in the hands of gangs (but unlike San Quentin these are African-American organizations rather than Chicano ones). As the *Tribune* reports, "So powerful are some inmate

---

[6] "More Blacks in their 20's Have Trouble with the Law," *New York Times,* October 5, 1995, p. 18.

[7] David Jacobson, "Mobility, Continuity, and Urban Social Organization," *Man* (n.s.) vol. 6, no. 4, 1971, p. 636.

[8] R. Theodore Davidson, *Chicano Prisoners: The Key to San Quentin* (New York: Holt, Rinehart, and Winston, 1974, pp.101–147).

leaders in state prisons that they can provide contraband items to other prisoners . . . The state prisons (are) run by the gangs that populate them." As Magnus Seng, a professor of criminal justice at Loyola University in Chicago noted, prison officials ". . . couldn't run the prisons otherwise . . . The inmates are running the place to some extent. There's a subrosa economy, a small town run by inmates."[9] And, as Bobby Gore, a Vice Lord leader from the 1960s, and now an activist with the Safer Foundation, noted, "That's the way it ought to be."[10]

We can see now how valuable gang membership is to ghetto men given the current political and economic situation in the inner city. On the streets, gangs provide a way to make a living for men with few job skills, fewer job opportunities, and a fast eroding welfare safety net. In prison, gangs can make the difference between easy time and hard time, protecting their members from violence and predation and organizing the allocation of scarce resources.

This double function is particularly important given the alternating pattern between the streets and jail that dominates the career paths of so many ghetto men. For gangs help make the transition both from the streets to jail, and from jail to the streets, relatively smooth for their members. Consequently, gang membership is a valuable resource, one made even more valuable by the punitive and repressive policies currently in favor in our country. The more jails we build, the more ghetto men we fill them with, the more we tear down the welfare system and the more jobs we cut, the more strong and vital groups like the Vice Lords, the Gangster Disciples, and the Black P-Stone Nation become. The very policies designed to destroy street gangs in fact have created phoenixes that rise ever stronger from their ashes.

One last note to all this. Federal prosecutors argue that arresting Larry Hoover and putting him behind federal bars will affect the Disciples's ability to function effectively because federal prisons are more restrictive on prisoner's movements, making it more difficult for Hoover to run his drug empire. In this light it's interesting to note a recent Associated Press release describing the growing influence of gangs in federal prisons. If history is any indication, putting such a skilled political leader as Larry Hoover in the federal prison system is like putting the fox in the chicken coup. It will come back to haunt us.

As I look at this, there are a number of missing threads that need to be woven into the argument. First, I need to discuss the phenomenon of oppression in greater detail. Some interesting work has been done in defining and honing our understanding of it.[11] Bringing this into the discussion would make my analysis stronger. Second, I need to think more about gangs in relation to inner-city street culture. I especially need to analyze how gangs re-

---

[9] "Peace Can Have Its Price: Gang Leaders Often Keep Prisons in Tow," *Chicago Tribune*, September 1, 1995, p. 7.

[10] ibid.

[11] Marilyn Frye, "Oppression" in Margaret L. Andersen and Patricia Hill Collins, eds. (Belmont, CA: Wadsworth, 1992).

late to the critical importance of respect and disrespect in the negotiation of social relationships.

Finally, I need to add an historical dimension to the argument by analyzing how the Vice Lords and other similar groups changed their focus over time from fighting to selling drugs. Prison is crucial in this transition, and I need to weave into my account how learning to control the underground prison economy provided gang members with the skills they needed to run a sophisticated drug operation. If I'm right about this, then sending the Vice Lords to the state penitentiary in the 1970s was like sending them to the Northwestern University Business School. At the time, the penitentiary was the educational institution with the best MBA program in the state in the illegal drug trade.

Review Questions

1. According to Keiser, how do U.S. authorities and the American media portray the organization, activities, and role of inner-city gangs?
2. How does Keiser explain the persistent rebirth of gangs in the face of official attempts by people in authority to eliminate them?
3. What functions do gangs perform for their members, both in cities and penitentiaries, in Keiser's opinion?
4. What do you think are the root factors that make gang membership especially attractive to inner-city males?

8

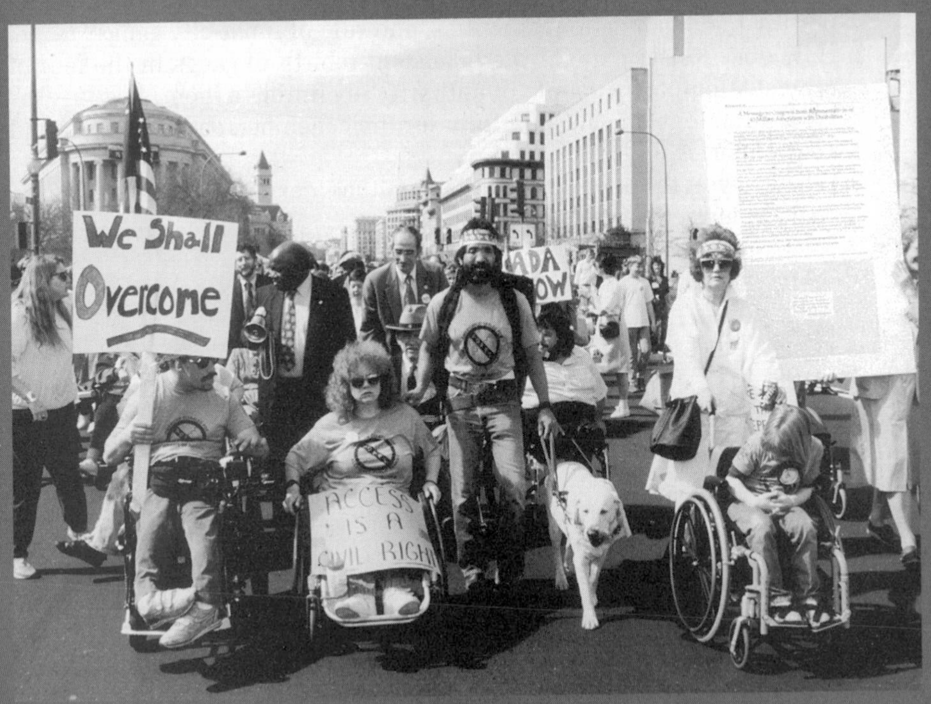

LAW AND POLITICS

Ideally, culture provides the blueprint for a smoothly oiled social machine whose parts work together under all circumstances. But human society is not like a rigidly constructed machine. It is made of individuals who have their own special needs and desires. Personal interest, competition for scarce resources, and simple accident can cause nonconformity and disputes, resulting in serious disorganization.

One way we manage social disruption is through the socialization of children. As we acquire our culture, we learn the appropriate ways to look at experience, to define our existence, and to feel about life. Each system of cultural knowledge contains implicit values of what is desirable, and we come to share these values with other people. Slowly, with the acquisition of culture, most people find they *want* to do what they *must* do; the requirements of an orderly social life become personal goals.

Enculturation, however, is rarely enough. Disputes among individuals regularly occur in all societies, and how such disagreements are handled defines what anthropologists mean by the legal system. Some disputes are *infralegal*; they never reach a point where they are settled by individuals with special authority. Neighbors, for example, would engage in an infralegal dispute if they argued over who should pay for the damage caused by water that runs off one's land into the other's basement. So long as they don't take the matter to court or resort to violence, the dispute will remain infralegal. This dispute may become *extralegal,* however, if it occurs outside the law and escalates into violence. Had the neighbors come to blows over the waterlogged basement, the dispute would have become extralegal. Feuds and wars are the best examples of this kind of dispute.

Legal disputes, on the other hand, involve socially approved mechanisms for their settlement. *Law* is the cultural knowledge that people use to settle disputes by means of agents who have the recognized authority to do so. Thus if the argument between neighbors cited above ended up in court before a judge or referee, it would have become legal.

Although we Americans often think of courts as synonymous with the legal system, societies have evolved a variety of structures for settling disputes. For example, some disputes may be settled by *self-redress,* meaning that wronged individuals are given the right to settle matters themselves. *Contests* requiring physical or mental combat between disputants may also be used to settle disputes. A trusted third party, or *go-between,* may be asked to negotiate with each side until a settlement is achieved. In some societies, supernatural power or beings may be used. In parts of India, for example, disputants are asked to take an oath in the name of a powerful deity or (at least in the past) to submit to a supernaturally controlled, painful, or physically dangerous test, called an *ordeal.* Disputes may also be taken to a *moot,* an informal community meeting where conflict may be aired. At the moot, talk continues until a settlement is reached. Finally, as we saw above, disputes are often taken to *courts,* which are formally organized and include officials with authority to make and enforce decisions.

Political systems are closely related to legal ones and often involve some of the same offices and actors. The *political system* contains the process for making and carrying out public policy according to cultural categories and rules; *policy* refers to guidelines for action. The *public* are the people affected by the policy. Every society must make decisions that affect all or most of its members. The Mbuti Pygmies of the Ituri Forest described by anthropologist Colin Turnbull, for example, occasionally decide to conduct a communal hunt. Hunters set their nets together and wait for the appearance of forest game. Men, women, and children must work together as beaters to drive the animals toward the nets. When the Mbuti decide to hold a hunt, they make a political decision.

The political process requires that people make and abide by a particular policy, often in the face of competing plans. To do so a policy must have *support,* which is anything that contributes to its adoption and enforcement. Anthropologists recognize two main kinds of support: legitimacy and coercion. *Legitimacy* refers to people's positive evaluation of public officials and public policy. A college faculty, for example, may decide to institute the quarter system because a majority feel that quarters rather than semesters represent the "right length" for courses. Theirs is a positive evaluation of the policy. Some faculty members will oppose the change but will abide by the decision because they value the authority of faculty governance. For them the decision, although unfortunate, is legitimate.

Coercion, on the other hand, is support derived from the threat or use of force or the promise of short-term gain. Had the faculty members adopted the quarter system because they had been threatened with termination by the administration, they would have acted under coercion.

There are also other important aspects of the political process. Some members of a society may be given *authority,* the right to make and enforce public policy. In our country, elected officials are given authority to make certain decisions and exercise particular powers. However, formal political offices with authority do not occur in every society. Most hunting and gathering societies lack such positions, as do many horticulturalists. *Leadership,* which is the ability to influence others to act, must be exercised informally in these societies.

The selections in this part illustrate several aspects of legal and political systems. The first article, by Mindie Lazarus-Black, looks at how poor women living on the Caribbean Island of Antigua use the state-sponsored legal system and child-support laws to reinforce informal kinship rules and to control men. In the second article, Anne Sutherland describes what happens when the substantive laws of two groups collide in court. A young Gypsy man is convicted for using another family member's social security number although he has no intention of defrauding anyone. The third article, by Elizabeth Eames, looks at the political institution of bureaucracy. Drawing on the theory of Max Weber, she notes that bureaucracy, which is designed to be impersonal and even-handed in Europe and America, is a personal institution in Nigeria. The final selection, by Norman Chance, describes the relationship between the United States government, oil companies, and the Iñupiat Eskimo of the Alaskan north slope. Forty years of change has resulted in the formation of an Iñupiat municipal government, Iñupiat-run private corporations, and direct political involvement of the Iñupiat in U.S. environmental legislation.

Key Terms

infralegal
extralegal
law
self-redress
contest
go-between
ordeal
moot
court
political system
policy
public
support
legitimacy
coercion
authority
leadership

Readings in This Section

Why Women Take Men to Magistrate's Court *Mindie Lazarus-Black,* page *270*

Cross-cultural Law: The Case of the Gypsy Offender *Anne Sutherland,* page *282*

Navigating Nigerian Bureaucracies *Elizabeth A. Eames,* page *290*

Government, Oil, and Political Transformation: The Iñupiat Eskimo Case *Norman A. Chance,* page *299*

25

Why Women Take Men to Magistrate's Court

Mindie Lazarus-Black

Part of every legal system is substantive law, *the legal statutes that define right and wrong. Such statutes may be written down or may simply be agreed-upon principles. When statutes are violated, the law comes into play. But people often use the legal system in ways that transcend the literal meaning of substantive law, as Mindie Lazarus-Black demonstrates in this article about how lower-class Antiguan women use the magistrate's court. Antiguan substantive law requires men to pay support for their children when the latter are born outside of formal marriage. Women, however, rarely take the fathers of their children to court for this reason. Instead, they use this statute against men who fail to meet a variety of other, less formally defined, kinship obligations or who refuse to treat the mothers of their children with proper respect. "Big men," who are most easily shamed by court proceedings, are the most likely targets. In this way, women use the court to control men's behavior and enforce important kinship values.*

Reprinted by permission from Mari Womack and Judith Marti, editors, *The Other Fifty Percent: Multicultural Perspectives on Gender Relations* (Prospect Heights, IL: Waveland Press); copyright © by the Waveland Press, 1993.

Every Thursday afternoon a list of "Order in Bastardy, Maintenance, and Arrears" is posted on the wall of the St. John's magistrate's court in Antigua, West Indies. In a typical week, six to eight new cases are scheduled for hearing, while twenty or thirty others are brought by the collecting officer of the state against men who have neglected to pay child support. There were 1,493 cases of maintenance and arrears in 1984, 1,287 cases in 1985. Given a population of approximately 65,000 in Antigua and Barbuda, such case loads indicate that the court is frequently utilized.

Academic, legal, and popular wisdom holds that these West Indian women are going to magistrate's court for money because the babies' fathers fail to support them or to pay regularly enough. They go to court because they are unemployed or underemployed with too many illegitimate children to raise and too few dollars with which to do so. But when I asked one woman if she went to court for money, her answer surprised me. She looked at me indignantly and said, "I carry my case up there for justice. I complain him for justice."

This article explores ideas about justice which are integral to kinship relations in Antigua and Barbuda. "Carrying a case" to the magistrate's court exemplifies the interaction between state forms and community norms and demonstrates that certain rules and judicial processes of the Antiguan state are now constituent of local family ideology and practice. That is, Antiguan women regularly take cases to court to demand justice in their kinship relations, to assert their autonomy and rights, and to resist the pervasive hierarchical structures of gender and class.

The Legacy of Colonialism

British and European colonists brought to the West Indies cultural traditions in which families were legally constituted and then duly went about relegislating kinship. In the case of Antigua, as early as 1672 and at regular intervals over the next three centuries, legal codes were absolutely critical to creating and maintaining different social ranks in the colony and to regulating families, gender and race. Local legislators wrestled with questions about who might marry whom, which persons constituted "family," and what rights and duties such connections bestowed. The kinship order these lawmakers instituted for Antiguans departed dramatically from the rules that guided kinship in Great Britain. The legacy of colonialism included both detailed kinship laws and an elaborate hierarchy of courts.

Antigua was first colonized in 1632, mainly by English and Irish adventurers, soldiers, farmers, and laborers. Early lawmakers and judges consisted of a very small group of men of property, most of them planters. The switch from tobacco and cotton to sugar began in the 1650s. At that time, the colony was comprised of small farmers and a good number of European indentured servants. A century later, 93.5 percent of the population were slaves and most worked on large sugar plantations. . . .

The kinship laws Antiguan planters wrote were directed at controlling marriage and human reproduction, and also at reproducing the hierarchical social and economic structure of capitalism. Codes made it illegal for slaves to marry free persons, prevented indentured servants from marrying without their masters' permission, granted the right to perform marriage ceremonies only to Anglican ministers, and made white men responsible for their white bastard children.

The *Leeward Islands Amelioration Act,* passed in Antigua in 1798, also set up a separate system of marriage for slaves. According to this act, a slave marriage was monogamous but not contractual, since the nuptials bestowed none of the rights and duties implied in marriages of free persons. Nor did a slave marriage convey upon children the status or title of the husband/father. The law did include provision for public declaration of a couple's intention to live together and for monetary awards from their masters.

The colonists also established a hierarchy of courts. By the end of the eighteenth century, there was a Court of Chancery, a Court of Error and Appeal, a Court of King's Bench and Grand Sessions, a Court of Common Pleas, a Court Ordinary, a Court Merchant, and a Court of Admiralty. In addition, complaints between indentured servants and masters, and masters and slaves, were heard by itinerant justices of the peace.

Slavery was abolished in Antigua in 1834. In reality, abolition brought few dramatic changes to the lives of the ex-slaves. Limited availability of free land and the infamous Contract Act, which set new terms between workers and planters, combined to make it difficult to leave the estates. The Contract Act not only made it arduous to find a new employer, it also directed who might legally reside with whom in the estate huts, and commanded labor from each member of a man's family. Other social welfare legislation of this period made the destitute, the infirm, and the elderly the economic responsibility of their kin, not of the government.

Lawmakers passed in 1875 *An Act for the Better Support of Natural Children, and to afford Facilities for obliging the Putative Father to assist in the Maintenance of such Children.* The statute set procedures for obtaining affiliation orders, bestowed power upon magistrates to establish relationships between illegitimate children and their fathers, and designated stipends for men to provide for their offspring. Any woman who delivered a bastard child could apply for a support order. The request had to be made within a year after the baby's birth unless she could prove that previously the man had cared for the child. At the hearing parties could bring witnesses and had the right to counsel.

Weekly support payments were limited to five shillings for the first six weeks and to two shillings and six pence thereafter until the child attained the age of twelve or until the mother married. Stipends were payable directly to the mother, and she had to apply for arrears within thirteen weeks or they were forfeited. The magistrate also had discretionary power to order the father to pay the costs of the case, a payment to the midwife, and funeral expenses if necessary. He could appoint a guardian for a child if the mother died, was of unsound mind, or went to prison. A putative father could appeal his case to the High Court, but the magistrate had power to send him to jail and to sell his property for failure to comply with the bastardy order.

With only slight modifications, the bastardy law still functions today. The act exemplifies both the continuous intervention of the state in matters of kinship and the hegemonic character of legalities in local communities. The bastardy law is regularly invoked by contemporary Antiguan women, although not always for reasons envisioned by nineteenth-century and later lawmakers.

The Economic and Political Context

Antigua's present population is almost entirely African-Caribbean. A few people have British and other European forefathers, others are descendants of Syrian and Lebanese traders who arrived early in the twentieth century, and there are some expatriate Americans and Canadians. English is the standard language, although there is a creole dialect. Most islanders are literate and most consider themselves Christian.

Historic dependence upon sugar exports prevented Antigua from achieving economic self-sufficiency. Agriculture remains in general decline today, despite a variety of efforts to revive it. Manufacturing and industry are developing slowly, but in the last two decades tourism has emerged as the most important economic sector. . . . Its direct value now accounts for approximately 21 percent of the gross domestic product, and at least 12 percent of the labor force works in tourism. . . . Government employs about 30 percent of all working persons. Unemployment remained at around 20 percent through the first half of the 1980s. . . .

Antiguan planters controlled local politics until labor unrest heralded a movement for social and economic reform early in this century. Unions were legalized in 1940 and adult suffrage was granted in 1951. Shortly thereafter, election rules were changed to allow greater representation of the working people. In 1979, the islands became an Associated State, gaining control over local affairs but still under British authority with respect to external relations and defense. Independence came in 1981. Antigua and Barbuda is now a parliamentary democracy with a Prime Minister, Senate, and House of Representative. The government proclaimed a non-aligned foreign policy at independence, but maintains strongest political and economic ties with Britain, Canada, and the United States.

Antigua's two social classes, middle and lower, can be differentiated into smaller strata based upon members' socioeconomic status and ability to wield formal political power. At the top of the present hierarchy is a small local elite which holds elected political authority. In contrast to the days when sugar dominated, this elite is Antiguan-born, black, and increasingly educated in the Caribbean. Within this same stratum are foreign businessmen and expatriates who play important roles in the economy but who are noticeably absent from the official political process. The lifestyle and domestic organization of the elite, however, are virtually indistinguishable from Antigua's middle class. Such similarities help explain why middle-class persons almost always say that Antigua has only two classes. Middle-class women rarely use the magistrate's court to order their kinship relations. Moreover, the ideology of class protects middle-class men from being named publicly as the fathers of illegitimate children.

Quite the opposite is true of the lower class, which uses the courts regularly. In some respects, the lower class is also more heterogeneous than the middle class. Its upper stratum consists of a petite bourgeoisie, "who own small amounts of productive resources and have control over their working conditions in ways that proletarians do not." . . . [1] Petite bourgeoisie men are often jacks-of-all-trades. They may own some land, raise a few cattle or goats, and work a job or two for weekly cash. Petite bourgeoisie women run their own small shops or work from their homes as seamstresses or hairdressers. In contrast, members of the working class have little or no property and only their own labor to sell. They include agricultural workers, fishermen, sales persons, domestics, hotel workers, and laborers. They are low-income, hard-working people for whom multiple jobs and job-sharing are common.

In contrast to Antigua, class is not relevant in Barbuda. Antigua's sister island was leased to the Codrington family in 1685 and 1705. The Codringtons used Barbuda as a supply depot and manufacturing center for their estates in Antigua. Until 1898 when the Antiguan legislature assumed financial responsibility for its government, Barbuda was virtually without political representation, welfare or educational services, or legal institutions.

The island has remained sparsely populated. Codrington, the only village, is home to approximately 1,200 people—almost all descendants of Codrington's slaves. Today many Barbudan men fish for their living. Others raise cattle. Both men and women work subsistence gardens and continue to insist upon communal ownership of land outside the village despite opposition from the government in Antigua. . . . Barbuda has a few shops, a couple of hotels where people find seasonal work, an elementary school, a health clinic, several churches, and a few government buildings. During my field work, a room in the police station served as a temporary courtroom upon the arrival of the magistrate.

The Courts, the Codes, and the Litigants

The organization of the courts and the legal codes partially determine who comes to the magistrate's court, the types of complaints that are filed, and how any particular case will fare. A four-tiered court system presently serves the islands. The first tier consists of the magistrate's courts. Affiliation and maintenance cases, arrears, disputes between persons over small property claims, personal grievances, traffic matters, and minor assaults are brought to

[1] R. Rapp, "Family and Class in Contemporary America: Notes Toward an Understanding of Ideology," in *Rethinking the Family: Some Feminist Questions,* edited by B. Thorne (New York: Longman 1982), 180.

these courts. In addition to the magistrate's court serving the capitol city of St. John's, three "country courts" meet weekly in the villages of Bolans, All Saints, and Parham. By law, the magistrate holds court in Barbuda four times a year for two or three days, depending upon the case load. The Barbuda court draws quite a crowd. Interested bystanders make humorous comments about the litigants and their cases, sometimes to the chagrin of the magistrate.

The second tier in the legal system is the High Court. The High Court also settles major property and criminal cases, and family matters such as divorce, adoption, and contested wills. The third tier, the Appellate Division of the Supreme Court of the Eastern Caribbean, meets intermittently in the different Leeward Islands. Finally, since Antigua and Barbuda is a member of the Commonwealth, cases decided by the Supreme Court may be appealed, as a last resort, to the Privy Council in England.

Kinship statutes instruct who shall use which of these courts to resolve family disputes. When I conducted field work, statutes distinguished persons on the basis of their marital status (single or married) and their birth status (legitimate or illegitimate). Married persons have the option of applying either to the High Court or the magistrate's court for legal remedy with respect to certain kinship disputes. For example, a married woman may apply to the magistrate for relief if a spouse has committed adultery or aggravated assault upon the applicant, or is guilty of persistent cruelty or desertion, or is a habitual drunkard. The magistrate has authority to order that the complainant no longer be bound to cohabit with the defendant, award legal custody of children to the applicant, and direct the defendant to pay weekly support for the plaintiff and any "children of the family" for whom the man is legally responsible. Only a woman in a legal union can ask for support for herself. . . . All conflicts between unmarried couples over child care and maintenance must be adjudicated in the magistrate's court.

The persistence of these two alternative legal channels preserves the hierarchical social structure. The system, in place since the nineteenth century, funnels women with illegitimate children through one set of processes and married women through another. The law also differentiates in practice between persons of different social classes, since the two courts are widely acknowledged to have quite different consequences for individuals' family ties and the economy of their households. When I asked whether the magistrate's court might be characterized as a "poor peoples' court," eighteen of twenty-one attorneys concurred.

There are structural, economic, and ideological reasons beyond the factor of legal jurisdiction as to why that characterization holds. First, the magistrate's court is more readily accessible to the lower class. It is cheap to take a case there: the cost of a three-dollar stamp. One need not hire an attorney and, indeed, the majority of litigants with maintenance cases are not represented. Second, in 1987 a magistrate could award a maximum of fifteen Eastern Caribbean dollars per week for child support ($5.67 U.S.) and up to twenty-five E.C. dollars per week ($9.36 U.S.) for support for a married woman. Such small sums are unlikely to draw middle-class women to the court. Moreover, since they are usually married, middle-class women prefer to divide their property and arrange for the welfare of their children at the High Court where judges have much greater discretion in awarding support. In contrast to magistrates, High Court judges investigate the income and property of both parties and the ages and educational needs of the children. Finally, there are ideological reasons why the middle class avoids the magistrate's court. Members of this class, and some lower-class persons as well, consider kinship cases analogous to "hanging one's dirty laundry in public." The court's long association with persons of low status—with rogues and criminals—also dissuades Antiguans concerned about reputation from bringing a case there.

For all of these reasons, the magistrates primarily hear kinship disputes of working-class persons. The large number of family cases is partly due to the frequency with which men who have been adjudged as legal fathers and ordered to pay weekly support fail to make those payments. When a man does not pay for five or six consecutive weeks, the collecting officer requests the magistrate to order the man to give reason why he has neglected to pay. At present, if he chooses not to pay he does not pay until the police track him down. Meanwhile, the number of cases against him continues to multiply on the books.

After cases of unpaid arrears, the most frequently heard family disputes are those in which a woman requests that the man be judged the putative father of her child and an order be made for the child's support. These petitions constituted about 70 percent of all new kinship cases brought before the magistrates each year between 1980 and 1986.

Excluding cases of arrears, almost all of the kinship cases heard by the court are brought by women. Women rely on the courts to establish affiliation and maintenance, to increase support orders, to deny husbands the right to cohabitation, to request maintenance for themselves and their children, to protect the financial interests of a child if a father is about leave the country, and to remove a youth from the home of a negligent parent. Men, on the other hand, file most of the requests for a discharge of a magistrate's order. They have that option as soon as a minor reaches the age of sixteen, if the child comes to reside with them, or if the mother takes the child out of the state.

The plaintiff with a kinship case in the magistrate's court is almost always a lower-class woman, finding herself at odds with a man and her children neglected. The woman may or may not have other children at home to support. In a great many instances, she juggles child care and some form of part-time employment to pay for shelter and food. Usually the union between the man and woman has not been a casual one; most frequently the couple have been seeing each other for over a year and up to several years. Of twenty-two such trials I observed in St. John's, seven involved one child, nine involved two children, four involved three children, and two involved four children. The parties tend to be young, commonly eighteen to thirty-five years of age, but the vast majority were not pregnant teens. Most plaintiffs had never been to court before and most were uncertain about what was expected of them.

The litigants usually did know, however, that a magistrate could award only up to $15 E.C. per week for child support. Indeed, the amount is so low that it can make a difference only to the most indigent. Moreover, if financial considerations were the primary cause for women going to court, we would expect to see a steady rise in the number of cases filed after 1982 when the stipend was raised from $7 to $15 E.C. That was not the case. There was an immediate but temporary rise in the number of requests for affiliation and maintenance in St. John's right after the stipend increased, probably due to the publicity surrounding the change in the law. This may have encouraged some women with easy access to this court to apply for aid for the first time and others to request an increase in the support they already received. Within two years of the passage of the bill, however, the number of new requests had dropped to earlier levels. The court records also show that over the relevant five-year period there were no significant changes in the number of new cases filed in any of the country courts or in Barbuda. Apparently neither urban nor village women were motivated to go to court for purely financial reasons.

Why Women Use the Magistrate's Court

Case histories, interviews with litigants and lawyers, and observations of trials at the magistrate's courts show that Antiguan women take men to court when those men violate local norms about respect, support, and appropriate relations between the sexes. Women invoke the state in the name of justice, using law and forensic processes to ritually enact the meaning, rights, and responsibilities of kin. Two case histories illustrate this phenomenon.

In 1985, Cicely was 38, unmarried, with four children, each of whom had a different father. Cicely supported herself and the children by cleaning offices two days a week, working in a private home one afternoon, and sometimes selling candy, cigarettes, drinks, and other small items on a street-corner from a tray perched upon a styrofoam cooler. Her regular salary was only $95 E.C. per week (about $35 U.S.), and she frequently needed help from her mother, who worked as a kitchen aid, or from her younger sister, a primary school teacher.

Her situation had improved somewhat a year later. She had a full-time cleaning job for which she earned $108 E.C. per week. She had also obtained some funds from an American organization which assisted poor children. The composition of her household had changed as well. Her oldest daughter had returned to live with her, but a little girl she had been "minding" in 1985 had gone to live with her father's sister. One thing was unchanged; Cicely had virtually no support for her children from their fathers. Yet Cicely took only two of those men to court. The first man was a bartender, the second was a police officer. The other fathers were laborers.

Josephine's story reveals some interesting parallels to Cicely's case. Her father, Tyronne, was a carpenter and electrician. Tyronne had no formal training, but he was a master at fixing and inventing things, and could connect a house to the government electricity without its knowledge. Tyronne ran a small shop and drove a big car. When he died in 1981, Josephine met siblings at his funeral that she had never known.

Josephine's mother, Evelyn, worked as a domestic servant. Evelyn and Tyronne had not stayed together long. When Evelyn married for the second time at the age of 44, she had had eight children by six different men. Only her first husband had consistently supported his two children. The other men, laborers and fishermen, went their separate ways. Only Tyronne, however, was taken to court. By coincidence, two other women also summoned Tyronne to court for maintenance on the same day and all three were awarded the maximum that the law allowed.

The timing of Tyronne's cases may have been coincidental; the fact that he and two of the fathers of Cicely's children were brought to court, was not. The case studies show that women use the courts selectively. The profiles of these men are keys to identifying ideas about family, gender, and status that explain why Antiguan women to go to court and why these particular men received summons. Moreover, these notions are intrinsic to family ideology and to the even flow of family life in the community.

In the Antiguan lower class, men and women are held to have distinctly different natures. Although West Indians highly value individual autonomy and economic independence for both men and women, I found that Antiguans repeatedly stressed the biological and social differences between men and women and used those differences to support the premise that there is a proper domain for each sex. Both men and women distinguish between the "inside" world of women and the "outside" world of men, and neither views those two domains as equal in any respect. The creed of gender hierarchy within the family contributes to the subordinate position of women in this society. Nevertheless, as we shall see, a highly developed sense of justice ensures there are limits beyond which a man may not assert the special privileges accorded to his sex.

Antiguan men and women love and need each other—children are one consequence of that fact—but because their natures are so different, men and women parent in different ways. Women nurture children, cook for them, wash them, teach them, and discipline them. Men provide some of this care, but their primary responsibility is to "feed a child," which means that the man maintains a particular kind of relationship with the child and the mother. An alliance exists in the first place because the man and the child share the same blood. Antiguan men are proud of their children and boast about their number. As another indication of their willingness to accept fatherhood, men rarely deny paternity at court, even if there are raging disagreements about how much they can afford in weekly payments.

A child generally uses his or her father's surname in the community and is entitled to that man's attention and "support." Support may take the form of cash, gifts, food, clothing, school supplies, or services provided by either the man or members of his family. For example, a woman generally does not take a man to court if his mother babysits or provides clothing for her grandchild. In contrast to the law, community norms are flexible with respect to the amount and type of support due to an illegitimate child. Support may vary in amount or kind from month to month, but it must be given somewhat regularly to maintain the alliance.

Finally, in addition to support, a man owes the mother of his child "respect." Like the notion of feeding a child, respect embodies a host of expectations. It means that even after their separation the man speaks politely about his child's mother and the people she is close to, that he acknowledges them publicly if the occasion arises, that he acts with discretion, and that he never flaunts a new relationship in her presence.

Breaking the norms which govern the alliances between men, women, and children sometimes results in a man being hauled to court. One woman I interviewed, for example, took the father of her child to court only after he had insulted her publicly in the market. Often, however, a norm involving respect is broken in conjunction with another which speaks directly about principles of hierarchy within the lower class. Consider the men whom Cicely and Evelyn brought to court: the bartender, the policeman, and Tyronne, the electrician. These men share a social stature that distinguishes them from the other fathers of Cicely's and Evelyn's illegitimate children. Locally, they are called "big men." A "big man" in Antigua has a respectable job with a steady income. Beyond this, he has won admiration by virtue of his leadership qualities, command of language, intelligence, wit, education, and generosity. He can maintain multiple unions, even when married, keep his women "in order," and father and "feed" many children. Big men uphold certain standards in their family relationships. They provide gifts to their wives and "outside" women and support all of their children in a manner which accords with their standing in the community.

Violating this code of behavior makes a big man an Antiguan woman's choice for a trip to the magistrate's court for a ritual shaming. The courtroom becomes for these men what Garfinkel[2] . . . calls a "degradation ceremony." When a man's name is called in court, his position as a big man is challenged. The trial indicates that he is not generous, not responsible, not a suitable father, and incapable of controlling his women.

By all accounts and my own observations, the shaming of men at the magistrate's court undeniably achieves this aim. Often a woman need only file legal papers and the man changes his ways. Those who come to court are chastised and warned that they may face prison if they fail to pay for their children. Some men refuse to attend, but in that case the suit is heard in their absence and the effect upon their reputation in the community is the same. The shaming ceremony, then, renews and validates legally constituted kinship responsibilities while mitigating the prestige of a big man.

Inversion of Gender Relations

The court ritual that challenges a man's personal competence and his status among his peers also inverts the usual hierarchical status between men and women. When she brings a man to the magistrate's court, a woman forces a

---

[2] H. Garfinkel, "Conditions of Successful Degradation Ceremonies," *The American Journal of Sociology* 61 (1956):89.

conjuncture of the domestic and the public spheres; the dirty laundry is made public. During the case, she uses law, courts, forensic processes, and legal personnel to manage male behavior and to lay claim to the rights due her and her children. If only for the duration of the ritual, she is a status equal and the public spokesman and representative for her children. Such behavior has its costs. A woman may be chided for going to court; she may be accused of spite. Nonetheless, the achievement of equality, the validation of individual rights, and the recognition of moral duty—central elements of Antiguan family ideology—are proclaimed during the trial. These constitute a vital part of the "justice" for which Antiguan women go to court.

Ironically, the expressed intent of the lawmakers—the regular provision of support for illegitimate children—is not nearly as effective as the threat or the actual performance of the shaming ceremony. Almost every woman I spoke with during my follow-up study complained about not receiving weekly payments. Their complaints were borne out by the collecting officer's records. Most women waited weeks between payments; some waited months. Women who take policemen to court face an added difficulty because officers are reluctant to hand warrants for failure to pay child support to fellow officers.

One last issue with respect to kinship cases at the magistrate's courts needs to be raised. There is a point at which a big man is too big a man to impugn in court, which accounts for the infrequency of inter-class family disputes in the lower courts. For at least three reasons, upper-middle-class status shields a man against the justice that lower-class women seek from the courts. First, charges of corruption against public officials occur frequently enough that the lower class remains cynical about the justice that poor people can expect at court when their opponents are wealthy and powerful people. In their view, pragmatism teaches that there is not much use in suing a middle-class man whose fancy lawyer will break your case or who is himself a friend of a friend of the judge. Second, rich and powerful men are likely to be married to rich and powerful women, who are formidable adversaries in their own right because they wield considerable influence over employment and educational opportunities in the community. Finally, some lower-class women do not take the wealthy fathers of their illegitimate children to court because they cherish the hope that some day these men will "rediscover" their children, come to love them, and provide them with their rightful due. That hope is part of the ideology of Antiguan family life and is crucial to understanding why a woman has a child "for" a man.

Although a maintenance case may appear to be a request for cash, it is in fact a way to substantiate familial alliances and to shame men who purport to be "big men" but who break a "big man's" code of conduct. A woman brings a case to magistrate's court to claim normative rights which regulate family, gender, and hierarchy within the lower class. Women rely on and use a literal translation of Antiguan kinship law to manage male behavior, to voice objections to their own inequality, and to reaffirm the rights of their children. They "carry" their cases for "justice."

Review Questions

1. How is the Antiguan legal system organized, and how did it come to be this way?
2. What is the nature of the Antiguan class system, and how is it related to the kinds of cases heard in different courts?
3. What are the substantive rules that lower-class women use to take the fathers of their children to court?
4. What are the real reasons why women take the fathers of their children to court?
5. Which men are most likely to be taken to court for failure to pay child support?

26

Cross-cultural Law: The Case of the Gypsy Offender

Anne Sutherland

Every society recognizes a list of legal statutes, which anthropologists call substantive law, that define right from wrong. In America, for example, it is against the law for an individual to marry more than one person at a time. But what is proper in one country may be a crime in another. Unlike the United States, for example, in Nepal it is legal for a person to be married simultaneously to more than one person. So what happens when members of one society live within and under the legal jurisdiction of another? This is the question explored by Anne Sutherland in this article on the legal plight of a young Gypsy man who is arrested for using the social security number of a relative on a car loan application. Despite the claim that using different identities of family members is a common Gypsy practice designed to hide their identities, and that he had no intention to defraud anyone by doing so, the young man receives a six-month jail term.

From "Gypsy Identity, Names and Social Security Numbers," *PoLAR*, vol. 17, no. 2, November 1994, pp. 75–83. Copyright © by the American Anthropological Association, 1994. Reprinted by permission of the American Anthropological Association.

It is often the case that a law made for one set of purposes has another, unintended impact on a particular group. A recent law making the use of a false social security number a federal felony is intended to help prosecution of major drug crime syndicates, but it has a special impact on Gypsies in the United States. Gypsies, traditionally a nomadic people, frequently borrow each others' "American" names and social security numbers, viewing them as a kind of corporate property of their kin group or *vitsa*. They also often lack birth certificates and must obtain midwife or baptismal certificates to use for identification purposes when they try to obtain credit, enter school, or apply for welfare.

In this article, I shall examine the case of a nineteen-year-old Gypsy man who was convicted under the new social security law and served six months in jail. Arguments for the defense in the case followed three lines of reasoning: 1) that this law unfairly singled out Gypsies for punishment; 2) that there was no intent to commit a crime; and 3) that in using the social security numbers of relatives, Gypsies were following a time-honored tradition to remain anonymous and separate from non-Gypsy society.

Facts of the Case

In the fall of 1991 in St. Paul, Minnesota, a nineteen-year-old Gypsy man was convicted of the crime of using his five-year-old nephew's social security number to obtain credit to purchase a car. When the purchase was questioned by the car dealership, he returned the car and was arrested on a felony charge of using a false social security number. After he was arrested, police searched the apartment where he was staying. They found lists of names, addresses and social security numbers, leading them to suspect an organized crime ring.

In *The United States of America v. S.N,*[1] it was "alleged that the defendant, S.N., while in the process of obtaining a new Ford Mustang from a car dealership, used a social security number that was not his own with intent to deceive." Under the statute 42 U.S.C. 408 (g)(2), a person who, with intent to deceive, falsely represents his or her number to obtain something of value or for any other purpose, is a felon.

In Mr. S.N.'s case there is no specific allegation that he intended to deprive another person permanently of property because the focus of the charging statute is false representation of numbers. The underlying purpose which motivates a person to falsely represent his or her number may be an essentially innocent purpose, but the statute, at least as it has been interpreted, does not appear to impose a burden of proof as to wrongful purpose.

---

[1] *United States v. Sonny Nicholas,* U.S. District Court, State of Minnesota, CR 4–91–137 (1991). Quotes from Philip Leavenworth, memorandum in support of a motion to declare 42 U.S.C. 408 (g) (2) unconstitutional.

The statute punishes the means (false number) which a person may employ to achieve any number of ends and it punishes those means as a felony. The lawyer for the defense argued that the statute's failure to address the nature of the purpose to which false credentials are used is a serious flaw in the law and may punish those who would use the number for petty misconduct as felons. He also argued that there is a potential for discriminatory impact on Gypsies who use false credentials to conceal themselves from mainstream society. A Gypsy household may obtain a telephone by providing a false social security number and even if they pay the telephone bill without fail for years, they are felons under this law. S.N. not only made the payments for his car, but he returned it when the number was questioned. He is still a felon under this law.

The defense lawyer argued that the law is objectionable for two reasons. First, the law's disproportionate impact on the Gypsies is objectionable under the equal protection guarantees in the Fifth Amendment of the U.S. Constitution. He argued that the law denies Gypsies equal protection of the law by irrationally and disproportionately punishing at the felony level certain traditional Gypsy actions which cause no positive injury to anyone. As evidence he used material from my book, *Gypsies: The Hidden Americans,* for testimony that Gypsies routinely use false social security numbers to acquire credit but do pay their bills and are available for repossession in case of default of payment. They get phone service, buy houses and cars and other household items on credit and have a record of payment that is probably better than the general population (*United States v. Sonny Nicholas,* 1991). They do this primarily to remain unknown by mainstream society rather than to cause loss or injury to any person.

Second, as the defense lawyer pointed out, there is a Supreme Court decision that requires the government to prove felonious intent when it seeks to punish a person for wrongful acquisition of another's property. S.N. maintained that he used a false social security number because of a Gypsy tradition to remain anonymous and because his own number had been used by other Gypsies. The government argued that there was a "ring" of Gypsies in the area where S.N. was living. At S.N.'s residence a number of false credentials and social security numbers were found which had been used to obtain cars illegally. Some of these cars are still missing. In other words, there was evidence that false identity had been used recently in the area to steal. In this case, however, S.N. had not stolen anything and was not being accused of stealing, but only of using a false social security number.

Because of the evidence of a ring of car thieves in the area, the prosecution hoped to use the threat of prosecution against S.N., the only Gypsy they had been able to arrest, to plea bargain for information regarding the other people involved in the alleged ring. These other people had disappeared immediately as soon as S.N. was arrested.

One of the problems in the case was that both the prosecution and even the defense had difficulty obtaining complete and accurate information on S.N. For example, they had difficulty determining his "real" name, a moot point for the Gypsies since they have a practice of using many "American" names although they only have one "Gypsy" name (*nav romano*). The Gypsy name of *o Spiro le Stevanosko* (or Spiro the son of Stevan) uses the noun declension characteristic of the Sanskrit-rooted Rom language and is not immediately translatable into English since it does not employ a surname. Spiro's identity can be pinned down by finding out what *vitsa* (a cognatic descent group) he belongs to so that he will not be confused with any other Spiro le Stevanoskos. The Spiro of our example is a *Kashtare* which is part of a larger "nation" of Gypsies or *natsia* called *Kalderasha* (coppersmith). For his "American" names he may take any of a number used by his relatives such as Spiro Costello, John Costello, John Marks, John Miller, Spiro John or Spiro Miller. His nickname is Rattlesnake Pete.

The Anthropologist as Cultural Broker

S.N.'s defense attorney contacted me after finding that he was less confused about S.N. after reading my book about Gypsies. He sought my help in determining whether S.N. was a Gypsy, what his name was, and any other cultural information (such as the use of social security numbers by Gypsies) that would help him with his case.

Consequently, one cold autumn day I drove to the federal holding prison, one and a half hours from the city, and met S.N. He was a thin young man, perpetually fearful of pollution from contact with non-Gypsies and suffering from the effects of several months of what for him was solitary confinement since he had not seen any of his people since being incarcerated. The telephone was his only link with people to whom he could relate, people from his own culture who spoke his language. His main contact was with a non-Gypsy woman who lived with one of his relatives. She was his link with the world he had known and the only "American" household he had been in before prison. Since my primary task was to determine if he was a Gypsy, first I talked to him about his relatives in Los Angeles and his *vitsa* (Yowane) and tried to establish what section of the *vitsa* I personally knew. This exchange of information about *vitsa* and Gypsies of mutual acquaintance is a normal one between Gypsies. The purpose was to establish a link between us.

Then I asked him about why he was in Minnesota. He talked about a seasonal expedition he and his brothers and cousins make to Minnesota to buy and sell cars and fix fenders before winter sets in. He claimed not to know where his brothers and cousins had gone or how he got into his present predicament.

For S.N., the most immediately effective action I could take was to see that he got the food he needed to stay "clean" in jail. When I met him he had lost fifteen pounds and was suffering demonstrable distress and nervousness. He was upset at being cut off from his culture and people for the first time in his life. In addition, he was distressed at being incarcerated and fearful for his safety. More importantly, he was worried he would become defiled or *marime*.

A major concern of his was that if he ate food prepared by non-Gypsies who did not follow rules of cleanliness considered essential in the Gypsy culture, he would become *marime,* a condition of ritual impurity that would result in his being shunned by his relatives and other Gypsies. To protect himself, he avoided eating prison food in the hopes that when he was released from prison he would be able to return to his family without a period of physical exile, also called *marime* (or "rejected" as the Gypsies translate it into English). I arranged for his lawyer to provide him with money to buy food from the concession because it is packaged and untouched by non-Gypsies and therefore considered clean by Gypsy standards. He bought milk in cartons, candy bars and soft drinks and other packaged foods that, though they may lack in nutrition, at least were not defiling and kept him from starvation.

A further complicating factor for S.N. was that he spoke English as a second language. He had only a rudimentary ability to read, thus straining his grasp of his defense. And his only contact with relatives was by telephone since neither he nor they could write with any ease. Even though his limited English made it difficult for him to follow his own trial, the court did not provide a translator.

The Trial

The trial was held in Federal Court and centered around the constitutionality of a law that unfairly targets a particular ethnic group and the question of intent to commit a crime. My testimony was intended to establish that Gypsies may use false identification for a number of cultural reasons which may have no connection to any intent to commit a crime. For a traditionally nomadic group with pariah status in the wider society and a pattern of secretiveness and autonomy, concealing identity is a long-established pattern.

This pattern is widespread in all Gypsy groups in Eastern Europe, Western Europe, Russia, Latin America and the United States. It is a mechanism they have developed over centuries to protect themselves from a wider society that has persecuted them or driven them away. The recent case of the German government paying large sums to Romania to take back Gypsy refugees is only the latest in an historically established tradition of discrimination against Gypsies. The persecution of Gypsies in the Holocaust, in medieval Europe and in the early part of the 20th century in the United States has been well documented. Current events in Eastern Europe have shown a resurgence of extreme prejudice against Gypsies. Interviews in recent *New York Times* articles have pointed to a hatred of Gypsies so deep that there is talk of extermination.[2] Because of the history of violence against them, Gypsies have developed elaborate mechanisms of secrecy and have hidden their identity in order to survive. It will not be easy to get them to change this pattern that has stood them in good stead for so many centuries.

---

[2] See *New York Times,* November 17 and 28, (1993) for recent accounts of extreme prejudice against Gypsies.

The purpose of my testimony was to establish that S.N. *was* a Gypsy and that Gypsies often use false identification without intent to defraud. They do so because as members of a *vitsa,* or cognatic descent group, identification is corporate in nature. Members of the group have corporate access to property owned by other members of the group. That property includes forms of identification.

An additional problem in the S.N. case was the question of identification from photographs. Here we encountered the age-old problem that members of one culture and race have trouble identifying individuals from another culture and race. In simple terms, to many non-Gypsies, all Gypsies look alike. Part of the case involved clearing up erroneous identification of S.N. in photos provided by the prosecution.

I was also asked to testify on my own personal experience with discrimination against Gypsies by the Minneapolis Police Department. One instance of discrimination I related to the court occurred during a talk I gave to some twenty police officers to help them understand Gypsy culture. When I had spoken about the strong sense of family and community among the Gypsies and how much they value their children, a police officer suggested that since the main problem law enforcement officers have is how to detain the Gypsies long enough to prosecute them, removing Gypsy children from their homes on any pretext would be an effective way to keep the parents in town.

Prejudice against Gypsies often goes unrecognized even by culturally and racially sensitive people. The assistant district attorney prosecuting S.N. offered me an article that he used to understand the Gypsies, entitled "Gypsies, the People and their Criminal Propensity,"[3] which quotes extensively from my work, including the fact that Gypsies have several names and that the same or similar non-Gypsy names are used over and over. The article concentrates on "criminal" behavior and never mentions the possibility that there are Gypsies who may not engage in criminal activities. In one section, quotations from my book on the ways Gypsies deal with the welfare bureaucracy were placed under the title, "Welfare Fraud," although by far most of the practices I described were legal. These concluding words in Part II are representative of the tone of the article:

> Officers should not be misled into thinking these people are not organized. They are indeed organized and operate under established rules of behavior, including those that govern marriage, living quarters, child rearing, the division of money and participation in criminal acts.

The implication of such statements is inflammatory. Gypsies have a culture, history, language and social structure, but that fact is distorted to imply that their social organization is partly for the purpose of facilitating criminal behavior. Their culture is viewed as a criminal culture. Gypsies have been fighting this view for hundreds of years. It is the view that they still combat in their relations with law enforcement and the criminal justice system. It is the view that was promoted by the prosecution in this case.

---

[3] Terry Getsay, *Kansas State FOP Journal,* Parts I, II, and III, (1982) pp. 18–30.

In spite of the best efforts of S.N.'s attorney and my testimony that use of a false social security number did not necessarily indicate intent to commit a crime, he was convicted of illegally using a social security number and served about six months in jail.

Conclusions: Anthropology and Cultural Differences in the Courtroom

Anthropologists are often called in as expert witnesses in cases involving cultural difference. Most Native American legal cases, such as the *Mashpee* case reported by James Clifford,[4] center around Indian status, treaties and land rights. In St. Paul, a number of Hmong legal cases highlighted the conflict between traditional marriage (specifically, the age at which children may marry) and the legal status of minors in American law. With the Gypsies, there is yet another set of cultural issues in their contact with American law.

First is the question of the cultural conflict between a historically nomadic group and the state bureaucracy of settled people. Identification—a serious legal issue in a bureaucratic society composed of people with fixed abodes and a written language—has virtually no meaning for the nomadic Gypsies who consider descent and extended family ties the defining factor for identification.

Second is the conflict between Gypsy religious rules regarding ritual pollution and prison regulations. The Gypsies avoid situations, such as a job or jail, that require them to be in prolonged contact with non-Gypsies. Jail presents special problems for the Gypsies can become *marime,* that is, defiled by unclean food and living conditions. The psychological trauma that results from isolation from their community is compounded if they then emerge from jail and have to undergo a further isolation from relatives because of becoming *marime* in jail.

Finally there is a cultural clash between the Gypsy value of corporate kinship and the American value of individual rights. The rights and status of an individual Gypsy are directly linked to his or her membership in a *vitsa* which is determined by birth. Furthermore, the status of the all members of the *vitsa* is effected by the behavior of each individual *vitsa* member. Since they are so intricately linked, reciprocity between *vitsa* members is expected. Members of a *vitsa* and family share economic resources, stay in each other's homes, help each other in work and preparation of rituals and loan each other cars, information, identification and money. They also share the shame of immoral or incorrect behavior by one member. For the Gypsies, the American idea that each individual has only one name, one social security number, or one medical identification number is contrary to their experience and culture. Unfortunately for the Gypsies in America, it is now a felony to think this way.

---

[4] "Identity in Mashpee," in *The Predicament of Culture,* Cambridge: Harvard University Press, (1988) pp. 277–346.

Review Questions

1. What aspect of the "crime" committed by a young Gypsy man is due to cross-cultural difference, according to Sutherland?
2. How did the police interpret the lists of social security numbers and other evidence found in the young man's apartment? How did their interpretation of this evidence differ from the Gypsy's?
3. How does this case illustrate the role cultural anthropologists can play in everyday American life?
4. Can you think of other cases where immigrants or culturally different people of run afoul of American substantive law?

27

Navigating Nigerian Bureaucracies

Elizabeth A. Eames

Anthropologists regularly study different political institutions, from the informal systems of foragers to the more highly structured organization of chiefdomships, kingdoms, and democracies. One important topic of anthropological study is the growth and operation of bureaucracies in complex societies, the subject of this selection by Elizabeth Eames. During fieldwork in Africa, Eames discovered that Nigerian bureaucracies work differently from those found in the west. Whereas the American plan is organized on the principle of what Max Weber called legal domination, *one characterized by impersonality and ideally the application of the same rules for everyone, the Nigerian system revolves around* patrimonial domination, *where transactions depend on establishing and cultivating social relations.*

From Elizabeth A. Eames, "Navigating Nigerian Bureaucracies, or 'Why Can't You Beg?' She Demanded," in *Work in Modern Society: A Sociology Reader.* Edited by Lauri Perman (Dubuque, IA: Kendall/Hunt, 1986). Copyright © by Elizabeth A. Eames, 1985. Reprinted by permission of the author.

Americans have a saying: "It's not *what* you know, it's *who* you know." This aphorism captures the usually subtle use of old-boy networks for personal advancement in the United States. But what happens when this principle becomes the primary dynamic of an entire social system? The period of three years I spent pursuing anthropological field research in a small Nigerian city was one of continual adjustment and reordering of expectations. This paper discusses a single case—how I discovered the importance personal ties have for Nigerian bureaucrats—but also illustrates the *general process* by which any open-minded visitor to a foreign land might decipher the rules of proper behavior. I was already familiar with Max Weber's work on bureaucracy and patrimony, yet its tremendous significance and explanatory power only became clear to me following the incidents discussed below. Accordingly, the paper concludes with a discussion of Weber's concept of *patrimonial authority.*

I heard the same comment from every expatriate I met in Nigeria—U.S. foreign service officers, U.N. "experts," and visiting business consultants alike: "If you survive a stint in Nigeria, you can survive *anywhere.*" The negative implications of this statement stem from outsiders' futile attempts to apply, in a new social setting, homegrown notions of how bureaucratic organizations function. This is indeed a natural inclination and all the more tempting where organizational structure *appears* bureaucratic. Yet in Nigeria, the office-holders behaved according to different rules; their attitudes and sentiments reflected a different moral code. A bureaucratic organizational structure coexisted with an incompatible set of moral imperatives. The resulting unwieldy, inflexible structure may be singled out as one of the British Colonialism's most devastating legacies.[1]

Please bear in mind, the problem of understanding another culture works both ways. Any Nigerian student reading for the first time the following passage by a prominent American sociologist would probably howl with laughter:

> The chief merit of a bureaucracy is its technical efficiency, with a premium placed on precision, speed, expert control, continuity, discretion and optimal returns on input. The structure is one which approaches the complete elimination of personalized relationships and nonrational considerations (hostility, anxiety, affectual involvements, etc.).[2]

Even those well-educated administrative officers who had once been required to incorporate such notions into their papers and exams do not *live* by them.

To many foreigners who have spent time in Nigeria, "the system" remains a mystery. What motivating principles explain the behavior of Niger-

---

[1] One common misunderstanding must be clarified: *bureaucratic organization is not a recent Western invention.* Even during the Han Dynasty (3rd century B.C.), China had developed an efficient bureaucracy based on a system of official examinations. This was the start of a "modern" type of civil service system based on merit. It was almost two thousand years before the West adopted such a system, partly inspired by the Chinese example.

[2] Robert K. Merton, *Social Theory and Social Structure* (New York: Free Press, 1969), 250.

ian administrative officers? How do local people understand the behavior of their fellow workers? Why do some people successfully maneuver their way through the system while others founder?

Recently I attended a party. As often happens at a gathering of anthropologists, we started swapping fieldwork stories, and meandered onto a topic of our most unpleasant sensation or unsettling experience. That night, I heard tales of surviving strange diseases, eating repulsive foods, losing one's way in the rain forest, being caught between hostile rebel factions or kidnapped by guerrilla fighters. As for me? All that came to mind were exasperating encounters with intransigent clerks and secretaries. I began to ponder why these interactions had proved so unsettling.

My discipline—social anthropology—hinges on the practice of "participant observation." To a fledgling anthropologist, the "fieldwork" research experience takes on all the connotations of initiation into full membership. For some, a vision-quest; for others, perhaps, a trial-by-ordeal: the goal is to experience another way of life from the inside and to internalize, as does a growing child, the accumulating lessons of daily life. But the anthropologist is not a child; therefore, he or she experiences not conversion, but self-revelation.

I came to understand my American-ness during the period spent coming to terms with Nigerian-ness. I found that I believed in my right to fair treatment and justice simply because I was a human being. I believed in equal protection under the law. But my Nigerian friends did not. What I found was a social system where status, relationships, and rights were fundamentally negotiable, and justice was *never* impartial. In the United States, impersonalized bureaucracies are the norm: we do not question them; our behavior automatically adjusts to them. But just imagine spending a year working in a corporation where none of these rules applied.

You see, a Nigerian immigration officer will only sign your form *if* doing so will perpetuate some mutually beneficial relationship or *if* he wishes to initiate a relationship by putting you in his debt. For those unlucky enough to be without connections (this must necessarily include most foreigners), the only other option is bribery—where the supplicant initiates a personal relationship of sorts and the ensuing favor evens matters up.[3]

Hence, Nigeria becomes labeled "inefficient," "tribalistic," and "corrupt." And so it is.[4] Yet this system exists and persists for a profound reason: Whereas in Europe and Asia, power and authority always derived from own-

---

[3] Bribery exists for several reasons: it initiates a personal relationship, unlike a tip, which terminates all intimacy; if not dedicated to "duty," a worker must be given added incentive to perform a service; the poor salary scale aggravated by the unpredictable nature of extended kin obligations means everyone is desperately in search of extra cash.

[4] Corruption is condemned only in the abstract, when far removed and on a grand scale. But anyone and everyone knows someone "well-placed," and that person is now powerful precisely because he or she has been generous. Moreover, one is more likely to be condemned for going by the book than for corruption. If, for instance, the brother of the man married to one of my cousins (my mother's father's sister's daughter's husband's brother) did not see to it that his colleague signed my tax form with the minimum of fuss, life could be made quite miserable for him indeed!

ership of landed property, in West Africa the key ingredient was a large number of loyal dependents. Because land was plentiful and agriculture of the extensive slash-and-burn variety,[5] discontented subordinates could simply move on. The trick was to maintain power over subordinates through ostentatious displays of generosity. This meant more than simply putting on a lavish feast—you must demonstrate a willingness to use your influence to support others in times of need. Even now, all Nigerians participate in such patron-client relationships. In fact, *all legitimate authority derives from being in a position to grant favors and not the other way around.*

Actually, only a minuscule portion of my time in the field was spent dealing with Nigeria's "formal sector." My research entailed living within an extended family household (approximately a dozen adults and two dozen children), chatting with friends, visiting women in their market stalls, even at times conducting formal or informal interviews. And during the years spent researching women's economic resources and domestic responsibilities, I came to understand—indeed to deeply *admire*—their sense of moral responsibility to a wide-ranging network of kin, colleagues, neighbors, friends, and acquaintances. Even now, I often take the time to recall someone's overwhelming hospitality, a friendly greeting, the sharing and eating together. Such warm interpersonal relations more than made up for the lack of amenities.

The longer I stayed, however, the clearer it became that what I loved most and what I found most distressing about life in Nigeria were two sides of the same coin, inextricably related.

The first few months in a new place can be instructive for those with an open mind:

Lesson One: The Strength of Weak Ties

My first exposure to Nigerian civil servants occurred when, after waiting several months, I realized my visa application was stalled somewhere in the New York consulate. Letter-writing and telephoning proved futile, and as my departure date approached, panic made me plan a personal visit.

The waiting room was populated with sullen, miserable people—a roomful of hostile eyes fixed on the uniformed man guarding the office door. They had been waiting for hours on end. Any passing official was simultaneously accosted by half a dozen supplicants—much as a political celebrity is accosted by the news media. Everyone's immediate goal was to enter through that door to the inner sanctum—so far, they had failed. But I was lucky—I had the name of an acquaintance's wife's schoolmate currently employed at the consulate. After some discussion, the guard allowed me to telephone her.

Mrs. Ojo greeted me cordially, then—quickly, quietly—she coaxed my application forms through the maze of cubicles. It was a miracle!

---

[5] Also known as shifting cultivation or swidden agriculture: small pieces of land are cultivated for a few years, until the natural fertility of the soil diminishes. When crop yields decline, the field must be abandoned. This has obvious implications for the concepts of private property, ownership, and monopoly.

"What a wonderful woman," I thought to myself. "She understands." I thought she had taken pity on me and acted out of disgust for her colleagues' mishandling of my application. I now realize that by helping me, she was reinforcing a relationship with her schoolmate. Needless to say, my gratitude extended to her schoolmate's husband, my acquaintance. As I later came to understand it, this natural emotional reaction—gratitude for favors granted—is the currency fueling the system. Even we Americans have an appropriate saying: "What goes around comes around." But at this point, I had merely learned that, here as elsewhere, connections open doors.

Lesson Two: No Impersonal Transactions Allowed

Once on Nigerian soil I confronted the mayhem of Muritala Muhammad airport. Joining the crowd surrounding one officer's station, jostled slowly forward, I finally confronted her face-to-face. Apparently I was missing the requisite currency form. No, sorry, there were none available that day. "Stand back," she declared: "You can't pass here today." I waited squeamishly. If I could only catch her eye once more! But then what? After some time a fellow passenger asked me what was the problem. At this point, the officer, stealing a glance at me while processing someone else, inquired: "Why can't you beg?" The person being processed proclaimed: "She doesn't know how to beg![6] Please, O! Let her go." And I was waved on.

A young post office clerk soon reinforced my conclusion that being employed in a given capacity did not in and of itself mean one performed it. Additional incentive was required. Again, I was confronted with a mass of people crowded round a window. Everyone was trying to catch the clerk's attention, but the young man was adept at avoiding eye contact. Clients were calling him by name, invoking the name of mutual friends, and so on. After some time, he noticed me, and I grabbed the opportunity to ask for stamps. In a voice full of recrimination yet tinged with regret, he announced more to the crowd than to me: "Why can't you greet?" and proceeded to ignore me. This proved my tip-off to the elaborate and complex cultural code of greetings so central to Nigerian social life.[7] In other words, a personal relationship is like a "jump-start" for business transactions.

Lesson Three: Every Case Is Unique

Mrs. Ojo had succeeded in obtaining for me a three-month visa, but I planned to stay for over two years. Prerequisite for a "regularized" visa was university affiliation. This sounded deceptively simple. The following two months spent registering as an "occasional postgraduate student" took a terrible toll on my nervous stomach.[8] The worst feeling was of an ever-receding target, an ever-thickening

---

[6] It turns out that "begging" means throwing yourself on someone's mercy, rubbing one's hands together, eyes downcast, even kneeling or prostrating if necessary, and literally begging for a favor.

[7] Nigerians coming to the United States are always taken aback by our positively inhuman greeting behavior.

[8] A few years later, I timed my registration as a graduate student at Harvard. The result: three offices in twelve minutes! Even a foreign graduate student could probably register in less than a day.

tangle of convoluted mazeways. No one could tell me what it took to register, for in fact, no one could possibly predict what I would confront farther down the road. Nothing was routinized, everything personalized, no two cases could possibly be alike.

Lesson Four: "Dash" or "Long-Leg" Gets Results

This very unpredictability of the process forms a cybernetic system with the strength of personal ties, however initiated. *Dash* and *Long-Leg* are the locally recognized means for cutting through red tape or confronting noncooperative personnel. *Dash* is local parlance for gift or bribe. *Long-Leg* (sometimes called *L-L* or *L-squared*) refers to petitioning a powerful person to help hack your way through the tangled overgrowth. To me, it evokes the image of something swooping down from on high to stomp on the petty bureaucrat causing the problem.

Lesson Five: Exercise Keeps Ties Limber

During my drawn-out tussle with the registrar's office, I recounted my problem to anyone who would listen. A friend's grown son, upon hearing of my difficulties, wrote a note on his business card to a Mr. Ade in the Exams Section. Amused by his attempt to act important, I thanked Ayo politely. When I next saw him at his mother's home, he took the offensive, and accused me of shunning him. It came out that I had not seen Mr. Ade. But, I protested, I did not know the man. Moreover, he worked in exams not the registry. That, I learned, was not the point. I was supposed to assume that Mr. Ade would have known someone at the registry. Not only had I denied Ayo the chance to further his link to Mr. Ade, but ignoring his help was tantamount to denying any connection to him or—more important for me—his mother.

This revelation was reinforced when I ran into a colleague. He accused me of not greeting him very well. I had greeted him adequately, but apologized nonetheless. As the conversation progressed, he told me that he had heard I had had "some difficulty." He lamented the fact that I had not called on him, since as Assistant Dean of Social Science he could have helped me. His feelings were truly hurt, provoking his accusation of a lackluster greeting. Indeed, things were never the same between us again, for I had betrayed—or denied—our relationship.

Lesson Six: Your Friends Have Enemies

Well, I did eventually obtain a regularized visa, and it came through *Long-Leg.*[9] But the problems inherent in its use derive from the highly politicized and factionalized nature of Nigerian organizations, where personal loyalty is everything.

Early on, I became friendly with a certain sociologist and his family. Thereby, I had unwittingly become his ally in a long, drawn-out war between himself and his female colleagues. The disagreement had its origins ten years before in accusations of sex discrimination, but had long since spilled over into every aspect of departmental functioning. Even the office workers had chosen sides, and would perform only for members of the proper faction. More significant, though, was the fact that my friend's chief antagonist and I had similar theoretical interests.

---

[9] I never paid *dash* in Nigeria.

Though in retrospect I regret the missed opportunity, I realize that I was in the thick of things before I could have known what was happening. Given the original complaint, my sympathies should have been with the other camp. But ambiguous loyalty is equivalent to none.

Early in the century, Max Weber, the great pioneering sociologist, articulated the difference between systems of *legal* and *patrimonial domination*. Within systems of legal domination, organized bureaucratically, authority is the property of a given office or position (not an attribute of the person) and is validated by general rules applying to the whole structure of offices. Assignment to an office is based on merit: rights and duties are properties of the office not its incumbent. The system functions according to routine and is therefore predictable and efficient. Great stress is placed on making relationships impersonal.

In contrast, patrimonial authority (from the Latin term for personal estate) pertains to the form of government organized as a more or less direct extension of the noble household, where officials originate as household servants and remain personal dependents of the ruler. Note how the following passage summarizing Weber's characterization of patrimonial administration fits with my own observations of Nigerian life:

> *First,* whether or not the patrimonial ruler and his officials conduct administrative business is usually a matter of discretion; normally they do so only when they are paid for their troubles. *Second,* a patrimonial ruler resists the delimitation of his authority by the stipulation of rules. He may observe traditional or customary limitations, but these are unwritten: indeed, tradition endorses the principled arbitrariness of the ruler. *Third,* this combination of tradition and arbitrariness is reflected in the delegation and supervision of authority. Within the limits of sacred tradition the ruler decides whether or not to delegate authority, and his entirely personal recruitment of "officials" makes the supervision of their work a matter of personal preference and loyalty. *Fourth* and *fifth,* all administrative "offices" under patrimonial rule are a part of the ruler's personal household and private property: his "officials" are servants, and the costs of administration are met out of his treasury. *Sixth,* official business is transacted in personal encounter and by oral communication, not on the basis of impersonal documents.[10]

Weber himself believed that bureaucracy would supplant patrimonial authority. He believed that the world was becoming progressively more rationalized and bureaucratized. But there are several different dimensions along which I dispute this contention:

> Bureaucracy has been invented, declined, and re-invented, several times over the millennia.
>
> We have seen how patrimonial ties persisted within a bureaucratic structure of offices in Nigeria. This is also true in America. Within certain organizational structures, personal loyalty remains important, favoritism prevails, connections count, and nepotism or corruption abounds. For instance, urban "political ma-

[10] Max Weber quoted from Reinhard Bendix, *Max Weber: An Intellectual Portrait* (Berkeley: University of California Press, 1960), 245; emphasis added.

chines" function according to a patrimonial logic. Bureaucracy and patrimonialism may be opposite poles on a continuum (Weber called them "ideal types"), but they are *not* mutually exclusive. Most institutions combine both types of authority structures, with a greater emphasis on one or the other. Personal connections can help in either society, but in America, their use is widely perceived as *illegitimate.*

The system I have outlined is not irrational by any means—but rational actions are based on a different set of assumptions.

Ties of kinship and clientship have an ally in human nature.

By the latter, I mean Weber's ideal types cannot be mutually exclusive for emotional/cognitive reasons: an individual's cognitive understanding of hierarchy is necessarily patterned on the relationship between infant and caretaker. Whatever the form of the earliest pattern (and child-rearing practices vary tremendously between and within cultures), it leaves a residual tendency for personal attachment to develop between authority figures and dependents. Clients in the Unemployment Office naturally wish to be considered individuals and resent cold, impersonal treatment. Each bureaucrat wages his or her own private struggle with the temptation to treat each case on its merits.

This is why most Nigerians' finely honed interpersonal skills stand them in good stead when they arrive in the United States. They easily make friends with whomever they run across, and naturally friends will grant you the benefit of the doubt *if* there is room to maneuver. The psychological need remains, even in our seemingly formalized, structured world, for a friendly, personable encounter. On the other hand, anyone adept at working this way suffers tremendous pain and anxiety from the impersonal enforcement of seemingly arbitrary rules. For instance, a Nigerian friend took it as a personal affront when his insurance agent refused to pay a claim because a renewal was past due.

Once I learned my lessons well, life became much more pleasant. True, every case was unique and personal relationships were everything. But as my friends and allies multiplied, I could more easily make "the system" work for me. As a result of my Nigerian experience, I am very sensitive to inflexible and impersonal treatment, the flip-side of efficiency.

Leaving Nigeria to return to Boston after 2½ years, I stopped for a week in London. I arrived only to find that my old college friend, with whom I intended to stay, had recently moved. Playing detective, I tried neighbors, the superintendent, directory assistance. Tired and bedraggled, I thought of inquiring whether a forwarding address had been left with the post office. Acknowledging me from inside his cage, the small, graying man reached for his large, gray ledger, peered in, slapped it shut, and answered:

"Yes."

"But . . . what is it?" I asked, caught off guard.

He peered down at me and replied: "I cannot tell you. We are not allowed. We must protect him from creditors."

I was aghast. In no way did I resemble a creditor. Noticing my reaction, he conceded:

"But, if you send him a letter, I will forward it."

Bursting into tears of frustration, in my thickest American accent, displaying my luggage and my air ticket, I begged and cajoled him, to no avail. I spent my entire London week in a Bed 'n Breakfast, cursing petty bureaucrats as my bill piled up. "THAT," I thought, "COULD NEVER HAPPEN IN NIGERIA!"

Review Questions

1. What is the difference between American and Nigerian bureaucracies? How does this difference relate to Weber's concepts of *legal* and *patrimonial domination?*
2. If Nigerians use personal relationships to navigate through bureaucracies, why do such practices as *dash* and *Long-Leg* exist?
3. What are the six features of patrimonial domination suggested by Weber? Do all six apply to the Nigerians?
4. What problems do bureaucracies like the ones found in Nigeria pose for members of the international business world?

28

Government, Oil, and Political Transformation: The Iñupiat Eskimo Case

Norman A. Chance

The relationship between the United States government and Native Americans is often viewed as one of exploitation, leading to the destruction of Native culture and political and territorial independence. More recently, however, this relationship has grown complex as the American awareness of past injustices and a political sophistication among Native Americans has grown. This is the case for the association between the U.S. government, oil companies, and the Alaskan Iñupiat Eskimo described by Norman Chance in this article. The discovery of oil in 1967 and the Alaska Native Claims Settlement Act led the Iñupiat to form a borough municipal organization capable of taxing the oil, and for profit corporations to invest the money received in exchange for land rights. Since 1958, the Iñupiat have managed to increase their political strength, raise their standard of living, and affirm their traditional culture.

From "The Iñupiat Eskimo and Arctic Alaska: A Cultural Update," by Norman A. Chance, *General Anthropology,* vol. 2, no. 2, spring 1997. Copyright © by the American Anthropological Association, 1997. Reprinted by permission of the American Anthropological Association.

June, 1958

Pitching a tent in the village of Kaktovik, located on the Arctic Coast 60 miles from the US-Canadian border, I settled in for my first ethnographic field work in the Alaskan North. The Iñupiaq-speaking families of this region relied on the products of the sea, along with seasonal caribou hunting trips inland for much of their daily sustenance. Although opportunities for cash employment linked to the construction of a small military installation adjacent to the village had begun to transform this subsistence pattern, extended families remained relatively autonomous, roughly equal in status, and with minimal local government. Transportation utilized dog sleds in winter and boat or foot in summer. The closest Iñupiat village was at Barrow, 300 miles to the northwest. Were village contacts with the outside world as limited as their geographical isolation suggested? Far from it.

Connections

Some Kaktovik residents had lived in the region for decades. Others from Barrow and Canada came more recently. All had older relatives who could tell stories of their contacts with whalers, traders, and missionaries up to a half a century or more. Formal education was introduced in Barrow in the late 1800s. Kaktovik, on the other hand, had only recently received its first teacher, a young Iñupiat World War II veteran who had agreed to come to the village, build a classroom, and begin instructing.

The local villagers' recent contact with non-Natives was less satisfactory. Several years prior to my arrival, the U.S. military had landed on a sand spit in front of the tiny village, informing the stunned residents that they would have to relocate immediately as their dozen or so driftwood and sod houses were to be bull-dozed into the sea to make room for an Air Force landing strip. Given the local Iñupiat's limited English-speaking skills, confusion over what was happening, and difficulty communicating directly with the outside world, little effective protest was mounted. But tensions remained, even as Iñupiat from Kaktovik, Barrow, and other North Slope villages were hired to help in the construction of a new military radar station.

These feelings were exacerbated a few years later when subsistence hunting and fishing activities came under government scrutiny with accompanying threats of fines and court action. On one well-known occasion at Barrow, an Iñupiat was arrested by a federal warden for shooting eider ducks out of season. In response, the local townspeople designed a unique protest. At a hearing shortly thereafter, the warden found himself surrounded by 300 Iñupiat, 138 of them holding eider ducks. Their spokesman presented the warden with a statement addressed to the President of the U.S. pointing out the absurdity of a migratory treaty ruling that designated a hunting season long after ducks had departed the Arctic for warmer climates. If the government's position was that the Iñupiat could not utilize water-fowl in their subsistence hunting, the government should also know that "hunger knows no law." Eventually, charges against the 139 defendants were dropped and no further arrests made.

A far more dramatic confrontation occurred in 1958, when, unbeknownst to the Iñupiat, the U.S. Atomic Energy Commission (AEC) inaugurated Project Chariot. Part of a larger program to demonstrate peaceful uses for nuclear explosives, the AEC selected a site 31 miles from the North Alaska village of Point Hope to detonate a massive thermonuclear device. Referred to as an experiment in "geographical engineering," the goal of the Project was to carve out a commercially viable harbor on Alaska's northwest coast. On learning of the proposed plan, angry Iñupiat leaders joined a growing public protest, eventually culminating in the AEC declaring a permanent "postponement."

At this time, Alaska Natives were generally perceived by non-Natives as being in a state of "transition" with Euro-American society carrying the responsibility for bringing the benefits of American knowledge to its outlying territory, as well as bringing "its" Native peoples into modern society. The Iñupiat, however, held quite a different perspective. While quickly acknowledging their desire for western technology, goods and services, they strongly disagreed with the notion that such an acceptance meant the loss of their cultural way of life. Nor was there any interest in relinquishing their subsistence activities for the supposed security of wage employment. In fact, men who were offered full time wage contracts usually turned them down unless they could be assured of regular time off to pursue their hunting and fishing interests. Women were never faced with such decisions, since employment opportunities for them, full or part time, were virtually non-existent. All that was to change, however, a short decade later.

December, 1967

On the 26th day of December in 30 degree below zero weather, workers exploring for oil at Prudhoe Bay on Alaska's North Slope decided to push below the 13,000 foot level. Soon, recalled the geologist member of the team, "We could hear the roar of natural gas like four jumbo jets flying overhead. It was a mighty sign that something big was down below." That something big was oil-rich sadlerochit sand, deposited 200 million years before when the North Slope was a tropical wilderness. It represented the largest petroleum deposit ever encountered in North America. And it was to change the region and its people profoundly.

Petroleum, Politics, and Profit

Following this discovery in 1968 the U.S. Congress was forced to address a long standing conflict with the Alaskan Native people over the legal ownership of Alaska's land, a dispute that had been simmering even prior to the territory's receiving Statehood in 1959. The final resolution of the dispute was concluded with the passage of the 1971 Alaska Native Claims Settlement

Act (ANCSA). Under this act, Alaska Natives retained 44 million acres of land and $962.5 million in compensation for the extinguishment of all other aboriginal claims totaling 330 million acres. The act obligated the Native population to establish regional profit-making corporations and over 200 village corporations to serve as vehicles for the ownership and management of the land and monies which then became corporate assets. By enacting ANCSA in this manner, Congress strongly rejected the concept of tribal government where land could be held "in trust" by the U.S. Department of the Interior, an arrangement the Congress considered a serious impediment to Native assimilation.

Immediately after federal passage of ANCSA, the Iñupiat formed the North Slope Borough, a municipal form of government that stretches from Point Hope on the west to the Canadian Border on the east. Geographically it is the largest city in North America. Much to the frustration of the oil companies, this enabled the borough's Iñupiaq leaders to tax oil revenues from Prudhoe Bay. As a borough, they also received state funds for city services, and sold municipal bonds on Wall Street. Millions of revenue dollars along with state transfer payments enabled the Iñupiat to plan their communities, including the building of houses with heating systems and running water, expanding schools in the region's villages, and providing other benefits of a modern lifestyle that had once been limited to localities far to the south. The borough also hired any Iñupiat wanting to work in construction, maintenance, and municipal services at competitively high wages with sufficient flexibility that men could take time off to engage in subsistence hunting and fishing.

Although the passing of ANCSA by Congress was primarily designed to allow oil to be extracted from Prudhoe Bay, it was also a source of new divisions among the Iñupiat. The economic basis for these divisions was formed when, under the terms of the act, the Iñupiat's major financial and natural resources were placed in the hands of the Native-owned Arctic Slope Regional Corporation (ASRC). The management skills required to run a highly complex multi-million dollar corporation such as ASRC were considerable. Eventually, a growing elite group of Iñupiat (along with a sizable contingent of non-Native managerial, fiscal, and legal associates) ascended to well paid positions of leadership, at which time they instituted initiatives which set the corporation on quite a different course from that of the borough.

Whereas borough leaders sought the support of their constituency based on a roughly equitable distribution of money and resources drawn from taxation, state transfer payments, and bonds, the ASRC's corporate leaders were required by their legal mandate to focus on the creation of profit as their key concern. In so doing, the regional corporation promoted the stratification of social status within Iñupiat society, while the borough, offering high-paying jobs broadly, had the effect of limiting the formation of these stratified relations.

Internal conflicts brought on by the conjunction of competitive, profit-generating activities on the one hand, with those of a more kin-based, cooperative, partially subsistence-oriented way of life on the other, presented the

Iñupiat with real difficulties. Not surprisingly, these problems were closely linked to another fear as well, that of co-optation. Might Native leaders working in the corporate sphere become so imbued with rewards flowing from their position that they could be drawn into seeking profits too single-mindedly, and in so doing, lose their concern for the broader interests of Iñupiat society? Needless to say, issues such as these continue up to the present time.

Other threats to Iñupiat culture followed the land claims settlement which extinguished aboriginal hunting and fishing rights. This enabled the state Department of Fish and Game to enforce rules for restricting hunting and fishing without regard to the local food needs of its Native citizens. Then, in 1980, the U.S. Congress passed the Alaska National Interest Lands Conservation Act, a bill that explicitly provided federal protection for subsistence hunting and fishing on federal lands. One premise underlying this act was of crucial importance to Iñupiat and other Native Alaskans for it clearly reaffirmed a federal commitment to protect Native Alaskan's subsistence interests:

> The Congress finds and declares that—the continuation of the opportunity for subsistence uses by rural residents of Alaska, including both Natives and non-Natives, on the public lands and by Alaska Natives on Native lands is essential to Native physical, economic, traditional, and *cultural* existence, and to non-Natives physical, economic, traditional and *social* existence.

(This must be one of the few times the federal government has recognized a distinction raised in every introductory anthropology class!)

This declaration turned out to be highly significant in that it set federal and state policies in direct conflict with one another. Whereas federal law provides a preference for subsistence uses of fish and game by all "rural Alaskans," most of whom are Native, the state constitution forbids such a geographical criterion. The resulting conflict has led the federal government to assume control over fish and wildlife resources under its jurisdiction (representing two-thirds of the state) until the state either changes its constitution or yields to federal law. In the minds of Alaska Federation of Native leaders, this is a historic issue of human rights and economic survival which will determine the quality of Native life in Alaska for years to come.

Mid–1980s

Petroleum geologists emphasize that the Coastal Plain of the Arctic National Wildlife Refuge [ANWR], located in the northeast corner of Alaska, holds the greatest potential for commercially viable new oil discoveries on the North Alaskan mainland. This projection set off a dramatic confrontation over appropriate natural resource utilization that today reverberates from Kaktovik (located in the center of the Refuge's Coastal Plain) all the way to the U.S. Congress and the White House.

Contested Terrain

Land has always been the centerpiece of Arctic Alaska. A territory of great beauty far removed from the industrial heartland of North America, it contains substantial wealth in minerals and other natural resources. As such, it has long been a prime target for economic development by corporations as well as a prime focus of protection by environmentalists and wildlife conservationists.

From the vantage point of Alaska's Native northerners, the region is viewed somewhat differently. As expressed by the Inuit Circumpolar Conference, an international indigenous organization founded at Barrow in 1977, the Arctic is not simply an exploitable frontier for economic growth. "It must allow for and facilitate spiritual, social, and cultural development." Of special significance is the linking of nature with *stewardship* in which societal groups are seen as active participants within natural systems rather than rulers over them.

Attempting to arbitrate conflicts between these rival groups are the various branches and agencies of the federal, state, and local governments. Yet, here too, conflicting interests are the norm. One agency within the federal government such as the Minerals Management Service, actively assists in developing natural resources, while another, e.g., the U.S. Fish and Wildlife Service, tries to protect the environment. As for the State of Alaska, it has been solidly behind oil development from the beginning, for 85 to 90 percent of its budget is drawn from petroleum revenues. Thus, whether the focus is political or economic, national or regional, both the federal and state governments have important vested interests in developing Alaska's mineral resources and assisting those corporations extracting them—for revenues from companies such as these are central to their continued welfare.

Petroleum Extraction and Wilderness Preservation

Prior to 1968, Alaska's North Slope was the largest intact wilderness area in the country. Since that time, oil development has transformed a segment of the region into a large industrial complex, including some 1,500 miles of roads and pipelines, and thousands of acres of industrial facilities covering hundreds of square miles. Environmentalists, drawing on numerous government and private agency reports, have shown that North Slope oil development has destroyed thousands of acres of local wildlife habitat, caused declines in local wildlife populations, and left hundreds of open pits containing millions of gallons of oil industry waste. Partly in response to these criticisms, oil companies on the North Slope have tried to improve their methods of operation in newer fields. However, most environmentalists consider these efforts as only minimally successful. Thus, the debate whether to explore for petroleum deposits in the Arctic Refuge continues unabated.

The area's Iñupiat Eskimo and Athabascan Gwich'in inhabitants are intimately involved in the debate as well, their particular views largely shaped by the nature of their relationship to the land and its resources. The Gwich'in, whose villages are located to the south and east of the Refuge, are unanimously opposed to oil exploration due to the damage that activity could bring to the Porcupine Caribou Herd on which they rely for much of their economic subsistence. In keeping with this view, they regularly mount publicity campaigns with environmental organizations, stressing that if the country's primary goal is to create a sustainable long-range energy policy, a far better way to achieve it is by improving the fuel efficiency of motor vehicles than by drilling for oil in the Refuge.

By contrast, corporate and borough Iñupiaq Eskimo leaders are unanimous in their support of oil exploration. Native shareholders of local and regional corporate stock also look forward to continuing their present standard of living which can only occur if oil exploration is allowed and petroleum found in commercial quantities. An oil spill is recognized as a potential hazard. But the eventual loss of income from the shrinking deposit of Prudhoe Bay oil is a reality.

This brief cultural update demonstrates how taxing of wealth from natural resource development can assist an indigenous population in achieving greater political strength, raise their standard of living, while affirming their culture in a manner quite unforeseen a few short decades ago. It also highlights how political, economic, and legal arrangements shape the structure within which the North Alaskan Iñupiat must operate in the present world economy. Today, the Iñupiat, in conjunction with a large corps of Euro-American experts, are actively directing large Native-owned corporations and managing borough and city budgets involving millions of dollars. They exert strong leadership in a school district composed of isolated villages where teachers and students are using the Internet and the world wide web to communicate over long distances. They have an active Commission on History, Language, and Culture committed to assuring that cultural knowledge will remain available for future generations, and a Department of Wildlife Management that works with other public and private agencies to insure sound resource utilization on the North Slope and adjacent sea. Together with other Native northerners, they organized the Alaskan Eskimo Whaling Commission, which works with the International Whaling Commission, a co-management program whose success is founded on mutual respect and equitable political relations. While the social and personal stresses accompanying these four decades of change should not be discounted, overall, the Iñupiat take great pride in their accomplishments . . . .

Review Questions

1. What were the initial relations between Iñupiat Eskimos and the U.S. government in 1958 like, according to Chance?
2. What impact did the discovery of north slope oil 1967 and the Alaska Native Claims Settlement Act have on Iñupiat political structure, culture, social organization, and standard of living?
3. What political and economic forces are at work in northern Alaska, and how have the Iñupiat used them to gain their own ends?
4. Why do the Iñupiat favor additional oil exploration on the north slope of Alaska?

9

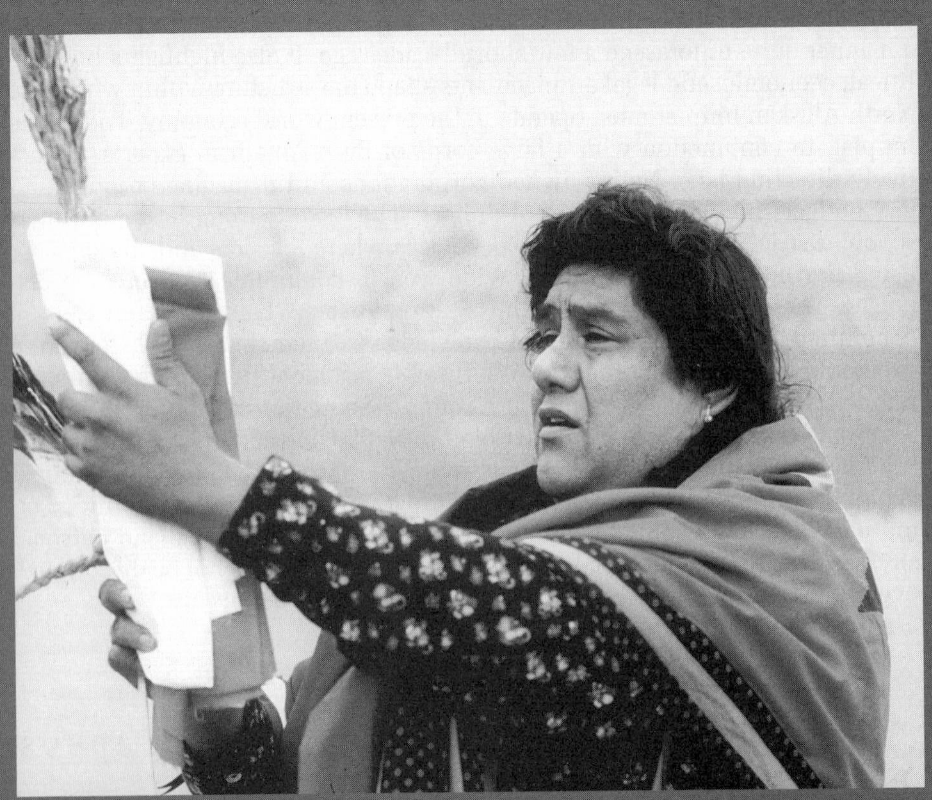

RELIGION, MAGIC, AND WORLDVIEW

People seem most content when they are confident about themselves and the order of things around them. Uncertainty breeds debilitating anxiety; insecurity saps people's sense of purpose and their willingness to participate in social activity. Most of the time cultural institutions serve as a lens through which to view and interpret the world and respond realistically to its demands. But from time to time the unexpected or contradictory intervenes to shake people's assurance. A farmer may wonder about his skill when a properly planted and tended crop fails to grow. A wife may feel bewildered when the man she has treated with tenderness and justice for many years runs off with another woman. Death, natural disaster, and countless other forms of adversity strike without warning, eating away at the foundations of confidence. At these crucial points in life, many people use religion to help account for the vagaries of their experience.

Religion is the cultural knowledge of the supernatural that people use to cope with the ultimate problems of human existence.[1] In this definition, the term *supernatural* refers to a realm beyond normal experience. Belief in gods, spirits, ghosts, and magical power often defines the supernatural, but the matter is complicated by cultural variation and the lack of a clear distinction in many societies between the natural and the supernatural world. *Ultimate problems,* on the other hand, emerge from universal features of human life and include life's meaning, death, evil, and transcendent values. People everywhere wonder why they are alive, why they must die, and why evil strikes some individuals and not others. In every society, people's personal desires and goals may conflict with the values of the larger group. Religion often provides a set of *transcendent values* that override differences and unify the group.

An aspect of religion that is more difficult to comprehend is its link to emotion. Ultimate problems "are more appropriately seen as deep-seated emotional needs," not as conscious, rational constructs, according to sociologist Milton

[1] This definition draws on the work of Milton Yinger, *Religion, Society, and the Individual: An Introduction to the Sociology of Religion* (New York: Macmillan, 1957).

[2] Yinger, 9.

Yinger.[2] Anthropologists may describe and analyze religious ritual and belief but find it harder to get at religion's deeper meanings and personal feelings.

Anthropologists have identified two kinds of supernatural power, personified and impersonal. *Personified supernatural force* resides in supernatural beings, in the deities, ghosts, ancestors, and other beings found in the divine world. For the Bhils of India, a *bhut,* or ghost, has the power to cause skin lesions and wasting diseases. *Bhagwan,* the equivalent of the Christian deity, controls the universe. Both possess and use personified supernatural force.

Impersonal supernatural force is a more difficult concept to grasp. Often called *mana,* the term used in Polynesian and Melanesian belief, it represents a kind of free-floating force lodged in many things and places. The concept is akin to the Western term *luck* and works like an electrical charge that can be introduced into things or discharged from them. Melanesians, for example, might attribute the spectacular growth of yams to some rocks lying in the fields. The rocks possess mana, which is increasing fertility. If yams fail to grow in subsequent years, they may feel that the stones have lost their power.

Supernatural force, both personified and impersonal, may be used by people in many societies. *Magic* refers to the strategies people use to control supernatural power. Magicians have clear ends in mind when they perform magic, and use a set of well-defined procedures to control and manipulate supernatural forces. For example, a Trobriand Island religious specialist will ensure a sunny day for a political event by repeating powerful sayings thought to affect the weather.

Sorcery uses magic to cause harm. For example, some Bhil *bhopas,* who regularly use magic for positive purposes, may also be hired to work revenge. They will recite powerful *mantras* (ritual sayings) over effigies to cause harm to their victims.

Witchcraft is closely related to sorcery because both use supernatural force to cause evil. But many anthropologists use the term to designate envious individuals who are born with or acquire evil power and who knowingly or unknowingly project it to hurt others. The Azande of Africa believe that most unfortunate events are due to witchcraft, and most Azande witches claim they were unaware of their power and apologize for its use.

Most religions possess ways to influence supernatural power or, if spirits are nearby, to communicate with it directly. For example, people may say *prayers* to petition supernatural beings. They may also give gifts in the form of *sacrifices* and offerings. Direct communication takes different forms. *Spirit possession* occurs when a supernatural being enters and controls the behavior of a human being. With the spirit in possession, others may talk directly with someone from the divine world. *Divination* is a second way to communicate with the supernatural. It usually requires material objects or animals to provide answers to human-directed questions. The Bhils of India, for example, predict the abundance of summer rainfall by watching where a small bird specially caught for the purpose lands when it is released. If it settles on something green, rainfall will be plentiful; if it rests on something brown, the year will be dry.

Almost all religions involve people with special knowledge who either control supernatural power outright or facilitate others in their attempt to influence it. *Shamans* are religious specialists who directly control supernatural power. They may have personal relationships with spiritual beings or know powerful secret medicines and sayings. They are usually associated with curing. *Priests* are religious specialists who mediate between people and supernatural beings. They don't control divine power; instead, they lead congregations in ceremonies and help others to petition the gods.

Worldview refers to a system of concepts and often unstated assumptions about life. It usually contains a *cosmology* about the way things are and a *mythology* about how things have come to be. World view presents answers to the ultimate questions: life, death, evil, and conflicting values.

The first article, by William Merrill, describes how a Mexican Indian group has transformed a foreign religion, Catholicism, to fit its original cultural beliefs and worldview, creating a new way to celebrate Easter. The second article, by George Gmelch, is a revision of his earlier classic article on the use of magic by American baseball players. He looks in detail at the rituals, taboos, and fetishes employed by the athletes. In the third article, William Beeman looks at the causes and nature of revitalization movements designed by people to create a more satisfying life. Focusing on current movements such as the American militias, Islamic fundamentalists, and the Native American ghost dance religion, he shows how deprivation can lead people to reformulate their own lives and oppose their perceived oppressors. The final selection, by Steven Leavitt, analyzes a specific revitalization movement, the cargo cults and beliefs of New Guinea. Noting that cargo movements originated as a response to changes and loss of power engendered by colonial government, he shows that cargo beliefs also connect people to their recently dead ancestors.

Key Terms

religion
supernatural
ultimate problems
transcendent values
personified supernatural force
mana
magic
sorcery
witchcraft
prayer
sacrifice
spirit possession
divination
shaman
priest
worldview
cosmology
mythology

Readings in This Section

God's Saviours in the Sierra Madre *William L. Merrill,* page *310*

Baseball Magic *George Gmelch,* page *320*

Revitalization Drives American Militias *William O. Beeman,* page *330*

Cargo Beliefs and Religious Experience *Steven C. Leavitt,* page *337*

29

God's Saviours in the Sierra Madre

William L. Merrill

One of the most important functions of religion is to reconcile life's contradictions. Life and death, good and evil, good fortune and adversity, all constitute paradoxes that people seek to explain, and it is often religion that deals with these basic oppositions. Yet the ways in which religion structures the answers to these questions vary markedly from one society to another, reflecting adaptive concerns and other cultural assumptions about life. Religious beliefs that work well for one society may seem incomprehensible to members of another. In this article by William Merrill, we see that Catholic beliefs about God and Christ, introduced to the Rarámuri Indians of Mexico by Jesuit missionaries, have been transformed to fit traditional religious beliefs and a world view that predate contact with the West. The Rarámuri have transformed the Christian definitions of God and the Devil, and especially the events that surround Easter, to fit their own concerns for balance, for a continued harmony between people and their social and natural world.

Originally published as "God's Saviours in the Sierra Madre." With permission from *Natural History*, vol. 93, no. 3. Copyright © by the American Museum of Natural History, 1983.

In 1607 the Catalan Jesuit Juan Fonte intervened in a conflict involving members of two Indian groups, the Tarahumaras and the Tepehuanes, who lived in the rugged Sierra Madre of northern New Spain, where the Mexican states of Chihuahua and Durango meet today. These Indians had previously remained beyond the influence of the Jesuits, except for missions established in the previous decade among the more southerly Tepehuanes. For the next nine years, Fonte devoted himself in converting them to Christianity, until the Tepehuanes revolted and killed him and five of his fellow missionaries. Almost immediately, other Jesuits arrived to replace the martyrs, and a vigorous mission system gradually spread throughout the region.

From the outset, converting the Tarahumaras required some modification of the strict orthodox line. The early missionaries apparently took Catholic doctrine and ritual, combined them with European folk beliefs and dances of the day, added their own innovations, adapted the whole to what they concluded the Tarahumaras would understand and accept, and presented it to them as the word and will of God. For their part, the Tarahumaras interpreted this complex of beliefs and actions in terms of their own ideas, adopting and modifying portions of it as they saw fit. In 1767 Charles III of Spain, distrustful of them, expelled the Jesuits from his New World domains. The Franciscans inherited the Tarahumara mission system, but financial difficulties and the disruptions of war and revolution led to its decline and abandonment by the mid-nineteenth century. Responsibility for their religious affairs reverted entirely to the Tarahumaras, who then developed, in their own fashion, the beliefs and rituals inherited from the mission period.

In 1900 the Jesuits reestablished the mission system, but in the years since, they have not attempted to force orthodoxy upon the Tarahumaras. The priests are peripheral to the Indians' religious life, performing baptisms and an occasional mass but little else, and few actually live in Tarahumara communities. Today the priests actively support the Tarahumaras in the practice of their own brand of Catholicism because they consider it a key element of Tarahumara cultural identity, which they hope to preserve. There is considerable pressure on the Tarahumaras to adopt the culture of the Mexicans who have settled in their area and who now number about 200,000, four times the Indian population. The Tarahumaras have maintained control of their religion, however. The settlers—joined in recent years by tourists from abroad—participate almost exclusively as onlookers at the Indians' elaborate holy day ceremonies, particularly those of Christmas and Easter.

The people whom outsiders have for centuries called Tarahumaras refer to themselves as Rarámuri, a word that means, on increasingly specific levels, human beings in distinction to nonhumans, Indians as opposed to non-Indians, the Rarámuri proper rather than some other Indian group, and finally, Rarámuri men in contrast to Rarámuri women. The Rarámuri version of the origin of their religion differs radically from the one just outlined. They maintain that almost everything they have and do, say and believe, was communicated by God to their ancestors soon after this world began. God, they say, is their father and they associate him with the sun. His wife, their mother, is affiliated with the moon and identified as the Virgin Mary. God's elder brother, and thus the Rarámuri's uncle, is the Devil. The Devil is the father of all non-Indians, whom the Rarámuri call *chabóchi,* "whiskered ones," an apt label since Rarámuri men have little facial hair. The Devil and his wife care for the *chabóchi* just as God and his wife care for the Rarámuri. At death, the souls of the Rarámuri ascend to heaven while those of the *chabóchi* join their parents on the bottom-most level of the universe, three levels below the earth.

The Rarámuri believe that people who commit misdeeds during their lives will be punished when they die, but they worry very little about their fate in the afterlife. They are far more concerned with the here and now and consider that their well-being depends almost entirely upon their ability to maintain proper relations with the other beings in their universe, particularly God and the Devil. God, as befits a parent, is benevolently inclined toward the Rarámuri, but he will withhold his beneficence if they fail to reciprocate his attentions adequately. The Devil's tendencies are just the opposite: he will send illness and misfortune to torment the Rarámuri unless they give him food.

The nineteenth-century Norwegian explorer and anthropologist Carl Lumholtz wrote of the Rarámuri, "The only wrong toward the gods of which he may consider himself guilty is that he does not dance enough." By "dance" Lumholtz meant that whole complex of dancing, chanting, feasting, and offerings that constitutes a Rarámuri religious fiesta. It is primarily through these fiestas that the Rarámuri balance accounts with God, who is pleased by the beauty of their performances and appreciates the offerings of food and maize beer they send to him. Typically they also bury bits of food during these fiestas to placate the Devil and deflect his malevolence.

Any Rarámuri with the resources and inclination can stage a fiesta any time of the year. People sometimes sponsor fiestas because God instructs them in their dreams to do so or because they feel in special need of his protection. They also hold them to send food, tools, clothing, and other goods to recently deceased relatives; to compensate Rarámuri doctors for curing the living; or to petition God to end a drought. There are also certain times of the year when fiestas or, at least, special rituals are required, particularly at points in the life cycle of the maize upon which the Rarámuri rely for their existence and on or near the more prominent holy days in the Catholic ritual calendar.

The fiestas associated with the maize crop take place in the hamlets where the Rarámuri live rather than at the churches around which the early missionaries had intended for them to settle. When the maize is a month or two old, neighboring households jointly sponsor a fiesta, during which a Rarámuri doctor and several assistants pass through the fields curing the maize. The doctor waves a knife and wooden cross to prevent hail from destroying the crop, while his assistants sprinkle a variety of medicines to protect the plants from pests and to enhance their growth. Periodically, the doctor stops to deliver a speech encouraging the maize to grow well and to have strength because the rains will soon commence. Later, in August, when the green ears of maize are ready to be eaten, a second fiesta is staged to offer the first fruits of the year to God, for he provided the Rarámuri with their first domesticated plants.

Despite these flurries of ritual activity during the maize-growing season, the major ceremonial activity does not get under way until the end of harvest. The most elaborate ritual events between harvest and planting are the Catholic holy day ceremonies, which begin in early December and follow one another in quick succession: Immaculate Conception (December 8), then Virgin of Guadalupe Day (December 12), Christmas Eve, and Epiphany (January 6), leading up to Candlemas (February 2), which marks for the Rarámuri the beginning of the Easter season (they do not observe Lent). The predominant theme of this winter round of celebration is the perpetuation of proper relations with God by recognizing and reciprocating his blessings. Although individual households may sponsor fiestas at their homes in conjunction with these holy days, the principal ritual activities on most take place at the thirty or so churches scattered across the 20,000 square miles of Rarámuri country.

Each fiesta is sponsored by one or more individuals who, at the conclusion of the same fiesta the year before, volunteered or were asked by others in the community to provide the food and maize beer. Together with the community's political and religious leaders, these fiesta sponsors direct the events. Men, women, and children, sometimes in the hundreds, converge on the local church from hamlets as much as fifteen miles away. Most of these people help by preparing or offering food, performing the often strenuous dances and rituals that are required, or providing encouragement and moral support to the major participants. Typically, a fiesta begins on the eve of the holy day in question and lasts all night long. If a Catholic priest arrives, mass is celebrated once or twice; if not, Rarámuri ritualists recite standard prayers. In most cases, large quantities of food and maize beer are distributed and consumed after first being offered to God.

The Rarámuri regard these celebrations as opportunities for socializing and having a good time. They joke with one another and often parody the leading ritual performers, but their frivolity does not detract from the importance they ascribe to the undertaking. They expect their efforts and even their jokes to please and satisfy God so that he will give them long lives, abundant crops, and healthy children. They also hope that their activities will convince him to postpone replacing the present world with a new one, an event that many Rarámuri, influenced by some of their Mexican neighbors, anticipate will come in the year 2000.

At this time of year, between February 2 and Easter, the theme of Rarámuri ritual begins to shift from an emphasis on the relationship between the Rarámuri and God to a concern with the relationship between God and the Devil. God and the Devil are brothers but, although they occasionally interact on a friendly basis, the Devil usually is bent on God's destruction. Most of the time God fends the Devil off, but each year the Devil succeeds by trick or force in rendering God dangerously vulnerable. Invariably this occurs immediately prior to Holy Week. From the Rarámuri point of view, their elaborate

Easter ceremonies are intended to protect and strengthen God so that he can recover and prevent the Devil from destroying the world. (The description that follows applies specifically to the community of Basíhuare, Chihuahua, where, more than in some other communities, the ceremonies deviate considerably from orthodox Catholicism. There is substantial regional variation in Rarámuri religion, owing to the different impact of Catholic missionaries in different areas and the rugged terrain, which has discouraged interaction among Rarámuri of separate regions.)

Soon after February 2, the men in Basíhuare assemble at the local church to appoint four of their number to the office of Pharisee. Each of the new Pharisees is paired with one of the four community officials known as Captains, who serve year-round as keepers of the peace and messengers for the top community officials. From the day of their selection until Easter Day, when their term of office ends, the Pharisees share police and messenger duties with the Captains and join with them as the principal organizers and performers of the Holy Week pageantry. The Pharisees, regarded as the Devil's allies, carry wooden swords painted white with ocher designs; the Captains, the allies of God, bear quivers made of coatis, the entrails replaced by bows and arrows.

In the weeks leading up to Easter, most men and older boys agree to assist either the Pharisees or the Captains during Holy Week. The reasons they join one group or the other are usually personal. For example, a man may choose to be a Pharisee this year because last year he was a Soldier, as the people who help the Captains are called. Or he may prefer the ceremonial roles or accouterments of one side to those of the other. Or he may follow the lead of friends or relatives. The usual outcome is a more or less equal division of the male community between the two groups.

The central theme of the Rarámuri's Holy Week—the conflict between God and the Devil and the Rarámuri's role as God's protector—is first expressed in a major way during the fiesta held in conjunction with Palm Sunday. A Palm Sunday ceremony I attended in Basíhuare gives some idea of the activities that will be taking place this year beginning on March 26. The preparations for the fiesta began at dusk on Saturday as, near the church, a bull was butchered by the men and its flesh, bones, and blood set to boiling by the women. Close by, several men removed stones and trash from a plot of ground to create what the Rarámuri call an *awírachi,* meaning "dance space" or "patio." Other men brought a bench about ten feet long from inside the church and placed it along the east side of the patio to hold the food that was to be offered to God. Behind it three crosses were erected and draped with necklaces, some of which bore small wooden crosses or metal crucifixes.

About 10:30 P.M., an old Rarámuri man wrapped in a hand-woven wool blanket stood at the western edge of the patio and began shaking a rattle and intoning the wordless phrases of the *tutubúri,* an indigenous rite thanking God for caring and providing for the Rarámuri and asking that he continue to bless them. Soon after the *tutubúri* got under way, a second, rather different kind of dance began on the opposite side of the patio. Known as the *mat-*

achín, a term possibly of Arabic origin, this dance presumably derives from one or more Renaissance European folk dances, but no one knows exactly when or in what form Catholic missionaries introduced it to the Rarámuri. The *matachín* dancers wear long capes and mirrored crowns and dance in two lines, whirling and crossing to the accompaniment of violins and guitars in a manner reminiscent of the Virginia reel. The *matachín* dance is said to please God because it is so beautiful. The same is true of the *tutubúri,* but, unlike the *matachín,* it is never performed within the church walls.

In the intervals between *matachín* and *tutubúri* performances, two troops of mostly young men and boys, designated as Pharisees and Soldiers, enacted the Pharisee dance, characterized by high, skipping steps executed in sinuous lines to the pounding of drums and the melody of sweet-sounding reed whistles. Some Soldiers carried bayonet-tipped staves while the Pharisees, who earlier had smeared their bodies with white earth, dragged wooden swords at their sides. The leading Pharisees donned twilled hats adorned with turkey feathers; the Rarámuri point out that the Pharisee dance bears certain similarities to the mating ritual of the turkey gobbler, but they are uncertain if the relationship is derivative or only coincidental.

About midnight, a Jesuit priest, who had arrived especially for the occasion, celebrated mass in Rarámuri and Spanish. The men knelt on the left side of the church, the women and small children on the right, and a few Mexicans stood at the rear. No Rarámuri partook of Holy Communion—in Basíhuare, they seldom do—but before and after the service, the *matachín* was danced in front of the altar.

Soon after sunrise, the first phase of the fiesta concluded. Earthen bowls of beef stew, together with stacks of tortillas and tamales and bundles of ground, parched maize, were taken to the patio and placed on the bench in front of the crosses. Seven men lifted the food to the cardinal directions, allowing the aroma and steam from the food to waft heavenward to be consumed by God. In this way, the Rarámuri acknowledged their debt to him and compensated for the sustenance he had provided them. The women then distributed the food among the people present so that all would be strengthened for the remaining activities and the journey home.

At mid-morning, one of the Rarámuri officials called *méstro,* who recite Catholic prayers and care for the accouterments of the church, rang the church bell three times. As they had done for as many years as anyone can remember, the Soldiers and Pharisees, working on opposite sides of the churchyard, began setting up wooden crosses at appropriate distances, marking the stations of the cross. Then all filed into the church for mass. At the conclusion of the service, the priest distributed palm leaves among the members of the congregation, who followed him in a procession around the churchyard, commemorating, in accordance with Catholic doctrine, Christ's entry into Jerusalem, when palm branches were strewn before him.

The Rarámuri attribute somewhat different significance to the palm. After bearing the fronds like scepters in the procession, they carry them home, for the leaves can be burned to prevent hail from destroying a crop or decocted and drunk to cure chest pains. They say the palm owes its special qualities to an event that occurred in the distant past. God, God's wife, and the Devil had been drinking maize beer for several hours when God fell asleep and the Devil succeeded in seducing God's wife, largely through his accomplished guitar playing. God awoke, catching them *in flagrante delicto,* and a fight ensued. The Devil pulled a knife and God fled, with the Devil in close pursuit. God would surely have been slain had a palm not offered its thick leaves as a hiding place. This event sealed an enduring friendship between God and the palm and established the palm's usefulness to the Rarámuri; however, it also determined that humans would fight and commit adultery in imitation of their deities.

Drums and reed whistles alternated with liturgy as the Palm Sunday procession passed through the various stations of the cross. At circuit's end, the priest retired to the house in which he stays during his visits to Basíhuare. The others assembled facing the front of the church, where their community leaders stood, grasping the wooden canes that signify their authority. The principal Rarámuri official called before him several men known to be accomplished dreamers and requested that they relate what their recent dreams had revealed about the coming year and especially the impending Holy Week. The dreamers reported that, as in years past at this time, God was in a weak and vulnerable state, this year because the Devil forced him to drink a great deal of maize beer and he had not yet recovered. The Rarámuri people must protect God and his wife until he was well again, they said, or the Devil would destroy them and the world. The official acknowledged the dreamers' advice and in a loud voice urged everyone to return to the church in three days for the Easter ceremonies to care for their parents, God and God's wife.

By mid-morning on Holy Wednesday, the Captains, Pharisees, and a few of their helpers were busy at work in the churchyard, making preparations for the Easter ceremonies. With saplings, leaves, and fibers gathered from nearby hills and canyons, they constructed archways, crosses, wreaths, and rosettes, positioning them in and around the church to mark the processional route, on two adjacent hilltops, and at the cemetery. A woman swept the church with a bundle of long grass stems while three men attended to the altar and its adornments: four candlesticks, two crosses, and a statue and portrait of the Virgin Mary. Another man cleared stones, branches, and trash from the processional path encircling the church.

The principal community officials and their families set themselves up in nearby huts and rockshelters, all of which are abandoned except on such ritual occasions. There they cleared dance patios, erected arches and crosses, and prepared the food and maize beer they would be obliged to serve in the days ahead. Like the other Rarámuri who were going to participate in the ceremony, they made sure that the clothes they would be wearing were either new or sparkling clean, as is expected during Holy Week.

The Rarámuri call Holy Week *Norírawachi,* meaning "when we walk in circles," because they spend much of Maundy Thursday, Good Friday, and

Holy Saturday morning circumscribing the church in formal procession. The point of the procession is to protect the church, and, by extension, God and God's wife. The fate of the universe rests on the Rarámuri's shoulders during this period, for they must prevent the Devil from vanquishing God and destroying the world. Their every action takes on cosmic significance. They must fast until past noon on Maundy Thursday and Good Friday because to eat would bloat God's stomach. Until Friday afternoon, fighting or chopping wood would bruise or cut God, so they must avoid both. They must dance and offer food to strengthen God, and they must guard the church and its paraphernalia, particularly the reproduction, hanging above the altar, of the miraculous portrait of the Virgin of Guadalupe, who is God's wife and their mother. Four Soldiers with bayonet-bearing staves are posted in front of the altar inside the church while a drum and whistle play behind them. Four Pharisees, wooden swords in hand, keep watch on the church steps. Replacements arrive every hour or so, and the guard is maintained much of Thursday and Friday.

Despite their efforts in guarding the church, the Pharisees are cast as the Devil's allies and as the opponents of the Soldiers, who are allied with God. The Pharisees reveal their association with the Devil most dramatically on Good Friday afternoon, when they appear with three figures made of wood and long grasses representing Judas, Judas's wife, and their dog. The Rarámuri say Judas is one of the Devil's relatives, and they call him Grandfather and his wife Grandmother. They also assign personal names to them each year: one recent Easter in Basíhuare, Judas was known as Ramón, his wife was María, and the dog, Monje, or Monk. Judas and his wife wear elements of Mexican-style clothing, as befits the Devil's kin, and display their oversized genitalia prominently. The Pharisees parade the figures around the church and dance before them, then turn them over to the Soldiers who do the same. The Pharisees then hide the figures away for the night.

In Basíhuare, as in many other Rarámuri communities, the Easter ceremonies conclude on Holy Saturday, not Easter Sunday. In the morning, the Soldiers and Pharisees engage in wrestling matches, battling symbolically for control of Judas. Regardless of the outcome, the Soldiers take possession, shooting arrows into the three figures and setting them afire. Then all remaining Easter paraphernalia is dismantled or destroyed. Such destruction is necessary, the Rarámuri say, to avert strong winds in the coming months. For the same reason, they place food and maize beer at ceremonial arches on two hilltops near the church, offerings to engender the good will of the Devil and the Wind, which they personify. By noon the church and its yard lie silent, deserted in favor of the many maize beer drinking parties being held in the surrounding countryside.

The Catholic missionaries who introduced Easter ceremonies to the Rarámuri presumably intended them to be reenactments of Christ's crucifixion and resurrection and dramatizations of the conflict between good and evil. The priests themselves probably adapted their teachings somewhat to what they knew of Rarámuri religion, but their original messages have been radically transformed by the Rarámuri to conform more closely to indigenous rituals, beliefs, and values. The Christian Trinity of Father, Son, and Holy Spirit has become in Rarámuri Catholicism a Duality of Father and Mother associated with the sun and moon, respectively. The Holy Spirit is never mentioned, and the events of Christ's life of which the Rarámuri are aware are attributed to God the Father. Because God created their ancestors, the Rarámuri regard themselves as his children, but they also maintain that God and his wife have many natural offspring who live with them in heaven. They apply the term "Jesus Christ" to all the males among these children and "Saint" to all the females, identifying the robes of saints (even male ones) as dresses.

The idea that Christ died on the cross to redeem the sins of humankind makes little sense to the Rarámuri. Ethnic affiliation rather than acceptance or rejection of Christ as Saviour determines a person's fate in the afterlife: the Rarámuri ascend to heaven after death to be with their parents, God and his wife, while the *chabóchi* (non-Indians) join the Devil and his wife below. According to the Rarámuri, *chabóchi* people want to live out eternity in the Devil's realm because it is a pleasant place to live, and the Devil and his wife are their parents. On the other hand, the souls of people who commit serious crimes such as murder or grand theft are completely destroyed soon after death. There is punishment for ill deeds in the Rarámuri cosmos, but no eternal damnation with its concomitant suffering.

To some degree God and the Devil personify good and evil for the Rarámuri, but in a much less absolute way than in Christian theology. Both God and the Devil can help or harm the Rarámuri depending on how the Rarámuri act toward them. The Rarámuri endeavor to perpetuate good relations with God and to placate the Devil by performing fiestas and making food offerings to them. By so doing they repay God for caring and providing for them and encourage the Devil to refrain from attacking them. If they fail in these obligations and overtures, God and the Devil will turn against them.

The basic purpose of their fiestas and offerings and of so much else the Rarámuri do, both in and outside their rituals, is to maintain balance in the world. This orientation, which almost certainly existed among the Rarámuri before Western contact, seems to have had a substantial impact on how they interpreted and adapted the Easter ceremonies that the missionaries taught them. Implicit throughout the Easter proceedings are expressions of the complementarity and mutual obligations that exist among various segments of Rarámuri society, between males and females, for example, or community officials and the people they lead and represent. While the most obvious message in the Easter celebration is the confrontation between God and the Devil, the Rarámuri have not followed the more orthodox Christian line of desiring the complete destruction of the Devil and his influence. Instead, their goal is to produce good relations between the Devil and themselves and to restore the balance between God and the Devil that existed before God fell victim to the Devil's machinations.

Review Questions

1. Why do you think it might have been difficult for the Rarámuri to adopt Catholicism?
2. What major changes did the Rarámuri Indians make in the teachings of the Catholic missionaries?
3. In the Rarámuri view, what is the purpose of the Easter ceremony? How is the ceremony organized to achieve this end?
4. What core value organizes Rarámuri religion? How is this value reflected in the Easter ceremony?

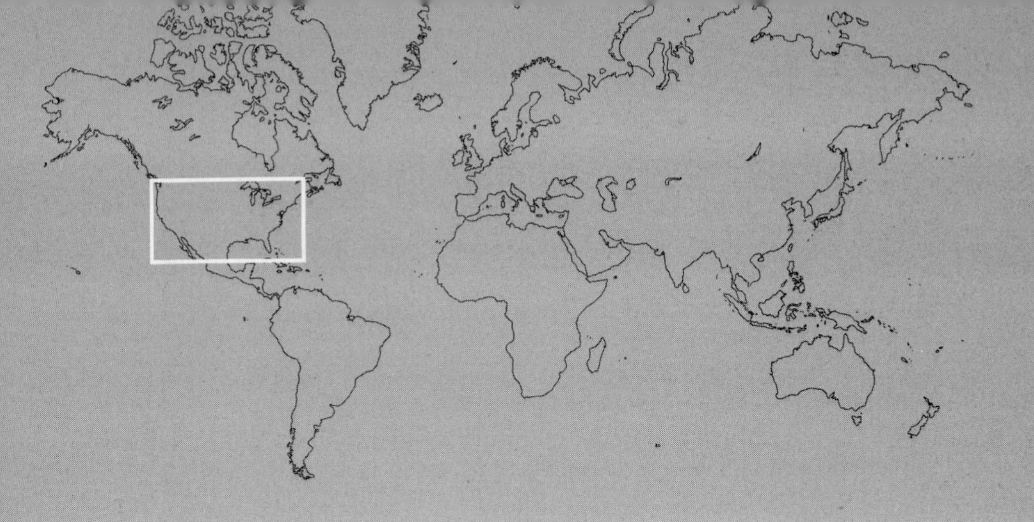

30

Baseball Magic

George Gmelch

Americans pride themselves on their scientific approach to life and problem solving. But as George Gmelch demonstrates in this article, American baseball players, much like people in many parts of the world, also turn to supernatural forces to ensure success in their athletic endeavors. Gmelch shows that magical ritual, taboos, and fetishes surround aspects of baseball that are least predictable, thus most likely to challenge human control.

On each pitching day for the first three months of a winning season, Dennis Grossini, a pitcher on a Detroit Tiger farm team, arose from bed at exactly 10:00 A.M. At 1:00 P.M. he went to the nearest restaurant for two glasses of iced tea and a tuna fish sandwich. Although the afternoon was free, he changed into the sweatshirt and supporter he wore during his last winning game, and one hour before the game he chewed a wad of Beech-Nut chewing tobacco. After each pitch during the game he touched his letters [the team name on his uniform] and straightened his cap after each ball. Before the start

"Baseball Magic" has been revised for this edition of *Conformity and Conflict*. Copyright © by George Gmelch, 1997. Printed by permission of the author.

of each inning he replaced the pitcher's rosin bag next to the spot where it was the inning before. And after every inning in which he gave up a run, he washed his hands.

When asked which part of the ritual was most important, he responded, "You can't really tell what's most important so it all becomes important. I'd be afraid to change anything. As long as I'm winning, I do everything the same. Even when I can't wash my hands (this would occur when he had to bat), it scares me going back to the mound. I don't feel quite right."

Trobriand Islanders, according to anthropologist Bronislaw Malinowski, felt the same way about their fishing magic. Among the Trobrianders, fishing took two forms: in the inner lagoon where fish were plentiful and there was little danger, and on the open sea where fishing was dangerous and yields varied widely. Malinowski found that magic was not used in lagoon fishing, where men could rely solely on their knowledge and skill. But when fishing on the open sea, Trobrianders used a great deal of magical ritual to ensure safety and increase their catch.

Baseball, America's national pastime, is an arena in which players behave remarkably like Malinowski's Trobriand fishermen. To professional baseball players, baseball is more than just a game. It is an occupation. Since their livelihoods depend on how well they perform, many use magic to try to control or eliminate the chance and uncertainty built into baseball.

To control uncertainty, for example, New York Yankees Wade Boggs eats chicken before every game (that's 162 meals of chicken per year), and he has been doing that for nine years. Chicago White Sox pitcher Jason Bere listens to the same song on his Walkman on the days he is to pitch. His teammate, Ozzie Guillen, doesn't wash his underclothes after a good game. San Francisco Giant pitcher Ron Bryant added a new stick of bubble gum to the collection in his bulging back pocket after each game he won. Jim Ohms, my teammate and pitcher on the Daytona Beach Islanders, put another penny in the pouch of his supporter after each win. Clanging against the hard plastic genital cup, the pennies made an audible sound as he ran the bases toward the end of a winning season.

Whether they are professional baseball players, Trobriand fishermen, soldiers, or even students taking final exams, people resort to magic in situations of chance, when they believe they have limited control over the success of their activities and the outcome is important. In technologically advanced societies that pride themselves on a scientific approach to problem solving, as well as in simple societies, rituals of magic are common. Magic is a human attempt to impose order and certainty on an otherwise uncertain situation. This attempt is irrational in that there is no causal connection between the rituals and instruments of magic and the desired consequences of the magical practice. But it is rational in that it creates in the practitioner a sense of confidence, competence, and control, which in turn helps them successfully execute their activity and achieve the desired result.

I have long had a close relationship with baseball, first as a participant and then as an observer. I devoted much of my youth to the game and played professionally as first baseman for five teams in the Detroit Tiger organization in the 1960s. It was shortly after the end of my last baseball season, that I took an anthropology course called "Magic, Religion, and Witchcraft." As my professor described the magic practiced by a tribe in Papua New Guinea, it occurred to me that what these so-called "primitive" people did wasn't all that different from what my teammates and I had done to give themselves luck while playing professional baseball.

In baseball there are three essential activities—pitching, hitting, and fielding. Each varies in the amount of chance and uncertainty associated with it. The pitcher is the player least able to control the outcome of his own efforts. His best pitch may be hit for a home run, while his worst pitch may be hit directly into the hands of a fielder for an out or be swung at and missed for a third strike. He may limit the opposing team to a few hits yet lose the game, or he may give up a dozen hits and still win. One has only to look at the frequency with which pitchers end a season with poor won–lost records but have good earned run averages, or vice versa. For example, in 1990 Dwight Gooden gave up more runs per game than his teammate Sid Fernandez but had a won–lost record nearly twice as good. Gooden won 19 games and lost only 7, while Fernandez won only 9 games while losing 14. They pitched for the same team—the New York Mets—and therefore had the same fielders behind them. Regardless of how well he performs, on every outing the pitcher depends upon the proficiency of his teammates, the ineptitude of the opposition, and caprice.

Hitting is also full of risk and uncertainty—Hall of Famer Ted Williams called it the most difficult single task in the world of sports. Consider the forces and time constraints operating against the batter. A fast ball travels from the pitcher's mound to the batter's box, just sixty and one-half feet, in three- to four-tenths of a second. For only three feet of the journey, an absurdly short two-hundredths of a second, the ball is in a position where it can be hit. And to be hit well the ball must be neither too close to the batter's body nor too far from the "meat" of his bat. Any distraction, any slip of a muscle or change in stance, can throw a swing off. Once the ball is hit chance plays a large role in determining where it will go into a waiting glove, whistling past a fielder's diving stab, or into the wide open spaces. In a quirky example of luck, some years ago Giant outfielder Willie Mays "dove for the dirt" to avoid being hit in the head by a fast ball. While he was falling, the pitch hit his bat and the ball went shooting down the left field line. Mays jumped up and ran, turning the play into a double, while the pitcher looked on in disgust.

Batters also suffer from the fear of being hit by a pitch—specifically, by a fast ball that often travels at speeds exceeding ninety miles per hour. Throughout baseball history the great fast ball pitchers like Sandy Koufax, Bob Gibson, Nolan Ryan, and Randy Johnson have thrived on this fear and on the level of distraction it causes hitters.

In fielding, on the other hand, the player has almost complete control over the outcome. Once a ball has been hit in his direction, no one can intervene and ruin his chances of catching it for an out. Infielders have approximately three seconds in which to judge the flight of the ball, field it cleanly, and throw it to first base. Outfielders have almost double that amount of time to track down a fly ball. The average fielding percentage (or success rate) of .975, compared with a .250 success rate for hitters (the average batting percentage), reflects the degree of certainty in fielding. Compared with the pitcher or the hitter, the fielder has little to worry about. He knows that in better than 9.7 times out of 10 he will execute his task flawlessly.

In sum, pitching and hitting involve a great deal of chance and are comparable to the Trobriand fishermen's open sea; fielding, on the other hand, involves little uncertainty and is similar to the Trobriander's inner lagoon. In keeping with Malinowski's hypothesis about the relationship between magic and uncertainty, I found that baseball players use magic for hitting and pitching, but not for fielding. Indeed, I observed a wide assortment of magic—rituals, taboos, and fetishes—associated with both hitting and pitching, but never observed the use of any directly connected to fielding. I have known only one player, a shortstop with fielding problems, who reported any ritual connected with fielding. Now let us look at the kinds of magic practiced by ballplayers.

Ritual

The most common form of magic in professional baseball is personal ritual—a prescribed behavior that players scrupulously observe in an effort to ensure that things go their way. These personal rituals, like those practiced by Trobriand fishermen, are performed in a routine, unemotional manner, much as players do non-magical things to improve their play: rubbing pine tar on their hands to improve their grip on the bat, or rubbing a new ball to make it more comfortable and responsive to the pitcher's grip. Rituals are infinitely varied since ballplayers may formalize any activity that they consider important or somehow linked to performing well.

Many hitters go through a series of preparatory rituals before stepping into the batter's box. These include tugging on their caps, touching their uniform letters or medallions, crossing themselves, tapping or bouncing the bat on the plate, swinging the weighted warm-up bat a prescribed number of times, and smoothing the dirt in the box. Mike Hargrove, former Cleveland Indian first baseman, had more than a dozen individual elements in the batting ritual. And after each pitch he would step out of the batter's box and repeat the entire sequence. His rituals were so time consuming that he was called "the human rain delay." Hargrove defended his routine, saying it was important to getting his concentration back after each pitch.

Rituals may become so important that they override practicality. Catcher Matt Allen, for example, was wearing a long sleeve turtle neck shirt on a cool evening in the New York-Penn League when he had a three-hit game. "I kept wearing the shirt and had a good week," he explained. "Then the weather got hot as hell, 85 degrees and muggy, but I would not take that shirt off. I wore it for another ten days—catching—and people thought I was crazy."

A popular ritual associated with hitting is tagging a base when leaving and returning to the dugout between innings. Mickey Mantle habitually tagged second base on the way to or from the outfield. Another player stepped on third base on his way to the dugout after the third, sixth, and ninth innings of each game. Asked if he ever purposely failed to step on the bag, he replied, "Never! I wouldn't dare. It would destroy my confidence to hit." A hitter who is playing poorly may try different combinations of tagging and not tagging particular bases in an attempt to find a successful combination.

When players are not hitting, some managers will rattle the bat bin, the large wooden box containing the team's bats, as if the bats are in a stupor and can be aroused by a good shaking. Similarly, some hitters rub their hands along the handles of the bats protruding from the bin, presumably in hopes of picking up some power or luck from those bats that are getting hits for their owners.

Rituals usually grow out of exceptionally good performances. When a player does well, he seldom attributes his success to skill alone. Although his skill remains constant, he may go hitless in one game and in the next get three or four hits. Many players attribute such inconsistencies in their performances to an object, the food they ate, or some behavior outside their play. Through ritual, players seek to gain control over their performance. Outfielder John White explained how one of his rituals started:

> I was jogging out to center field after the national anthem when I picked up a scrap of paper. I got some good hits that night and I guess I decided that the paper had something to do with it. The next night I picked up a gum wrapper and had another good night at the plate . . . I've been picking up paper every night since.

Like many hitters, John abandoned this ritual and looked for a new one when he stopped hitting.

Because most pitchers play only once every four days, they perform rituals less frequently than hitters. But the rituals are just as important, perhaps more so. A starting pitcher cannot make up for a poor performance the next day, and having to wait three days to redeem oneself can be miserable. Moreover, the team's performance depends more on the pitcher than on any other single player. Considering the pressures to do well, it is not surprising that pitchers' rituals are often more complex than those of hitters.

Most baseball fans observe ritual behavior, such as pitchers tugging their caps between pitches, touching the rosin bag after each bad pitch, smoothing the dirt on the mound before each new batter or inning, never realizing that these actions may be as important to the pitcher as actually throwing the ball.

Many other rituals take place off the field, out of public view. On the days they are scheduled to appear, many pitchers avoid activities that they believe sap their strength and therefore detract from their effectiveness, or that they otherwise link with poor performance. Many pitchers avoid eating certain foods on their pitching days. Some pitchers do not shave on the day of a game; some pitchers don't shave as long as they are winning. Early in the 1989 season Oakland's Dave Stewart had six consecutive victories and a beard before he finally lost. Ex-St. Louis Cardinal Al Hrabosky took this taboo to extremes; Samsonlike, he refused to cut his hair or beard during the entire season, which was part of the reason for his nickname, the "Mad Hungarian."

Mike Griffin begins his ritual preparation a full day before he pitches, by washing his hair. The next day, although he does not consider himself superstitious, he eats bacon for lunch. When Griffin dresses for the game he puts on his clothes in the same order, making certain he puts the slightly longer of his two outer, or "stirrup," socks on his right leg. "I just wouldn't feel right mentally if I did it the other way around," he explains. He always wears the same shirt under his uniform on the day he pitches. During the game he takes off his cap after each pitch, and between innings he sits in the same place on the dugout bench. He believes his rituals give him a sense of order which reduces his anxiety about pitching.

Some pitcher's involve their wives or girlfriends in their rituals. One wife reported that her husband insisted that she wash her hair each day he was to pitch. In her memoirs, Danielle Torrez reported that one "rule" she learned as a baseball wife was "to support your husband's superstitions, whether you believe in them or not. "I joined the player's wives who ate ice cream in the sixth inning or tacos in the fifth, or who attended games in a pink sweater, a tan scarf, or a floppy hat" (1983:79).

Taboo

The word *taboo* comes from a Polynesian term meaning prohibition. Breaking a taboo or prohibition leads to undesirable consequences or bad luck. Most players observe at least a few taboos. Some are careful never to step on the chalk foul lines or lines of the batters box. One teammate of mine would never watch a movie on a game day, despite the fact that we played nearly every day from April to September. Another teammate refused to read anything before a game because he believed that reading weakened his eyesight when batting.

Many taboos grow out of exceptionally poor performances, which players, in search of a reason or cause, attribute to a particular behavior. During my first season of pro ball I ate pancakes before a game in which I struck out four times. A few weeks later I had a similarly bad game, again after eating pancakes. The result was a pancake taboo: I never ate pancakes during the season from that day on. In earlier decades some baseball players believed that it was bad luck to go back and fasten a missed buttonhole after dressing for a game. They simply left missed buttons on shirts or pants undone. This taboo, however, is no longer observed by today's ballplayers.

There is a taboo against crossing bats, against permitting one bat to rest on top of another. Although this superstition appears to be dying out among ballplayers today, it was religiously observed by some of my teammates. One of my Hispanic teammates became quite annoyed when another player tossed a bat from the batting cage and it landed on top of his bat. Later he explained that the top bat might steal hits from the lower one. In his view, bats contained a finite number of hits, a sort of baseball "image of limited good." For Pirate shortstop Honus Wagner, a charter member of baseball's Hall of Fame, each bat contained only 100 hits and never more. Regardless of the quality of the bat, he would discard it after its 100th hit.

Hall of Famer Johnny Evers, of the Cub double-play trio Tinker to Evers to Chance, believed in saving his luck. If he was hitting well in practice, he would suddenly stop and retire to the bench to "save" his batting for the game. One player told me that many of his teammates on the Asheville Tourists in the Class A Western Carolinas League would not let pitchers touch or swing their bats, not even to loosen up. Poor-hitting pitchers were believed to pollute or weaken the bats.

Fetishes

Charms or fetishes are material objects believed to embody supernatural powers that can aid or protect the owner. Good luck fetishes are standard equipment for many ballplayers. They include a wide assortment of objects: horsehide covers from old baseballs, coins, chains, crucifixes, and old bats. Ordinary objects acquire power by being connected to exceptionally hot batting or pitching streaks, especially ones in which players get all the breaks. The object is often a new possession or something a player finds and holds responsible for his new good fortune. A player who is in a slump might find a coin or an odd stone just before he begins a hitting streak, then attribute an improvement in his performance to the influence of the new object, and come to regard it as a fetish.

While playing in the Pacific Coast League, Alan Foster forgot his baseball shoes on a road trip and borrowed a pair from a teammate. That night he pitched a no-hitter, which he attributed to the shoes. After he bought them from his teammate, they became a fetish. The prized rock of Expo farmhand Mark LaRosa has a very different origin and use:

> I found it on the field in Elmira after I had gotten bombed [pitched very poorly]. It's unusual, perfectly round, and it caught my attention. I keep it to remind me of how important it is to concentrate. When I am going well I look at the rock and remember to keep my focus, the rock reminds me of what can happen when I lost my concentration. For one season Marge Schott, owner of the Cincinnati Reds, insisted that her field manager rub her St. Bernard "Schotzie" for good luck before each game. When the Reds were on the road, Schott reportedly would sometimes send a bag of the dogs hair to the field manager's hotel room.

During World War II American soldiers used fetishes in much same way. Social psychologist Samuel Stouffer and his colleagues found that in the face of great danger and uncertainty, soldiers developed magical practices, particularly the use of protective amulets and good-luck charms (crosses, Bibles, rabbits' feet, medals), and jealously guarded articles of clothing they associated with past experiences of escape from danger. Stouffer also found that prebattle preparations were carried out in fixed "ritual" order, much as ballplayers prepare for a game.

Uniform numbers have special significance for some players. Many have a lucky number which they request. Since the choice is usually limited, players may try to get a number that at least contains their lucky number, such as 14, 24, 34, or 44 for the pitcher whose lucky number is four. Oddly enough, there is no consensus about the effect of wearing number 13. Some players will not wear it, others will, and a few, like Yankees David Cone, request it.

The way in which number preferences emerge varies. Occasionally a young player requests the number of a former star, hoping that—in a form of *imitative* magic—it will bring him a similar measure of success. Or he may request a favorite number that he has always associated with good luck. Vida Blue, former Athletic and Giant, changed his uniform number from 35 to 14, the number he wore as a high-school quarterback. When the new number did not produce the better pitching performance he was looking for, he switched back to his old number.

Clothing, both the choice of clothes and the order in which they are put on, combine elements of both ritual and fetish. Some players put on their uniform in a specified order. Expos farmhand Jim Austin always puts on his left sleeve, left pants leg, and left shoe before the right. Most players, however, single out one or two lucky articles or quirks of dress rather than ritualizing all items of clothing. After hitting two home runs in a game, for example, infielder Jim Davenport of the San Francisco Giants discovered that he had missed a buttonhole while dressing for the game. For the remainder of his career he left the same button undone. For Brian Hunter of the Cincinnati Reds, the focus is on his shoes: "I have a pair of high tops and a pair of low tops. Whichever shoes don't get a hit that game, I switch to the other pair." At the time of our interview, he was struggling at the plate and switching shoes almost every day. For Birmingham Baron pitcher Bo Kennedy the *arrangement* of the different pairs of baseball shoes in his locker is critical:

> I tell the clubs [clubhouse boys] when you hang stuff in my locker don't touch my shoes. If you bump them move them back. I want the Pony's in front, the turfs to the right, and I want them nice and neat with each pair touching each other . . . Everyone on the team knows not to mess with my shoes when I pitch.

During streaks—hitting or winning—many players wear the same clothes and uniforms for each game. Once I changed sweatshirts midway through the game for seven consecutive games to keep a hitting streak going. During a 16-game winning streak in 1954, the New York Giants wore the same clothes in each game and refused to let them be cleaned for fear that their good fortune might be washed away with the dirt. Taking this ritual to the extreme, Leo Durocher, managing the Brooklyn Dodgers to a pennant in 1941, spent three and a half weeks in the same black shoes, gray slacks, blue coat, and knitted blue tie. The opposite may also occur. Several of the Oakland A's players bought new street clothes in an attempt to break a 14-game losing streak.

Although most taboos are idiosyncratic, there are a few that all players hold and that do not develop out of individual experience or misfortune. These taboos are learned, some as early as Little League. Mentioning a no-hitter while one is in progress is a widely known example. It is believed that if a pitcher hears the words "no-hitter," the spell will be broken and the no-hitter lost. This taboo is still observed by many sports broadcasters, who use various linguistic subterfuges to inform their listeners that the pitcher had not given up a hit, never mentioning "no-hitter."

Such superstitions, like most everything else, change over time. Many of the rituals and beliefs of early baseball are no longer remembered. In the 1920s and 1930s sportswriters reported that a player who tripped en route to the field would often retrace his steps and carefully walk over the stumbling block for "insurance." A century ago players spent time off the field and on looking for items that would bring them luck. For example, to find a hairpin on the street assured a batter of hitting safely in that day's game (today women don't wear hairpins—a good reason why the belief has died out). To catch sight of a white horse or a wagon load of barrels were also good omens. In 1904 the manager of the New York Giants, John McGraw, hired a driver and a team of white horses to drive past the Polo Grounds around the time his players were arriving at the ballpark. He knew that if his players saw white horses, they'd have more confidence and that could only help them during the game. Belief in the power of white horses survived in a few backwaters until the 1960s. A gray-haired manager of a team I played for in Quebec would drive around the countryside before important games and during the playoffs looking for a white horse. When he was successful, he'd announce it to everyone in the clubhouse before the game.

B. F. Skinner's early research with pigeons sheds some light on how these rituals, taboos, and fetishes get established in the first place. Like human beings, pigeons quickly learn to associate their behavior with rewards or punishment. By rewarding the birds at the appropriate time, Skinner taught them such elaborate games as table tennis, miniature bowling, and how to play simple tunes on a toy piano.

On one occasion he decided to see what would happen if pigeons were rewarded with food pellets every fifteen seconds, regardless of what they did. He found that the birds tended to associate the arrival of the food with a particular action—tucking the head under a wing, hopping from side to side, or turning in a clockwise direction. About ten seconds after the arrival of the last pellet, a bird would begin doing whatever it had associated with getting the food and keep at it until the next pellet arrived.

In the same way, baseball players tend to believe there is a causal connection between two events that are linked only temporally. If a superstitious player touches his crucifix and then gets a hit, he may decide the gesture was responsible for his good fortune and follow the same practice the next time he comes to the plate. If he should get another hit, the chances are good that he will begin touching the crucifix each time he bats and that he will do so whether or not he hits safely each time.

The average batter hits safely approximately one quarter of the time. And if the behavior of Skinner's pigeons or of gamblers at a Las Vegas slot machine is any guide, that is more than enough to keep him believing in a ritual. Skinner found that once a pigeon associated one of its actions with the arrival of food or water, sporadic rewards would keep the connection going. One pigeon, apparently believing that hopping from side to side brought pellets into its feeding cup, hopped ten thousand times without a pellet before finally giving up.

Since the batter associates his hits at least to some degree with his ritual touching of a crucifix, each hit he gets reinforces the strength of the ritual. Even if he falls into a batting slump and the hits temporarily stop, he may continue to touch his crucifix in the hope that it will change his luck. If the slump lasts too long, however, he will soon change his behavior and look for a new practice to bring back his luck.

Skinner's and Malinowski's explanations are complementary. Skinner's research throws light on how a ritual develops and why a particular ritual, taboo, or fetish is maintained. Malinowski focuses on why human beings turn to magic in situations of chance and uncertainty. In their attempts to gain greater control over their performance, baseball players respond to chance and uncertainty in the same way as people in tribal societies. It is wrong to assume that magical practices are a waste of time for either group. The magic in baseball obviously does not make a pitch travel faster or more accurately, or a batted ball seek the gaps between fielders. Nor does the Trobriand brand of magic make the surrounding seas calmer and more abundant with fish. What both kinds of magic do is give their practitioners a sense of control, and with that confidence, at very little cost.

Review Questions

1. According to Gmelch, what is magic, and why do people practice it?
2. What parts of baseball are most likely to lead to magical practice? Why?
3. What is meant by the terms taboo and fetish? Illustrate these concepts using examples from this article.
4. How are Malinowski's and Skinner's theories of magic alike and different? What is each designed to explain?
5. Can you think of other areas of American life where magic is practiced? Do the same theories used in this article account for these examples, too?

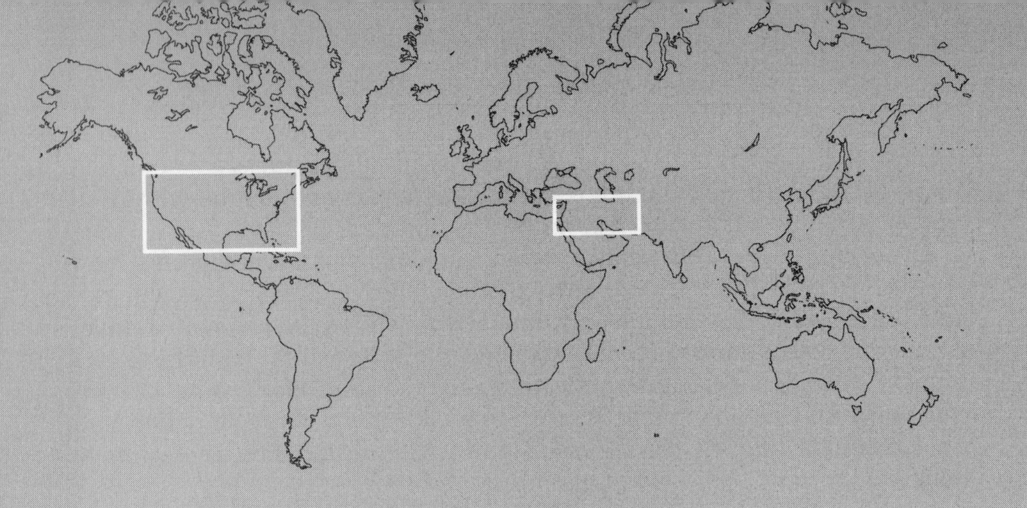

31

Revitalization Drives American Militias

William O. Beeman

When one cultural group becomes dominated by another, resulting rapid change and loss of authority may make its original meaning system seem thin, ineffective, and contradictory. The resulting state of deprivation often causes members to rebuild their culture along what they consider to be more satisfying lines. The process, which is called revitalization by anthropologists, has occurred over and over again among peoples throughout the world. Often couched in religious terms, movements prescribe rituals and beliefs designed to restore order to their existence. In this selection, William Beeman describes the process of revitalization and shows how it shapes the beliefs and actions of such groups as the militias that are springing up across America and the Islamic fundamentalists of the Middle East.

On April 19, 1995, the Federal Building in Oklahoma City, Oklahoma, was bombed killing 168 innocent adults and children. This was the

This article was written for *Conformity and Conflict*. Copyright © by William O. Beeman, 1997. Reprinted by permission of the author.

worst terrorist action ever committed on American soil to that date. The perpetrators of this crime apparently belonged to a para-military "militia" group based in Michigan. It was difficult for Americans to understand the ideology of a group that would sanction the bombing of innocent citizens. It is estimated that in the United States there are at least 15,000 active members of militia movements operating in 40 States.[1] This phenomenon is by no means unique to America. Groups like the militias are found all over the world. Indeed although they have different ideological underpinnings, the American militia groups have much in common with resistance groups in the Middle East, Ireland, India, and Japan.

Anthropologists identify these groups as the embodiments of "revitalization movements." These movements may be a natural consequence of human processes of cultural change. In every society on earth change proceeds at an uneven pace. Some society members embrace change with relish. Others find it oppressive and troubling. If people feel that change is being imposed on them, some will find it necessary to resist—sometimes violently.

The dynamics of revitalization thus are tied to inter-group dynamics. When one group in society perceives itself as having its power and authority usurped by another group, the first group comes to blame both internal and external causes for its fall from power. Internally, the group blames itself for its decline. Its leaders often point to internal decadence as the principal reason for its decline. They accuse members of society of becoming weak and irresolute to the point where they let others oppress them. This invariably results in the creation of physical and mental training programs to strengthen the character and resolve of those who want to become the vanguard to restore society to its former idealized state. These practices are extremely varied. They range from prayer and meditation to ascetic practices and military training.

Externally, the group blames the perceived oppressor, and usually advocates resistance—sometimes violent—to that group. The core operations of the revitalization movement may be varied ranging from guerrilla warfare and attacks on public figures and facilities, to more peaceful protests and non-violent action. Occasionally, revitalization movements embrace the outsiders, and direct their energies toward becoming more like them, or attracting their attention. Large scale religious conversions have had this quality.

Members of revitalization movements see themselves as saviors of society. For this reason they are able to justify almost any action, however violent, and any personal sacrifice, however great, for their cause. There is a tendency to see the world in black and white terms. People are clearly enemies or friends. Actions are good or bad. The unrelenting commitment and conviction of the members of the movement is eventually the element that makes them so dangerous for the rest of society.

---

[1] Reported in Halpern, Thomas, David Rosenberg and Irwin Suall, "Militia Movement: Prescription for Disaster." *U.S.A. Today Magazine,* vol. 124, January 1, 1996, pp. 16 ff.

Myths of a Golden Age

Revitalization movements invariably create a myth of a supposed Golden Age in the past when the members of the movement were strong, vital, and in control of the world. Their main goal is to return to that sense of group strength and wholeness. In seeking to do this, they adhere to no particular political ideology. They are as likely to be left-leaning as right-leaning in their solution to the problem.

The United States has seen a number of revitalization movements throughout its history. The peace movement of the '60s and early '70s was one important movement in recent history. The militia movement of the '90s has been another. These two movements are radically different in their political orientation, but eerily similar in their methods.

Allen J. Matusow, author of *The Unraveling of America: A History of Liberalism in the 1960's,* labels these groups as "moral extremists." "They believe the government is perpetrating evil in some way and that you must resist evil by carrying out guerrilla acts if necessary."[2] During the summer of 1970 nearly 20 explosions of public buildings a week were seen in California. None of these inflicted the horrible deaths seen in the Oklahoma City bombing, but the groups that carried them out were clearly trying to make the point that the American government, and the corporations that participated with the government in the Vietnam War, was the enemy. The Golden Age for these groups was an imagined time when peace and love reigned supreme—an Age of Aquarius, to coin a pop-culture image of the time.

The American militia groups of the '90s have at times been characterized as "neo-Nazis," "skinheads," or "white supremacists." These characterizations are not really accurate. However, the Golden Age for these groups does hearken back to a time when being white, male, and having a gun really meant something in American society. The militias idealize a set of values that most U.S. citizens would identify as historically important for American life—independence, freedom, and individualism. Above all they hate restrictions imposed by outsiders on their actions and use of resources. They want to instill these values in their progeny, and fiercely resist any attempt to regulate the moral and ideological education of their children.

These are the idealized values of an American Golden Age spanning the period from the American Revolution through the Westward expansion—the proudest moments in U.S. history. (The Civil War is seen as an aberration and is conveniently ignored.) The militias' values are also seen as the values that motivated Americans in war all over the planet in the twentieth century. The militia groups see the growth of government regulation, and the rise of legislation that overturns the social order of the past as debilitating for American life. Indeed, for many members life under present social conditions is increasingly losing its meaning.

---

[2] Quoted in Easton, Nina J. "America the Enemy; Their Politics are Light Years Apart, but the Bombers of the '60s and '90s Share Volatile Rhetoric, Tangled Paranoia and a Belief that Violence is a Legitimate Weapon." *Los Angeles Times,* June 18, 1995, p. 8.

Members of American militia groups are invariably located in rural areas. Their Golden Age includes a time when all that was good in American life was found outside of urban areas. Now our rural past is in deep decline. People whose ancestors made their living from the land are seeing that land decline in value and become encumbered by debt. They see a way of life slipping away in the face of rampant urbanization. The people of the city—including urban government officials—are seen as the enemy. They are the people who seize land for public works, prevent logging or farming on wetlands, and regulate the monetary and market systems that oppress the primary producers of the country. These urbanites are consequently distrusted and feared. There is no question that the enemies of the American way of life are to be found in cities.

Like the revolutionaries of the '60s, militia movement members of the '90s view the government as it has evolved since the 1940s as the enemy. They decry the increasing interference of government in every aspect of private and public life. Their particular complaints revolve around taxes, gun control, and government regulation. There is broad fear that the government is trying to disarm the population and create a "New World Order" that is contrary to traditional American values. The New World Order is believed to be one in which one-world government will replace individual nations. Americans would lose sovereignty and traditional freedoms. In this conspiracy theory, minority groups such as African Americans and Jews, and the United Nations figure prominently as agents of unwelcome change. In Arizona, Jack McLamb runs one militia group called Police Against the New World Order, and spreads his message of warning in a conspiracy tract entitled "Operation Vampire Killer 2000."[3]

The actions of both the '60s and the '90s governments are the natural targets of revitalization movements. They form an easy ideological target. Human governments are messy things. By nature their actions cannot be ideologically pure. There are too many mitigating factors and competing interests in any society to eliminate compromise. Members of revitalization movements thus see governmental bodies as proof of the devolution of society from the Golden Age. The most extreme zealots in these movements want to scorch the landscape clean of these impure bodies to allow the re-establishment of life as it should be.

Other Revitalization Movements

Americans can learn about these groups by studying other similar revitalization movements elsewhere. The Middle East offers a good example. The Islamic movement grew up 125 years ago as European powers gradually usurped economic and military power throughout the Middle East. The leaders of the movement idealized the Golden Age of the great Islamic Empires

---

[3] Halpern, Thomas, David Rosenberg and Irwin Suall, "Militia Movement . . ." See Kehoe, Alice Beck, *The Ghost Dance: Ethnohistory and Revitalization*. Ft. Worth: Holt, Rinehart, and Winston, 1989.

stretching from the eighth to the eighteenth centuries when Muslims were wealthy, independent, pious, and militarily strong. The leader of the Islamic movement was Jamal al-Din al-Afghani, an Iranian political leader who aroused Muslims throughout the Middle East and North Africa. Al-Afghani advocated a return to personal piety, reform of Islamic law to meet the requirements of a modern age, and violent resistance to Westerners who had usurped power from the Islamic world. He saw the governments in the Middle East as hopelessly corrupt—undermined by Western forces and Western values.

Al-Afghani's successors have included a variety of movements and social groups. On the positive side, they include far-sighted legal and social reformers, such as the eminent Egyptian jurist Muhammad Abduh. They also include relatively moderate reform groups such as the Islamic Brotherhood, now active throughout the Middle East. More violent fringe groups include the assassins of Egyptian president Anwar Sadat, and Palestinian nationalist groups, such as Hamas, a group responsible for a series of devastating suicide bombings of Israeli citizens in the spring of 1996.

Another famous revitalization movement far removed from the Middle East was the Ghost Dance religion that swept Native American peoples of the Plains in the late 1800s. A Paiute prophet, Wovoka, told Native Americans that if they practiced the Ghost Dance, a hypnotic spiritual dance, the White Man would disappear, and Native American civilization would be restored. The Lakota Sioux were influenced by the Ghost Dance. The practice was distrusted by the white soldiers stationed in South Dakota and eventually a confrontation between the two groups led to the famous massacre at Wounded Knee on December 29, 1890 where at least 200 Native American people were killed.

In the contemporary world, farmers outside of Tokyo whose land was appropriated to build Narita airport continue to engage in confrontation with the Japanese government. They are angry about losing their land, but they also see the building of the giant airport as symptomatic of the decline of Japanese civilization and religious strength. They constitute a fringe element of a much larger group of militant Japanese citizens who want to restore Japan to its previous pre-World War II might as an East Asian military power.

Elements of revitalization thinking can be seen in almost all armed struggle against standing governmental bodies. The Irish Republican Army, the Naxalite movement in India, and the Tamil nationalists in Sri Lanka are just a sampling of groups that are willing to use force to purify the societies under which they live.

Revitalization movements can be positive. Moreover, they do not always lead to violent action. In the Middle East, the Islamic revival has provided for a strong upsurge in religious faith. It has strengthened the family. It is the fringe elements that have carried out actions such as the assassination of President Sadat and the suicide bombings of Hamas. With widespread social approval of the values of the movement, it is difficult for the non-violent majority to keep the extremist fringe in check. Since martyrdom is proof of sincerity, arrest and execution of these individuals is never a deterrent.

The Anthropological Theory of Revitalization

Contemporary anthropological understanding of revitalization movements has been shaped by the work of Anthony F. C. Wallace who analyzed an important Native American revitalization movement centering around an Iroquois prophet named Handsome Lake in two important publications in 1956 and 1961.[4]

Wallace suggested that all revitalization movements go through five stages as follows.

I. Period of generally satisfactory adaptation
 Members of society are living in relative harmony.
II. Period of increased individual stress
 Changes in political or natural environment cause stressful living conditions for some individuals.
III. Period of cultural distortion
 Changes in the environment continue and gradually produce widespread deviation from normal cultural patterns. Violence, moral laxity, and family breakdown are examples of this distortion.
IV. Period of revitalization
 This is seen by Wallace to proceed in six stages:
 A. Reformulation of the basic cultural pattern by a prophet or set of prophets
 B. Communication of the reformulated pattern
 C. Organization of the new pattern
 D. Widespread adaptation of the new pattern
 E. Cultural transformation
 F. Routinization of the new pattern
V. New period of generally satisfactory adaption

Members of the militia movements in the United States see themselves as having come through the first four periods of this cycle and are now involved in the period of revitalization where they seem to be still in stage C, the organizational period. Like many revitalization movements, they may be prevented from reaching a period of full transformation because of resistance from the larger society.

A successful revitalization movement is tantamount to a revolution when it succeeds in transforming a whole society. The Islamic Movement had at least one full realization of revitalization in the Iranian Revolution of 1978–79 in which the Shah of Iran was toppled from power by a coalition of

---

[4] Wallace, Anthony F. C., "Revitalization Movements: Some Theoretical Considerations for their Comparative Study." *American Anthropologist* n.s. 58(2): 264–281; and "Cultural Composition of the Handsome Lake Religion." In William N. Fenton and John Gulick, eds., *Symposium on Cherokee and Iroquois Culture. B.A.E. Bulletin* 180, pp. 139–151. Washington: Smithsonian Institution.

religious and political forces united in the name of reform. The Revolution emphasized martyrdom in the service of the higher cause of reform. The explicit message of the Revolution was to return Iran to a period of harmony and strength that pre-existed the secular government of the Shah. Whereas Muslims in the rest of the Islamic World do not necessarily agree with the religious and political agenda of the Iranian revolutionaries, they have been inspired by the Revolution as proof that an Islamic revitalization can take place.[5]

Members of the American militias are undoubtedly a fringe group at present. Their revitalization is not widespread enough to ensure its eventual success throughout American society. Nevertheless, despite their outlying position in American social and political life they, like extremist Muslims in the Middle East, rest on a base of supporters in the United States who are sympathetic but not activist. If the overall political and social climate of opinion moves slowly to accept their ideology, their perceived mandate for action will also increase.

In the meantime, like their Islamic counterparts, the militia members will see arrest and punishment at the hands of the government as proof of the value of their actions. Thus violent actions such as the Oklahoma City bombing may increase, even as they are decried by the larger society.

Review Questions

1. What is meant by the term *revitalization movement?*
2. What are the five major stages of revitalization according to Anthony F. C. Wallace, as quoted in this paper? What are the six steps that mark the stage of revitalization?
3. What conditions are likely to give rise to revitalization?
4. Why do the beliefs and actions of American militias appear to fit the revitalization model?
5. Name several more movements that also fit the revitalization model and state why.

---

[5] See Beeman, William, "Religion and Development in Iran from the Qajar Era to the Islamic Revolution of 1978–9." In James Finn, ed., *Religion and Global Economics.* New Brunswick and London: Transaction Books, 1983.

32

Cargo Beliefs and Religious Experience

Stephen C. Leavitt

In the last selection, we saw that many new religious and political groups result from revitalization movements. Such movements usually respond to a feeling of loss and powerlessness caused by rapid change and colonial domination, and several have given rise to great world religions. One of the most unusual examples of revitalization movements, however, has occurred in New Guinea. These are cargo cults (cargo is pidgin for western goods) that attempt, through ritual, to generate cargo wealth thought to be under the control of ancestral spirits. In this article, Steven Leavitt reviews the history and social functions of cargo cults. But he goes a step further by showing how cargo cults meet the needs of individuals, especially the need for support from one's immediate ancestors.

In August 1984 I began two years' research among the Bumbita Arapesh in the East Sepik Province of Papua New Guinea. I had planned to

This article is written for *Conformity and Conflict.* Copyright © by Steven C. Leavitt, 1997. Printed by permission of the author.

study religious experience in a secret men's cult. Soon after I arrived, though, I was told that the men's cult was gone forever: only two months earlier several Bumbita acting in the name of Jesus, had revealed the cult secrets to women and children, making it impossible for the men to return to cult activities. Nevertheless, I had come at an opportune time, some said, for Jesus himself was due to arrive and usher in a new age in November.

The Bumbita and their neighbors were in the midst of what was locally known as a "revival," a period of widespread Evangelical Christianity. Missionaries had been in the area since the 1950s when the South Sea Evangelical Mission had established a station in Bumbita territory. However, they had had only limited success in converting local people; many people had been baptized at some point, but most had also left the church again after their enthusiasm had died down. All agreed, though, that 1984 was different. The revelation of cult secrets meant that there was no turning back to the old religion.

As time passed, I learned that some of the Bumbita Christian ideas were quite different from our own. Most Bumbita did find in Christianity a promise of a transformed world of happiness, and they believed that when Jesus came, there would no longer be illness, hunger or death. But many also hoped for the arrival of vast material wealth. In their view, Jesus would bring with him huge quantities of rice, tinned meat, clothing, housing materials and other goods. These are the kinds of goods that Europeans had brought with them into the area. As many Bumbita see it, all of this material wealth must have a magical or spiritual origin—it must be their own ancestors who really own the wealth, and somehow the Europeans figured out how to acquire some of it. Through Jesus' return, the ancestors would now be passing all their wealth onto their living descendants and rightful heirs.

These ideas were familiar to me because they were similar to those found in "cargo cults," the well-known religious movements that had been going on for generations in Papua New Guinea. Cargo cults are religious movements that involve attempts, usually through ritual, to attain vast amounts of material wealth thought to be under the control of ancestral spirits. In the early days of European colonization of the Pacific, when supplies of cargo were routinely unloaded from ships, the display of wealth made a strong impression on the local peoples. Although their own societies had complex ritual and social systems, and although they had developed intricate seafaring technologies, the Pacific islanders were truly amazed at what the Europeans possessed. It was not long before religious movements appeared, seeking to explain this seemingly miraculous access to wealth. Cult leaders would tell people that the Europeans must be following special rituals, that if they too could follow them carefully, the ancestors would return with the cargo. The rituals often involved imitating strange behaviors observed in Europeans, such as forming rigid lines and marching in unison or singing hymns for hours on end in church services. Frequently, cargo movements incorporated Christian ideas learned from missionaries, even though the missions opposed this kind of reinterpretation of the Christian message.

In some instances, the rituals became very elaborate. People built imitation communication centers and airstrips with bamboo control towers in hopes that cargo-laden planes would then land. In one well-known cult, now called the "Johnson cult," leaders even collected money from their followers to send to the United States in hopes of buying President Lyndon Johnson.

The largest movement to touch the Bumbita area occurred in 1971, when the cult leader Yaliwan claimed that the removal of two cement geological survey markers from the top of a well-known mountain would release cargo from the mountain. Yaliwan's organization collected membership fees from people over a wide area. The idea was that if one was an official member, one would be sure to get a share of the cargo when it came. On the appointed day villagers in even distant areas stayed in their houses, in fear of a terrible cataclysm. The markers were unearthed and carried down the mountainside, but the ancestors' failure to arrive did not stop the movement. In fact, Yaliwan was subsequently elected to represent his district in the national parliament.

The recurring cargo movements posed serious problems for colonial administrators because, although the cults were most active, people would neglect their gardens and other work in hopes that a new world would soon be upon them. There was also a concern that people would be duped into giving hard-earned money to cult leaders. In fact, money-collecting for cargo cult activity was made illegal by the colonial government, and when Papua New Guinea gained independence in 1975, those laws remained on the books. Today, although the term "cargo cult" has a bad name in Papua New Guinea, people continue to have strong beliefs in the ancestral control of cargo, and these beliefs continue to find expression in Christian religious movements like the Bumbita revival in 1984.

The seemingly bizarre beliefs typical of cargo cults have intrigued anthropologists interested in religious movements and the impact of colonial rule. Researchers saw similarities between these cults and religious movements in other parts of the world. The emphasis on ritual, the reliance on visions of charismatic leaders, and the hopes for a complete world transformation are common features of cults organized in response to colonial domination. In the nineteenth century for example, Native American religious movements such as the Ghost Dance sought to create a new world through the performance of key rituals. These movements had arisen in response to crises over the loss of cultural traditions and the disappearance of the buffalo. Anthropologists saw the cargo cult as another example of the way people try to regenerate meaning in a time of cultural crisis.

But the emphasis on ancestral control of cargo was distinctive, and to explain this feature anthropologists looked to the pre-existing cultural understandings of Pacific peoples. The traditional religions of Papua New Guinea emphasized the role of ancestral spirits in taking care of people. A family could produce a thriving crop of yams or sweet potatoes only with magical assistance from ancestral spirits. It therefore made sense to think that European food and other goods might also come from this supernatural source. In addition, traditional cultures in Papua New Guinea placed a great deal of emphasis on exchange and the giving of gifts as a basis for building relationships and achieving prestige. People cemented friendships, built alliances and resolved disputes by mounting large-scale exchanges of food with others. They also competed with rivals by engaging in competitive exchanges.

The Europeans who arrived did not share the same view of how relationships are built. They had control over extremely attractive material goods, but they refused to enter into proper exchange relations with the local people. Instead, they instituted colonial control and acted as superiors. Some anthropologists have argued, then, that the Papua New Guinean preoccupation with cargo is a way of rebuilding a sense of independence and prestige in the face of colonial rule.

My own research suggests that these explanations make sense, but that they cannot be the whole answer. Contemporary Papua New Guineans know quite a bit about how commerce works and where material goods come from. Many earn money through jobs or cash-cropping, and they buy Western goods for themselves. European colonial control has been replaced by an independent government. Nevertheless, many people today—people who have gone through schools, worked in plantations or factories, and participated in failed cargo cults—continue to look for a way to get cargo from ancestors. Why do cargo ideas persist after so many years?

Cargo ideology has to be understood as part of a religious world view that gives meaning to the larger questions in life while it also addresses the most deeply personal concerns of individual believers. Colonial rule is gone and some money is now available, but Papua New Guineans must still deal with the fact that they are relatively insignificant players on the world stage, and they have relatively little wealth in comparison to people elsewhere. Cargo ideology takes these diffuse and irresolvable existential problems and translates them into an idiom that is deeply personal. Instead of having to think about their position in the world at large, people can focus on their relations with those close to them. The "ancestors" that people turn to for cargo are not distant and anonymous supernatural beings; they are in fact the spirits of fathers, mothers, and other close kin. This means that to really understand the central idea behind cargo—that ancestors will bring wealth and bestow it upon the living—one needs to think in terms of what it means personally for a given individual. Cargo ideas are about relations with deceased parents. Often, getting cargo means receiving a sign, a gift, from one's own parents or grandparents showing that they forgive, that they still care.

When Bumbita men and women try to understand cargo in terms of their relationships with their own parents, they are looking for a way to give real meaning to all the bewildering changes that have been going on around them. It is a way for them to recast their colonial experience in terms that they can understand and deal with. But there is a cost. The problem is that for most people, the bulk of the cargo has not—and never will—arrive. As the Bumbita see it, the ancestors are for some unknown reason still holding back. This means that their religious experience remains filled with feelings of longing and remorse. It can be a difficult emotional predicament.

To illustrate the personal side to religious experience, my work focuses on detailed narratives or stories collected from several individuals. The idea is to speak with a few people in depth, recording their narratives carefully, so that I can later follow their line of thinking in detail. This method has the virtue of showing the personal side to religious belief while at the same time allowing people's words to stand for themselves. A major drawback is that such individual stories cannot be viewed as "representative" of the society as a whole. Personal stories must necessarily remain personal. Nevertheless, I believe this approach offers a richer sense of themes that might well be a part of other people's experience as well.

To illustrate, let's look at the stories of two older men who, when they converted, adopted the Christian names "Matthew" and "John." Each was around 60 years old when I did my interviews (some 25 hours total). I visited them at their houses or asked them to visit me, and we usually talked, alone, for one to two hours in a sitting. I tried not to guide them too much, but I did make it known that I was interested in their religious beliefs.

Matthew, a widower, first converted to Christianity in 1967, and he remains one of the most vocal proponents of the Christian cause in the Bumbita area. Before converting he was trained as a sorcerer, and he admits that he practiced sorcery. Matthew is well known for his preoccupation with the local missionaries and with Europeans in general. Everywhere he goes he carries a large sack containing Christian literature, calendars of years past, photographs of his favorite missionaries, and even some letters from them sent from various countries. Every item in his bundle is tattered, stained, and frayed, showing signs of frequent handling. His house also has mementos of his relations with missionaries, including a child's plastic gramophone with a stack of 78 r.p.m. records of sermons translated by the mission into the Bumbita Arapesh language. Matthew has been active in every cargo movement that has touched the Bumbita area.

Interviews with Matthew showed that one attraction of cargo beliefs for him was to resolve feelings of guilt that he had toward his father who had died some years before. Throughout his adult life, Matthew had a troubled relationship with his father. He says that his father once tried to seduce his fiancee, when she was living in their hamlet. Matthew claims that when he found out, he even tried to kill his father with a spear. As punishment, the father was banished for life from the village. Matthew believes that his father later retaliated with sorcery by killing Matthew's wife (she died in childbirth). Although he and his father were reconciled later, Matthew still longs for some sign that his father had forgiven him—a sign that he had not received before his father died.

Matthew's story will show that he was searching for a sign of forgiveness from his dead father by cultivating relationships with European missionaries. Matthew's most startling belief was that among these missionaries was one who was really that ghost of his own father. It is in fact a common belief among the Bumbita that some Europeans are the spirits of dead relatives. But Matthew, more than most people, appeared to be longing to find his personal ghost and to get from him a gift of cargo that would signal his father's forgiveness. All of this came out in a story Matthew told me about his parting with a local missionary who was going home to Germany. Matthew had brought the missionary some yams and greens as a farewell gift. He describes the subsequent interaction:

> [I asked the missionary about his leaving, and] he said that he would stay. But then when I asked him [again], he didn't answer and I sat down. He went and got a funnel and filled it with salt for me, and then I asked him. I said, "I think you are my father. I think you have the face of my father, Turingi, and your wife is like my mother, Tinga'wen. I can see the resemblance." And there was no answer. He did not answer me because he was ashamed. He said, "Just take the salt and go. You shouldn't come and blabber too much." [laughs] And now you see here, I have written their names in my book.

Matthew is claiming here that his father has returned from the dead as a European missionary. He says he can tell by the quiet way the man reacted when he gave him food—he was ashamed, so he silently gives Matthew a gift of salt and tells him to be quiet about this.

In reality, the missionary most likely thought he was paying Matthew for the yams and greens, but Matthew has come to see it in another way, as a gesture of intimate communication. The missionary says nothing, and Matthew takes it as a tacit confession, as if to say, "Yes, I am your father, you have guessed it, but say nothing to anyone about it." The gift was for Matthew a silent symbolic statement about the goodwill in their relationship. Although the gift of salt was a trivial one, Matthew's reaction to it shows his longing for more extensive cargo: he wants to be given material wealth by Europeans because he believes this cargo is really a gift from his own dead kin signaling their love for him.

My interviews with a second man, John, also showed that dreams of cargo had a deep personal significance. Unlike Matthew, John was a highly respected leader in his day. He was now sixty years old and retired. John was a short man by Bumbita standards, and he retained a lively demeanor. John also felt that his father would be the ultimate source of the cargo. But although Matthew looked for father figures among the missionaries, John saw God himself as his father.

John looked for God to give his approval by giving him secret knowledge as a key to material wealth. In the Bumbita view, it is proper to expect a father-ancestor to offer secrets and magical help, and John is extending this idea to include the concept of cargo. As John saw it, with the cargo he could then become a great and powerful leader by distributing it to others, just as traditionally Bumbita leaders had built power by giving away pigs and yams. Like Matthew, John feels that receiving the cargo will be final proof of his father's good will and approval.

John said God communicated with him mostly through dreams. In Bumbita culture, dreams are regarded as real experiences, albeit in a spiritual realm. People use dreams as omens to guide them in their hunting or in their pursuit of love relationships. Here John related to me one dream he had had some two months before the interview in which I recorded it. The dream went as follows:

> I dreamt that I had gone inside a house. I went and I sat like this. Everything here, the books, the money, were heaped around. I was on the edge of it all. It was a big house. A huge house. A house of iron. It had rooms that went on and on and I was sitting at the fence in front. Now I don't know how to write things; reading, yes, I can read some, but [someone else] would have to write [for me] . . . But my [dream] spirit, when I went into this house, I went and I myself wrote everything and I myself checked everything over. I wrote and straightened the books and put them aside . . . Then I got up to come back and a voice said, "Now you have come."—it was like a sign, right? When you can see it all. [It said,] "Later, when you come back, you will sit at this spot. Yes, you will straighten up everything later. Now you have seen it and written everything down and straightened it up and you will go. Later when you come back, you will straighten it all up, later, not now." . . . I woke up and remembered this and then went to sleep again, and a voice said, "This man, . . . he will come and stay at this house and check everything and distribute it to the people here . . . This man will become a king. The king for distributing everything, for checking everything."

In this dream, John identifies himself with the clerks in the warehouses, with those people he sees as controlling the material wealth. His view is that clerks are very powerful because they preside over the goods. He says that God made him a clerk to show him that he will in fact be like "a king" in the new age, doling out the fates of the people. His main activity in the dream is writing, a skill still associated with Europeans and a sore point for adults who see their children learning to write in school. In this dream John shows that he looks to God to make him a great leader by giving him the power to distribute cargo.

A second dream has some of the same messages, but here John's ideas about the dream show that, as with Matthew, the core emotional content has to do with his own father. The high position that John sees for himself in the new age must be given to him by God, and for John, that God is his actual father. In this account, I follow John's statements step by step to show how his thoughts lead him from a dream about cargo to his personal relationship with his own father. He begins,

> [One night] I took the Bible inside and made a fire and just lay down. I said, "God"—I prayed—"God, I want you to show me my present now, where is it? I want to see it. . . .
>
> I want you yourself to show me so I can see it . . . I want to see my present." All right, when I went to sleep, I went straight to it. Man, I went inside, they—a big house.

At this point, he stumbled over his words because he felt he had to hide part of the dream as he related it to me. He later revealed to me that it had not been "a big house" that he had seen in the dream, but actually a graveyard. The dead were presiding over the cargo in the graveyard. John said that he had originally hidden this fact from me because he had not wanted to be accused of being a "cargo cultist." He went on to say that he was not a cargo cultist but a "good man," that he had not sought out the details of the dream—God himself had given them to him. He wants me to take him seriously and not write him off as a cultist. What he is about to say is important to him. He continues:

> They had put up a cloth from Hong Kong. They had hung it up and it went down like this, at the door. When I went and lifted up this cloth and pulled it up—Sorry! Huge huge boxes, more and more of them, going up to the clouds. Many many boxes . . . In just one box, there would be so much inside. With two or three there would be even more. I just gazed up at them like this. When I looked down, I saw mushrooms growing on the boxes, and I thought, "They were good here, but some of them, I think they have already rotted. Everything has rotted so there are mushrooms growing there." . . . I checked the ones that were on top and they were still good. You know, they went up and up and then at the top—I looked up, and I thought, "Hey, I hope a box doesn't come off and fall and break my head." So I lifted my leg onto one of the boxes and climbed on up and up and then I started and I was there lying in my bed. Then what did I do? I cried and cried over the present that God had shown me.

This dream conveys well the awe inspired by visions of cargo. The cargo here was under the control of the ancestors since, as he later confessed, the setting of the dream was really a graveyard and not a "house." As often happens in Bumbita dreams about the dead, an image of rot and decay appears in the dream, along with some anxiety, evident here in his fear that a case might fall on top of him. But unlike with most dreams about the dead, John interprets these images in a way that avoids unpleasantness. He points out that the decay indicates that God was saying that there would be so much cargo that much of it would rot with no one to use it, and he also succeeds in waking up before any boxes fall. John's euphoria over having had this dream points to the emotional power of the cargo itself. The cargo is a "present" that has deep meaning.

As his narrative continues, John then goes on immediately to link these cargo images to childhood memories of the amassed food of men from his father's generation. In Bumbita society, the ability to grow and display huge quantities of yams is the highest expression of male achievement. John continues,

> [Our ancestors] used to fill up the yams, in a huge bin . . . We would dance and then go and give it to [our exchange partners]. So now I saw this image [of cargo in the dream], and it was just like what they used to do before, what [our fathers] did. It would go way up and up. Heaps and heaps of food, and given away. Now God has shown this to me. The present is hidden.

Here he links the heaps of food for exchange with the image of cargo from his dream. He talks of the mounds of food going "up and up," in what suggests a vision of a child's awe at the sight of such amounts of food. He links it with the awe he felt in the dream upon discovering the true extent of the wealth (the "present") controlled by the dead. Thus, the emotions he felt in his dream at the sight of the cargo were not unfamiliar—he remembers similar feelings from a time when senior men used to assemble food for exchange. In this way, John reveals what is for him a symbolic link between the ancestors of his dream and the senior adult male figures from his youth.

John then returns immediately to the significance of his having been shown the "present." He says:

> The present that [God] has shown me, the present here, it will all happen. You will see it, I am happy with him too. All of the time that I walk around my thinking dwells on only this. I don't stray from it. I think only of this that God has shown me. I think of it like this. If a man is no good, if a man has sins, if he prays and asks God for something, then God won't answer his prayer. No way. Because this thing, the sin, is there. It closes off the path to God . . . How is God going to tell you? . . . If you are a holy man, free, and you are with God, he will hear it and God will answer. You will see God.

By this point, John has gone from a dream's image of splendid cargo to a sense of awe at the power of older generations, and finally to the argument that seeing cargo proves he is right with God. All that remains is for him to make the transition to his own father. And indeed, immediately following the passage cited above, he continues:

> A good man will see [God] here. God, I know, the God of the Christians. My God is—if I am Christian, then my God is Christian. Now he has died, and now I have seen him. I know now. It is finished. [laughs] Sorry, if I talk on like this, then the happiness is going to well up now! He will come. My God . . . [overcome with emotion, he laughs to avoid crying. He pauses]
>
> SL: You said you have seen him, what does he look like, God?
>
> My God? A big man, a big man. Before he was short, but now that he has gone, he's a big man. Happiness. I am happy with him True, if before, he weren't Christian, yes, he would have gone and been lost . . . But he was already Christian when he died. So now he's there. He will look after me, he is with me. He was Christian already. Now he has shown me everything. Who is he? God the father.

As he becomes absorbed with what he is saying, his description of God's position on revealing secrets to sinners becomes almost a reverie in the memory of his own father, of a short man who now seems big to him, of someone who looks after him, and above all, of someone who has shown him an image of the mass of wealth that the ancestors control. John is overcome by the recognition that his father/God has decided to reserve a special place for him in the new age, that he, John, will be the new leader.

Thus John's Christianity, with its concern about cargo and its inspired hopes for reunion with the dead, also works its way back to a personal relationship with his own father. John's God is his father, and the cargo is his sign of reassurance. John has become convinced that by being a Christian he will acquire that cargo.

For the Bumbita, Christian doctrines preach that the ancestors have good will, that in the end, in the transformation that will come with the return of Christ, they will demonstrate that good will and they will deliver. In his final summation of his thoughts about his father, John expresses with some eloquence the personal significance of getting the cargo, of knowing about and seeing God. He says in a whisper, again fighting tears:

> Now [in my life] I am just the same as I was before. But in my dreams, yes, I get it all. Life will go on until Jesus comes. Then I will get it, I will know about him, I will see him. His thinking. His wishes. The eyes of my father. Me and him. The eyes of father God, I will know them.

Although each of these stories bears the stamp of two different personalities, they both reveal a perspective that is a well-known part of New Guinean ideas about cargo. At the heart of it is the hope that the world will be transformed by renewed relationships with spirits of the dead. What these narrative suggest is that when some Bumbita think about their futures, whether it be their own personal lives or their larger place on the world stage, they do so in terms of a familiar family scenario, with parental figures (spirits) sharing or withholding gifts. By thinking of the situation in this way, they can take the bewildering and difficult problems of coping with the colonial experience and translate them into a much more personal and familiar set of ideas about love and nurture. In the end, cargo is important because it is a visible sign that the spirits are there and that they do care.

The stories of Matthew and John show how beliefs about cargo in Papua New Guinea can take the shape they do from the role they play in giving meaning to individuals. Although it is dangerous to make broad generalizations from the accounts of two people, their stories do point to a personal side of cargo ideas that has not been emphasized in most anthropological explanations. To have a more complete understanding of religious experience, one has to pay close attention to what individual believers say about the significance of their beliefs for their own lives. In the case of cargo beliefs, we can see that there is more going on than one might at first think. It is not just that the Bumbita have come to some unusual conclusions about how to interpret the changes in their world—they are also making an active effort to integrate the changes into their deepest personal sense of who they are.

Review Questions

1. What are the main attributes of most cargo cults, according to Leavitt? Give some examples of the form cargo cults can take
2. How have anthropologists tried to explain cargo cults?
3. Under what conditions do cargo cults occur, and what is their goal?
4. In what ways do cargo cults embrace the teaching of Christian missionaries?
5. Why does Leavitt think cargo cults persist? What is their religious function for individuals?

10

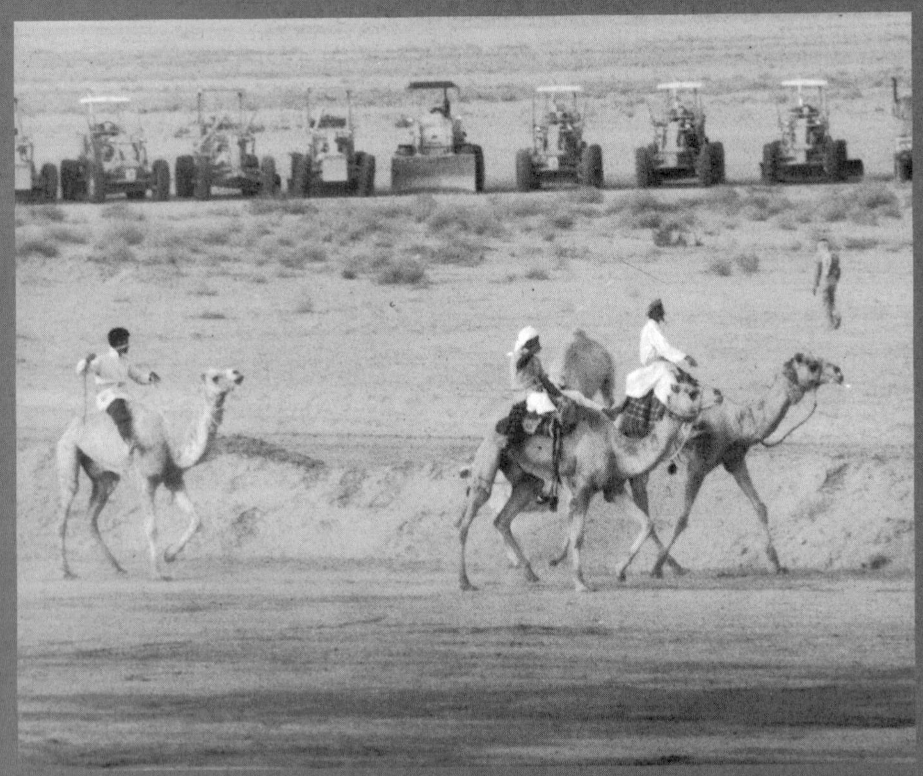

CULTURE CHANGE AND APPLIED ANTHROPOLOGY

Nowhere in the world do human affairs remain precisely constant from year to year. New ways of doing things mark the history of even the most stable groups. Change occurs when an Australian aboriginal dreams about a new myth and teaches it to the members of his band; when a loader in a restaurant kitchen invents a way to stack plates more quickly in the dishwasher; or when a New Guinea Big Man cites the traditional beliefs about ghosts to justify the existence of a new political office devised by a colonial government. Wherever people interpret their natural and social worlds in a new way, cultural change has occurred. Broad or narrow, leisurely or rapid, such change is part of life in every society.

Culture change can originate from two sources: innovation and borrowing. *Innovation* is the invention of qualitatively new forms. It involves the recombination of what people already know into something different. For example, Canadian Joseph-Armand Bombardier became an innovator when he mated tracks, designed to propel earth-moving equipment, to a small bus that originally ran on tires, producing the first snowmobile in the 1950s. Later, the Skolt Lapps of Finland joined him as innovators when they adapted his now smaller, more refined snowmobile for herding reindeer in 1961. The Lapp innovation was not the vehicle itself. That was borrowed. What was new was the use of the vehicle in herding, something usually done by men on skis.

Innovations are more likely to occur and to be adopted during stressful times when traditional culture no longer works well. Bombardier, for example, began work on his snowmobile after he was unable to reach medical help in time to save the life of his critically ill son during a Canadian winter storm. Frustrated by the slowness of his horse and sleigh, he set out to create a faster vehicle.

The other basis of culture change is *borrowing*. Borrowing—or *diffusion*, as it is sometimes called—refers to the adoption of something new from another group. Tobacco, for example, was first domesticated and grown in the New World but quickly diffused to Europe and Asia after 1492. Such items as the umbrella, pajamas, Arabic numerals, and perhaps even the technology to make steel came to Europe from India. Ideologies and religions may diffuse from one society to another.

An extreme diffusionist view has been used to explain most human achievements. For example, author Erik Von Däniken argues that features of ancient New World civilizations were brought by space invaders. Englishman G. Elliot Smith claimed that Mayan and Aztec culture diffused from Egypt. Thor Heyerdahl sailed a reed boat, the *Ra II,* from Africa to South America to prove that an Egyptian cultural origin was possible for New World civilization.

Whether something is an innovation or borrowed, it must pass through a process of *social acceptance* before it can become part of a culture. Indeed many, if not most, novel ideas and things remain unattractive and relegated to obscurity. To achieve social acceptance, an innovation must become known to the members of a society, must be accepted as valid, and must fit into a system of cultural knowledge revised to accept it.

Several principles facilitate social acceptance. If a change wins the support of a person in authority, it may gain the approval of others. Timing is also important. It would have made little sense for a Lapp to attempt the introduction of snowmobiles when there was no snow or when the men who do the reindeer herding were scattered over their vast grazing territory. Other factors also affect social acceptance. Changes have a greater chance of acceptance if they meet a felt need, if they appeal to people's prestige (in societies where prestige is important), and if they provide some continuity with traditional customs.

Change may take place under a variety of conditions, from the apparently dull day-to-day routine of a stable society to the frantic climate of a revolution. One situation that has occupied many anthropologists interested in change is *cultural contact,* particularly situations of contact where one society politically dominates another. World history is replete with examples of such domination, which vary in outcome from annihilation, in the case of the Tasmanians and hundreds of tribes in North and South America, Africa, Asia, and even ancient Europe, to the political rule that indentured countless millions of people to colonial powers.

The study of change caused by these conditions is called *acculturation.* Acculturation is the process of change that results from cultural contact. Acculturative change may affect dominant societies as well as subordinate ones. After their ascendance in India, for example, the British came to wear *khaki* clothes, live in *bungalows,* and trek through *jungles*—all Indian concepts.

But those who are subordinated experience the most far-reaching changes in their way of life. From politically independent, self-sufficient people, they usually become subordinate and dependent. Sweeping changes in social structure and values may occur, along with a resulting social disorganization.

Although the age of colonial empires is largely over, the destruction of tribal culture continues at a rapid pace today. As we saw in Reed's article in Part 4 of this book, hundreds of thousands of Amazonian Indians have already perished in the last few years because of intrusive frontier and development programs. Following almost exactly the pattern of past colonial exploitation, modern governments bent on "progress" displace and often kill off indigenous tribal populations. The frequent failure of development, coupled with its damaging impact on native peoples, has caused many anthropologists to reassess their role. As a result, more and more anthropologists have become part of native resistance to outside intrusion.

A less dramatic, but in many ways no less important, agent of change is the world economy. No longer can most people live in self-sufficient isolation. Their future is inevitably tied in with an overall system of market exchange. Take the Marshall Islanders described by anthropologist Michael Rynkiewich, for example. Although they cultivate to meet their own subsistence needs, they also raise coconuts for sale on the world market. Receipts from the coconut crop go to pay for outboard motors and gasoline, cooking utensils, and a variety of other goods they don't manufacture themselves but have come to depend on. Recently several major American food companies have eliminated coconut oil from their products because of its high level of saturated fat. This loss has created lower demand for copra (dried coconut meat), from which the oil is pressed. Reduced demand, in turn, may cause substantial losses to the Marshall Islanders. A people who once could subsist independently have now become prisoners of the world economic system.

Anthropologists may themselves become agents of change, applying their work to practical problems. Applied anthropology, as opposed to academic anthropology, includes any use of anthropological knowledge to influence social interaction, to maintain or change social institutions, or to direct the course of cultural change. There are four basic uses of anthropology contained within the applied field: adjustment anthropology, administrative anthropology, action anthropology, and advocate anthropology.

Adjustment anthropology uses anthropological knowledge to make social interaction more predictable among people who operate with different cultural codes. For example, take the anthropologists who consult with companies and government agencies about intercultural communication. It is often their job to train Americans to interpret the cultural rules that govern interaction in another society. For a business person who will work in Latin America, the anthropologist may point out the appropriate culturally defined speaking distances, ways to sit, definitions of time, topics of conversation, times for business talk, and so on. All of these activities would be classified as adjustment anthropology.

Administrative anthropology uses anthropological knowledge for planned change by those who are external to the local cultural group. It is the use of anthropological knowledge by a person with the power to make decisions. If an anthropologist provides to a mayor knowledge about the culture of constituents, he or she is engaged in administrative anthropology. So would advisers to chief administrators of U.S. trust territories such as once existed in places like the Marshall Islands.

Action anthropology uses anthropological knowledge for planned change by the local cultural group. The anthropologist acts as a catalyst, providing information but avoiding decision making, which remains in the hands of the people affected by the decisions.

Advocate anthropology uses anthropological knowledge by the anthropologist to increase the power of self-determination of a particular cultural group. Instead of focusing on the process of innovation, the anthropologist centers attention on discovering the sources of power and how a group can gain access to them. James Spradley took such action when he studied tramps in 1968. He discovered that police and courts systematically deprived tramps of their power to control their lives and of the rights accorded normal citizens. By releasing his findings to the Seattle newspapers, he helped tramps gain additional power and weakened the control of Seattle authorities.

Whether they are doing administrative, advocate, adjustment, or action anthropology, anthropologists take, at least in part, a qualitative approach. They do ethnography, discover the cultural knowledge of their informants, and apply this information in the ways discussed previously. In contrast to the quantitative data so often prized by other social scientists, they use the insider's viewpoint to discover problems, to advise, and to generate policy.

The articles in this part illustrate several aspects of cultural change and applied anthropology. The first, by Jack Weatherford, deals with the impact of the world market on the social organization and economy of the indigenous peoples of Peru, Bolivia, and Colombia who grow coca and prepare the drug for market. In the second article, Terence Turner relates the case of how one people, the Kayapo of the Brazilian Amazon have successfully resisted external threats to their existence as a people. By uniting Indians, environmental groups, and legislators, and using the international media, they have managed to protect and expand their forest area and advance the international environmental cause. The third article, by David McCurdy, discusses the modern uses of anthropology. From studies of General Motors workers, to program assessment for people with AIDS, to participation in government health projects to international counseling, professional anthropologists put their discipline to work. In this article, McCurdy looks at one way in which the ethnographic perspective can be put to work in a business setting. Finally, Eric Bailey, an applied anthropologist himself, describes how he used his training as a medical anthropologist to consult on two health fair outreach programs. His work illustrates how training in graduate-level applied anthropology programs can be put to use in the world outside of academia.

Key Terms

innovation	applied anthropology
borrowing	adjustment anthropology
diffusion	administrative anthropology
social acceptance	action anthropology
cultural contact	advocate anthropology
acculturation	

Readings in This Section

Cocaine and the Economic Deterioration of Bolivia *Jack McIver Weatherford,* page *354*

The Kayapo Resistance *Terence Turner,* page *365*

Using Anthropology *David W. McCurdy,* page *383*

The Medical Anthropologist as Consultant *Eric J. Bailey,* page *395*

33

Cocaine and the Economic Deterioration of Bolivia

Jack McIver Weatherford

The demands of the world market have eroded local subsistence economies for centuries. Lands once farmed by individual families to meet their own needs now grow sugarcane, cotton, grain, or vegetables for market. Deprived of their access to land, householders must work as day laborers or migrate to cities to find jobs. Villages are denuded of the men, who have gone elsewhere for work, leaving women to farm and manage the family. The rhythm and structure of daily village life are altered dramatically. In this article, Jack Weatherford describes the impact of a new world market for cocaine on the structure and lives of rural Bolivians. Fed by an insatiable demand in Europe and the United States, the Bolivian cocaine trade has drawn males from the countryside, disrupted communications, destroyed families, unbalanced the local diet, and upset traditional social organization.

"They say you Americans can do anything. So, why can't you make your own cocaine and let our children come home from the coca

This article was written especially for this book. Copyright © by Jack McIver Weatherford, 1986.

plantations in the Chapare?" The Indian woman asked the question with confused resignation. In the silence that followed, I could hear only the rats scurrying around in the thatched roof. We continued shelling corn in the dark. The large house around us had once been home to an extended clan but was now nearly empty.

There was no answer to give her. Yet it was becoming increasingly obvious that the traditional Andean system of production and distribution built over thousands of years was now crumbling. Accompanying the destruction of the economic system was a marked distortion of the social and cultural patterns of the Quechua Indians. Since early in Inca history, the village of Pocona where I was working had been a trading village connecting the highlands, which produced potatoes, with the lowlands, which produced coca, a mildly narcotic plant used by the Incas. Over the past decade, however, new market demands from Europe and the United States have warped this system. Now the commodity is cocaine rather than the coca leaves, and the trade route bypasses the village of Pocona.

Bolivian subsistence patterns range from hunting and gathering in the jungle to intensive farming in the highlands, and since Inca times many parts of the country have depended heavily on mining. In the 1980s all of these patterns have been disrupted by the Western fad for one particular drug. Adoption of cocaine as the "drug of choice" by the urban elite of Europe and America has opened up new jungle lands and brought new Indian groups into Western economic systems. At the same time, the cocaine trade has cut off many communities such as Pocona from their traditional role in the national economy. Denied participation in the legal economy, they have been driven back into a world of barter and renewed isolation.

The vagaries of Western consumerism produce extensive and profound effects on Third World countries. It makes little difference whether the demand is for legitimate products such as coffee, tungsten, rubber, and furs marketed through legal corporations, or for illegal commodities such as opium, marijuana, cocaine, and heroin handled through criminal corporations. The same economic principles that govern the open, legal market also govern the clandestine, illegal markets, and the effects of both are frequently brutal.

Before coming to this Bolivian village, I assumed that if Americans and Europeans wanted to waste their money on cocaine, it was probably good that some of the poor countries such as Bolivia profit from it. In Cochabamba, the city in the heart of the cocaine-producing area, I had seen the benefits of this trade among the *narco chic* who lived in a new suburb of houses styled to look like Swiss chalets, Spanish haciendas, and English country homes. All these homes were surrounded by large wrought-iron fences, walls with broken glass set in the tops, and with large dogs that barked loudly and frequently. Such homes cost up to a hundred thousand dollars, an astronomical sum for Bolivia. I had also seen the narco elite of Cochabamba wearing gold chains and the latest Miami fashions and driving Nissans, Audis, Ford Broncos, an occasional BMW, or even a Mercedes through the muddy streets of the city. Some of their children attended the expensive English-speaking school; much of Cochabamba's meager nightlife catered to the elite. But as affluent as they may be in Bolivia, this elite would probably not earn as much as working-class families in such cities as Detroit, Frankfurt, or Tokyo.

Traveling outside of Cochabamba for six hours on the back of a truck, fording the same river three times, and following a rugged path for the last twenty-five kilometers, I reached Pocona and saw a different face of the cocaine trade. Located in a valley a mile and a half above sea level, Pocona is much too high to grow the coca bush. Coca grows best below six thousand feet, in the lush area called the Chapare where the eastern Andes meet the western edge of the Amazon basin and rain forest.

Like the woman with whom I was shelling corn, most of the people of Pocona are older, and community life is dominated by women together with their children who are still too young to leave. This particular woman had already lost both of her sons to the Chapare. She did not know it at the time, but within a few months, she was to lose her husband to the same work as well. With so few men, the women are left alone to plant, work, and harvest the fields of potatoes, corn, and fava beans, but with most of the work force missing, the productivity of Pocona has declined substantially.

In what was once a moderately fertile valley, hunger is now a part of life. The daily diet consists almost exclusively of bread, potato soup, boiled potatoes, corn, and tea. The majority of their daily calories comes from the potatoes and from the sugar that they put in their tea. They have virtually no meat or dairy products and very few fresh vegetables. These products are now sent to the Chapare to feed the workers in the coca fields, and the people of Pocona cannot compete against them. The crops that the people of Pocona produce are now difficult to sell because truck drivers find it much more profitable to take goods in and out of the Chapare rather than face the long and unprofitable trip to reach such remote villages as Pocona.

Despite all the hardships caused by so many people being away from the village, one might assume that more cash should be flowing into Pocona from the Chapare, where young men easily earn three dollars a day—three times the average daily wage of porters or laborers in Cochabamba. But this assumption was contradicted by the evidence of Pocona. As one widowed Indian mother of four explained, the first time her sixteen-year-old son came home, he brought bags of food, presents, and money for her and the younger children. She was very glad that he was working in the Chapare. On the second visit home he brought only a plastic bag of white powder for himself, and instead of bringing food, he took away as much as he could carry on the two-day trip back into the Chapare.

The third time, he told his mother that he could not find enough work in the Chapare. As a way to earn more money he made his mother bake as much bread as she could, and he took Mariana, his ten-year-old sister, with him to sell the bread to the workers in the Chapare. According to the mother, he beat the little girl and abused her repeatedly. Moreover, the money she made disappeared. On one of Mariana's trips home to get more bread, the mother had no more wheat or corn flour to supply her son. So, she sent Mariana away to

Cochabamba to work as a maid. The enraged son found where Mariana was working and went to the home to demand that she be returned to him. When the family refused, he tried but failed to have her wages paid to him rather than to his mother. Mariana was separated from her family and community, but at least she was not going to be one more of the prostitutes in the Chapare, and for her mother that was more important.

The standard of living in Pocona was never very high, but with the advent of the cocaine boom in Bolivia, the standard has declined. Ten years ago, Pocona's gasoline-powered generator furnished the homes with a few hours of electric light each night. The electricity also allowed a few families to purchase radios, and occasionally someone brought in a movie projector to show a film in a large adobe building on the main square. For the past two years, the people of Pocona have not been able to buy gasoline for their generator. This has left the village not only without electricity but without entertainment and radio or film contact with the outside world. A few boys have bought portable radios with their earnings from the Chapare, but their families were unable to replace the batteries. Nights in Pocona are now both dark and silent.

In recent years the national economy of Bolivia has been virtually destroyed, and peasants in communities such as Pocona are reverting to barter as the only means of exchange. The value of the peso may rise or fall by as much as 30 percent in a day; the peasants cannot take a chance on trading their crops for money that may be worth nothing in a week. Cocaine alone has not been responsible for the destruction of the Bolivian economy, but it has been a major contributor. It is not mere coincidence that the world's largest producer of coca is also the country with the world's worst inflation.

During part of 1986, inflation in Bolivia varied at a rate between 2,000 and 13,000 percent, if calculated on a yearly basis. Prices in the cities changed by the hour, and on some days the dollar would rise at the rate of more than 1 percent per hour. A piece of bread cost 150,000 pesos, and an American dollar bought between two and three million pesos on the black market. Large items such as airplane tickets were calculated in the billions of pesos, and on one occasion I helped a man carry a large box of money to pay for such a ticket. It took two professional counters half an hour to count the bills. Workers were paid in stacks of bills that were often half a meter high. Because Bolivia is too undeveloped to print its money, the importation of its own bills printed in West Germany and Brazil was one of the leading imports in the mid-1980s.

Ironically, by no longer being able to participate fully in the money economy, the villagers of Pocona who have chewed coca leaves for centuries now find it difficult to afford the leaves. The narcotics industry pays such a high price that the people of Pocona can afford only the rejected trash from the cocaine industry. Whether chewed or made into a tea, the coca produces a mild lift somewhat like a cup of coffee but without the jagged comedown that follows a coffee high. Coca also reduces hunger, thirst, headaches, stomach pains, and the type of altitude sickness known as *sorroche*.

Were this all, coca use might be viewed as merely a bad habit somewhat like drinking coffee, smoking cigarettes, or overindulging in chocolates, but unlike these practices coca actually has a number of marked health benefits. The coca leaf is very high in calcium. In a population with widespread lactose intolerance and in a country without a national system of milk distribution, this calcium source is very important. The calcium also severely reduces cavities in a population with virtually no dental services outside the city. Coca also contains large amounts of vitamins A, C, and D, which are often lacking in the starchy diets of the mountain peasants.

Without coca, and with an excess of corn that they cannot get to market, the people of Pocona now make more *chicha,* a form of home-fermented corn beer that tastes somewhat like the silage that American dairymen feed their cows. It is ironic that as an affluent generation of Americans are decreasing their consumption of alcohol in favor of drugs such as cocaine, the people of Pocona are drinking more alcohol to replace their traditional coca. *Chicha,* like most beers, is more nutritious than other kinds of distilled spirits but lacks the health benefits of the coca leaves. It also produces intoxication, something that no amount of coca leaves can do. Coca chewing is such a slow process and produces such a mild effect that a user would have to chew a bushel of leaves to equal the impact of one mixed drink or one snort of cocaine.

In many ways, the problems and complaints of Pocona echo those of any Third World country with a cash crop, particularly those caught in the boom-and-bust cycle characteristic of capitalist systems. Whether it is the sisal boom of the Yucatán, the banana boom of Central America, the rubber boom of Brazil, or the cocaine boom in Bolivia, the same pattern develops. Rural villages are depleted of their work forces. Family and traditional cultural patterns disintegrate. And the people are no longer able to afford certain local products that suddenly become valued in the West. This is what happened to Pocona.

Frequently, the part of a country that produces the boom crop benefits greatly, while other areas suffer greatly. If this were true in Bolivia, benefits accruing in the coca-producing area of the Chapare would outweigh the adjustment problems of such villages as Pocona. As it turns out, however, the Chapare has been even more adversely affected.

Most of the young men who go to the Chapare do not actually work in the coca fields. The coca bush originated in this area and does not require extensive care. One hectare can easily produce eight hundred kilograms of coca leaves in a year, but not much labor is needed to pick them. After harvesting, the leaves are dried in the sun for three to four days. Most of these tasks can easily be done by the farmer and his family. Wherever one goes in the Chapare one sees coca leaves spread out on large drying cloths. Old people or young children walk up and down these cloths, turning the drying leaves with their whisk brooms.

The need for labor, especially the labor of strong young men, comes in the first stage of cocaine production, in the reduction of large piles of leaves into a small quantity of *pasta,* or coca paste from which the active ingredient, cocaine, can then be refined. Three hundred to five hundred kilograms of leaves must be used to make one kilogram of pure cocaine. The leaves are made into *pasta* by soaking them in vats of kerosene and by applying salt, acetone, and sulfuric acid. To make the chemical reaction occur, someone must trample on the leaves for several days—a process very much like tromping on grapes to make wine, only longer. Because the corrosive mixture dissolves shoes or boots, the young men walk barefooted. These men are called *pisacocas* and usually work in the cool of the night, pounding the green slime with their feet. Each night the chemicals eat away more skin and very quickly open ulcers erupt. Some young men in the Chapare now have feet that are so diseased that they are incapable of standing, much less walking. So, instead, they use their hands to mix the *pasta,* but their hands are eaten away even faster than their feet. Thousands and possibly tens of thousands of young Bolivian men now look like lepers with permanently disfigured hands and feet. It is unlikely that any could return to Pocona and make a decent farmer.

Because this work is painful, the *pisacocas* smoke addictive cigarettes coated with *pasta.* This alleviates their pain and allows them to continue walking the coca throughout the night. The *pasta* is contaminated with chemical residues, and smoking it warps their minds as quickly as the acids eat their hands and feet. Like Mariana's brother, the users become irrational, easily angered, and frequently violent.

Once the boys are no longer able to mix coca because of their mental or their physical condition, they usually become unemployed. If their wounds heal, they may be able to work as loaders or haulers, carrying the cocaine or transporting the controlled chemicals used to process it. By and large, however, women and very small children, called *hormigas* (ants), are better at this work. Some of the young men then return home to their villages; others wander to Cochabamba, where they might live on the streets or try to earn money buying and selling dollars on the black market.

The cocaine manufacturers not only supply their workers with food and drugs, they keep them sexually supplied with young girls who serve as prostitutes as well. Bolivian health officials estimate that nearly half of the people living in the Chapare today have venereal disease. As the boys and girls working there return to their villages, they take these diseases with them. Increasing numbers of children born to infected mothers now have bodies covered in syphilitic sores. In 1985, a worse disease hit with the first case of AIDS. Soon after the victim died, a second victim was diagnosed.

In an effort to control its own drug problem, the United States is putting pressure on Bolivia to eradicate coca production in the Andean countries. The army invaded the Chapare during January of 1986, but after nearly three weeks of being surrounded by the workers in the narcotics industry and cut off from their supply bases, the army surrendered. In a nation the size of Texas and California combined, but with a population approximately the size of the city of Chicago, it is difficult for the government to control its own territory. Neither the Incas nor the Spanish conquistadores were ever able to conquer and administer the jungles of Bolivia, where there are still nomadic bands of Indians who have retreated deep into the jungle to escape

Western encroachment. The army of the poorest government in South America is no better able to control this country than its predecessors. The government runs the cities, but the countryside and the jungles operate under their own laws.

One of the most significant effects of the coca trade and of the campaigns to eradicate it has come on the most remote Indians of the jungle area. As the campaign against drugs has pushed production into more inaccessible places and as the world demand has promoted greater cultivation of coca, the coca growers are moving into previously unexplored areas. A coca plantation has been opened along the Chimore river less than an hour's walk from one of the few surviving bands of Yuqui Indians. The Yuquis, famous for their eight-foot-long bows and their six-foot arrows, are now hovering on the brink of extinction. In the past year, the three bands of a few hundred Yuquis have lost eleven members in skirmishes with outsiders. In turn, they killed several outsiders this year and even shot the missionary who is their main champion against outside invaders.

According to the reports of missionaries, other Indian bands have been enlisted as workers in cocaine production and trafficking, making virtual slaves out of them. A Bolivian medical doctor explained to me that the Indians are fed the cocaine in their food as a way of keeping them working and preventing their escape. Through cocaine, the drug traffickers may be able to conquer and control these last remnants of the great Indian nations of the Americas. If so, they will accomplish what many have failed to do in the five-hundred-year campaign of Europeans to conquer the free Indians.

The fate of the Indians driven out of their homelands is shown in the case of Juan, a thirteen-year-old Indian boy from the Chimore river where the Yuquis live. I found him one night in a soup kitchen for street children operated in the corner of a potato warehouse by the Maryknoll priests. Juan wore a bright orange undershirt that proclaimed in bold letters Fairfax District Public Schools. I sat with him at the table coated in potato dust while he ate his soup with his fellow street children, some of whom were as young as four years old. He told me what he could remember of his life on the Chimore; he did not know to which tribe he was born or what language he had spoken with his mother. It was difficult for Juan to talk about his Indian past in a country where it is a grave insult to be called an Indian. Rather than talk about the Chimore or the Chapare, he wanted to ask me questions because I was the first American he had ever met. Was I stronger than everyone else, because he had heard that Americans were the strongest people in the world? Did we really have wolves and bears in North America, and was I afraid of them? Had I been to the Chapare? Did I use cocaine?

In between his questions, I found out that Juan had come to Cochabamba several years ago with his mother. The two had fled the Chapare, but he did not know why. Once in the city they lived on the streets for a few years until his mother died, and he had been living alone ever since. He had become a *polilla* (moth), as they call such street boys. To earn money he washed cars and sold cigarettes laced with *pasta*. When he tired of talking about himself and asking about the animals of North America, he and his two friends made plans to go out to one of the nearby *pasta* villages the next day.

Both the Chapare (which supplied the land for growing coca) and highland villages such as Pocona (which supplied the labor) were suffering from the cocaine boom. Where, then, is the profit? The only other sites in Bolivia are the newly developed manufacturing towns where cocaine is refined. Whereas in the past most of this refining took place in Colombia, both the manufacturers and the traffickers find it easier and cheaper to have the work done in Bolivia, closer to the source of coca leaves and closer to much cheaper sources of labor. The strength of the Colombian government and its closeness to the United States also make the drug trafficking more difficult there than in Bolivia, with its weak, unstable government in La Paz.

Toco is one of the villages that has turned into a processing point for cocaine. Located at about the same altitude as Pocona but only a half-day by truck from the Chapare, Toco cannot grow coca, but the village is close enough to the source to become a major producer of the *pasta.* Traffickers bring in the large shipments of coca leaves and work them in backyard "kitchens." Not only does Toco still have its young men at home and still have food and electricity, but it has work for a few hundred young men from other villages.

Unlike Pocona, for which there are only a few trucks each week, trucks flow in and out of Toco every day. Emblazoned with names such as Rambo, El Padrino (The Godfather), and Charles Bronson rather than the traditional truck names of San José, Virgen de Copacabana, or Flor de Urkupina, these are the newest and finest trucks found in Bolivia. Going in with a Bolivian physician and another anthropologist from the United States, I easily got a ride, along with a dozen Indians, on a truck which was hauling old car batteries splattered with what appeared to be vomit.

A few kilometers outside of Toco we were stopped by a large crowd of Indian peasants. Several dozen women sat around on the ground and in the road spinning yarn and knitting. Most of the women had babies tied to their shoulders in the brightly colored *awayu* cloth, which the women use to carry everything from potatoes to lambs. Men stood around with farm tools, which they now used to block the roads. The men brandished their machetes and rakes at us, accusing us all of being smugglers and *pisacocas.* Like the Indians on the truck with us, the three of us stood silent and expressionless in the melee.

The hostile peasants were staging an ad hoc strike against the coca trade. They had just had their own fields of potatoes washed away in a flash flood. Now without food and without money to replant, they were demanding that someone help them or they would disrupt all traffic to and from Toco. Shouting at us, several of them climbed on board the truck. Moving among the nervous passengers, they checked for a shipment of coca leaves, kerosene, acid, or anything else that might be a part of the coca trade. Having found nothing, they reluctantly let us pass with stern warnings not to return with cocaine or *pasta.* A few weeks after our encounter with the strikers, their strike ended and most of the men went off to look for work in the Chapare and in Toco; without a crop, the cocaine traffic was their only hope of food for the year.

On our arrival in Toco we found out that the batteries loaded with us in the back of the truck had been hollowed out and filled with acid to be used in making *pasta. Chicha* vomit had been smeared around to discourage anyone from checking them. After removal of the acid, the same batteries were then filled with plastic bags of cocaine to be smuggled out of Toco and into the town of Cliza and on to Cochabamba and the outside world.

Toco is an expanding village with new cement-block buildings going up on the edge of town and a variety of large plumbing pipes, tanks, and drains being installed. It also has a large number of motorcycles and cars. By Bolivian standards it is a rich village, but it is still poorer than the average village in Mexico or Brazil. Soon after our arrival in Toco, we were followed by a handful of men wanting to sell us *pasta,* and within a few minutes the few had grown to nearly fifty young men anxious to assist us. Most of them were on foot, but some of them circled us in motorcycles, and many of them were armed with guns and machetes. They became suspicious and then openly hostile when we convinced them that we did not want to buy *pasta.* To escape them we took refuge in the home of an Indian family and waited for the mob to disperse.

When we tried to leave the village a few hours later, we were trapped by a truckload of young men who did not release us until they had checked with everyone we had met with in the village. They wondered why we were there if not to buy *pasta.* We were rescued by the doctor who accompanied us; she happened to be the niece of a popular Quechua writer. Evoking the memory of her uncle who had done so much for the Quechua people, she convinced the villagers of Toco that we were Bolivian doctors who worked with her in Cochabamba, and that we were not foreigners coming to buy *pasta* or to spy on them. An old veteran who claimed that he had served in the Chaco War with her uncle vouched for us, but in return for having saved us he then wanted us to buy *pasta* from him.

The wealth generated by the coca trade from Bolivia is easy to see. It is in the European cars cruising the streets of Cochabamba and Santa Cruz, and in the nice houses in the suburbs. It is in the motorcycles and jeeps in Toco, Cliza, and Trinidad. The poverty is difficult to see because it is in the remote villages like Pocona, among the impoverished miners in the village of Porco, and intertwined in the lives of peasants throughout the highland districts of Potosí and Oruro. But it is in communities such as Pocona that 70 percent of the population of Bolivia lives. For every modern home built with cocaine money in Cochabamba, a tin mine lies abandoned in Potosí that lost many of its miners when the world price for tin fell and they had to go to the Chapare for food. For every new car in Santa Cruz or every new motorcycle in Toco, a whole village is going hungry in the mountains.

The money for coca does not go to the Bolivians. It goes to the criminal organizations that smuggle the drugs out of the country and into the United States and Europe. A gram of pure cocaine on the streets of Cochabamba costs five dollars; the same gram on the streets of New York, Paris, or Berlin costs over a hundred dollars. The price increase occurs outside Bolivia.

The financial differential is evident in the case of the American housewife and mother sentenced to the Cochabamba prison after being caught with six and a half kilograms of cocaine at the airport. Like all the other women in the prison, she now earns money washing laundry by hand at a cold-water tap in the middle of the prison yard. She receives the equivalent of twenty cents for each pair of pants she washes, dries, and irons. In Bolivian prisons, the prisoner has to furnish his or her own food, clothes, medical attention, and even furniture.

She was paid five thousand dollars to smuggle the cocaine out of Bolivia to the Caribbean. Presumably someone else was then to be paid even more to smuggle it into the United States or Europe. The money that the American housewife received to smuggle the cocaine out of the country would pay the salary of eighty *pisacocas* for a month. It would also pay the monthly wages of two hundred fifty Bolivian schoolteachers, who earn the equivalent of twenty U.S. dollars per month in pay. Even though her price seemed high by Bolivian standards, it is a small part of the final money generated by the drugs. When cut and sold on the streets of the United States, her shipment of cocaine would probably bring in five to seven million dollars. Of that amount, however, only about five hundred dollars goes to the Bolivian farmer.

The peasant in the Chapare growing the coca earns three times as much for a field of coca as he would for a field of papayas. But he is only the first in a long line of people and transactions that brings the final product of cocaine to the streets of the West. At the end of the line, cocaine sells for four to five times its weight in gold.

The United States government made all aid programs and loans to Bolivia dependent on the country's efforts to destroy coca. This produces programs in which Bolivian troops go into the most accessible areas and uproot a few fields of aging or diseased coca plants. Visiting drug-enforcement agents from the United States together with American congressmen applaud, make their reports on the escalating war against drugs, and then retire to a city hotel where they drink hot cups of coca tea and cocktails.

These programs hurt primarily the poor farmer who tries to make a slightly better living by growing coca rather than papayas. The raids on the fields and cocaine factories usually lead to the imprisonment of ulcerated *pisacocas* and women and children *hormigas* from villages throughout Bolivia. Local authorities present the burned fields and full prisons to Washington visitors as proof that the Bolivian government has taken a hard stance against drug trafficking.

International crime figures with bank accounts in New York and Zurich get the money. Bolivia ends up with hunger in its villages, young men with their hands and feet permanently maimed, higher rates of venereal disease, chronic food shortages, less kerosene, higher school dropout rates, increased drug addiction, and a worthless peso.

Review Questions

1. List and describe the major effects of the cocaine trade on rural Bolivian life.
2. Why have the production of coca and the manufacture of cocaine created a health hazard in Bolivia?
3. Why has the cocaine trade benefited the Bolivian economy so little?
4. How has the cocaine trade disrupted village social organization in Bolivia?

34

The Kayapo Resistance

Terence Turner

Until about 200 years ago, vast areas of the world were inhabited by native, mostly hunter-gatherer or horticultural, peoples. Few native groups, however, have survived the ravages of colonial and economic expansion, and those who are left seem destined to become victims of "progress." In this article, however, Terence Turner argues that "fourth world" peoples, in this case the Kayapo of the Brazilian Amazon, have acted to conserve their own political autonomy while simultaneously aiding the world conservation movement. Apparently doomed to extinction by the relentless encroachment of Brazilian settlers, loggers, miners, and dam builders, the Kayapo have managed to mobilize not only themselves, but other Indians, environmentalists, legislators, and the world press in a united effort to defend the forest and their right to live in it.

As increasing numbers of people have become aware of the imminence of the destruction of the world's tropical forests and the probable consequences for the atmosphere and climate of the planet, voices have

From "The Role of Indigenous Peoples in the Environmental Crisis: The Example of the Kayapo of the Brazilian Amazon," *Perspectives in Biology and Medicine,* vol. 36, no. 3, spring 1993, pp. 526–545. Copyright © by the University of Chicago, 1993.

increasingly been heard drawing attention to the need for concern for human populations of forest dwellers, as well as the floral and faunal components of the ecosystem. This has been motivated in part by humanitarian concerns, in part by more specific concerns for indigenous political and legal rights, in part by an awareness that native forest peoples may possess valuable knowledge of their environments, and also, at times, by a realization that the traditional adaptive activities of such peoples may make important functional contributions to the ecosystems in which they live. Whatever their specific point of departure, however, advocates of native forest peoples have tended to assume that recognition of the rights and contributions of the native inhabitants of the forests, as well as their physical and cultural survival, would depend, like the salvation of the forests themselves, upon them. That native forest peoples themselves, many of whom number among the most primitive and remote human societies on earth, should come to play an important role as allies and even leaders in the world struggle to save the forests is a prospect so apparently remote as to seem only a little less improbable than Martians arriving to lend a hand. Yet this is precisely what has been happening in the last few years, nowhere with more impressive scope and success than in the case of the Kayapo Indians of the Brazilian Amazon.

The Kayapo: Ethnographic and Historical Background

The Kayapo are a nation of Ge-speaking Indians who inhabit the middle and lower reaches of the valley of the Xingu River, one of the major southern tributaries of the Amazon. Their total population is currently around 2,500, divided among 14 mutually independent communities. The largest of these communities, Gorotire, has about 800 inhabitants, but several others are little more than hamlets. Kayapo country is a mixture of forest and savannah land, with rather more forest than open country around most of the villages. The total area covered by Kayapo communities and their associated land-use patterns is about the size of Scotland.

The massive destruction of the Amazonian environment represented by the cutting and burning of the forest, the cutting of roads, and the soil erosion and river pollution caused by mining and the building of giant hydroelectric dams, have had a shattering impact on the environment and way of life of many forest Indians of the Amazon. Even groups whose lands have not yet been reached by these activities, or are just beginning to be affected by them, now live in the permanent shadow of the threat. To understand the meaning of this threat for indigenous peoples like the Kayapo, one must stand in a Kayapo village under the dense clouds of smoke that now darken the sky over Kayapo country at the end of every dry season, as Brazilian squatters and ranchers burn off vast stretches of previously forested land to the east and south, rapidly approaching the traditional borders of Kayapo territory along a 700-mile front. It is to feel one's world burning, with the ring of fire drawing even tighter.

For members of modern industrial societies, one of the most difficult points to grasp about the relation of native tropical forest peoples to their environment, as articulated through their modes of subsistence production, is that the relationship is not felt or conceived to comprise a separate, "economic" sphere in our sense. Rather, it forms an integral part of the total social process of producing human beings and social life. The threatened annihilation of such a society's environmental base of subsistence is therefore not felt merely as an "economic" threat, nor one that can be located and confined in an external, "environmental" sphere. It is a threat to the continuity and meaning of social life. Understanding this point is essential, not only to appreciate the traumatic effects of wholesale ecological devastation on traditional societies of subsistence producers like the Kayapo, but also to understand the nature of their political response and resistance to such threats.

The Relation of the Kayapo to the Environment through Subsistence Production

For the Kayapo, like most other contemporary Amazonian native peoples, traditional patterns of subsistence adaptation are still the basic way of life. The Kayapo produce their means of subsistence by a combination of slash-and-burn horticulture, hunting, fishing, and foraging. According to the division of labor by gender and generation, men engage in all productive pursuits incompatible with the care of young children, while women perform those which can be carried out while caring for children. This means that men hunt, fish, do the heavy and dangerous work of clearing gardens, and gather certain wild forest products that grow at great distances, requiring overnight journeys. Women do the planting, weeding, and harvesting of gardens; cut firewood; cook the food; build traditional shelters (now done almost exclusively in trekking camps); forage for such wild products as can be found within a day's round-trip walk from the village or camp; and care for children. Girls begin to help their mothers with household and garden chores while still children, but boys do little productive labor until they are inducted into the men's house, a bachelors' dormitory and men's club which stands apart from the family houses in the middle of the round village plaza.

Kayapo gardens must be cleared from fresh forestland and produce for about three years for most crops. The Kayapo raise an impressive variety of garden produce: manioc (both the bitter and sweet varieties), maize, bananas, yams, sweet potatoes, fava beans, squash, *cissus* (a leafy creeper that is a unique domesticate of their own), tobacco, *urucu* (used to make red body paint), and cotton (used to make string, but not woven). In recent years, many Kayapo have added Brazilian-introduced crops such as papaya, rice, various species of beans, pineapples, watermelon, avocado, and mango. Most families maintain about three gardens in production at any one time and clear a new one every year. After a garden is abandoned, it requires about 25 years for reforestation to render it ready for reuse. A sizable village therefore needs an extensive area of forestland for the rotation of its garden plots.

The Kayapo supplement their horticultural diet with large quantities of fish and game. Included among the latter are wild pig, tapir, deer, monkey, tortoise, armadillo, and various species of birds and rodents. Gathered wild produce is also seasonally important, and includes *babassu* coconuts (used for body and hair oil), *piki, tucum,* and brazil nuts, honey, palmito, *acai, bacaba,* and a variety of less important fruits. Hunting or fishing for the men, and gardening for the women, are more or less daily activities while the community is settled in its base village.

For considerable periods of the year, however, the Kayapo abandon their base villages and go off on collective seminomadic treks through the surrounding forest and savannah. These may last from one to three months, and may take one of several forms. Individual age-sets (most frequently, the male bachelors' set) may be sent out to gather seasonally ripening nuts or fruits; the whole village may go together; the individual senior men's societies may trek as separate groups, each with its associated women, children, and bachelor dependents; or only part of the village may go on trek to gather food for a ceremonial feast, while the rest remain behind in the village. A community may go on two or three such treks per year, so that at least some of the village may spend as much as half the year on trek. Large areas may thus be covered by all the treks undertaken by the members of a single village in a given year. In spite of the low population density of Kayapo country, therefore, most of the area is actually used by the mobile trekking groups which continually sally forth from the widely scattered base villages.

The regular alternation between trekking and base village occupation thus appears to be an integral aspect of Kayapo social organization. Why this should be so is not immediately apparent. Trekking by large collective groups is a relatively inefficient way to exploit the wild floral and faunal resources of an area. Only the adult men of the camp do any hunting. The bachelors and younger boys are typically occupied either with clearing the trail to the next day's campsite and the campsite itself, or bringing up horticultural produce from the village gardens, while the women occupy themselves with pitching or breaking camp, cutting firewood, preparing food, and tending children. The camp is moved every one or two days, but usually only for a distance of one or two kilometers, about a 15-minute walk. More game could doubtless be captured by small groups of men working alone, free to move more rapidly over greater distances. Hunting and fishing are routinely done in this way while the community is residing in the base village, and it is certainly no less productive than the hunting done on trek. Trekking by whole communities or large groups, in other words, cannot be accounted for as the most efficient available method of acquiring needed protein or other foodstuffs.

A similar question arises over the frequency with which Kayapo bands moved their village sites in the days before peaceful relations were established with the Brazilians. There is in fact no ecological reason why Kayapo villages as large as two thousand would ever need to move as a group from their permanent village sites to remain supplied with the foods they require. Notwithstanding this fact, Kayapo villages before pacification tended to move as often as every two, or more usually five to ten years. A given community would have as many as a dozen village sites, and occupy most of them over a twenty-year period. This frequency of movement, again, cannot be accounted for simply as a result of material necessity. In common with trekking, it seems part of a dynamic inherent in Kayapo social organization.

The Social Meaning of Subsistence Production

. . . The high mobility of Kayapo society, and the large amounts of territory it requires in consequence, thus cannot be understood, as some have attempted to do, as the result of nutritional deficiencies in the soil or lack of protein or other nutrients in the faunal or floral environment. They are, rather, the corollaries and effects of the organization of Kayapo society, with its central tension between female-centered and male-centered forms of social grouping. These forms themselves, however, are articulated in terms of their complementary roles in production, although this is production understood in the Kayapo sense of the social production of human beings and social relations, which includes but is not reducible to, material subsistence. This notion of social production calls for a more extended exegesis as it is essential to an understanding of the Kayapo relationship to their natural environment and their society per se.

Kayapo patterns of environmental adaptation and subsistence production are intricately interwoven with their ways of producing human individuals. This process of human production includes what we call "socializing" children, but continues through the life cycle and the final rites of death. This individual process, in turn, is treated by the Kayapo as an integral part of the process of reproducing collective social units like extended-family households, age-sets, and ceremonial organizations, and thus of society as a whole. As I have already indicated, the division of labor in the production of material subsistence is defined in relation to the division of labor in the production of social persons and relations, with women specializing in the socialization of children. It must be clearly understood that this is not simply a natural result but a culturally imposed social pattern. Women who do not happen to be raising young children nevertheless do not go hunting and fishing. At a higher level of organization, the nuclear family forms the social unit of cooperation in the production and consumption of material subsistence, but as a social unit it owes its form primarily to its role in producing new social persons, not its functions in expediting subsistence activities. Subsistence production thus finds its place as an integral part of the global process of social production, which also includes the socialization of children, the recruitment and reconstitution of families and collective groups, and the celebration of the great communal ceremonies. In these two-to-four month long symbolic dramas, all of these levels of activity are performed in an orchestrated pattern that asserts their essential interdependence as parts of a single whole.

The Kayapo attitude toward the nonhuman natural environment must be understood as a part of this same global pattern. The Kayapo do not oppose "nature" to human society as mutually exclusive, externally related domains; nor can they be said to possess a single, uniform concept of "nature" in our sense. They recognize that the forest and savannah beyond their village clearings are products of forces that are independent of humans and not under social control. They further recognize that they depend upon these natural forces and products for their own social existence, and that social persons are in fact largely "natural" beings, whose physical bodies, senses, and libidinal energies are as extra-social in origin as any forest tree or wild animal. Disease, death, shamanic trance, insanity, and periods of transition in left-crisis ritual are seen as moments when the continuity between the internal natural core of human social actors and the external natural environment of the forest and animal world asserts itself, short-circuiting and blacking out the interposed, insulating social veneer. At such times, the social person reverts to a "natural" state, here conceived as one of entropic dissolution of social form. At other times, as in the rituals of initiation at puberty or the everyday bringing in of game, gathered nuts, or garden produce from the forest, displacing or penetrating the boundary between nature and society has the opposite result: an infusion of energy which, directed into social channels, enables society to exist and renew itself. Human beings and society itself, in sum, are seen as partly "natural" entities, dependent on continual infusions of energy from their natural surroundings. The reproduction of human society, the reproduction of socialized human beings, and the reproduction of the natural forest and savannah environment are thus interconnected parts of a single great process.

Society and its members, in sum, are essentially seen as appropriating and channeling natural energy, and are thus dependent on the ability of the natural world (meaning the forest, animals, birds, rivers, and fish) to reproduce itself and continue as a great reservoir and source of the energy society must continually draw upon to live. The destruction of the forest, the killing or driving away of its animals, or the pollution of the rivers and killing of their fish, therefore, are not seen by the Kayapo simply as an attack on "the natural environment" in our sense, but as a direct assault upon them as a society and as individuals.

This view, it should immediately be added, is fully compatible with the destruction of trees and animals on a considerable scale for appropriation by the Kayapo of the energy stored in their flesh, fruits, or the soil on which they stand. The Kayapo operate with a rough rule of thumb derived from millenia of experience, a sense of the ability of the local environment to accommodate a certain level of destruction, inflicted by their traditional modes and levels of subsistence activity, and still regenerate itself. They have no mystical sense of reverence or respect for individual trees or animals and feel no hesitation about chopping them down or taking them as game whenever their interests demand. What concerns the Kayapo is nature in the aggregate, or more specifically, the survival and reproduction of a sufficient slice of the natural environment to support their traditional way of life. It was only when they realized that this aggregate capacity for regeneration was threatened by the vast scale of the destruction now being inflicted on the area that the Kayapo became aroused over the fate of the forest environment as such. Similarly, ecological concerns for tropical rain forests became transformed into urgent political issues in the developed world only when peoples of the developed countries realized the probable consequences of this destruction from the rest of the world's climate and population. Kayapo and First World modes of "ecological" consciousness and concern converged, in short, when, starting from very different premises, the members of both societies realized that the survival of their societies was at stake. The dramatic results of this convergence are the subject of the rest of this paper.

The Kayapo Resistance and the Environmentalist Movement

The Kayapo area of Southern Para state is a representative microcosm of the destructive processes at work in the Amazon as a whole. Beginning in the late 1960s, the Kayapo have been confronted with virtually every major form of environmental destruction and land depredation found elsewhere in the region.

The Kayapo Face the End of Their World

Since the 1960s there has been constant pressure from small squatters and large ranchers attempting to infiltrate Kayapo areas and clear small farms by burning off patches of forest. Land speculators have attempted to build illegal airstrips and to survey and sell off large chunks of Kayapo land to which they did not even hold legal title. In 1971, the Brazilian government built a major road of the Trans-Amazonica highway system through Kayapo country, secretly altering the route so as to amputate the Kayapo area of the Xingu National Park, which it then attempted to sell off to private owners, mostly speculators, would-be ranchers, and farmers. The road brought heavy truck and bus traffic carrying settlers and supplies to the new settlements farther west, bringing with them the perils of infectious disease and the potential for conflict with the Indians. Timber companies interested in the large stands of virgin mahogany within the boundaries of the remaining officially delimited Kayapo reserve, the Kayapo Indigenous Area, sought and obtained logging concessions for large tracts from Kayapo leaders in exchange for sizable money payments and the construction of modern housing and other facilities in Kayapo villages. Most of the money went into communal accounts in banks in neighboring frontier towns. These accounts were either explicitly or tacitly controlled by chiefs or the few literate Kayapo able to keep the accounts. Some of these individuals began to draw heavily on these "communal" funds for personal use, giving rise to tension and resentment by the rest of their communities. Rivalries between competing companies and their respective Kayapo sponsors almost led to war between two Kayapo villages in 1986.

The discovery of gold at the huge mine of Serra Pelada near the eastern border of the Kayapo Indigenous Area led to intense prospecting and exploratory gold-mining activity within the eastern borders of the Kayapo Indigenous Area. This culminated in 1983 with the opening of two large illegal gold mines only ten kilometers from Gorotire village. Three thousand Brazilian miners swarmed onto Kayapo land, and neither the Brazilian Indian Service (FUNAI) nor any other arm of the Brazilian government seemed willing or able to do anything to stop it. Tons of mercury from the mining operations began to pollute the Rio Fresco, the main fishery of several Kayapo communities. Then, in 1986, an even more ominous form of pollution threatened, when radioactive waste from a cancer treatment facility in the city of Goiania caused two dozen fatalities, and the federal government attempted to dump the material on the western border of Kayapo country.

As if all this were not enough, the Kayapo began to hear rumors that the Brazilian government was planning to build a series of hydroelectric dams along the Xingu and its tributaries, which would result in the flooding of large areas of Kayapo land and end the value of most of the river system as a fishery. The scheme was to be funded by loans from the World Bank. Repeated attempts to learn the truth about the government's plans were met with stonewalling and denials that any such plan existed. The rumors persisted, however, and construction sites began to be cleared at certain points along the river. The Kayapo were outraged by the government's disregard for their political and legal rights to be consulted about a project which would so heavily affect their lands and livelihood. They were equally concerned about the ecological effects. While Kayapo leaders strove unsuccessfully to penetrate the government's cover-up about the dam project, however, they were confronted by an even more direct threat to their legal and political rights, as Indians, to challenge governmental or private Brazilian infringements of their land rights, resources, or communal interests. At the convention called to draw up the new Brazilian constitution, a measure was introduced calling for the redefinition of any Indian who demonstrated the capacity to bring a legal action in a Brazilian court as an "acculturated" person who could no longer be considered an Indian, and therefore could no longer represent or bring an action on behalf of an Indian community in court. This "catch–22" provision would have destroyed the possibility of any legal or political resistance by native peoples against abuses of their rights, persons, lands, or environments within the terms of the Brazilian legal and political process.

This daunting array of threats to the Kayapo environment, communal lands and resource base, political and civil rights is a representative sample of the human face of the environmental crisis in the Amazon. The Kayapo confronted this apparently overwhelming onslaught beginning in the early 1970s as a still largely monolingual people of Ge-speakers scattered over a vast area in 14 mutually autonomous and politically uncoordinated settlements. In most of the villages, some of the men (but almost no women) spoke Portuguese, and a handful had learned to read, write, and do simple arithmetic. A few leaders had obtained some experience of Brazilian administrative and political ways through working in the Indian Service or as members of Brazilian expeditions to contact other tribes. They had a few contacts with the outside world through anthropologists and indigenous advocacy groups, and the Brazilian Indian Service (FUNAI) offered some support, although it could not be counted upon to represent the Indians' interests against the more threatening forms of economic development mounted by government or powerful private interests. Aside from this slender array of assets, the Kayapo had no political resources with which to defend themselves and their forest beyond their own largely intact tribal institutions and culture. These, however, were to serve them well in the trials that lay ahead.

The Kayapo Resistance

This is what they did. The two western communities whose land had been severed by the road began an unrelenting campaign of armed attacks on all Brazilian intruders who attempted to open ranches or settle in the separated area. After 15 years and perhaps 50 Brazilian dead, with no Kayapo casualties, no Brazilian settler remained in the entire area. The leaders of the two Kayapo groups meanwhile carried out a campaign of diplomacy, making repeated trips to Brasília to pressure the government to return the stolen land and thus end the violent standoff in the area. The government capitulated in 1985, returning the area to the Kayapo and ceding an additional area immediately to the north of the old area (this became the Capoto Indigenous Area). The two communities of the region joined again into a single large village and have resolutely banned all Brazilian mining, timber, and agricultural interests and settlers from their reclaimed areas.

Also in 1985, the two illegally opened gold mines were assaulted and captured by 200 Kayapo, armed with a mixture of firearms and traditional weapons. The larger mine was accessible only by air, so the Kayapo seized and blockaded the landing strip, confronting the Brazilian government with a choice: either cede title and administrative authority over the mines to the Kayapo, together with a significant percentage of the proceeds (10% was the amount initially demanded), and legally demarcate the boundaries of the Kayapo Indigenous Area (thus making the government unambiguously responsible for the defense of the area against any further such incursions), or the Kayapo would allow no more planes to land or take off, either to supply or evacuate the three thousand miners at the site. After a tense ten-day standoff, the government gave in to the Kayapo demands.

The leaders of Gorotire, the nearest and largest Kayapo village, used the first income from the mine to purchase a light plane and hire a Brazilian pilot. They put the plane to use to patrol their borders from the air to spot intruders and would-be squatters. If any were seen, patrols were dispatched to expel or eliminate the invaders. Within a year, invasions effectively ceased. They have also used the plane to fly to other Kayapo villages and to Brazilian cities to purchase goods and bring people out for medical assistance. In the nearest town of Redencao, and the state capital of Belem, they have bought houses for the use of Kayapo travelers and shoppers, and in the former they have established a tribal office to deal with their bank accounts and official relations with the local office of FUNAI.

All timber concessions on Kayapo land were suspended by the Indian Service (FUNAI) at the end of 1987, at the urging of the most influential Kayapo leaders, Payakan and Ropni. Some concessions, however, were surreptitiously continued by a few other leaders who have lined their own pockets with the fees paid by the companies. Still other communities and leaders not previously involved with lumbering companies are under great pressure from the companies to grant new concessions. Meanwhile, resistance to any new concessions continues to be strong, and one community (A'Ukre) has declared its part of the Kayapo Indigenous Area an "extractive reserve" closed to all ecologically destructive forms of timber and mineral exploitation. This remains a conflicted issue, with the ultimate outcome in doubt. Meanwhile, a substantial area of the Kayapo Indigenous Area has been clear-cut. The fate of the captured gold mines has also proved a divisive issue. Not only have the Kayapo not closed them down, as they originally said they would do within two years of taking them over, but some Kayapo have opened a couple of small new mines on their own land. Other Kayapo vigorously oppose this and have strictly prohibited all mining activity, whether by Brazilians or Kayapo, from their areas of the reserve. Meanwhile, five Gorotire Kayapo have become wealthy enough from the gold and timber revenues to buy private houses for themselves in Redencao, where they live for much of the time, keeping Brazilian servants and, in two cases, acquiring large ranches outside the reserve. This phenomenon has been paralleled by the chief of the village of Kikretum, who owns an airplane, houses, and a hotel in the neighboring town of Tucuma. The rise of this embryonic "new class" has already given rise to significant tensions within Kayapo society and is a factor in the unresolved conflicts over the future form of accommodation between Kayapo society and the Brazilian economy.

Most of the other threats posed by the enveloping national society proved less divisive, and the Kayapo were able to mount concerted, well-organized responses to them without internal dissension or conflict. When the government's plan to dump the radioactive waste on traditional Kayapo land was announced, the Kayapo sent a hundred men to Brasília to demonstrate against the plan. Suitably painted and feathered, they staged a sit-in in the president's palace. Nothing like this had happened in Brazil in the twenty years since the coup d'etat that established the military regime that was then in the process of relinquishing power. The initial incredulity and indignation of the authorities, however, gave way to acquiescence to the Kayapo's demands, and the dumping plan was abandoned. Pressing their advantage, the Kayapo next sent a deputation of some 50 chiefs and leading citizens to the Constitutional Convention to lobby for the defeat of the "catch–22" acculturation clause and other provisions injurious to Indian interests. Presenting themselves as always, in traditional paint and feathers and carrying traditional weapons, they patiently attended the weeks of debates on the sections bearing on indigenous peoples' rights, gave press conferences, and lobbied the deputies. When the acculturation clause was defeated, and surprisingly strong safeguards of indigenous rights, lands, and resources were adopted by the Convention, the Kayapo received much of the credit in the Brazilian press.

In 1988, two Kayapo leaders were invited to the United States to participate in a conference on tropical forest ecology. From there, they traveled to Washington, met with members of Congress, and spoke with World Bank officials about the effects of the proposed Xingu dam scheme on the peoples and environment of the area. They were able to obtain copies of the entire dam project, the very existence of which the Brazilian government had continued to deny, from the Bank. Shortly after the Kayapos' visit, the World Bank announced that it was deferring action on the Brazilian loan request. Enraged, elements of the Brazilian national security and political establishment had criminal charges brought against them and their American interpreter under a law prohibiting participation in political activity in Brazil by foreigners. The charges were ridiculous in strictly legal terms; since the actions in question had taken place in the United States, the American had been acting in his own country, and the Kayapo were not in any case foreigners. The transparent attempt at legal terrorism boomeranged, as nongovernment organizations (NGOs), anthropologists, and the congressmen whom the Kayapo had met on their tour organized an international outcry.

When one of the Kayapo leaders came to Belem, the capital of the state of Para, where the charges had been brought, to be arraigned, the Kayapo organized a massive protest demonstration. More than five hundred Kayapo men and women danced through the streets and massed in the square before the Palace of Justice to support their kinsman and denounce Brazilian political repression. The defiance turned to ridicule when the judge refused to allow the Kayapo leader to enter the courthouse for arraignment until he changed his paint and feathers for "civilized" (Brazilian) clothes. The Kayapo refused and told the judge he would have to come to the Kayapo village of Gorotire if he wanted another chance to arraign him on the charges. Meanwhile, Kayapo orators unrolled the map of the Xingu dam scheme obtained from the World Bank in Washington on an easel erected in the square and explained the entire secret project in Kayapo and Portuguese for the benefit of the many Brazilian onlookers, who included reporters and TV crews. The government never again dared to try to arraign the Kayapo leader, and eventually dropped all the charges.

With the World Bank still actively considering the Brazilian government's request for a loan to enable the building of the Xingu dams, the proposed multi-dam hydroelectric scheme in the Xingu River valley now appeared to the Kayapo as the greatest threat, not only to their environment, but to their political and legal control over their lands and resources. Since the government still refused to disclose its plans to build the dams, the Kayapo resolved to force it to reveal its intentions and to receive, before an audience of national and world news media, their criticisms of the human and environmental effects of the dams, as well as of its deceit in attempting to conceal and deny its plans. To accomplish this, they decided to convene a great congress of Amazonian peoples at the site of the first of the dams the government hoped to build: Altamira, near the mouth of the Xingu. To the meeting would be invited representatives of the Brazilian government; representatives of the World Bank; representatives of the national and world news media; nongovernmental organizations active in the environmentalist, human rights, and indigenous peoples' support fields; delegates from as many indigenous nations of Amazonia as possible; and as many Kayapo as could be transported and accommodated. At the meeting, the government representatives would be asked to present their plans, to give an account of their probable effects on the environment and the human inhabitants of the region (Brazilian as well as native), and to explain why they had tried for so long to keep their plans secret from those who would be most affected by them.

The Kayapo leaders who envisioned this project saw that its success would depend on international public opinion, press attention, and financial support. Only the attendance of a large number of media and NGO representatives, they felt, would compel the Brazilian government to send its representatives to face certain humiliation at such a meeting. The leader chiefly responsible for the plan, Payakan, therefore embarked on a tour of seven European and North American countries (sponsored and coordinated by Friends of the Earth, the World Wildlife Federation, and the Kayapo Support Group of Chicago) in November, 1988, to publicize the Altamira gathering and appeal for support. At a more general level, Payakan also sought to bring the crisis of the Amazon forest and its native peoples to wider public attention, and to lobby government and international development bank officials against supporting economic development projects (such as the Xingu dam scheme) that would irreversibly damage the environment and require the expropriation or destruction of native lands.

Payakan, at the same time, also sought to bring about greater mutual trust, cooperation, and unity of purpose among the various kinds of nongovernmental organizations and sectors of public opinion involved in supporting the Indians and the environmental struggle. These included human rights, indigenous peoples' advocacy, anthropological, and environmentalist organizations. Among the latter were some groups specifically devoted to defending tropical rain forests, others concerned with saving endangered animal species, and still others dedicated to conservation and environmental quality in a more general sense. Payakan, in his dealings with these groups or their representatives, had quickly realized that they tended to work in isolation from one another, often mistrusted one another's politics, or viewed one another's work as irrelevant to their own concerns. With other Kayapo leaders, Payakan saw this situation as not only damaging the effectiveness of the work of these organizations, but as out of touch with the real interconnections of the issues with which the groups were attempting to deal. For both reasons, they felt, the support of the NGOs was less effective than it might otherwise be. Payakan therefore devoted much effort on his tour to appealing to these groups to join forces and recognize that they were really all involved in a single great struggle. As he put it in a speech at the University of Chicago:

> The forest is one big thing; it has people, animals, and plants. There is no point saving the animals if the forest is burned down; there is no point saving the forest if the people and animals who live in it are killed or driven away. The groups trying to save the races of animals cannot win if the people trying to save the forest lose; the people trying to save the Indians can not win if either of the others lose; the Indians cannot win without the support of these groups; but the groups cannot win either without the support of the Indians, who know the forest and the animals and can tell what is happening to them. No one of us is strong enough to win alone; together, we can be strong enough to win.

Payakan's message was widely heard. His tour became a concrete example of the intergroup cooperation he preached. For many indigenous advocacy organizations, environmentalist groups, human rights groups, Latin Americanist social scientists and anthropologists, helping to organize Payakan's tour and attending his speeches was their first practical experience of cooperating and coming together around a common set of interests and commitments. This experience has been continually repeated since then in a series of cooperative efforts to support the Altamira meeting, aid new organizational initiatives by the Kayapo and other forest peoples in Brazil, and help with subsequent tours by Payakan and other Kayapo leaders. It is generally recognized by activists of the various support organizations concerned that the Kayapo campaign has become an important catalyst of increased contact and cooperation among them at the national and international level, and that this cooperation has brought increased efficacy in lobbying, fund-raising, and public opinion outreach efforts.

Payakan's tour successfully achieved all its goals. Enough money was raised to defray all the costs of the Altamira gathering (which eventually approached $100,000) without drawing upon any of the funds derived from timber or gold concessions, which Payakan and most of his closest Kayapo supporters opposed. Much publicity and media attention was generated, guaranteeing a strong international media presence at the Altamira gathering itself. The support base of the Kayapo campaign among European and American nongovernmental organizations, public opinion, and politicians was greatly strengthened. The stage was now set for one of the most remarkable events in the history of Amazonia, the environmentalist movement, and modern popular protest politics.

From February 19–24, 1989, 600 Amazonian Indians and a roughly equal number of Brazilian and international journalists, photographers, TV crews, documentary filmmakers, Brazilian and foreign politicians, and representatives of various nongovernmental support organizations converged on the small river town of Altamira. Among the Indians were some 500 Kayapo and 100 members of 40 other indigenous nations, whom the Kayapo had invited to join them in confronting the Brazilian government, and to make their own views on the issues of dams and the destruction of the forest known to the government representatives, the news media, and one another. Five days of meetings, speeches, press conferences, and ritual performances by Kayapo and other indigenous groups were programmed and carried out without a major hitch. The event represented an impressive feat of organization and political coordination. It required the transportation, lodging, and feeding of hundreds of indigenous participants, which involved constructing a large encampment with traditional Kayapo shelters outside the town and daily busing of its inhabitants to the meeting hall in the center. Much of the credit for the event belongs to the Brazilian indigenous peoples' support organization, The Ecumenical Center for Documentation and Information (CEDI), which effectively cooperated with Payakan and the rest of the indigenous leadership in handling many of the logistical tasks essential to the success of the meeting.

Some elements of the regional Brazilian populace, especially those linked with landowning and commercial interests who stood to gain from the construction of the dams, were hostile to the Indians and (even more) their Brazilian and foreign environmentalist supporters. There were fears that violent incidents might occur and spread out of control. That this did not happen can be attributed in part to the foresight and discipline of the Kayapo, who carefully sited their encampment far outside of town and refrained from street demonstrations within the city limits, but also in large measure to the presence of so many foreign and domestic media personnel and observers.

The event took on the aspect of an international media circus. The Pope sent a telegram of support. The rock star Sting flew in for a day and gave a press conference at the Kayapo encampment, denouncing the destruction of the forest and promoting his own project for the creation of a new Kayapo reserve. No doubt because this project depended on the goodwill of the Brazilian government, Sting avoided directly committing himself in support of the Kayapo campaign against the dams. Since this was the whole purpose of the Altamira meeting, his Kayapo hosts roundly criticized him for using their platform for his own project and then skipping off. A British member of Parliament, a Belgian member of the European Parliament, and a half-dozen Brazilian deputies of the National Congress, however, mounted the platform and gave unreserved support. A final communique was issued, on behalf of all native peoples of Amazonia, condemning the dam project. By the time the conference closed with a dance from the Kayapo New Corn ceremony (joined in by assorted Indians of other tribes, European and Brazilian activists and media personnel, momentarily giving it the air of a 1960s hippie love-in), the Altamira gathering had become an international media success of such proportions as to generate serious political pressure against any international funding of the dam scheme, or indeed any attempt to go on with the plan by the Brazilian government. Within two weeks after the end of the meeting, the World Bank announced that it would not grant the Brazilian loan earmarked for the dam project, and the Brazilian National Congress had announced plans for a formal investigation and debate on the whole plan.

The Kayapo have not rested on their laurels since Altamira. One major line of effort was the drive to get a large area of the west bank of the Xingu demarcated as a third major Kayapo reserve, linking the two largest existing reserves (the Capoto and Kayapo Indigenous Areas) in a continuous area the size of Britain. In this effort, the Kayapo were supported by Sting and his recently founded Rainforest Foundation, which raised close to two million dollars to support the project. President Sarney of Brazil made several public statements vaguely in favor of the plan, but in January 1990, when Sting came to Brazil with the money from the Rainforest Foundation to present to the government to start the demarcation of the reserve, Sarney noncommittally passed the buck by merely extending the official period for administrative decision on the proposal into the new administration of President-elect Collor without taking action. Collor finally proclaimed the new reserve in 1991; the actual demarcation of the boundary was finished in September 1992. The demarcation of the new reserve bears witness to the political pressure the Kayapo, and the Rainforest Foundation with its international and Brazilian support, were able to bring to bear. Meanwhile, Payakan established a Kayapo Foundation (the "Fundacao Mebengokre") to administer and raise money for the support of a series of programs, including the establishment of an "extractive reserve" within the Kayapo Indigenous Area. This is an area off-limits to all lumbering and mining operations, devoted exclusively to environmentally sustainable forms of forest exploitation such as the gathering of Brazil nuts and other wild forest products.

The Kayapo also made some attempt to follow up on the links of solidarity with other indigenous Amazonian peoples forged at Altamira. In November 1989, several Kayapo leaders and a Kayapo video-cameraman flew (in a Kayapo plane) to Boa Vista in the northern frontier state of Rondonia to investigate an incident in which Yanomamo villagers had been attacked and driven from their land by Brazilian gold miners. The Kayapo denounced the government policies leading to the incident and declared their support for the survivors. The government had banned the area to all non-Indians after the occurrence, attempting to cover up the affair and keep it out of the press. The government was clearly thinking only of local Yanomamo Indians, but the Kayapo, seizing upon the loophole opened up by the wording of the ban and capitalizing on their undeniable identity as "Indians," were able to penetrate the official smokescreen with their fact-finding and support mission.

Wider Implications: The Kayapo Achievement in World Perspective

The Environmentalist Movement

At the level of international environmentalist politics, the Kayapo are now an established presence. In 1990 alone, Kayapo spokesmen have traveled to various European countries, Canada, the U.S.A., and Japan. They were accorded audiences by heads of state (Mitterand of France), cabinet ministers responsible for loans, aid and financial dealings with Brazil, and members of parliaments and national assemblies (Canada, France, Belgium, England, and the

U.S.A.). They have also met with indigenous groups and leaders in North America, notably the Cree of Northern Quebec in 1991 and 1992. All of this notoriety and attention has generated for them a measure of immunity from the cruder forms of abuse and exploitation that have so often been the lot of indigenous peoples in Amazonia and elsewhere.

A mere ten years ago, however, they themselves were the targets of many such abuses, as recounted above. They have succeeded, against fantastic odds, in turning the tables on their would-be exploiters and seizing the political advantage, drawing upon the support of international and urban Brazilian public opinion. The strength of this support owes much to the worldwide wave of concern for the fate of the tropical forests, but the Kayapo would not have been able to capitalize so effectively on the general climate of environmental concern without their shrewd grasp of the possibilities of contemporary news and informational media and their effective presentation of themselves and their cause through them. Other factors in the Kayapo successes have been the effective support of numerous nongovernmental organizations and the impressive capacity of the Kayapo themselves for mass organization and militant but disciplined confrontational tactics, as exemplified by their bold but nonviolent demonstrations in Brasília, Belem, and Altamira.

The success of the Kayapo in furthering their own cause, at the same time, has had an important effect upon the politics of the developed world, and in particular, of the environmentalist movement. The support of environmentalist groups and public opinion has been essential to the Kayapo victories, but it is equally true that the Kayapo have won important victories for the environmentalist movement, and partly as a result have exercised an important influence upon its thinking, strategies, and organizational tactics. Perhaps most importantly, in a few short years they have revolutionized the consciousness of many activists and ordinary persons concerned with the fate of the world's tropical forests, teaching them that indigenous forest-dwelling peoples are not just a passive part of the problem, but an active part of the solution. By their own example, they have demonstrated that native forest peoples, no matter how apparently primitive, remote, or numerically insignificant, can become potent combatants and allies in the struggle to avert ecological disaster. In addition, they have helped bring about working relations of mutual trust and collaboration between members of a number of important organizations, scientific specialists, and politicians, who had previously never considered working together, and in many cases mistrusted one another's politics and policies.

Before the advent of the Kayapo on the international stage, many environmentalists had realized that there could be no solution to the problem of saving the forests that did not include the human inhabitants of the forests. Many who had arrived at this relatively enlightened opinion, however, continued to think of aboriginal forest peoples, and even forest-dwelling members of national societies like the Brazilian rubber-tappers, as historical basket cases, with all the capacity for political action in their own behalf of endangered animal species like the black cayman or the Amazonian giant otter. It has been a humbling, disconcerting, but delightful surprise to many of these same good people suddenly to discover that some of these supposedly hapless victims of progress have assumed a leading role in the struggle environmentalists had thought (perhaps a tad condescendingly) *they* were leading, and that these same native peoples have even succeeded in bringing to the effort a degree of unity and effectiveness that had previously eluded its familiar leadership.

The Rise of Ecological Resistance in the Fourth World

The Kayapo are not a unique case. Their story, in fact, conforms in its essential features to an emerging pattern of ethnic self-assertiveness and ecological militancy on the part of native forest peoples in the Amazon and other parts of the world. It is not new for native peoples (to refer, by this term, to the tribal societies and ethnic minorities comprising the "Fourth World") to attempt to resist the wholesale appropriation of their lands and resources by the peoples and governments of modern states. What is new is the combination of political, economic, environmental, and ideological pressures with revolutionary new media technologies that has enabled native peoples to take their case directly to the peoples and governments of the world, and to find a receptive hearing because of the convergence of their cause with the new levels of popular concern over the environment.

One major manifestation of this worldwide pattern is the organization, over the past twenty years, of many federations of native peoples, for the most part consisting of groups speaking the same or related languages. Over 50 such groups now exist in the Amazon alone. They typically unite around a program of defense of native land and resources, respect for civil and political rights, and the assertion of traditional values and cultural identity. These groups are increasingly in touch with one another, and in some areas intergroup coordinating organizations, such as the recently organized Coordinating Group of the Amazon Basin, COICA, have begun to appear.

The rise of these organizations and the political consciousness they express has been catalyzed by many factors. Among them are the extension of modern transportation and communications networks to many previously inaccessible areas inhabited by tribal peoples; improved medical technology and assistance; greater availability of manufactured tools and goods; the extension of effective national government administrative control over the contiguous national populations; the increase in the strength and effectiveness of nonindigenous, nongovernmental advocacy and support organizations; the increased interest and ability of national and international media to publicize abuse of native lands, rights and peoples; the increase in international economic and political interdependence, which has made many governments more sensitive to the repercussions of bad publicity over indigenous issues; and last but not least, the influence of a steady trickle of anthropological researchers, who have helped both to catalyze native groups' awareness of the value of their traditional cultures in the eyes of the outside world and to inform them of the existence of potential sources of support in that world for their struggles to resist economic, political, and cultural oppression.

These factors have converged in recent years with growing concern in world public opinion for human rights and environmental issues, which have favored the causes of native groups struggling to defend their traditional lands and resource bases. None of these external factors, however, would have been sufficient by themselves to generate the cultural and social resources, or the political organization and will to act, that have been shown by so many native peoples. This is the part of the story that remains least well known to the world at large. It is important that it become known, as an antidote to the hopelessness induced by apocalyptic but often inaccurate news stories of "genocide" and widespread romantic clichés like the inevitable disappearance of primitive peoples in the path of progress. (The two often have more in common than meets the eye.) These myths have had the harmful effect of discouraging support for the struggles of many native peoples with a fighting chance to win. As the Kayapo case shows, such support can make an enormous difference.

That is the rosy side of a picture which is in the main far from rosy. For every indigenous people who have found the courage, leadership, and ability to respond constructively to the threat of despoliation of their ecological bases or the theft of their lands, others have been or are being decimated, dispossessed, or destroyed. In spite of some shining cases of successful resistance to threats to the ambient life-world, other battles have been, or are being, lost. The sheer volume of environmental destruction, and the variety of its forms and causes, make the struggle appear almost hopeless. Nowhere, however, has this been more true than in the Kayapo area of the Amazon. What the Kayapo have managed to do shows that even the most apparently hopeless odds can be faced and overcome.

Review Questions

1. How do the Kayapo Indians of Brazil subsist in their Amazon forest environment?
2. What forces threaten the livelihood and social existence of the Kayapo as a cultural group?
3. How have the Kayapo reacted to defend their forest environment and their existence as a cultural group?
4. Turner argues that the Kayapo have tried to unite and enlist the aid of several kinds of local and world groups in their fight to preserve their forest and lands. What are these groups? Use the case of the encampment at Altimira to illustrate how they could work together.
5. How have the Kayapo affected the world environmentalist movement?

35

Using Anthropology

David W. McCurdy

Some disciplines, such as economics, have an obvious relationship to the nonacademic world. Economic theory, although generated as part of basic research, may often prove useful for understanding the "real" economy. Anthropology, on the other hand, does not seem so applicable. In this article, David McCurdy discusses some of the professional applications of anthropology and argues that there is a basic anthropological perspective that can help anyone cope with the everyday world. He uses the case of a company manager to illustrate this point, asserting that ethnographic "qualitative" research is an important tool for use in the nonacademic world.

Recently, a student, whom I had not seen for fifteen years, stopped by my office. He had returned for his college reunion and thought it would be interesting to catch up on news about his (and my) major depart-

---

This article was adapted from "The Shrink-Wrap Solution: Anthropology and Business," by David W. McCurdy and Donna F. Carlson in *Conformity and Conflict: Readings in Cultural Anthropology,* 5th ed. (Boston: Little, Brown and Company, 1983). It was written especially for this volume. Copyright © by David W. McCurdy, 1990.

ment, anthropology. The conversation, however, soon shifted from college events to his own life. Following graduation and a stint in the Peace Corps, he noted, he had begun to study for his license as a ship's engineer. He had attended the Maritime Academy, and worked for years on freighters. He was finally granted his license, he continued, and currently held the engineer's position on a container ship that made regular trips between Seattle and Alaska. He soon would be promoted to chief engineer and be at the top of his profession.

As he talked, he made an observation about anthropology that may seem surprising. His background in the discipline, he said, had helped him significantly in his work. He found it useful as he went about his daily tasks, maintaining his ship's complex engines and machinery, his relationships with the crew, and his contacts with land-based management.

And his is not an unusual case. Over the years, several anthropology graduates have made the same observation. One, for example, is a community organizer who feels that the cross-cultural perspective he learned in anthropology helps him mediate disputes and facilitate decision making in a multiethnic neighborhood. Another, who works as an advertising account executive, claims that anthropology helps her discover what products mean to customers. This, in turn, permits her to design more effective ad campaigns. A third says she finds anthropology an invaluable tool as she arranges interviews and writes copy. She is a producer for a metropolitan television news program. I have heard the same opinion expressed by many others, including the executive editor of a magazine for home weavers, the founder of a fencing school, a housewife, a physician, several lawyers, the kitchen manager for a catering firm, and a high school teacher.

The idea that anthropology can be useful is also supported by the experience of many new Ph.D.'s. A recent survey has shown, for the first time, that more new doctorates in anthropology find employment in professional settings than in college teaching or scholarly research, and the list of nonacademic work settings revealed by the survey is remarkably broad. There is a biological anthropologist, for example, who conducts research on nutrition for a company that manufactures infant formula. A cultural anthropologist works for a major car manufacturer, researching such questions as how employees adapt to working overseas, and how they relate to conditions on domestic production lines. Others formulate government policy, plan patient care in hospitals, design overseas development projects, run famine relief programs, consult on tropical forest management, and advise on product development, advertising campaigns, and marketing strategy for corporations.

This new-found application of cultural anthropology comes as a surprise to many Americans. Unlike political science, for example, which has a name that logically connects it with practical political and legal professions, there is nothing in the term *anthropology* that tells most Americans how it might be useful.

The research subject of anthropology also makes it more difficult to comprehend. Political scientists investigate political processes, structures, and motivations. Economists look at the production and exchange of goods and services. Psychologists study differences and similarities among individuals. The research of cultural anthropologists, on the other hand, is more difficult to characterize. Instead of a focus on particular human institutions, such as politics, law, and economics, anthropologists are interested in cross-cultural differences and similarities among the world's many groups.

This interest produces a broad view of human behavior that gives anthropology its special cross-cultural flavor. It also produces a unique research strategy, called *ethnography,* that tends to be qualitative rather than quantitative. Whereas other social sciences moved toward *quantitative methods* of research designed to test theory by using survey questionnaires and structured, repetitive observations, most anthropologists conduct *qualitative research* designed to elicit the cultural knowledge of the people they seek to understand. To do this, anthropologists often live and work with their subjects, called *informants* within the discipline. The result is a highly detailed ethnographic description of the categories and rules people consult when they behave, and the meanings that things and actions have for them.

It is this ethnographic approach, or cultural perspective, that I think makes anthropology useful in such a broad range of everyday settings. I particularly find important the special anthropological understanding of the culture concept, ethnographic field methods, and social analysis. To illustrate these assertions, let us take a single case in detail, that of a manager working for a large corporation who consciously used the ethnographic approach to solve a persistent company problem.

The Problem

The manager, whom we will name Susan Stanton, works for a large multinational corporation called UTC (not the company's real name). UTC is divided into a number of parts, including divisions, subdivisions, departments, and other units designed to facilitate its highly varied business enterprises. The company is well diversified, engaging in research, manufacturing, and customer services. In addition to serving a wide cross-section of public and private customers, it also works on a variety of government contracts for both military and nonmilitary agencies.

One of its divisions is educational. UTC has established a large number of customer outlets in cities throughout the United States, forming what it calls its "customer outlet network." They are staffed by educational personnel who are trained to offer a variety of special courses and enrichment programs. These courses and programs are marketed mainly to other businesses or to individuals who desire special training or practical information. For example, a small company might have UTC provide its employees with computer training, including instruction on hardware, programming, computer languages, and computer program applications. Another company might ask for instruction on effective management or accounting procedures. The outlets' courses for individuals include such topics as how to get a job, writing a resume, or enlarging your own business.

To organize and manage its customer outlet network, UTC has created a special division. The division office is located at the corporate headquarters and is responsible for developing new courses, improving old ones, training customer outlet personnel, and marketing customer outlet courses, or "products" as they are called inside the company. The division also has departments that develop, produce, and distribute the special learning materials used in customer outlet courses. These include books, pamphlets, video and audio tapes and cassettes, slides, overlays, and films. These materials are stored in a warehouse and are shipped, as they are ordered, to customer outlets around the country.

It is with this division that Susan Stanton first worked as a manager. She had started her career with the company in a small section of the division that designed various program materials. She had worked her way into management, holding a series of increasingly important positions. She was then asked to take over the management of a part of the division that had the manufacture, storage, and shipment of learning materials as one of its responsibilities.

But there was a catch. She was given this new management position with instructions to solve a persistent, although vaguely defined, problem. "Improve the service," they had told her, and "get control of the warehouse inventory." In this case, "service" meant the process of filling orders sent in by customer outlets for various materials stored in the warehouse. The admonition to improve the service seemed to indicate that service was poor, but all she was told about the situation was that customer outlet personnel complained about the service; she did not know exactly why or what "poor" meant.

In addition, inventory was "out of control." Later she was to discover the extent of the difficulty.

> We had a problem with inventory. The computer would say we had two hundred of some kind of book in stock, yet it was back ordered because there was nothing on the shelf. We were supposed to have the book but physically there was nothing there. I'm going, "Uh, we have a small problem. The computer never lies, like your bank statement, so why don't we have the books?"

If inventory was difficult to manage, so were the warehouse employees. They were described by another manager as "a bunch of knuckle draggers. All they care about is getting their money. They are lazy and don't last long at the job." Strangely, the company did not view the actions of the warehouse workers as a major problem. Only later did Susan Stanton tie in poor morale in the warehouse with the other problems she had been given to solve.

Management by Defense

Although Stanton would take the ethnographic approach to management problems, that was not what many other managers did. They took a defensive stance, a position opposite to the discovery procedures of ethnography. Their major concern—like that of many people in positions of leadership and responsibility—was to protect their authority and their ability to manage and to get things done. Indeed, Stanton also shared this need. But their solution to maintaining their position was different from hers. For them, claiming ignorance and asking questions—the hallmark of the ethnographic approach—is a sign of weakness. Instead of discovering what is going on when they take on a new management assignment, they often impose new work rules and procedures. Employees learn to fear the arrival of new managers because their appearance usually means a host of new, unrealistic demands. They respond by hiding what they actually do, withholding information that would be useful to the manager. Usually, everyone's performance suffers.

Poor performance leads to elaborate excuses as managers attempt to blame the troubles on others. Stanton described this tendency.

> When I came into the new job, this other manager said, "Guess what? You have got a warehouse. You are now the proud owner of a forklift and a bunch of knuckle draggers." And I thought, management's perception of those people is very low. They are treating them as dispensable, that you can't do anything with them. They say the workers don't have any career motives. They don't care if they do a good job. You have to force them to do anything. You can't motivate them. It's only a warehouse, other managers were saying. You can't really do that much about the problems there so why don't you just sort of try to keep it under control.

Other managers diminished the importance of the problem itself. It was not "poor service" that was the trouble. The warehouse was doing the best it could with what it had. It was just that the customers—the staff at the customer outlets—were complainers. As Susan Stanton noted:

> The people providing the service thought that outlet staff were complainers. They said, "Staff complain about everything. But it can't be that way. We have checked it all out and it isn't that bad."

Making excuses and blaming others lead to low morale and a depressed self-image. Problems essentially are pushed aside in favor of a "let's just get by" philosophy.

Ethnographic Management

By contrast, managers take the offensive when they use ethnographic techniques. That is what Stanton did when she assumed her new managerial assignment over the learning materials manufacturing and distribution system. To understand what the ethnographic approach means, however, we must first look briefly at what anthropologists do when they conduct ethnographic field research. Our discussion necessarily involves a look at the concepts of culture and microculture as well as ethnography. For as we will shortly point out, companies have cultures of their own, a point that has recently received national attention; but more important for the problem we are describing here, companies are normally divided into subgroups, each with its own microculture. It is these cultures and microcultures that anthropologically trained managers can study ethnographically, just as fieldworkers might investigate the culture of a !Kung band living in the Kalahari Desert of West Africa or the Gypsies living in San Francisco.

Ethnography refers to the process of discovering and describing culture, so it is important to discuss this general and often elusive concept. There are numerous definitions of culture, each stressing particular sets of attributes. The definition we employ here is especially appropriate for ethnographic fieldwork. We may define culture as the acquired knowledge that people use to generate behavior and interpret experience. In growing up, one learns a system of cultural knowledge appropriate to the group. For example, an American child learns to chew with a closed mouth because that is the cultural rule. The child's parents interpret open-mouthed chewing as an infraction and tell the child to chew "properly." A person uses such cultural knowledge throughout life to guide actions and to give meaning to surroundings.

Because culture is learned, and because people can easily generate new cultural knowledge as they adapt to other people and things, human behavior and perceptions can vary dramatically from one group to another. In India, for example, children learn to chew "properly" with their mouths open. Their cultural worlds are quite different from the ones found in the United States.

Cultures are associated with groups of people. Traditionally, anthropologists associated culture with relatively distinctive ethnic groups. Culture referred to the whole life-way of a society and particular cultures could be named. Anthropologists talked of German culture, Ibo culture, and Bhil culture. Culture was everything that was distinctive about the group.

Culture is still applied in this manner today, but with the advent of complex societies and a growing interest among anthropologists in understanding them, the culture concept has also been used in a more limited way. Complex societies such as our own are composed of thousands of groups. Members of these groups usually share the national culture, including a language and a huge inventory of knowledge for doing things, but the groups themselves have specific cultures of their own. For example, if you were to walk into the regional office of a stock brokerage firm, you would hear the people there talking an apparently foreign language. You might stand in the "bull pen," listen to brokers make "cold calls," "sell short," "negotiate a waffle," or get ready to go to a "dog and pony show." The fact that events such as this feel strange when you first encounter them is strong evidence to support the notion that you don't yet know the culture that organizes them. We call such specialized groups *microcultures.*

We are surrounded by microcultures, participating in a few, encountering many others. Our family has a microculture. So may our neighborhood, our college, and even our dormitory floor. The waitress who serves us lunch at the corner restaurant shares a culture with her coworkers. So do bank tellers at our local savings and loan. Kin, occupational groups, and recreational associations each tend to display special microcultures. Such cultures can be, and now often are, studied by anthropologists interested in understanding life in complex American society.

The concept of microculture is essential to Susan Stanton as she begins to attack management problems at UTC because she assumes that conflict between different microcultural groups is most likely at the bottom of the difficulty. One microculture she could focus on is UTC company culture. She knows, for example, that there are a variety of rules and expectations—written and unwritten—for how things should be done at the company. She must dress in her "corporates," for example, consisting of a neutral-colored suit, bow tie, stockings, and conservative shoes. UTC also espouses values about the way employees should be treated, how people are supposed to feel about company products, and a variety of other things that set that particular organization apart from other businesses.

But the specific problems that afflicted the departments under Stanton's jurisdiction had little to do with UTC's corporate culture. They seemed rather to be the result of misunderstanding and misconnection between two units, the warehouse and the customer outlets. Each had its own microculture. Each could be investigated to discover any information that might lead to a solution of the problems she had been given.

Such investigation would depend on the extent of Stanton's ethnographic training. As an undergraduate in college, she had learned how to conduct ethnographic interviews, observe behavior, and analyze and interpret data. She was not a professional anthropologist, but she felt she was a good enough ethnographer to discover some relevant aspects of microcultures at UTC.

Ethnography is the process of discovering and describing a culture. For example, an anthropologist who travels to India to conduct a study of village culture will use ethnographic techniques. The anthropologist will move into a community, occupy a house, watch people's daily routines, attend rituals, and spend hours interviewing informants. The goal is to discover a detailed picture of what is going on by seeing village culture through the eyes of informants. The anthropologist wants the insider's perspective. Villagers become teachers, patiently explaining different aspects of their culture, praising the anthropologist for acting correctly and appearing to understand, laughing when the anthropologist makes mistakes or seems confused. When the anthropologist knows what to do and can explain in local terms what is going on or what is likely to happen, real progress has been made. The clearest evidence of such progress is when informants say, "You are almost human now," or "You are beginning to talk just like us."

The greatest enemy of good ethnography is the preconceived notion. Anthropologists do not conduct ethnographic research by telling informants what they are like based on earlier views of them. They teach the anthropologist how to see their world: the anthropologist does not tell them what their world should really be like. All too often in business, a new manager will take over a department and begin to impose changes on its personnel to fit a preconceived perception of them. The fact that the manager's efforts are likely to fail makes sense in light of this ignorance. The manager doesn't know the microculture. Nor have they been asked about it.

But can a corporate manager really do ethnography? After all, managers have positions of authority to maintain, as we noted earlier. It is all right for professional anthropologists to enter the field and act ignorant; they don't have a position to maintain and they don't have to continue to live with their informants. The key to the problem appears to be the "grace period." Most managers are given one by their employees when they are new on the job. A new manager cannot be expected to know everything. It is permissible to ask basic questions. The grace period may last only a month or two, but it is usually long enough to find out valuable information.

This is the opportunity that Susan Stanton saw as she assumed direction of the warehouse distribution system. As she described it:

> I could use the first month, actually the first six weeks, to find out what was going on, to act dumb and find out what people actually did and why. I talked to end customers. I talked to salespeople, people who were trying to sell things to help customer outlets with their needs. I talked to coordinators at headquarters staff who were trying to help all these customer outlets do their jobs and listened to what kinds of complaints they had heard. I talked to the customer outlet people and the guys in the warehouse. I had this six-week grace period where I could go in and say, "I don't know anything about this. If you were in my position, what would you do, or what would make the biggest difference, and why would it make a difference?" You want to find out what the world they are operating in is like. What do they value. And people were excited because I was asking and listening and, by God, intending to do something about it instead of just disappearing again.

As we shall see shortly, Stanton's approach to the problem worked. But it also resulted in an unexpected bonus. Her ethnographic approach symbolized unexpected interest and concern to her employees. That, combined with realistic management, gave her a position of respect and authority. Their feelings for her were expressed by one warehouse worker when he said:

> When she [Susan] was going to be transferred to another job, we gave her a party. We took her to this country-and-western place and we all got to dance with the boss. We told her that she was the first manager who ever tried to understand what it was like to work in the warehouse. We thought she would come in like the other managers and make a lot of changes that didn't make sense. But she didn't. She made it work better for us.

Problems and Causes

An immediate benefit of her ethnographic inquiry was a much clearer view of what poor service meant to customer outlet personnel. Stanton discovered that learning materials, such as books and cassettes, took too long to arrive after they were ordered. Worse, material did not arrive in the correct quantities. Sometimes there would be too many items, but more often there were too few, a particularly galling discrepancy since customer outlets were charged for what they ordered, not what they received. Books also arrived in poor condition, their covers ripped or scratched, edges frayed, and ends gouged and dented. This, too, bothered customer outlet staff because they were often visited by potential customers who were not impressed by the poor condition of their supplies. Shortages and scruffy books did nothing to retain regular customers either.

The causes of these problems and the difficulties with warehouse inventory also emerged from ethnographic inquiry. Stanton discovered, for example, that most customer outlets operated in large cities, where often they were housed in tall buildings. Materials shipped to their office address often ended up sitting in ground-level lobbies, because few of the buildings had receiving docks or facilities. Books and other items also arrived in large boxes, weighing up to a hundred pounds. Outlet staff, most of whom were women, had to go down to the lobby, open those boxes that were too heavy for them to carry, and haul armloads of supplies up the elevator to the office. Not only was this time-consuming, but customer outlet staff felt it was beneath their dignity to do such work. They were educated specialists, after all.

The poor condition of the books was also readily explained. By packing items loosely in such large boxes, warehouse workers ensured trouble in transit. Books rattled around with ease, smashing into each other and the side of the box. The result was torn covers and frayed edges. Clearly no one had designed the packing and shipping process with customer outlet staff in mind.

The process, of course, originated in the central warehouse, and here as well, ethnographic data yielded interesting information about the causes of the problem. Stanton learned, for example, how materials were stored in loose stacks on the warehouse shelves. When orders arrived at the warehouse, usually through the mail, they were placed in a pile and filled in turn (although there were times when special preference was given to some customer outlets). A warehouse employee filled an order by first checking it against the stock recorded by the computer, then going to the appropriate shelves and picking the items by hand. Items were packed in the large boxes and addressed to customer outlets. With the order complete, the employee was supposed to enter the number of items picked and shipped in the computer so that inventory would be up to date.

But, Stanton discovered, workers in the warehouse were under pressure to work quickly. They often fell behind because materials the computer said were in stock were not there, and because picking by hand took so long. Their solution to the problem of speed resulted in a procedure that even further confused company records.

> Most of the people in the warehouse didn't try to count well. People were looking at the books on the shelves and were going, "Eh, that looks like the right number. You want ten? Gee, that looks like about ten." Most of the time the numbers they shipped were wrong.

The causes of inaccurate amounts in shipping were thus revealed. Later, Stanton discovered that books also disappeared in customer outlet building lobbies. While staff members carried some of the materials upstairs, people passing by the open boxes helped themselves.

Other problems with inventory also became clear. UTC employees, who sometimes walked through the warehouse, would often pick up interesting materials from the loosely stacked shelves. More important, rushed workers often neglected to update records in the computer.

The Shrink-Wrap Solution

The detailed discovery of the nature and causes of service and inventory problems suggested a relatively painless solution to Stanton. If she had taken a defensive management position and failed to learn the insider's point of view, she might have resorted to more usual remedies that were impractical and unworkable. Worker retraining is a common answer to corporate difficulties, but it is difficult to accomplish and often fails. Pay incentives, punishments, and motivation enhancements such as prizes and quotas are also frequently tried. But they tend not to work because they don't address fundamental causes.

Shrink-wrapping books and other materials did. Shrink-wrapping is a packaging device that emerged a few years ago. Clear plastic sheeting is placed around items to be packaged, then through a rapid heating and cooling process, shrunk into a tight covering. The plastic molds itself like a tight skin around the things it contains, preventing any internal movement or external contamination. Stanton described her decision.

> I decided to have the books shrink-wrapped. For a few cents more, before the books ever arrived in the warehouse, I had them shrink-wrapped in quantities of five and ten. I made it part of the contract with the people who produced the books for us.

On the first day that shrink-wrapped books arrived at the warehouse, Stanton discovered that they were immediately unwrapped by workers who thought a new impediment had been placed in their way. But the positive effect of shrink-wrapping soon became apparent. For example, most customer outlets ordered books in units of fives and tens. Warehouse personnel could now easily count out orders in fives and tens, instead of having to count each book or estimate numbers in piles. Suddenly, orders filled at the warehouse contained the correct number of items.

Employees were also able to work more quickly, since they no longer had to count each book. Orders were filled faster, the customer outlet staff was pleased, and warehouse employees no longer felt the pressure of time so intensely. Shrink-wrapped materials also traveled more securely. Books, protected by their plastic covering, arrived in good condition, again delighting the personnel at customer outlets.

Stanton also changed the way materials were shipped, based on what she had learned from talking to employees. She limited the maximum size of shipments to twenty-five pounds by using smaller boxes. She also had packages marked "inside delivery" so that deliverymen would carry the materials directly to the customer outlet offices. If they failed to do so, boxes were light enough to carry upstairs. No longer would items be lost in skyscraper lobbies.

Inventory control became more effective. Because they could package and ship materials more quickly, the workers in the warehouse had enough time to enter the size and nature of shipments in the computer. Other UTC employees no longer walked off with books from the warehouse, because the shrink-wrapped bundles were larger and more conspicuous, and because taking five or ten books is more like stealing than "borrowing" one.

Finally, the improved service dramatically changed morale in the division. Customer outlet staff members, with their new and improved service, felt that finally someone had cared about them. They were more positive and they let people at corporate headquarters know about their feelings. "What's happening down there?" they asked. "The guys in the warehouse must be taking vitamins."

Morale soared in the warehouse. For the first time, other people liked the service workers there provided. Turnover decreased as pride in their work rose. They began to care more about the job, working faster with greater care. Managers who had previously given up on the "knuckle draggers" now asked openly about what had got into them.

Stanton believes the ethnographic approach is the key. She has managers who work for her read anthropology, especially books on ethnography, and she insists that they "find out what is going on."

Conclusion

Anthropology is, before all, an academic discipline with a strong emphasis on scholarship and basic research. But, as we have also seen, anthropology is a discipline that contains several intellectual tools—the concept of culture, the ethnographic approach to fieldwork, a cross-cultural perspective, a holistic view of human behavior—that make it useful in a broad range of nonacademic settings. In particular, it is the ability to do qualitative research that makes anthropologists successful in the professional world.

A few years ago an anthropologist consultant was asked by a utility company to answer a puzzling question: Why were its suburban customers, whose questionnaire responses indicated an attempt at conservation, failing to reduce their consumption of natural gas? To answer the question, the anthropologist conducted ethnographic interviews with members of several families, listening as they told him about how warm they liked their houses and how they set the heat throughout the day. He also received permission to install several video cameras aimed at thermostats in private houses. When the results were in, the answer to the question was deceptively simple: Fathers fill out questionnaires and turn down thermostats; wives, children, and cleaning workers, all of whom, in this case, spent time in the houses when fathers were absent, turn them up. Conservation, the anthropologist concluded, would have to involve family decisions, not just admonitions to save gas. The key to this anthropologist's success, and indeed to the application of cultural anthropology by those acquainted with it, is the ethnographic approach. For it is people with experience in the discipline who have the special background needed to, in the words of Susan Stanton, "find out what is going on."

Review Questions

1. What kinds of jobs do professional anthropologists do?
2. What is special about anthropology that makes fundamental knowledge of it valuable to some jobs?
3. What is meant by *qualitative research?* Why is such research valuable to business and government?
4. What difficulties did the company manager described in this article face? What solutions did she invent to deal with them? How did her knowledge of anthropology help her with this problem?
5. Why is ethnography useful in everyday life? Can you think of situations in which you could use ethnographic research?

36

The Medical Anthropologist as Consultant

Eric J. Bailey

In the last article, we saw how a general background in cultural anthropology can aid in business management. Recently, many graduate anthropology departments have introduced special programs designed to train applied anthropologists in specific areas such as business consulting and medical anthropology. It is experience based on this latter training that is the subject of Eric Bailey's article. Trained as a medical anthropologist, he relates how his background in medical anthropology enabled him to design health fairs for African American communities and to eventually start his own consulting business.

Medical anthropology is often poorly understood by those who are not a part of the discipline. When working with other health care professionals, medical anthropologists are commonly asked to explain what

From "Medical Anthropologist as Health Department Consultant," *Practicing Anthropology*, vol. 16, no. 1, 1994, pp. 13–15. Copyright © by the Society for Applied Anthropology, 1994. Reprinted by permission of the Society for Applied Anthropology.

their field is, what they do, and how they can assist clinicians and public health officials in appropriating better health care for their patients/clients. Many assume that medical anthropologists are always on excavations like archaeologists or that we are very similar to biologists. To counteract such misconceptions and misinterpretation, we need to develop practical applications of our work so that others can benefit from our expertise, and we need to market our skills better. In sum, practical strategies are needed in *applied* medical anthropology in order to justify our existence in economic and sociopolitical terms with various health organizations.

Trained as an applied medical anthropologist at Wayne State University, I felt that my academic training was transferable to the real world. I thought that I could use my skills, if necessary, to get a job outside of academia—for example, as a consultant or program director of a major health care project. Although at the time my role was perceived more as student than consultant, I had had the chance to collaborate with a local health care organization for my dissertation research.

The United Health Care Organization had been co-sponsoring annual health fairs throughout metropolitan Detroit for the previous twenty years with a great deal of success. Interestingly, however, the organization had had little success in African American communities. In fact, African Americans participating in the annual health fairs had declined from 20 percent in 1976 to a mere 6 percent in 1984. As an African American resident in Detroit and trained as an applied medical anthropologist, I felt I could be of help in this "practical" and real life health care situation. In order to show the organization's administrators my commitment to this project, however, I had to "sell" or "market" my idea that I could improve the Annual Free Health Fair.

I addressed one major question: What had United Health Organization been doing wrong in the African American communities? To provide an answer and practical suggestions, my strategy consisted of the following:

1. To conduct cultural-historical background research on Detroit's African American population;
2. To engage in informal observation in the local communities where the screening sites existed;
3. To carry out informal interviewing of key informants in the African American communities; and
4. To implement formal quantitative and qualitative data collection.

My cultural-historical research revealed that many institutions which had provided health care for African Americans through the 1950s were in decline by the 1970s. Those institutions currently accessible to African Americans tended to be large teaching hospitals with a high turnover of medical staff. Many African Americans, especially the elderly accustomed to the medical institutions of the fifties, reported feeling a lack of trust and rapport in the facilities available to them in the eighties. Consequently, they often avoided seeking medical care until a health problem had grown serious.

When I went into communities in which United Health Care Organization had been holding annual health fairs and asked people why they had not frequented them, they often told me they were not aware of the fairs. Those who were aware of them often saw the fairs as an occasion for outside organizations to do something for their own benefit, and not really for the benefit of the local population. Key informants also indicated that health screening staff failed to work "with" the local residents; it only worked "for" them. This difference has important psychological implications. When African Americans perceive a health service as strictly a "hand-out," they believe that the service is of poor quality and demeaning to the psyche of the individual. This perception caused many not to participate in the local health screenings.

Local residents and key informants also observed that the staff at the health fairs were not of the same ethnic background as the local population, their promotion materials were not culturally sensitive, and their advice was not in tune with the realities of life in these communities. The health screenings provided only a tentative diagnosis; those with possible health problems were told, "See your physician," ignoring the fact that most had no physician and no regular access to the health care system. Health fair organizers also failed to recognize that people who have multiple economic and social problems may not want to know about as yet imperceptible health problems. To attract more participants, some health fairs had been held in shopping malls. People found the setting incongruous, however, and told me, "I didn't come to the mall to find out that something else is wrong with me!"

At the conclusion of my research, I recommended the following:

1. utilize more local community leaders;
2. locate influential community leaders to endorse the program;
3. incorporate other community services into the health fairs;
4. include work site screenings;
5. create incentives with local businesses; and
6. advertise and educate through innovative means.

To what degree United Health Organization actually used my recommendations, I cannot state, since I left the area at the end of the internship. Nonetheless, this experience provided me with the incentive to develop my skills as a consultant to various public health care organizations.

The opportunity to use my skills as a consultant or program director did not present itself at graduation, so I took an assistant professor's position at the University of Houston. I taught the normal course load for a junior faculty member and participated in a number of academic activities. Of course, being a junior faculty member and an African American at a major university meant that much of my professional time centered around university service activities and functions. As each day passed, my identity as an academic professional became more solidified.

Yet my desire to do applied work and to work with "real" people and "real" issues continued. In order to do applied anthropology at a non-applied anthropology department, I sought out opportunities to volunteer with local health and social organizations in the Houston area. Fortunately, in 1989 I became associated with the Houston Health Department. I first served on an advisory board at the Riverside Health Center to assist with the development of a health fair. Once the planning phase started, I was elected chairman of the 1989 Riverside Health Fair.

My job was to organize, coordinate, and direct all the operations of the health fair. The prospect of organizing this event while also maintaining my academic duties at the University of Houston was a bit intimidating. Nonetheless, I accepted this job because I knew that it would be a very good learning experience for me and that a successful health fair would have a direct impact on the health status of the local African American community.

I felt that it was critical to conduct some basic field work and background research on the community surrounding Riverside Health Center. Cultural-historical documents and health department statistics led to identification of the following socioeconomic factors in the Riverside area (Houston's Third Ward):

1. Riverside's population totaled nearly 70,000. Blacks accounted for 77.5 percent of the population, whites for 12.9 percent, Hispanics for 7.5 percent, and others for 2.1 percent.
2. The average age of the population as a whole and of blacks fell within the 25–29 year age group. The average age of Hispanics and others was within 20–24 years, and whites had an average age within the 30–34 year age group.
3. Socioeconomic indicators listed 24 percent of families as under the poverty level and 36 percent of households as headed by single females. The median household income for 1989 was $15,666.

To find out more about Riverside's African American community, I established a working dialogue and association with three key informants in this area: Shannon Jones (Riverside Medical Director), Dr. Brobbey (Riverside Medical Director), and Mrs. Helen Hall Kinard (President of the Advisory Board for the Riverside Health Center). These three informants provided substantive qualitative data about Houston Health Department's program procedures and Riverside residents' needs.

As in Detroit, by 1989 the African American health care system that developed in Houston during the period of segregation had all but disappeared. Of the four African American hospitals still operating in the city in 1970, only two, Riverside General Hospital and Charles Drew Hospital, were still open. In an effort to improve the health care available to African Americans and other ethnic populations, the city of Houston's Department of Health and Human Services had expanded their operation of health clinics.

To get to know more of the personal and health care dynamics of local community residents, I spent many hours at the Riverside health clinic. The information I gathered from those who worked at the clinic and from those who lived in the neighborhood suggested that for the average household the priority placed on maintaining "health" had to be adjusted in light of economic and social needs. I concluded that since unemployment and public safety were major issues affecting most community residents, residents needed information on job opportunities and public safety strategies for the young and elderly as much as they needed traditional health messages.

The advisory board at the Riverside Health Center consisted of local residents, Houston Health Department officials, and local business leaders. Charged with overseeing the operations of the clinic and developing community programs, the board met once a month. Initially, board members thought that a health fair should offer strictly medical services to local residents. Cholesterol screening, blood pressure screening, vision screening, and height/weight measurements were the "norm" for a public health fair. After much debate, the health fair was finally expanded to include a wider array of health care and social services and was designed as a "community festival." As chairman and acting consultant, I proposed and strongly supported this modification because my background research had shown that the previous model was outdated and not oriented to the needs of the local African American community.

In cooperation with Houston's Department of Health and Human Services and eighteen local agencies, basic tests and preventative health services offered at the health fair were height and weight screening, dental screening, pulmonary function screening, prenatal and child care counseling, law enforcement child identification screening, social service counseling, AIDS counseling, and an AIDS educational play. In addition, this day-long, free community event provided food and prizes to all participants. An initial projection was for seventy participants. To our surprise, well over two hundred local residents of all age groups participated. Approximately 90 percent of the participants were African American, 5 percent Anglo American and 5 percent Hispanic. The proportion of African American participants was even higher than their proportion in the local population.

Advisory board members, staff personnel from the Riverside clinic, local businesses, and community volunteers all contributed to the success of this modified health fair. Yet, ultimately its success depended upon the application of anthropological concepts. Developing a more "culturally oriented" and "culturally sensitive" approach in reaching out to and working with the African American community was responsible for the high rate of participation. This approach consisted of three major steps:

1. Increasing the number of African American health care and social service personnel who could participate in the fair;
2. Promoting the event through African American media; and
3. Educating African Americans in a style and pattern which they could understand and to which they are accustomed.

All agencies were encouraged strongly to have a diversified staff work their booth. This strategy helped many of the participants feel more comfortable asking questions and helped them develop an immediate rapport with the agency's workers. The advisory board also enlisted the services of the local African American radio station not only to announce the health fair on the air but also to bring their special mobile van to play music. In addition, we advertised the health fair in the local, well-established African American newspaper.

The AIDS educational play provided an example of how to educate and to discuss serious health issues with an entertaining and culturally sensitive approach. The playwright was an African American male, and the performers were young adults. Thus, the play had dialogue and issues directly reflecting young African American life-styles.

I also used anthropological concepts and data in working with the Riverside Advisory Board. The ethnographic data and the cultural-historical information helped me show the board that other health, social, and cultural issues are of major importance to the design of a health fair. If health fairs are to be successful in this community, "health" must be defined broadly, and the fair must include local cultural institutions and agencies and local leaders.

From these experiences using anthropology in applied settings, I realized that my skills as a health care consultant are definitely needed, and I have continued to work in the public health area. My association with Detroit's United Health Organization, with Houston's Riverside Health Center, and later with Indiana State Health Department has been very productive, rewarding, and eye-opening. Trained as an applied medical anthropologist, I realized that if one wants to become a consultant, one must learn to modify and adapt skills to the organizational environment in which one works. This does not mean that the applied medical anthropologist disregards his/her approach entirely. What it does mean is that applied medical anthropologists need to appreciate, to understand, and to work with different sociocultural, medical, and public health personnel in order to gradually introduce change from "within" as oppose to demanding change from the "outside." By doing this, more applied medical anthropologists and more public health departments (city and state) can benefit from collaboration.

Review Questions

1. What was Bailey's first research project like? Why did he feel that health fairs were not working for African Americans in Detroit, and how did he find out what was going on?
2. What were Bailey's recommendations for improving the success of Detroit health fairs?
3. When Bailey acted as a consultant to the Houston Health Department, what field methods did he use to find out about the black community and its members' lack of attendance at previous health fairs?
4. What were his recommendations about improving health fair attendance? Did they work?
5. What is especially anthropological about the style of research employed by Bailey in his consulting work?

Glossary

Acculturation The process that takes place when groups of individuals having different cultures come into first-hand contact, which results in change to the cultural patterns of both groups.

Action Anthropology Any use of anthropological knowledge for planned change by the members of a local cultural group.

Adjustment Anthropology Any use of anthropological knowledge that makes social interaction between persons who operate with different cultural codes more predictable.

Administrative Anthropology The use of anthropological knowledge for planned change by those who are external to a local cultural group.

Advocate Anthropology Any use of anthropological knowledge by the anthropologist to increase the power of self-determination for a particular cultural group.

Affinity A fundamental principle of relationship linking kin through marriage.

Agriculture A subsistence strategy involving intensive farming of permanent fields through the use of such means as the plow, irrigation, and fertilizer.

Allocation of Resources The knowledge people use to assign rights to the ownership and use of resources.

Applied Anthropology Any use of anthropological knowledge to influence social interaction, to maintain or change social institutions, or to direct the course of cultural change.

Bilateral (Cognatic) Descent A rule of descent relating someone to a group of consanguine kin through both males and females.

Caste A form of stratification defined by unequal access to economic resources and prestige, which is acquired at birth and does not permit individuals to alter their rank.

Clan A kinship group normally comprising several lineages; its members are related by a unilineal descent rule, but it is too large to enable members to trace actual biological links to all other members.

Class A system of stratification defined by unequal access to economic resources and prestige, but permitting individuals to alter their rank.

Consanguinity The principle of relationship linking individuals by shared ancestry (blood).

Contest A method of settling disputes requiring disputants to engage in some kind of mutual challenge such as singing (as among the Inuit).

Cosmology A set of beliefs that defines the nature of the universe or cosmos.

Court A formal legal institution in which at least one individual has authority to judge and is backed up by a coercive system to enforce decisions.

Cultural Contact The situation that occurs when two societies with different cultures somehow come in contact with each other.

Cultural Ecology The study of the way people use their culture to adapt to particular environments, the effects they have on their natural surrounding, and the impact of the environment on the shape of culture, including its long-term evolution.

Cultural Environment The categories and rules people use to classify and explain their physical environment.

Culture The knowledge that is learned, shared, and used by the people to interpret experience and generate behavior.

Culture Shock A form of anxiety that results from an inability to predict the behavior of others or act appropriately in cross-cultural situations.

Descent A rule of relationship that ties people together on the basis of reputed common ancestry.

Descent Groups Groups based on a rule of descent.

Detached Observation An approach to scientific inquiry stressing emotional detachment and the construction of categories by the observer in order to classify what is observed.

Diffusion The passage of a cultural category, culturally defined behavior, or culturally produced artifact from one society to another through borrowing.

Distribution The strategies for apportioning goods and services among the members of a group.

Divination The use of supernatural force to provide answers to questions.

Division of Labor The rules that govern the assignment of jobs to people.

Ecology The study of the way organisms interact with each other within an environment.

Economic System The provision of goods and services to meet biological and social wants.

Egalitarian Societies Societies that, with the exception of ranked differences between men and women and adults and children, provide all people an equal chance at economic resources and prestige. Most hunter-gatherer societies are egalitarian by this definition.

Endogamy Marriage within a designated social unit.

Ethnocentrism A mixture of belief and feeling that one's own way of life is desirable and actually superior to others'.

Ethnography The task of discovering and describing a particular culture.

Exogamy Marriage outside any designated group.

Explicit Culture The culture that people can talk about and of which they are aware. Opposite of tacit culture.

Extended Family A family that includes two or more married couples.

Extralegal Dispute A dispute that remains outside the process of law and develops into repeated acts of violence between groups, such as feuds and wars.

Family A residential group composed of at least one married couple and their children.

Functional Integration The various aspects of a society, such as its culturally defined behaviors, beliefs, and artifacts, that affect and support each other to create an organized system.

Go-Between An individual who arranges agreements and mediates disputes.

Grammar The categories and rules for combining vocal symbols.

Horticulture A kind of subsistence strategy involving semi-intensive, usually shifting, agricultural practices. Slash-and-burn farming is a common example of horticulture.

Hunting and Gathering A subsistence strategy involving the foraging of wild, naturally occurring foods.

Incest Taboo The cultural rule that prohibits sexual intercourse and marriage between specified classes of relatives.

Industrialism A subsistence strategy marked by intensive, mechanized food production and elaborate distribution networks.

Inequality A human relationship marked by differences in power, authority, prestige, and access to valued goods and services, and by the payment of deference.

Informant A person who teaches his or her culture to an anthropologist.

Infralegal Dispute A dispute that occurs below or outside the legal process without involving regular violence.

Innovation A recombination of concepts from two or more mental configurations into a new pattern that is qualitatively different from existing forms.

Kinship The complex system of social relationships based on marriage (affinity) and birth (consanguinity).

Language The system of cultural knowledge used to generate and interpret speech.

Law The cultural knowledge that people use to settle disputes by means of agents who have recognized authority.

Lineage A kinship group based on a unilineal descent rule that is localized, has some corporate powers, and whose members can trace their actual relationships to each other.

Magic Strategies people use to control supernatural power to achieve particular results.

Mana An impersonal supernatural force inherent in nature and in people. Mana is somewhat like the concept of "luck" in American culture.

Market Economies Economies in which production and exchange are motivated by market factors: price, supply, and demand. Market economies are associated with large societies where impersonal exchange is common.

Market Exchange The transfer of goods and services based on price, supply, and demand.

Marriage The socially recognized union between a man and a woman that accords legitimate birth status rights to their children.

Matrilineal Descent A rule of descent relating a person to a group of consanguine kin on the basis of descent through females only.

Microculture The system of knowledge shared by members of a group that is part of a larger national society or ethnic group.

Monogamy A marriage form in which a person is allowed only one spouse at a time.

Moot A community meeting held for the informal hearing of a dispute.

Morpheme The smallest meaningful category in any language.

Mythology Stories that reveal the religious knowledge of how things have come into being.

Naive Realism The notion that reality is much the same for all people everywhere.

Nonlinguistic Symbols Any symbols that exist outside the system of language and speech; for example, visual symbols.

Nuclear Family A family composed of a married couple and their children.

Ordeal A supernaturally controlled, painful, or physically dangerous test, the outcome of which determines a person's guilt or innocence.

Pastoralism A subsistence strategy based on the maintenance and use of large herds of animals.

Patrilineal Descent A rule of descent relating consanguine kin on the basis of descent through males only.

Personified Supernatural Force Supernatural force inherent in Supernatural beings such as goddesses, gods, spirits, and ghosts.

Phoneme The minimal category of speech sounds that signals a difference in meaning.

Phonology The categories and rules for forming vocal symbols.

Phratry A group composed of two or more clans. Members acknowledge unilineal descent from a common ancestor but recognize that their relationship is distant.

Physical Environment The world as people experience it with their senses.

Policy Any guideline that can lead directly to action.

Political System The organization and process of making and carrying out public policy according to cultural categories and rules.

Polyandry A form of polygamy in which a woman has two or more husbands at one time.

Polygamy A marriage form in which a person has two or more spouses at one time. Polygyny and polyandry are both forms of polygamy.

Polygyny A form of polygamy in which a man is married to two or more wives at one time.

Prayer A petition directed at a supernatural being or power.

Priest A full-time religious specialist who intervenes between people and the supernatural, and who often leads a congregation at regular cyclical rites.

Production The process of making something.

Public The group of people a policy will affect.

Racial Inequality Inequality based on reputed biological characteristics of the members of different groups.

Ramage A cognatic (bilateral) descent group that is localized and holds corporate responsibility.

Rank Societies Societies stratified on the basis of prestige only.

Reciprocal Exchange The transfer of goods and services between two people or groups based on their role obligations. A form of nonmarket exchange.

Redistribution The transfer of goods and services between a group of people and a central collecting service based on role obligation. The U.S. income tax is a good example.

Religion The cultural knowledge of the supernatural that people use to cope with the ultimate problems of human existence.

Respondent An individual who responds to questions included on questionnaires; the subject of survey research.

Rite of Passage A series of rituals that move individuals from one social state or status to another.

Role The culturally generated behavior associated with particular statuses.

Sacrifice The giving of something of value to supernatural beings or forces.

Self-redress The actions taken by an individual who has been wronged to settle a dispute.

Semantics The categories and rules for relating vocal symbols to their referents.

Sexual Inequality Inequality based on gender.

Shaman A part-time religious specialist who controls supernatural power, often to cure people or affect the course of life's events.

Slash-and-Burn Agriculture A form of horticulture in which wild land is cleared and burned over, farmed, then permitted to lie fallow and revert to its wild state.

Social Acceptance A process that involves learning about an innovation, accepting an innovation as valid, and revising one's cultural knowledge to include the innovation.

Social Situation The categories and rules for arranging and interpreting the settings in which social interaction occurs.

Social Stratification The ranking of people or groups based on their unequal access to valued economic resources and prestige.

Sociolinguistic Rules Rules specifying the nature of the speech community, the particular speech situations within a community, and the speech acts that members use to convey their messages.

Sorcery The malevolent practice of magic.

Speech The behavior that produces meaningful vocal sounds.

Spirit Possession The control of a person by a supernatural being in which the person becomes that being.

Status A culturally defined position associated with a particular social structure.

Stratified Societies Societies that are at least partly organized on the principle of social stratification. Contrast with egalitarian and rank societies.

Subject The person who is observed in a social or psychological experiment.

Subsistence Economies Economies that are local and that depend largely on the nonmarket mechanisms, reciprocity and redistribution, to motivate production and exchange.

Subsistence Strategies Strategies used by groups of people to exploit their environment for material necessities. Hunting and gathering, horticulture, pastoralism, agriculture, and industrialism are subsistence strategies.

Substantive Law The legal statutes that define right and wrong for members of a society.

Supernatural Things that are beyond the natural. Anthropologists usually recognize a belief in such things as goddesses, gods, spirits, ghosts, and *mana* to be signs of supernatural belief.

Support Anything that contributes to the adoption of public policy and its enforcement.

Symbol Anything that humans can sense that is given an arbitrary relationship to its referent.

Tacit Culture The shared knowledge of which people usually are unaware and do not communicate verbally.

Technology The part of a culture that involves the knowledge that people use to make and use tools and to extract and refine raw materials.

Transcendent Values Values that override differences in a society and unify the group.

Ultimate Problems Universal human problems, such as death, the explanation of evil and the meaning of life, and transcendent values that can be answered by religion.

Unit of Production The group of people responsible for producing something.

Witchcraft The reputed activity of people who inherit supernatural force and use it for evil purposes.

Worldview The way people characteristically look out on the universe.

Photo Credits

Unless otherwise noted, all photographs are the property of Scott Foresman and Company.

Page 2 David Falconer/David R. Frazier Photolibrary

Page 12 Peggy & Yoram Kahana/Peter Arnold, Inc.

Page 56 Jeff Greenberg/MRP/Peter Arnold, Inc.

Page 100 Michele Burgess/The Stock Market

Page 152 Milt & Joan Mann/Cameramann International Ltd.

Page 190 Jason Laure

Page 230 Sylvain Grandadam/Photo Researchers, Inc.

Page 266 Cynthia Johnson/Gamma-Liaison

Page 306 David R. Frazier Photolibrary

Page 348 Mehmet Biber/Photo Researchers, Inc.

Index

'ard (female honor), 240–241
Abbot, Nabia, 37
Academic anthropology, 351
Acculturation, 350–351
Action anthropology, 352
Adaptation biological, 101
Adaptation, cultural, 101
Adjustment anthropology, 351
Administrative anthropology, 352
Advocate anthropology, 352
Affinity, 191. *See also* Marriage
Africa
  male and female power in, 245–246, 248–249
  Nigerian bureaucracy in, 290–298
  Tiv storytelling in, 34–43
African hunter/gatherers, 26–33, 105–118
African Americans, 395–400.
Agriculture
  definition of, 102–103
  horticulture as a kind of, 120–129
Alcoholic beverages, 122, 358
Alliance, marriage, 207–208
Allocation of resources, 153
Amazon forest, 365–382
  destruction of, 366, 371–373
Amazonian Indians, 351
American culture, study of, 3
Ancestors, 338–340, 343–346
Anonymity and the veil, 239
Anthropologist as consultant, 395–400
Anthropologists as expert witnesses, 288
Anthropology, uses of, 383–399
Anthropology, application to America, 3-6
Anthropology, 394. *See also* Cultural anthropology
Antigua, 270–281
  political history of, 273–274
  economic history of, 273–274
Appadurai, Arjun, 94

Applied anthropology, 351
Applied anthropology, 282–289, 395–400
Arak (Bhil word for clan), 209
Arrogance, among the !Kung, 32–33
Aspiration, use in pronunciation, 58
Authority, 268–269

Barbados, rural life in, 47–48
Barbados, 44–55
Barbuda, 274
Baseball, magic in, 320–329
Behavior
  cultural, and television 93–98
  drinking, 35
  ethnocentric, 11
  homocentric, 11
Bell Curve, The, 252–254
Betrothal, 209–210
Bhil, 4, 192, 205–213, 308, 388
Bilateral descent, 192
Biological adaptation, 101
Blumer, Herbert, 24–25
Body language, learning of, 67–69
Body movement and culture, 62–63
Bolivia, effect of cocaine on, 354–364
Bombardier, Joseph-Armand, 349–350
Bombay, 164–170
Boreholes, 118–119
Borrowing, cultural, 349–350
Botswana, 106
Brazil, 96, 365–382
  and television, 96
Bribery, of bureaucrats, 292
Brideprice, 210
Brown, Roger, 86
Bumbita, 337–346
Bureaucracy, 291, 296–297
Bushman. *See* !Kung

Cargo Cult, 337-346
  cultural basis of 339–340
  forms of, 338
  ideology of, 340
  personal meanings of, 343–346
Caribbean, 270–281
Cash labor, impact on kinship, 211
Caste, 232
Catholicism, 310–19
Cattle. 130–140. *See also* Cows, Oxen, Pastoralism
  American, energy efficiency of, 135
  breeding programs for, 134
  energy efficiency of, 137
  manure production of, 136
Central America, 180–189
Change,
  cultural, 349
  among the Dobe Ju/'hoansi, 118–119
  environmental, 141–150
Charms. See Fetishes
Chicha (corn beer), 358
Child support, 270–281
  laws concerning, 272–273
Child care, 195–204
Chinese, 22–228
Christianity,
  Bumbita interpretations of, 342–346
  conversion to, 341–342
Civil service, Nigerian 293–297
Civilization, disappearance of, 141–150
Clan, 192, 208–209,
Class, social, 51–52, 232, 252–258, 273–274
Class, race, and IQ, 252–258
Cocaine, 354–364
  control of, 360
  impact on Indians of, 360–361
  production of, 358–360
Coercion, 268
Cognatic descent. *See* Bilateral descent
Cognitive map, 24
Colonialism
  in Antigua, 271–273
  impact of on rain forests, 125–128

Colonos (colonists in Paraguay), 125–128
Color categories, 84–85
Communication,
and language, 57–59
nonverbal, 61–70
Complex society, 5
Conflict, 8-9.
Consanguinity, 191. *See also* Descent
Conservation programs, 127–128
Consultant, anthropologist as, 395–400
Contests, in dispute settlement, 268
Conversation, styles of, 71–79
Conversation and gender, 72
Cook, Captain James, 143
Corporate kin group among Gypsies, 287
Corporations, ethnographic management in, 387–392
Cosmology, 308–309
Courts, 268, 270–281
types of, 274–277
uses of, 274–277
Cow protection, reasons for, 139
Cows, 130-140. *See also* Cattle, Oxen
harsh treatment of, 134
love for, 130–140
milk production of, 132
sacredness of, 130–131
worship of, 130–131
Crack cocaine, 172
Cross-cultural misunderstanding, 26–43
Cultural bias, in IQ tests, 255–257
Cultural adaptation, 101
Cultural anthropology, 3
Cultural artifacts, 21
Cultural behavior, 21
Cultural borrowing, 349
Cultural code, 101
Cultural contact, 365–382
Cultural diversity, 9
Cultural ecology, 101
Cultural knowledge, 22
Cultural relativism, 7–8
Culture, 4-6, 13-17, 388
and adaptation, 101–102
definition of, 4–6, 14
explicit, 16
tacit, 16
and television, 93–98
and values, 6–11
Culture shock, 16

Dam building, 372
Dapa (Bhil word for bride price), 210
Dash (bribe in Nigeria), 295
Death, 195–204. *See also* Infant death
mothers' indifference to, 195–201
officials' reaction to, 202-203
Deforestation, 120–129, 365–382
Degradation ceremony, 280
Demography, of the !Kung, 112
Descent, 191
bilateral, 191
groups, 191–192
matrilineal, 191
patrilineal, 191, 209
Detached observation, 15, 18
Development, impact on forests, 125–128
Devil, 312–319
Diet selectivity, of the !Kung, 110
Diffusion, cultural, 349
Disputes, 267-268
extralegal, 267
infra legal, 267
kinship, 276
legal, 268
Distance, speaking
intimate, 66
personal, 66
social, 66
public, 66
Distribution, economic, 154
Divination, 321
Division of labor, 158
by sex, 245–246

Dobe. *See* !Kung
Domestic labor, 164–170
Dominance, male, 243–245
Drinking behavior, 35
Drug dealing, 171–179
Drugs, sale of, 259–265
Dyson-Hudson, Rada, 159

East Asia, 222–228
Easter, 312-19
Easter Island, 141–150
  discover of, 142
  subsistence patterns on, 143
Ecological resistence, 381–382
Ecology, 101–102
Economic system, 153
Economy
  definition of, 153
  inner city, 171–179
  service, 175–176
  shadow, 164–170
Ecozones, 130–31
Education, respect for, 53–54
Education, fieldwork and, 53–54
Egalitarian society, 233
Emotional attachment, 195–204
Endogamy, 192
Environment. *See also* Development, Ecology, Subsistence strategies
  cultural, 101
  Kayapo relation to, 369–371
  physical, 101
Environmental degredation, 141–150
Environmental movement, 379–381
Eskimo, 249–250
Ethnocentrism, 5, 16
Ethnographic management, 387–390
Ethnography, 5, 14, 18–25, 387–390
  and culture, 18–25
  definition of, 5, 14, 388
  among the !Kung, 27–33
Euphemisms, effect on meaning of, 81–85
Exchange 340
Exchange, 154–155
  reciprocal, 154
  redistributive, 155
  market, 154
Exogamy, 192
Exogamy, village, 208
Expert witness, anthropologist as, 288
Explicit culture, 16, 23
Extended family, 192
  on Taiwan, 224–225
Extralegal disputes, 267

Family, 192, 222–228
  Antiguan examples of, 277-278
  extended, 192
  nuclear, 192
  uterine, 222-225
Family loyalty, in India, 212
Famine relief program, United Nations, 116
Fathers, obligations of, 279–280
Feast, among !Kung, 26–33
Feminal kin, 208
Fieldwork, 18–19. *See also* Ethnography
  on Barbados, 44–55
  and education, 53–54
  among the !Kung, 26–33
Fiestas, 312–13
FIRE economy, 175–176
Flenley, John, 145
Foraging, 26–33, 102, 105–119, 246–247
Forest
  Amazonian, 365–382
  destruction of, 146–147
Fraternal polyandry, 214–221
FUNAI (Brazilian Indian Service), 372–373

Gangs, 259–265
Garfinkel, H., 279
Gender, 49-50. *See also* Male dominance, Sex roles
  and conversation styles, 71–79

Gender relations, 270–281
  inversions of, 270–281
Gender stereotypes, 78
Genderism, 73
General intelligence, 255
Genetic code, 101
Ghost dance religion, 334
Gift giving, 157–163, 340
  as academic citations, 161
  as foreign aid, 162–163
  as a way to fight, 160
Giving, meanings of, 26–33. *See also* Reciprocity, Reciprocal exchange
Gleason, H. A., 84–85
Go-between, 268
Goffman, Irving, 73
Grammar, 58–59
Grammatical effects on perception, 82–84
Green sea turtles, 180–181,184
Group differences, explanations of, 13–14
Guarani, 120–129
Gypsies, American, 282–289

Hall, Edward, 24
Hanunoo, 85
Heston, Alan, 138
Health fairs, 395–400
Hess, Eckhard, 64
Hicks, George, 19, 24
Hindi phonemes, 58
Hindu cow worship, 130–140
Honor, for men and women, 240–241
Hopi, 82–84
Horticulture, 102–103
  Guarani, 120–129
  Kayapo, 365–382
  and women, 250
Human environment, 10
Human Relations Area Files, 5
Hunter/gatherers, 26–33, 102, 105–118, 154, 243–251
  types of, 246–251
  value on equality among, 26–33
Hunting and gathering
  among the !Kung, 105–118
  loss of dependence on, 118–119

Idealization, of the past, 332
Imitative magic, 327
Incest taboo, 193
India, 13–15, 130–140, 164–170
  place of cattle in, 130–140
Indian giver, 158–159
Indian gift, 158
Indians and cocaine production, 360
Indo-European language family, 87–88
Industrial societies and women, 262–63
Industrialism, 103
Inequality, 232–234
Infant death, church's reaction to, 202–203
Infanticide, female, 217
Inflation, as a result of cocaine production, 356–357
Informant, 15, 16. *See also* Respondent, Subject of experiment
Informant, 15
Infralegal dispute, 267
Inheritance, 209
Inmates, prison, 263–264
Innovation, 349
Intelligence persistence tests, 254–258
Intelligence, general, 255
Interaction, ritual nature of, 73
International languages, 86
Intimate speaking distance, 66
IQ (Intelligence quotent), 252–258
  and poverty, 253–254
  tests, validity of, 254–258
  Iroquois, 4, 245
  Islam, 235
  and the seclusion of women, 237–238

Ju/'hoansi, Dobe, 118–119

Kalahari desert, 106
Kanguijy (alcoholic beverage), 122
Kayapo resistence to development, 369–371
Kayapo, 365–382
 and the Brazilian government, 373–375
 and environmental groups, 373–379
Kin, feminal, 208
Kin groups, 192
Kinesics, 68
King, Sarah, 145
Kinship, 1991–193
 as an adaptation to agriculture, 206
 impact of cash labor on, 211
 in India, 205–213
Kinship disputes, 276
Kinship network, 207
Kinship statutes, 275
Kinzel, Augustus, 65
Kula, 160
!Kung, 26-33, 105-118, 154
!Kung San. *See* !Kung
Kwakiutl, 4

Labor, domestic, 164–170
Language, 16, 58
 affect on perception of, 80–92
 and gender,
 imprecision of, 90–91
 international, 86
 political, 91–92
 subsystems of, 58–59
 Law, 267
 and Gypsies, 282–289
 and magistrate's court, 270–281
 substantive, 282
Legal channels, 275–276
Legal domination, principle of,290, 296–298
Legitimacy, 268
Legs, styles of crossing, 68
Leisure, amount of, 113–114
Life expectancy, 197
Lineage, 192, 208
Long-leg (influence of a powerful person in Nigeria), 295
Love, mothers' for infants, 195–204
Lovedu, 245

Magic, 308
 in baseball, 320–329
 function of, 321
 imitative, 327
 theories of, 321
 as a way to reduce anxiety, 321
 in WW II, 326–327
Magistrate's court, 275–277
Male dominance, 243–251
Male power, 245–246
Male/female behavior, 71–79
Malinowski, Bronislaw Kaspar, 321, 329
Mana, 308
Management
 by defense, 397
 ethnographic approach to, 385–394
Mantras (powerful ritual chants in India), 308
Marime (Gypsy word for pollution), 286–287
Market
 intrusion of, 182–183
 as a kind of exchange, 154
 system, 164
Marriage, 192, 214–221
 alliance, 207–208
 arranged, 207–211
 endogamous, 192–193
 exogamous, 192–193
 polyandrous, 214–221
 polygamous, 193
 polygynous, 193
Masculinity, 50
Materialism, 48–49
Matrilineal descent, 198
Mbuti (Pygmy), 268
Men
 control of by women, 280–281

nature of, 278–279
shaming of, 280–281
Meaning, cultural, 23–24
Meat
distribution of, 29–30
prestige of, 246
Medical Anthropology, 395–400
Men and women, talk between, 71–79
Men's and women's roles, 240
Mexico, 310–319
Microculture, 15, 387
Middle East, 235–242
Midwives, 200
Militia movements, 330–333
Miskito, 180–189
Misunderstanding, cross-cultural, 26–43
Mongongo nuts, !Kung subsistence on, 108–110
Monogamy, 193, 215–216. *See also* Marriage
Moot, 268
Morphemes, 59
Mother-in-law, relations with on Taiwan, 225
Mothering, 195–204
Movements, revitalization, 330–336
Mukogodo, 159
Multi cultural society, 9
Mythology, 309

Naive realism, 16, 20–21
Tiv example of, 34–43
Narco chic (new class of Latin American drug barons), 355
Natural environment, 10
Need,economic, 153
Nepal, 214–221
New Guinea, 337–346
Nigeria, 290–298
Nonverbal communication, 61–70
based on body movement, 62–63
based on pupillary reflex, 63–64
based on speaking distance, 64–65
based on touching, 67–68
evolution of, 62
Nuclear family, 192

Objectivity, in ethnographic research, 6–7

Omens, among the Tiv, 37, 40

Oppression, 261–263, 265

Ordeals as a way to settle disputes, 268

Oxen. 132–133. *See also* Cattle, Cows, Pastoralism
role in feast, 26–33
shortage of in India, 132–133
treatment of in India, 134

Paraguay, 120–129
Participant observation, 292
Pasta (cocaine paste), 357
Pastorialism, 103
Patriarchy, 245
Patrilineal descent, 191, 209
Patrilineal extended family, 222–228
Patrilineal systems, 229–35
Patrimonial domination,290–291, 296–297
Patrones (Latin American land owners), 127
Perception and language, 80–92
Personal speaking distance, 66–67
Personified supernatural force, 308
Phonemes, 16, 58
Hindi example of, 58
Phonology, 58
Phratry, 192. *See also* Descent groups
Physical environment, 101
Pitt-Rivers, Julian 240
Policy, public, 268
Political language, 90–91
Political system, limitation of, 268

Pollen, analysis of, 145, 147
Pollution, Gypsy beliefs about, 285
Polyandry, 193, 214–221
explanation of, 217–220
and female infanticide, 217–218
material advantages of, 219–220
as a means of population control, 218–219
Polygamy, 193
Polygyny, 193
Polynesia, 141–150
Population density, 112
Population growth
effects of, 148–149
on Eastern Island, 148
Postmodern
definition of, 94
classroom, 93–98
Potlatch, 160-161
Poverty, urban, 164–170
Prayer, 308
Priests, 309
Primogeniture, 216
Principles of social acceptance, culture change, 350
Prison, and gangs, 259–265
Production, 153
Public, definition of, 268
Public policy, 268
Public speaking distance, 66–67
Pupillary reflex, 63–64
Purdah, 235–242
and the veil, 239
Pygmy. *See* Mbuti

Qualitative research, 385
Quechua, 355

Rajput, 4
Ramage, 192. *See also* Bilateral descent
Rank societies, 233
Rapp, R., 274
Reciprocal exchange, 154
Reciprocal gift giving, 157–163
Reciprocity, 157–163
Recognition distance, 64
Redistribution exchange, 154
Religion, 130–140, 307–308
Resources, use of by hunter/gatherers, 105–118
Respondent, 15
Ritual
in baseball, 351–361
of children, 225
function of, 352
magical, 341–50
personal, 354–55
roles, 222-228,231, 240
of women, 222–228
Race, 50–51
Race, class, and IQ, 252–258
Rarámuri, religion of, 310–319
Religion, 307
Rarámuri, 310–319
syncretic, 312–319
Remlinger, Kate, 77
Respect behavior, between in-laws, 210–211
Respondent, 15
Revitalization
Islamic movement as, 333–334
militia movement as, 333–334
movement, 330–336, 337–346
theory of, 335–336
Ritual, 310-319
in baseball, 323–325
Ritual and conversation, 73
Roggeveen, Jacob, 142–144
Rural and urban, differences between, 47–48

Sapir, Edward, 82

Sapir-Whorf hypothesis, 80–92
criticisms of, 80–92
Seclusion, *See also* Purdah
and the veil, 238
of women, 236–238.
Self redress, 268
Semai, 268
Semantics, 59

Service Economy, 175–176
Sex roles, 222–228
Sexual division of labor, 243–244
Sexual inequality, 233
Shadow economy, 64–170, 171–179
Shaman, 308
Sharaf (male honor), 240
Shaw, Nancy Stoller, 332
Skinner, B. F., 328–329
Slash-and-burn agriculture, 108. *See also* Horticulture
Slavery, 271–272
Social situation, 231–232
Social speaking distance, 66
Social role, 231
Social status, 231
Social stratification, 232. *See also* Caste, Class
Social organization, 191–193
Social class, 51
Social relationships, 47
Social organization, of the Kayapo, 369–371
Social acceptance of change, 350
Social class
Social impact of market exchange, 186–188
Sociolinguistic rules, 59
Sorcery, 308
Space, meaning of, 65–66
Speaking distance, 66–67
Speech, 57
Spirit possession, 308
Standard of living, 157
Starvation, 201
Statues, on Easter Island, 143–144, 148
Status, 231
Steadman, David, 142, 146
Story telling, among the Tiv, 36
Stratified society, 233
Student fieldwork, 44–55
Styles of walking, 69
Subculture, 5
Subject, 15
Subject, of experiment, 15
Subsistence
  Guarani, 123–125
  !Kung, 105–118
Subsistence economy, 180–182
Subsistence patterns, on Easter Island, 143
Subsistence strategy, 102–103
Subsistence, 367–369
Substantive law, 282
Supernatural, 307
Supernatural force, personal, 308
Support, political, 268
Symbolic interaction, premises of, 24–25
Symbols, 24, 57
  nonlinguistic, 59
  vocal, 58

Taboo
  in baseball, 325–326, 328
  definition of, 355
  incest, 193
Tacit culture, 16, 24
Taiwan, 222–228
Taiwanese, 222–228
Talking, 63
Tamoi (Guarani ritual and political leader), 122–123, 127
Tanzania, 248–249
Technology, 153
Teleconditioning, 95
Television, impact of, 93–98
  impact of in Brazil, 96
Tibetans, 214–221
Tillion, Germaine, 236
Tiv, 34–43
Tiwi, 248
Tourism, 53
Touch, 67
Trance dance, 115
Transcendent values, 307
Trial, of a Gypsy, 286–287
Tribal peoples, 353
Tropical forest, subsistence in, 120–129
Taboo, 325–326, 328

Tswana, 26, 28
Turnbull, Colin 268
Turtles
economy based on, 180–189
techniques for hunting, 184–186
Tylor, Edward B., 14

Ultimate problems, of human existence, 307–308
Underground economy, 171–179
Unit of production, 154
United States, study of in anthropology, 5
Urban poverty, 164–170
Uterine family, 222–228

Values
and cultural relativisim, 7–8
and culture, 6–11
definition of, 6
functions of, 7
Veil, symbolic meaning of, 235–242
Vice Lords, 259–265
Vietnam war, movement against, 332
Vitsa (Gypsy corporate kin group), 283, 285
Vocal symbols, 58

Walking styles, 68-69
Wallace, Anthony F. C. , 335
Want, economic, 153
Ward, Barbara, 10
Washo, 247
Weber, Max, 291, 296–297
West Indies, 270–281
Whorf, Benjamin Lee, 80–84
Witchcraft, 40
Women
and child support, 270–281
community of, 226–228
effect of poverty on, 164–170
and family, 222–228
in India, 164–170
lower class, 270–281
nature of, 278–279
participation in shadow economy by, 164–170
in patrilineal systems, 222–228
respect for, 270–281
seclusion of, 236–238. *See alsoPurdah*
and work, among the !Kung, 115–116
Workplace, conversation in, 71–79
World languages, 86
Worldview, 309

Xingu River, 365–382

Yanomamo, 243–244
Yerba mate (caffeinated tea), 124–126
Yinger, Milton, 307

Zebu cattle, 131
Zombie, 38-39